Y0-CCR-694

Under the editorship of

HEROLD C. HUNT

Harvard University

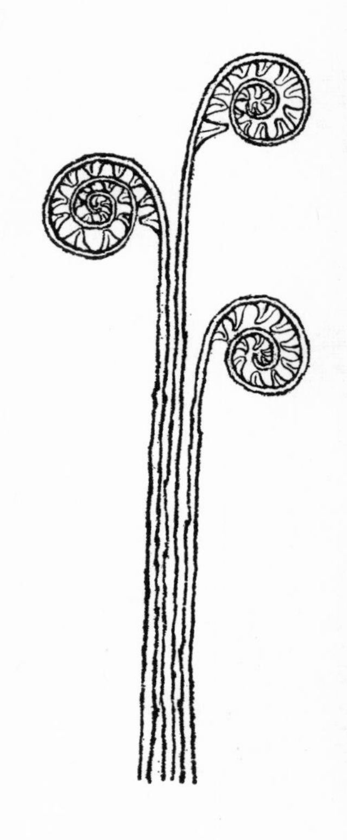

The Junior

Houghton Mifflin Company · Boston

Nelson L. Bossing

DISTINGUISHED VISITING PROFESSOR OF EDUCATION,
SOUTHERN ILLINOIS UNIVERSITY

Roscoe V. Cramer

FORMER PRINCIPAL OF WEST JUNIOR HIGH SCHOOL,
KANSAS CITY, MISSOURI, AND SOMETIME SUMMER
LECTURER IN EDUCATION, UNIVERSITIES OF
MISSOURI, MINNESOTA, AND MARYLAND

High School

HOUGHTON MIFFLIN COMPANY • BOSTON

Printed in the U.S.A.

Preface

The junior high school is now in the midst of a renaissance. It has served for too long as a small imitation of the upper division of the secondary school, influenced in its development more by the concepts and recommendations of the report of the powerful Committee of Ten of 1893 that provided its historic birth than by the educational concepts developed after the turn of the century which inspired its growth.

The clearer understanding of the nature of adolescence and the rapidly changing conceptions of the nature of learning within recent decades, plus the fact of the near complete school enrollment saturation of the junior high school, have forced upon the school a reappraisal of the needs of early adolescence. This in turn has necessitated a realistic re-examination of the educational and organizational requirements of the school unit that serves this unique age group. It calls for some radical changes in the traditional curriculum and structure of the junior high school. It is anticipated that the next two decades, particularly, will witness a profound revolution in this institution and its program.

Throughout this book the authors have tried to suggest the general direction they believe this modification of the junior high school should take. They have presented their thinking in seventeen chapters concerned with the history, purposes, and functions of the junior high school; the unique nature of early adolescence; the curriculum and instructional program; student personnel problems; problems of staff and housing; articulation problems; school-community relations; and program evaluation.

The study of these problems is imperative for all who are immediately concerned with the education of early adolescents — for citizens who wish to become informed about the separate school units, as well as for teachers and administrators.

The authors wish to express their thanks to the hundreds of persons who have been members of their many graduate courses on the junior high school and from whom, during these hours of shared experience, they have learned much. Appreciation is due particularly to Dr. Cramer's daughter, Mrs. A. Lee Copeland, for her invaluable assistance.

Acknowledgment is made here to the many published and unpublished sources that have contributed to the content of this book. All quotations and references are duly documented.

NELSON L. BOSSING

ROSCOE V. CRAMER

January 10, 1964

Contents

PART TWO

Curriculum and Instruction

PART THREE

Student Personnel Administration

PART FOUR

Staff and Facilities

PART FIVE

School Relationships and Evaluation

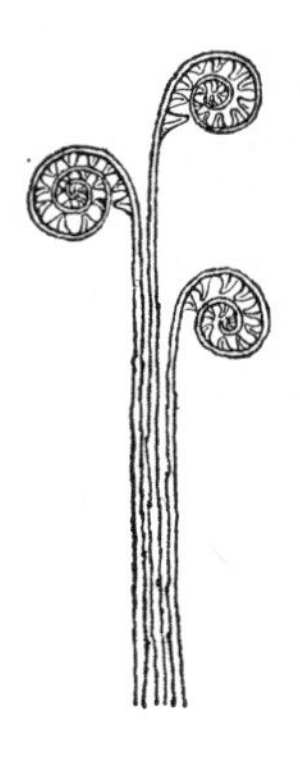

Part One

GROWTH AND DEVELOPMENT

1

Development of the Junior High School

Institutionalized secondary education began in the American colonies with the Latin Grammar School of Boston in 1635. Because it enrolled those of the approximate ages of present junior high school pupils, it has sometimes been superficially linked with the modern junior high school. The junior high school did not appear on the American educational scene full blown or because of the genius of one man or a few men. It is the product of both long evolutionary educational thought and varied educational innovations. Educational ferment seldom, if ever, has been confined to a few people, to a single place, or even to one country.

1. What are some possible European antecedents of the junior high school?

Some scholars have thought that they could trace the germinal ideas associated with the origins of the junior high school to educational thinkers of Europe; the names of Comenius, Rousseau, Basedow, Pestalozzi, Herbart, and Herbert Spencer are most frequently mentioned. All of these men and others of Europe have influenced American educational thinking and practice, but it would be difficult to identify any one of them even remotely with our junior high school. Because Rousseau discussed educational ideas and their specific application to the education of the early adolescent years in the famous book *Émile,* his influence has been considered particularly strong, for this school includes the ages twelve to fifteen and embraces some educational ideas advocated by Rousseau.

It is easier, however, to see the junior high school emerging out of our own educational matrix, at first somewhat dimly, then much more clearly as we near the time of its general acceptance as a distinct rung on the educational ladder.

2. *How did the junior high school grow out of our evolving school system?*

The early days

In the beginning of the colonial period[1] and for a considerable time thereafter the colonies as a group had nothing approaching an educational system. Not until near the middle of the nineteenth century did a somewhat tenuous national pattern begin to emerge.

Reflecting their divergent European antecedents, the colonies offered many forms of education. At the outset, education was usually considered solely a family responsibilty, and under the rigorous living conditions of the time, in many homes it was neglected.

Several devices were used to promote education, at first in homes — in the so-called dame school, where a housewife boasting a little erudition and some leisure would undertake the instruction of a few neighbor children, for a price, in the rudiments of reading and writing. Public-spirited citizens began, too, to support charity schools, pauper schools, and Sunday schools, where the less fortunate could be taught. The reading school, the writing school, the infant school appeared.

Early in the colonial period Massachusetts, alone of the colonies, introduced an educational plan that, according to many scholars, formed the basis for our present educational system. As Bunker has pointed out, "Within eight years after the founding of Boston a college with a system of preparatory schools was established, and within 17 years, the foundation, in theory at least, of our entire American public school system was laid."[2]

In 1642 Massachusetts passed the first colony-wide school law. This law placed a definite obligation upon parents, guardians, and masters of apprentices to teach children and youth the rudiments of learning and trade competence, including the ability "to read and understand the principles of religion and the capital laws of the country." Penalties were provided for neglect of these responsibilities. This is the first time among English-speaking

[1] For a more complete discussion of this period see Nelson L. Bossing, *Principles of Secondary Education* (Englewood Cliffs, N.J.: Prentice-Hall, Inc., rev. ed., 1955), Chap. 2; Frank F. Bunker, *Reorganization of the Public School System* (Washington: U.S. Bureau of Education, Bulletin No. 8, 1916), Chaps. 1-2; and Paul Munroe, *Founding of the American Public School System* (New York: The Macmillan Company, 1940), Chaps. 1-7.

[2] Bunker, *ibid.*, p. 2.

peoples that any political unit had ever required universal education of its children.

Because the enforcement of this law proved difficult, the now famous Law of 1647, known as the "Old Deluder" law, was enacted by Massachusetts. In conjunction with the 1642 measure, it established our first system of public elementary and secondary schools. The part of the Law of 1647 important for our purpose reads as follows:

> It is therefore ordered, that every township in this jurisdiction, after the Lord hath increased them to the number of 50 householders, shall then forthwith appoint one within their town to teach all such children as shall report to write and read, whose wages shall be paid either by the parents or masters of such children, or by the inhabitants in general, by way of supply, as the major part of those that order the prudentials of the town shall appoint: provided, those that send their children be not oppressed by paying much more than they can have them taught for in other towns; and it is further ordered, that where any town shall increase to the number of 100 families or householders, they shall set up a grammar school, the master thereof being able to instruct so far as they may be fitted for the University, provided that if any town neglect the performance hereof above one year, that every such town shall pay 5 pounds to the next school till they shall perform this order.

Within a short time the essentials of the Law of 1647 became a part of the educational system of most of the New England colonies. Even within these colonies, particularly in the elementary schools, marked differences existed as to the curriculum offered and the number of years associated with each school division.

Cubberley, probably this country's most eminent educational historian, comments on the significance of the Massachusetts education laws of 1642 and 1647:

> It can safely be asserted that these two Massachusetts laws of 1642 and 1647 represent not only new educational ideas in the English-speaking world, but that they also represent the very foundation stones upon which our American public school systems have been constructed.[3]

The earliest schools known in the colonies were secondary in character. In fact, before the Massachusetts school laws of 1642 and 1647, Latin grammar schools were already in existence. The first, the Boston Latin Grammar School, claims an origin dating back to 1635. These schools were avowedly college preparatory institutions. They were generally known throughout the colonies although most popular in New England. Because of their popularity and their established character educational historians assume

[3] Ellwood P. Cubberley, *Public Education in the United States* (Boston: Houghton Mifflin Company, 1919), p. 18.

that the grammar schools founded pursuant to the Law of 1647 were Latin grammar schools.

Since the Latin grammar schools were usually six to seven years in length, and admission to college was at a relatively early age, these schools may likewise well have taken very young entrants, probably below the present equivalent fifth or sixth grades, or at the age of ten years, possibly even younger. It is pertinent at this point to note that the influential Boston Latin Grammar School did not change from a seven- to a four-year school until 1789, and then presumably owing to the pressures of an elementary school that was extending upward the length of its term of years.

The Latin grammar school

The Latin grammar schools, as the name reveals, had a curriculum that consisted mostly of Latin. Some Greek was taught, since Latin and Greek were the principal subjects of the colleges for which the schools existed. These schools were the college preparatory schools of England and their prototype for the European countries, transferred to America because they were what the educated colonists had known and attended in the homeland. That they did not meet the needs of the typical pioneers in a New World environment was not at first recognized by those who established them. As new generations replaced the old, a more general type of education was demanded and fewer youth attended these schools possessed of an Old World curriculum.

Here began the historic struggle between the colleges and universities, for a secondary school oriented primarily toward college preparation, and the masses, for a more practical form of secondary education. In the opening statement of his discussion of our developing public school system Bunker declares:

> The story of the development of this system is the story of the conflict between two demands. That for a college preparation on the one hand, and on the other for a non-collegiate preparation extending beyond the elementary grades. As in every country developing a system of education, the colleges reached downward to find a means of preparation for the few, while the elementary schools reached upward in order to secure an extension of a general, practical education for the many.[4]

It is in this conflict that much of the genesis of the junior high school movement may be found, and from which it ultimately has evolved as an early but separate segment of secondary education.

The academy

The dissatisfaction of second- and third-generation descendants of the original colonists with the extreme limitations of the Latin grammar schools

[4] Bunker, *op. cit.,* p. 1.

brought about the appearance of a new type of secondary school. As early as 1723 New York City was reported to have a school offering such subjects as reading, writing, arithmetic, and mariner's art, geometry, surveying, ethics, rhetoric, logic, and natural philosophy, in addition to Latin, Greek, and Hebrew. In 1732 the English Grammar School was established in New York. It included in its curriculum writing, all branches of mathematics, Latin, algebra, geometry, geography, navigation, and merchant's bookkeeping.

The general educational unrest in the colonies was further aggravated by a similar unrest in Europe over the limited purpose and curriculum which the Latin grammar school and the Gymnasium there represented. In England particularly, an effort to develop a more practical secondary school had found expression in the academy movement. It is not surprising, therefore, that an "academy" was founded in 1726 in Pennsylvania, or that the eminently practical Benjamin Franklin in 1743 espoused the cause of this type of secondary education and in 1751 became instrumental in establishing what became known as Franklin's Academy. With a curriculum directed primarily to the needs of youth for whom it would be terminal, this school offered writing, arithmetic, merchant's accounts, history, geography, natural history, logic, mechanics, farming, navigation, algebra, geometry, surveying, astronomy, and natural and mechanical philosophy, as well as Greek, Latin, English, French, and German. Like the early Latin grammar schools, the academy served those in the early adolescent period. Let a few quotations from Franklin's "Proposals Relating to the Education of Youth in Pennsylvania" indicate the uniqueness of his ideas for this academy:

> That a House be provided for the ACADEMY, if not in the Town, not many Miles from it: the Situation high and dry, and if it may be, not far from a River, having a Garden, Orchard, Meadow, and a Field or two.
>
> That the House be furnished with a Library (if in the Country, or if in the Town, the Town Library may serve) with Maps of all Countries, Globes, some Mathematical Instruments, an Apparatus for Experiments in Natural Philosophy, and for Mechanics; Prints, of all Kinds, Prospects, Buildings, Machines, etc.
>
> . . . .
>
> All should be taught to write a fair Hand, and swift, as that is useful to All. And with it may be learned something of Drawing by Imitation of Prints, and some of the first Principles of Perspective.
>
> Arithmetick, Accounts, and some of the first principles of Geometry and Astronomy.
>
> The English Language might be taught by Grammar, in which some of our best Writers, as Tellotson, Addison, Pope, Algernon Sidney, Cato's Letters, etc. should be Classicks. . . .
>
> . . . .

While they are reading Natural History, might not a little Gardening, Planting, Grafting, Inoculating, etc., be taught and practiced, and now and then Excursions made to the neighboring Plantations of the best Farmers, their Methods observ'd and reason'd upon for the Information of Youth. . . .[5]

The influence of this school spread rapidly through the colonies. The first fifty years of its history witnessed, also, a rapid expansion of the curriculum so as to meet the widely practical needs of non-college as well as college oriented youth.

The high school

As the popularity of the academy increased, it began to replace the Latin grammar school. The result was an intensified struggle between the colleges, which needed college preparatory schools, and those who tried to protect the needs of the larger non-college-bound clientele of the academy, where limited economic resources made extended curricular service of widely divergent interests difficult. Gradually the academy was brought predominantly into the orbit of the college preparatory function, to the neglect of the larger needs of the masses of youth.

There were sporadic attempts to correct this situation. The establishment of the English Classical School in Boston in 1821 is accepted as the historic beginning of another secondary school, completely dedicated to the needs of the youth who did not plan a college career but who wanted to go beyond the elementary school.

This school, three years in length, accepted youth at approximately the age of twelve and covered the age range now served by the junior high school. Three years later, in 1824, its name was changed to the English High School. It did not offer foreign languages, then a basic requirement for college admission. Its curriculum consisted of such subjects as composition, declamation, geography, advanced arithmetic, algebra, geometry, trigonometry, ancient and modern history, logic, navigation, surveying, history of the United States, and natural philosophy including astronomy. Except for the languages, the curriculum closely resembled that of the first academies.

Because the high school offered a relatively practical curriculum, was tax supported, and was open to all youth, rich and poor alike, it appealed to most citizens. At first slow to take hold because of the hesitancy of tax units to undertake its support, after the middle of the century it spread rapidly. Shortly after the Civil War it eclipsed the fast waning Latin grammar school and twenty-five years later bypassed the academy, which had succeeded the Latin grammar school.

[5] T. H. Montgomery, *A History of the University of Pennsylvania, 1749-1770* (Philadelphia: George W. Jacobs and Company, 1900), pp. 497-500.

3. *What was the school organization pattern in the late nineteenth century?*

Like Topsy our American educational system just grew. The independent approach to school development in the several colonies caused organizational patterns to vary greatly, a condition much abetted by the early hands-off policy of the federal government.

Slowly the elementary school developed into three general types in different sections of the country. In New England it tended to become a nine-year school. When the English Classical School of Boston was established in 1821, however, it was based, apparently, upon a seven-year grammar (elementary) school. In the South, until recent times, the seven-year elementary school has been the dominant pattern, while in the Middle West and West the eight-year elementary school developed in the first half of the nineteenth century.

The secondary schools, which began to take form earlier than the elementary schools, generally ranged from three to seven years in length. The Boston Latin Grammar School, for example, was a seven-year school until 1789, when it was reduced to a four-year school. On the other hand, the English Classical School began as a three-year school, but the high school movement gradually shifted to a predominantly four-year pattern. However, such a wide variation in the length of the secondary school continued to exist near the end of the last century that in 1888 at the National Meeting of the Department of Secondary Education a resolution was passed urging "that it is of the greatest importance in the education of our youth that every effort should be made to secure a four-years' course in all high schools of the nation, to the end that their graduates shall be better prepared for college, for the training school, for the teacher's profession, and the duties of business."[6]

Why the Department of Secondary Education in 1888 felt it was so important to have a four-year secondary school is not revealed. Nor is there unequivocal evidence to indicate why the four-year secondary school came to be the dominant pattern of the high school, or why it should have been related primarily to an eight-year elementary school.

While historians have disagreed as to the origin of the 8-4 plan, Frank F. Bunker has amassed a formidable array of evidence to document the claim that the 8-4 ladder system, so prevalent in our educational organization toward the end of the last century, had its antecedents in Prussia. A large number of influential American educators were studying the Prussian system in the first half of the nineteenth century, some of whom claim to have been

[6] National Education Association, *Journal of Proceedings and Addresses,* 1888, pp. 403-404.

influenced by what they saw there as they participated in setting up educational systems here at home. Too, there is a remarkable similarity between the early 8-4 plan as established in the 1830's and 1840's in America and the Prussian system of the same time.[7]

4. *What was the junior high school organizational idea?*

At first criticisms were directed against the lack of uniformity of the length of the secondary school in practice and particularly against the emerging 8-4 plan. As had been true in the past, the major censure arose from the college and university sector, which had frowned upon every previous effort to provide a more practical type of secondary education to meet the needs of non-college-bound youth.

The role of Charles Eliot

Early leadership of the colleges in their criticism of the school situation centered in the person of the able, dynamic, scholarly Charles W. Eliot, president of Harvard University. For at least two decades he became the principal spokesman of higher education and led the movement to reform the pattern of America's public education.

There had been an effort made on the part of the colleges and universities to meet the problem of the irregular patterns of educational preparation which entrants to colleges presented, and at the same time to maintain the transitional standards of the college envisioned by college leaders. Some universities had established a three-year program for the bachelor's degree, as had Harvard University at the time of its founding, Brown University in 1850, and Johns Hopkins University in 1876. Harvard had long since lengthened its college course to four years. Other colleges followed suit because they found it necessary to include in their program courses which they felt rightly belonged to the preparatory school but in which secondary school graduates were deficient when they presented themselves for admission. Even entrance requirements were made more flexible in an effort to adjust to the situation.

On the other hand, the progressive extension of the total period of elementary and secondary education was being reflected in the gradual advance in the ages at which students entered college. In his report to the Board of Trustees of Harvard in 1872-1873, President Eliot pointed out the fact that the "average age of admission has gradually risen until it is now a little over 18 years."[8] In President Eliot's report of 1885-1886 he again called attention

[7] For the arguments favoring the Prussian origin of the 8-4 plan see Bunker, *op. cit.*, Chaps. 1-2.

[8] *Harvard Reports,* 1872-1873, p. 10, quoted in Bunker, *op. cit.*, p. 44.

to the late age at which students enter the university. By that time two-fifths of the freshmen were "over 19 at entrance."[9]

It was not in the nature of the dynamic president to let his case rest with his own institution's problems. In February, 1888, Eliot made his now famous addresss before the annual meeting of the Department of Superintendents of the National Education Association in Washington on the subject "Can School Programmes Be Shortened and Enriched?"[10] For the preceding sixty years, he said, the average age of college admission had steadily risen until at Harvard it had reached eighteen years, ten months. Students of European universities were being graduated much earlier than their American college peers. Likewise, the tendency for professional courses to be lengthened to four years made it almost impossible for a young man to begin a learned profession before the age of twenty-seven. Eliot pleaded for a shortening and enriching of the elementary and secondary school programs to enable youth to enter the university at least a year earlier — at the age of eighteen.

The address was widely read and had a profound influence on the thinking of educational leaders. President Eliot was quite conscious of the reception his words had had when four years later, in 1892, he again spoke before a National Education Association meeting. With satisfaction, he commented:

> On reviewing the progress of this reform since I had the honor of discussing the question "Can School Programmes Be Shortened and Enriched?" before this Department of Superintendents, four years ago, I see many evidences that a great and beneficent change in public school programmes is rapidly advancing. The best evidence is to be found in the keen interest which superintendents and teachers take in the discussion of the subject.[11]

This talk was but an amplification and reinforcement of his 1888 address. He spoke on the subject "Shortening and Enriching the Grammar School Course." Now, however, he got down to specifics. Three recommendations were made to shorten the program of the elementary school. The first involved a reduction of grades "from ten to nine, or from nine to eight, so that the combined primary- and grammar-school periods shall end at fourteen or thirteen." The second suggested that capable pupils be allowed to progress as rapidly as possible — so that many might complete two grades in one year. The third advised the elimination of some useless work. President Eliot argued, for example, that too much arithmetic was taught, "indeed, much more than most of us ever use."

Then he turned his attention to enrichment. First, he called for the intro-

[9] *Harvard Reports,* 1885-1886, pp. 7-9, quoted in Bunker, *op. cit.*, p. 44.

[10] Charles William Eliot, *Educational Reform: Essays and Addresses* (New York: The Century Company, 1901), pp. 151-176.

[11] *Ibid.*, p. 269.

duction of certain subjects earlier in the school program: elementary natural history earlier than now offered, elementary physics in the later years of the program, algebra and geometry at age twelve or thirteen, the opportunity to study French, German, or Latin after age ten. He further recommended the use of improved classroom methods, greater flexibility in pupil choice of subjects, and more flexibility in promotion and graduation.[12]

Largely because of the stimulus felt from the 1888 address and the widespread discussion of the issues raised in the four-year interval by influential educational groups, the address of 1892 was climaxed by the appointment of a committee by the National Education Association to study the issues and report back the next year. This committee, which came to be known as the Committee of Ten, had a far-reaching impact on the future development of elementary and secondary education in America — an impact, indeed, which is still felt by our public school system. It has greatly affected the pattern of development of the junior high school.

It frequently happens that the person instrumental in getting a committee or project under way finds himself immediately identified with it. President Eliot was made a member and chairman of the Committee of Ten. It should occasion little surprise, therefore, to find many of the things advocated in the two addresses referred to above reappearing in the recommendations of this committee.

The Committee of Ten — 1893

The Committee of Ten, appointed by the National Education Association in July, 1892, held its initial meeting in New York City in November of that year. Five college and university presidents, one college professor, two headmasters of private secondary schools, one high school principal, and the U.S. Commissioner of Education were members of the Committee.

At their first meeting they decided to form nine conferences covering as many subject-matter areas, with ten members on each conference. With President Eliot serving as general chairman and each original member of the Committee of Ten serving as a conference chairman, the conferences were as top-heavy on the college and university interest side as was the membership of the Committee of Ten. The personnel of the nine conferences were as follows:

47 were college administrators and professors
21 were headmasters of private schools
14 were principals of public high schools
2 were superintendents of schools
4 were representatives of normal schools
1 was a director of a public school department
1 was head of the U.S. Weather Bureau, formerly a university professor

[12] *Ibid.*, pp. 253-269.

At least seventy-three members of the conferences were representatives of the interests of higher education, with a small minority of seventeen presumably concerned with the broad democratic functions of the public schools. This disproportionate representation is clearly evidenced in the conference recommendations.

There was a definite ambivalence in the statements of the Committee respecting the functions of the secondary school. In one breath it declared that "the secondary schools of the United States taken as a whole, do not exist for the purpose of preparing boys and girls for colleges. . . . The preparation of a few pupils for college or scientific school should in the ordinary secondary school be the incidental, and not the principal object." In the same paragraph it suggested that "the recommendations of the Nine Conferences, if well carried out, might fairly be held to make all the main subjects taught in the secondary schools of equal rank for the purposes of admission to college or scientific school." Further on in this same paragraph is found the statement that in the setting up of four recommended four-year curriculums "the Committee had in mind . . . the requirements for admission to colleges."[13]

All conferences wanted their subjects taught earlier in the school curriculum, all pleaded for uniformity in entrance requirements, and all but three wanted a greater time allotment for their subjects. Likewise the Committee unanimously declared that "every subject which is taught at all in a secondary school should be taught in the same way and to the same extent to every pupil so long as he pursues it, no matter what the probable destination of the pupil may be, or at what point his education is to cease."

Not only was the Committee of Ten determined upon excessive uniformity of the organization and method of handling the secondary school curriculum but it recognized what President Eliot had been advocating for some time, that the college entrance problem could not be effectively solved in the framework of an 8-4 plan. It therefore made a direct attack upon the problem in this far-reaching recommendation:

> In preparing these programmes, the Committee were perfectly aware that it is impossible to make a satisfactory secondary school programme, limited to a period of four years, and founded on the present elementary school subjects and methods. In the opinion of the Committee, several subjects now reserved for high schools — such as algebra, geometry, natural science, and foreign languages — should be begun earlier than now, and therefore within the schools classified as elementary; or, as an alternative, the secondary school period should be made to begin two years earlier than at present, leaving six years instead of eight for the elementary school period. Under the present

[13] National Education Association, *Report of the Committee of Ten on Secondary School Studies* (New York: American Book Company, 1894), pp. 51-52.

organization, elementary subjects and elementary methods are, in the judgment of the Committee, kept in use too long.[14]

Throughout the report there is the clear indication that administratively the high school was to maintain its four-year pattern and that the two years below it should become an intermediate school — the seventh and eighth grades paralleling the usual grammar school years to be set apart from the six-year elementary school — to absorb the departmentalized subjects dropped into these years, with the possible exception of elective modern languages and concrete geometry, which might be begun as low as the fifth grade.[15]

It is in this recommended framework that the organizational beginning of the junior high school is seriously suggested. As an intermediate or lower secondary school between the elementary school and the high school, it would be departmentalized as to subjects and teachers, utilize accepted high school methods, and in every way conform to the organizational pattern and spirit of the high school, yet serve as a means of better articulation between the elementary and secondary levels.

For approximately the next twenty-five years a series of national committees struggled with the problem of a closer articulation of the work of the secondary school with that of the college, and with streamlining the program of the six-year secondary school to achieve an economy of time for those desiring admission to college — in other words to make the secondary school an effective college preparatory institution. Along the way, however, counterirritants developed as it was increasingly recognized that the intermediate secondary school should have distinctive functions of its own.

The Committee of Fifteen — 1895

The Committee of Fifteen, composed principally of superintendents, was appointed in 1893 by the Department of Superintendence to consider further the readjustment of the elementary school. It grappled with the question of whether the elementary school should be reduced to a six-year school or remain an eight-year school.

The Committee, reporting in 1895, decided in favor of retaining the eight-year organization. It recommended the introduction of a modified form of algebra in place of advanced arithmetic in the seventh and eighth grades, and of Latin in place of English grammar in the eighth grade. This, it was emphasized, would represent a proper transition from the general work of the elementary to the departmentalized work of the secondary school: "Hitherto the change from the work of the elementary school has been too abrupt, the pupil beginning three formal studies at once, namely algebra, physical geography,

[14] *Ibid.*, p. 45.
[15] *Ibid.*, p. 44.

and Latin."[16] This willingness to push certain high school subjects down into the upper elementary years and to begin partial departmentalization in the seventh and eighth grades as a means of better articulation between the elementary and high school marks the Committee report as a forerunner of the junior high school idea.

The Committee on College Entrance Requirements — 1899

At this point it may be pertinent to mention that the Committee of Fifteen was the last major National Education Association group to advocate the continuance of the eight-year elementary school. In 1895 the Committee on College Entrance Requirements, appointed by the Department of Secondary Education and made up of members of the Department of Secondary Education of Higher Education, was commissioned to explore the problem of better relations between the two groups on matters of college admission requirements. It made its report in 1899.

Our primary concern with its recommendations is focused on the projection of the secondary school downward. The Committee strongly favored a unified six-year secondary school beginning with the seventh grade. It took advance ground on the reasons given for the proposed change:

> The most necessary and the most far reaching reforms in secondary education must begin in the seventh and eighth grades of our schools. Educators agree that these grades must be enriched by eliminating non-essentials and adding new subjects formerly taught only in the high school. These reforms require the highest pedagogic knowledge and the most efficient supervision. In our opinion these problems can be solved most quickly and surely by making the seventh and eighth grades parts of the high school under the immediate direction of the high school principal.
>
> The seventh grade rather than the ninth, is the natural turning point in the pupil's life, as the age of adolescence demands new methods and wise direction. . . . The transition from the elementary to the secondary period may be made from the one-teacher regimen to the system of special teachers, thus avoiding the violent shock now commonly felt upon entering the high school.
>
> The inspiration afforded by a well equipped high-school principal and by a special teacher in languages, science, mathematics, would do much to retain desirable students in the high school, thus raising the educational standard of American citizenship.[17]

[16] National Education Association, *Report of the Committee of Fifteen on Elementary Education* (New York: American Book Company, 1895), p. 95. See also National Education Association, *Journal of Proceedings and Addresses,* 1895, pp. 232-237.

[17] National Education Association, "Report of the Committee on College Entrance Requirements," *Journal of Proceedings and Addresses,* 1899, pp. 659-660.

The significance of the Committee's report as it relates to the junior high school idea may be summarized thus:

1. Addition of the seventh and eighth grades to the high school in a six-year sequence — the first definite proposal of an administrative organization of a six-year high school.
2. Elimination of non-essentials from these grades and the addition of new subjects formerly taught in the high school, as had been recommended by the Committee of Ten and the Committee of Fifteen.
3. Recognition that the seventh grade rather than the ninth grade represents the point of psychological change in the life of the pupil.
4. Recognition that the age of adolescence requires a different educational approach from that found in the elementary school.
5. The need for a more gradual transition from the one teacher elementary school to the departmentalized high school.
6. The possible increased holding power of such a reorganized secondary school. Evidence from practice is claimed to support this advantage.

These ideas in part became the basis for the future development of the educational institution historically known as the junior high school.

Contribution of Nicholas Murray Butler

In the late nineties President Butler of Columbia University became a formidable champion, both in speech and in writing, of the reorganized secondary school idea. His educational prestige and energetic advocacy of reform were powerful influences in creating sentiment for change. His particular contribution to the movement for reorganization flowed from his clear recognition of the functions of the elementary and secondary schools and the significance of adolescence in relation to the proposed inclusion of Grades 7 and 8 in the secondary school. It was possibly his emphasis upon the peculiar nature of adolescence that influenced the pronouncements on this point of the Committee on College Entrance Requirements.

In a notable address made in 1898 President Butler differentiated between the functions of elementary and secondary education thus:

> Elementary education I define as that general training in the elements of knowledge that is suitable for a pupil from the age of 6 or 7 to the period of adolescence. . . . I have never known a child who needed more than six years' time in which to complete the elementary course, and I have known but few who have, as an actual fact, ever taken longer than that. . . .
>
> The secondary school period is essentially the period of adolescence, of what may be called active adolescence as distinguished from the later and less violent manifestations of physical and mental change that are now usually included under the term. The normal years are, with us, from 12 to 16, or from 13 to 17. The normal boy or girl who is going to college ought to enter at 17 at the latest. . . . It is in this elimination of elementary studies from the

secondary school and the frank recognition of the paramount advantages of the elective system that I see the way of highest usefulness opening before the secondary school.[18]

5. *What were the emerging junior high school ideas — 1900-1920?*

After the turn of the century there was a definite upsurge in the volume of pronouncements on the reorganization of education from the elementary school through the college. The issues sharpened and a consensus began to appear.

Contribution of John Dewey

Another stalwart in the reorganization movement that gave impetus to the junior high school idea was John Dewey. At the fifteenth educational conference held at the University of Chicago in 1901 under the leadership of President Harper, devoted to reorganization problems of education, Dewey presented a memorable paper on the subject "Current Problems of Secondary Education."

Dewey maintained that articulation was a major problem of the secondary school. Caught in the center, it has to adjust to the elementary school on the one hand and to the college on the other. The adjustment problem arose because the "elementary school is the outgrowth of the democratic movement in its ethical aspects"; since the middle of the eighteenth century it had been influenced by the democratic demand "for equality of intellectual and moral opportunity and development." Prior to that time the elementary school had been little more than a device for "instructing little children of the lower classes in some of the utilities of their future callings — the mere rudiments of reading, writing, and numbers." The high school, on the other hand, is, in many of its phases, "the outgrowth of exactly the same impulse. It has the same history and stands for the same ideals; but only in part. It represents also the tradition of the learned class . . . it embodies the aristocratic idea."[19] This tradition, according to Dewey, has been handed down to the high schools through the colleges. Further, both the elementary school and the high school have struggled against the conflicting ideals that form their historic background.

Dewey prophesied that the discussion of the past fifteen years of the relation of the high school and the college would soon shift to the relationship of the high school to the elementary school. And he further predicted that the issues would shift to the effect of what was taught upon the growth of the

[18] Nicholas Murray Butler, "The Scope and Function of Secondary Education," *Educational Review,* 16:15-27, June, 1898.

[19] John Dewey, "Current Problems in Secondary Education," *School Review,* 10:13-28, January, 1902.

individual, and to the study of the psychological makeup of the individual and his social relations. In this way he pointed to the new focus of the secondary school centered in the junior high school idea within the decade.

The following year, 1902, at a similar conference held under the auspices of the University of Chicago Dewey spoke on the topic "Shortening the Years of the Elementary School."[20] In this discussion he supported the six-year elementary school. He attacked the wasted time in the upper grades of drill on rudiments already mastered, and challenged the idea that the function of the grades was the amassing of information. In his view the purpose of the elementary school was "to organize the instincts and impulses of children into working interests and tools" and "to organize certain modes of activity in observation, construction, expression, and reflection." If this purpose were accepted, the high school, which now has "no defiinite task of its own," would then be able to set up definite aims for itself.

Contribution of William Rainey Harper

President Harper of the University of Chicago began to focus the thinking of the annual educational conferences held under the auspices of the university upon these problems. The conferences, with one exception, favored limiting the elementary school to six years. President Harper, in 1903, declared that the elementary division should end about the twelfth year, or at Grade 6, and the secondary school should end at about the eighteenth year, or at Grade 12.

Contributions of Hanus, Snedden, and Lyttle

Several other leaders expressed the conviction that the secondary school should begin with the seventh grade. P. H. Hanus believed that some pupils might profitably be given vocational training in the seventh and eighth grades as well as at the upper end of the secondary school.[21] Strongly supporting Hanus' advocacy of a differentiated curriculum beginning at the seventh grade, D. S. Snedden felt that this was the best way to adjust to the needs of the individual pupil, noting that many stop school at an early age.[22] E. W. Lyttle, of the State of New York Education Department, in an address before the Department of Secondary Education of the National Education Association in 1905, came out strongly for the 6-6 plan:

> Is there any pedagogical point where secondary education should begin? There is. Secondary education should begin as soon as the elementary pupil has acquired the tools with which he may gain a higher education. Approxi-

[20] John Dewey, "Shortening the Years of the Elementary School," *School Review*, 11:17-20, January, 1903.

[21] P. H. Hanus, "A Six Year High School Program," *Educational Review*, 25:455-463, May, 1903.

[22] D. S. Snedden, "The Six Year High School," *Educational Review*, 26:525-529, December, 1903.

mately this point in civilized countries very nearly coincides with the dawn of adolescence.[23]

The Committee on Six-Year Course of Study — 1908

Three years later the "Report of the Committee on Six-Year Course of Study" under the chairmanship of Lyttle was made to the Department of Education of the National Education Association.[24] It called attention to the fact that the 6-6 plan was in successful operation in at least ten cities and that a member of the Board of Education of New York City had published an argument in one of the city papers for a 6-3-3 type of school organization. The Committee outlined a suggested curriculum for the seventh and eighth grades, with 70 per cent of the courses required and 30 per cent elective; it recommended a careful study of vocational offerings for the secondary division and promotion by units rather than by years, to facilitate shortening or lengthening of the six-year period to meet the needs of youth of varying ability. While not expressing an opinion, the Committee was obviously impressed with the proposed 6-3-3 organizational plan. However, the Committee confined its recommendations to the seventh and eighth grades. The program was as follows:

Subjects Required	*Periods Weekly 30 Minutes*
English, including spelling, literature, composition, grammar	6-8
Arithmetic with concrete geometry and algebra	5
Geography and history	5-7
Music	2
Drawing	2
Physical training (required of those whose physical condition needs it as a corrective; optional for others)	2
Electives	
Manual training	3
Science	3
Foreign language (for each one given)	5

The Committee on Equal Division of the Twelve Years in the Public Schools — 1907

Another important committee of the Department of Secondary Education on the 6-6 plan had reported a year earlier under the chairmanship of Gilbert B. Morrison, principal, William McKinley High School, St. Louis, Missouri. The report centered around two aspects of the problem "educational and pedagogic" and "economic." It dismissed the economic aspect by

[23] E. W. Lyttle, "Should the Twelve-Year Course of Study Be Equally Divided Between the Elementary School and the Secondary School?" National Education Association, *Journal of Proceedings and Addresses,* 1905, pp. 428-433.

[24] National Education Association, "Report of the Committee on Six-Year Course of Study," *Journal of Proceedings and Addresses,* 1908, pp. 625-628.

saying that the longer secondary division was more expensive but that its advantages were worth the cost. The advantages of the educational and pedagogic phase were outlined in ten points abbreviated as follows:

1. Pupils would have superior instruction by teachers who were subject specialists.
2. Instead of being subjected to one teacher, pupils would have the enriched experience of contact with several teachers.
3. Laboratory experiences in science could be made available earlier.
4. Manual training could be provided for seventh and eighth grades in their own secondary schools.
5. Languages could be begun earlier and studied longer.
6. Easy transition from elementary to secondary school would be less abrupt, with reduced loss of pupils.
7. It would cause more pupils to enter the ninth grade.
8. "An equal division of the twelve years would make the system more nearly self-consistent" and save "two years of valuable time."
9. It would give the pupil more time to prepare for college.
10. It "would help to solve the problem of the outward extension of the course of study and the crowded curriculum." [25]

Third report of the Committee on Six-Year Course of Study — 1909

Another committee under the chairmanship of Morrison reported in 1909. It further confirmed the growing demand for the 6-6 plan and expressed a strong sentiment in favor of the beginning of differentiated pupil work at the end of the sixth grade.[26] These reports clearly support the junior high school idea as later developed.

The Committee on Economy of Time — 1913

The first national committee to advocate a 6-3-3 type of organization was the National Council of Education Committee on Economy of Time in Education. In its report in 1913 Henry Suzzalo, at this time professor of educational philosophy at Columbia University, in a special section on "Educational Principles Involved," asserted that the six-year secondary school should be equally divided into "two administrative sections: (1) a junior high school of three years, extending from the twelfth to the fifteenth year; and (2) a senior high school, also of three years, covering the period from the fifteenth to the eighteenth year." [27]

[25] National Education Association, "Report of the Committee on Equal Division of the Twelve Years in the Public Schools Between the District and High Schools," *Journal of Proceedings and Addresses,* 1907, pp. 705-710.

[26] National Education Association, *Journal of Proceedings and Addresses,* 1909, pp. 498-503.

[27] James H. Baker, *Economy of Time in Education,* Report of the Committee of the National Council of Education (Washington: U.S. Bureau of Education, Bulletin No. 38, 1913), p. 20.

In a real sense this report brought to a close the effort begun by the Committee of Ten to reduce the age of admission to college and firmly fixed the seventh grade as the beginning of secondary education. The Committee on Economy of Time was also one of the first national groups to give recognition to the three-year junior high school organization, although by this time the 6-3-3 type of junior-senior high school organization was already in operation in a few places.

The Commission on the Reorganization of Secondary Education — 1918

A listing of reports of committees of national importance would not be complete without the statement on the junior high school of the historic Commission on the Reorganization of Secondary Education of the National Education Association, made in 1918 in *Cardinal Principles of Secondary Education.* Educators have regarded this report in many ways as the "Magna Carta" declaration of freedom of the secondary school from domination by the college and university, which major committee reports since 1893 had assumed to be the relation of the high school to the college. The opening sentence of the report declared, "Secondary education should be determined by the needs of the society to be served, the character of the individuals to be educated, and the knowledge of educational theory and practice available." Reinforcing the statement of the independence of the secondary school from higher educational domination, the Commission went on:

> In view of the important role of secondary education in achieving the objectives essential in American life, it follows that higher institutions of learning are not justified in maintaining entrance requirements and examinations of a character that handicap the secondary school in discharging its proper functions in a democracy.[28]

The Commission approved the 6-6 plan of school organization and further recommended the three-year junior high school, embracing Grades 7 through 9. In very small schools where the 3-3 type of secondary program could not readily be maintained, a four-year junior high school was suggested. The functions of the junior and senior high school were made clear in these words:

> In the junior period emphasis should be placed upon the attempt to help the pupil to explore his own aptitudes and to make at least provisional choice of the kinds of work to which he will devote himself. In the senior period emphasis should be given to training in the fields thus chosen. . . . In the junior

[28] National Education Association, *Cardinal Principles of Secondary Education,* Report of the Commission on the Reorganization of Secondary Education (Washington: U.S. Bureau of Education, Bulletin No. 35), 1918, pp. 7, 19-20.

high school there should be the gradual introduction of departmental instruction, some choice of subjects under guidance, promotion by subjects, prevocational courses, and a social organization that calls forth initiative and develops the sense of personal responsibility for the welfare of the group.[29]

Although this section has given recognition to the recommendations of major committees and educational leaders of national status, it should not be assumed that these only were occupied with the problem of school organization. A survey of the educational writings even in the early nineties reveals a widespread concern with the curriculum and organization of education from the elementary to the college level. After the turn of the century regional, state, and local groups became increasingly involved. Primary emphasis was placed on the original problem of President Eliot — that of reducing the time necessary for a student to meet college admission requirements. Attention from the beginning was naturally focused upon administrative and curriculum problems. As one writer declared, "The Committee of Ten started a generation of curriculum making by national committees of subject-matter specialists."[30] This was in part true; in most committees a heavy concentration of subject specialists was in evidence, although the total range of educational leadership was involved.

As the discussion progressed more fundamental issues came to the fore: the purpose of education in a democratic society which should control the curriculum and organization of the educational agencies, including the college; the nature of the educand and his needs at various stages of his social and educational development; the growing awareness of individual differences; and the ever-widening range of needs and interests of a rapidly growing school population representative of every segment of society. These larger issues, forming the basis of the junior high school idea, were fully reflected in the various committee reports and the addresses and writings of key educational leaders of the period.

6. *What other factors influenced the junior high school idea?*

School elimination studies

The problem of the holding power of the schools during the last years of the elementary school was generally recognized in the nineties. C. M.

[29] *Ibid.*, pp. 18-19.

[30] See Harold Rugg, "Three Decades of Mental Discipline: Curriculum Making via National Committees," in *The Foundations and Technique of Curriculum Construction*, Twenty-Sixth Yearbook of the National Society for the Study of Education, Part I (Bloomington, Ill.: Public School Publishing Company, 1926), Chap. 3.

Woodward, president of the St. Louis Board of Education, had presented data on the problems in the St. Louis schools as early as 1894. Again in 1900 he made a similar report, showing how rapid the dropouts became after the first four years in the elementary grades. Data were marshaled from as far back as the years 1879-1881 to indicate that of every 100 pupils in the second grade in St. Louis there were 44 in the fifth, 20 in the sixth, 9 in the seventh, and 8 in the eighth, 5 in the first year of high school and only 2 in the fourth year (see Table 1). The pattern had remained almost unchanged over a twenty-year period.

Woodward attributed these conditions to lack of interest because of (1) a school curriculum that did not challenge the children of the higher grammar grades and (2) general dissatisfaction that practical courses such as domestic science and manual training were not offered in the upper grades and high school.

As school attendance burgeoned, increased attention was given to the rate of dropouts. In 1905 Lyttle, addressing the Department of Secondary Education of the National Education Association, pointed out the fact that between the ages of thirteen and fifteen in Chicago and St. Louis, and between the ages of fourteen and sixteen in Boston, school dropouts each year range from 20 to 40 per cent of the total enrollment. Further, in St. Louis withdrawals are most numerous in the sixth and seventh grades, and 34 per cent of them occur "not because of necessity but for lack of interest." Lyttle attributes the major cause of this heavy dropout ratio to lack of appropriateness of the curriculum and methods used to challenge early adolescent boys and girls.[31]

In 1904 Superintendent William H. Maxwell of New York City found 39 per cent of the children of the elementary schools retarded. In 1908, A. S. Draper, Commissioner of Education of New York State, estimated that only

TABLE 1

St. Louis Schools — Attendance by Grades, November, 1899 and 1900

Grades	1	2	3	4	5	6	7	8	I	II	III	IV
1899	13,337	11,070	9,536	9,249	5,013	3,045	2,133	1,296	668	366	260	215
1900	12,970	11,238	10,089	9,134	5,677	3,012	2,143	1,468	733	353	255	214

From C. M. Woodward, "When and Why Pupils Leave School," in *Report of the U.S. Commissioner of Education,* 1899-1900, Vol. 2, pp. 1366-1367. See also C. M. Woodward, "At What Age Do Pupils Withdraw from the Public Schools?" in *Report of the U.S. Commissioner of Education,* 1894-1895, Vol. 2, Chap. XXIV.

[31] Lyttle, *op. cit.,* p. 431.

one-third to two-fifths of the pupils entering the first grade remained to complete the eighth grade.

Maladjustment and dropout facts such as these, observed on every hand, led to a number of extended studies to obtain more precise data on existing conditions. The first was made by Edward L. Thorndike of Columbia University, and its results were published in a monograph by the U.S. Bureau of

TABLE 2

Estimated Percentage of Pupils Entering School Who Continue to the Fourth, Fifth, etc., Grades in Each of 23 Cities

City	Grammar School Grade						High School Year			
	4	5	6	7	8	9	1	2	3	4
Baltimore	71.0	53.0	32.0	22.0	14.4	...	8.2	5.0	3.0	2.3
Boston	85.0	80.5	76.3	65.8	52.2	47.0	31.3	15.7	12.5	6.3
Cambridge	90.3	82.0	62.9	57.8	55.7	41.9	29.4	21.0	15.8	13.9
Chicago	86.3	85.2	62.3	49.2	35.0	...	14.0	9.8	6.6	5.5
Cleveland	97.2	79.6	61.9	45.3	33.1	...	19.9	12.6	10.0	7.4
Denver	98.0	86.0	78.0	57.0	44.0	...	...	...	...	...
Jersey City	75.9	65.5	50.6	35.6	26.4	...	9.2	5.0	2.9	2.4
Kansas City, Mo.	96.5	75.3	62.4	49.4	...	...	40.0	25.9	17.6	16.5
Los Angeles	95.4	95.0	80.0	61.5	45.1	...	39.0	21.6	11.7	6.2
Malden	86.7	85.4	79.8	65.9	62.4	54.0	42.8	28.9	18.5	14.9
Minneapolis	85.7	69.7	57.1	45.7	32.0	...	24.0	16.0	12.6	10.3
Newport	91.7	85.6	71.4	58.1	53.0	44.9	35.7	23.5	12.0	8.2
Newark	78.0	58.3	45.8	33.3	25.0	...	17.9	8.3	5.6	3.8
New Haven	85.0	76.0	68.0	57.0	35.0	...	24.0	17.0	14.0	9.1
New York	90.0	77.0	58.0	43.0	33.7	...	...	...	...	...
Paterson	86.4	71.8	52.4	32.0	19.4	...	10.9	6.8	5.1	3.7
St. Louis[a]	94.0	63.0	35.0	27.0	21.0	...	14.1	4.2	4.1	3.2
Springfield	99.0	82.4	78.0	66.2	53.4	38.5	30.0	24.6	18.2	12.8
Trenton	86.6	73.2	57.3	48.0	30.6	...	22.0	15.2	14.2	11.6
Washington[a]	93.4	86.9	70.6	57.5	52.1	...	...	...	...	...
Waterbury	84.0	81.0	64.0	54.0	43.0	...	32.0	26.0	14.0	8.0
Wilmington	90.6	81.1	73.8	51.6	39.0	...	33.7	11.6	8.4	...
Worcester	99.0	94.0	94.0	72.0	72.0	58.0	43.0	34.5	28.3	26.4
Medians	90.0	80.5	63.0	51.5	37.0[b]	...	27.0	16.0	12.5	8.0
Medians estimated in view of this and all other available information	90.0	81.0	68.0	54.0	40.0[c]	...	27.0	17.0	12.0	8.0

[a] White.
[b] Median of last grammar grades (7, 8, or 9) 38.5.
[c] Last grammar.

From Edward L. Thorndike, *The Elimination of Pupils from School* (Washington: U.S. Bureau of Education, Bulletin No. 4, 1907), p. 15.

Education in 1907.[32] Thorndike pointed out that the data of his study were inexact inasmuch as the statistical device used was to take the comparative enrollment data for each grade of a school system as of a specific date, which must account for holdovers of retarded pupils in a given grade as well as additions to the grade. Consequently this was not a precise study of the actual pupils who remained in a given grade out of those originally enrolled in Grade 1. Thorndike estimated that an exact study would show (1) that at least twenty-five out of every one hundred children (white) in the country who enter school stay only long enough to read simple English, to spell the words of common usage, and to learn to use the four basic operations of arithmetic, and that a fifth of the white children stayed only to the fifth grade, and (2) that less than one in ten graduate from the high school. He found great variation in the holding power of the schools in different communities, as revealed in Table 2.

A second study frequently quoted, which largely substantiated the Thorndike study, was made by Leonard P. Ayres in 1908. Confining himself to the larger cities, he found the general conditions of elimination to be approximately those found by Thorndike. His conclusions were slightly more optimistic as regards conditions in the elementary schools. The enrollment percentage medians for grades and high school of fifty-nine cities are shown in Table 3.

Ayres found extreme variations in the holding powers of the cities. For example, in Quincy, Massachusetts, for every one hundred pupils who entered the first grade eighty-two continued to the eighth grade, whereas in Camden, New Jersey, only seventeen out of every one hundred who began the first grade finished the eighth grade. The basic reason for the variation, Ayres concluded, lay in the school curriculum.

A much more extensive study of retardation and elimination was made by George D. Strayer, and based upon U.S. Census data collected in De-

TABLE 3

Percentage of Elimination, Grades 1-12

Grades	Elementary Grades									High School			
	1	2	3	4	5	6	7	8	9	1	2	3	4
Enrollment percentage medians	173	129	128	120	106	90	71	51	57	40	19	14	10

From Leonard P. Ayres, *Laggards in Our Schools* (New York: Russell Sage Foundation, 1909), p. 57.

[32] Edward L. Thorndike, *The Elimination of Pupils from School* (Washington: U.S. Bureau of Education, Bulletin No. 4, 1907).

cember, 1908. Strayer's findings were remarkably similar to those of Thorndike and Ayres.[33]

A plethora of lesser studies over the next ten years revealed, as might be expected, the same conditions. These were uniformly laid at the door of an unrealistic curriculum and a poor administrative organization of the educational system.

Growing recognition of problems of adolescence and individual differences

Two trends in educational thinking became increasingly noticeable as the agitation for educational reform gained momentum. The first concerned the nature of adolescence. The early interest in the adjustment of the program of elementary and secondary education to facilitate admission to college, as symbolized in the Committee of Ten recommendations, rapidly gave way at the turn of the century to the larger question of adjusting the school program to the changing interests and needs of adolescents.

Butler and Dewey had given prominent leadership in focusing attention upon the importance of adolescent development in the consideration of educational adjustments for the upper grades and high school. Then came the monumental two-volume study of *Adolescence* by G. Stanley Hall.[34] This document not only brought together the wealth of research by Hall and others on the subject but stimulated study, thinking, and discussion of the implications of the adolescent period and its characteristics for education.

Publication of Hall's work gave impetus to a parallel growing awareness of the larger problem of individual differences as they affected the educational program, though awareness of the wide variations in ability, aptitudes, and interests was based more on empirical observation than on specific research. However, the studies in this area then being carried on were a little later (1914) to be emphasized by Thorndike in his notable *Mental Work and Fatigue and Individual Differences and Their Causes*. The significance of the adolescent period and the related but more inclusive problem of individual differences have had an important influence in the development of the junior high school.

[33] For details see George D. Strayer, *Age and Grade Census of Schools and Colleges: A Study of Retardation and Elimination* (Washington: U.S. Bureau of Education, Bulletin No. 5, 1911), p. 135. An extended bibliography on retardation and elimination covering the years 1900-1910 is included, pp. 141-144.

[34] G. Stanley Hall, *Adolescence* (New York: Appleton Company, 1904).

7. *What were the emerging organizational practices of the junior high school before 1920?*

Developments to 1910

What these developments were depends upon what is accepted as a junior high school. Table 4 indicates the discrepancies between early reports of studies of the junior high school.

If the concept of the junior high school is not restricted to the middle term of the 6-3-3 form of administrative organization, but the Committee of Ten recommendation is accepted — that a six-year elementary school be followed by a two-year school associated with a four-year high school, forming together a six-year secondary school departmentalized with subject specialist teachers — then Richmond, Indiana, may properly lay claim to having established the first junior high school. Here a new school building was erected in 1895 to house a newly formed unit of the school system (evidently begun in 1896) made up of Grades 7 and 8. The departmental plan was introduced. The curriculum was vitalized by the introduction of modified algebra, modified English using units of literature in place of a formal reading course, and a more rigorous course in United States history. Elective choice could be made among Latin, French, English, music, art, and practical arts, available to both boys and girls. Subject specialists, promotion by subject, organization into homerooms with faculty advisers, and the beginning of an organized system of activities characterized this school.[35]

TABLE 4

Years in Which Junior High Schools Were Reportedly Established, 1890-1910

Date	1896	1898	1899	1900	1902	1904	1905	1907	1908	1909	1910	Total
Douglass	1	2	1	1	2	1		2	3	2	4	21
Briggs[a]	(2)?						1	1	3	3	11	19

[a] Briggs lists two before 1900 but does not specify dates.

Adapted from data in Aubrey A. Douglass, *The Junior High School,* Fifteenth Yearbook of the National Society for the Study of Education, Part III (Bloominton, Ill.: Public School Publishing Company, 1917), p. 25; and Thomas H. Briggs, *The Junior High School* (Boston: Houghton Mifflin Company, 1920), p. 32.

[35] See editorial in *The School Review* 47:564-566, October, 1939. Data based upon a "statement prepared in 1935 by N. C. Heironimus, principal of this intermediate school in Richmond, Indiana, in 1896 and until his death a principal in the Richmond schools. Also N. C. Heironimus, "Is This the Earliest Known Junior High School?" *The Clearing House* 14:518-519, May, 1940.

G. Vernon Bennett listed school systems in various stages of reorganization, 1896-1910. If some form of segregation of grades of the intermediate years with some departmentalization and elective subject offerings are taken as minimal features of a junior high school, then possibly Providence, Rhode Island, in 1898, with a 6-2-4 plan; Baltimore in 1902, with a 6-3-2 plan; Kalamazoo, Michigan, in 1902, with a 7-3-2 plan; Muskegon, Michigan, in 1903, with a 6-1-2-3 plan; Roanoke, Virginia, in 1910, with a 6-2-4 plan; Concord, New Hampshire, in 1910, with a 6-2-3 plan; Los Angeles in 1910, with a 6-2-4 plan; and Alameda, California, in 1910, with a 6-2-4 plan, also can be said to have moved definitely in the direction of the junior high school idea.[36]

The first three-year junior high school appeared in 1909-1910. Frank F. Bunker, then superintendent of schools at Berkeley, California, has claimed the honor of having first established a three-year junior high school (at that time called an intermediate school) in January, 1910. It featured separate housing, departmentalization, specialized teachers, promotion by subject, and an enriched curriculum with some elective privilege. However, in Columbus, Ohio, it is asserted that a separate three-year school was authorized in the summer of 1909 and began operation the following September as the Indianola Junior High School, antedating the Berkeley school by four months.

Developments between 1910 and 1920

It is clear from the accounts of Bunker and the superintendent of schools of Los Angeles that plans for a junior high school were being considered before Bunker left Los Angeles to take over the superintendency of the Berkeley schools. Thus Los Angeles was the next to organize a three-year school, in 1911, and other cities in rapid succession adopted forms of the three-year junior high school pioneered in Columbus and Berkeley.

Table 5 indicates the extent to which the junior high school organizational movement gathered momentum within the next few years.

It is necessary to add to this sampling the statement of Briggs, based upon a comprehensive study of all junior high schools reported by states in 1917, that "up to the spring of 1917, 800 junior high schools had been reported."[37]

Not all so-called junior high schools established after 1910 were three-year units. Table 6 indicates the variations of combinations called junior high schools that were reported for the period 1914-1918. Obviously a number of them did not meet the definition of a junior high school adopted in 1918 by the North Central Association of Colleges and Secondary Schools:

[36] See G. Vernon Bennett, *The Junior High School* (Baltimore: Warwick and York, 1919), pp. 31-32.

[37] Thomas H. Briggs, *The Junior High School* (Boston: Houghton Mifflin Company, 1920), p. 60.

TABLE 5

Growth of the Junior High School Movement in Cities Before 1920

Year	Number
Before 1900	2
1905	1
1907	1
1908	3
1909	3
1910	11
1911	9
1912	21
1913	27
1914	44
1915	76
1916	68
1917	6
	272

Adapted from data shown by Thomas H. Briggs, *The Junior High School* (Boston: Houghton Mifflin Company, 1920), p. 32.

Resolved, That the term Junior High School, as used by this Association, shall be understood to apply only to schools including the ninth grade combined with the eighth grade, or with the eighth and seventh grades, in an organization distinct from the grades above and the grades below.[38]

This definition gave attention only to the organizational framework of grade combinations of the junior high school. Matters of function, articulation, curriculum, and departmentalization, among other characteristics that had been emphasized as important to this period for almost two decades, were not mentioned. The advanced and vital educational ideas stressed in the Columbus, Ohio, and Berkeley, California, reorganization plans were overlooked in the effort of the North Central Association to bring some simple limitations to the grade combination pattern.

However, a year later the North Central Association defined the junior high school more rigorously:

A junior high school is a school in which the seventh, eighth, and ninth grades are segregated in a building (or portion of a building) by themselves, possess an organization and administration of their own that is distinct from

[38] North Central Association *Bulletin,* 1918, p. 6.

TABLE 6

Distribution of Grade Combinations in Junior High Schools, 1914-1918

Studies	U.S. Commissioner of Education[a]		Davis[b]		Douglass[c]	
Grade Combination	Number	Per Cent	Number	Per Cent	Number	Per Cent
5-7					1	0.5
5-8					1	0.5
6-6					10	5.4
6-7					1	0.5
6-8	3	1.1	22	7.5	11	6.0
7	2	0.8				
7-8	71	26.6	133	45.4	77	41.8
7-9	174	65.2	89	30.7	64	34.8
7-10					7	3.8
7-12			18	6.1		
8	6	2.2	11	3.5	3	1.6
8-9	8	3.0	8	2.7	8	4.3
8-10	1	0.4				
9	2	0.8			1	0.5
Others			11	3.8		
Total	267	100.1	292	99.7	184	99.7

This table is adapted from the following sources:

[a] Report of the United States Commissioner of Education, 1914, pp. 148-149.

[b] Calvin O. Davis, "Junior High Schools in the North Central Association Territory," *The School Review*, 26:324-336, May, 1918.

[c] Aubrey A. Douglass, *The Junior High School,* Fifteenth Yearbook of the National Society for the Study of Education, Part III (Bloomington, Ill.: Public School Publishing Company, 1917), p. 88.

the grades above and grades below, and are taught by a separate corps of teachers. Such schools, to fall within the classification of junior high schools, must likewise be characterized by the following:

1. A program of studies decidedly greater in scope and richness of content than that of the traditional elementary school.
2. Some pupil choice of studies, elected under supervision.
3. Departmental teaching.
4. Promotion by subject.
5. Provision for testing out individual aptitudes in academic, prevocational, and vocational work.
6. Some recognition of the peculiar needs of the retarded pupil of adolescent age, as well as special consideration of the supernormal.
7. Some recognition of the plan of supervised study.[39]

[39] *Ibid.*, 1919, p. 4.

This definition set high standards for schools professing to be junior high schools. Judged by a study of junior high schools made by C. O. Davis and reported to the North Central Association at its twenty-third annual meeting in 1918, a large number of such schools fell far short of these standards. Of 293 professed junior high schools that formed the basis of this study, 45 per cent included Grades 7 and 8 only; 30 per cent included Grades 7, 8, and 9; 7.5 per cent included Grades 6, 7, and 8; 6 per cent maintained an undifferentiated six-year school; and the rest utilized other grade combinations.

Placement of the junior high school in separate buildings or portions of a building was another standard inadequately met. Only 17 per cent were housed in separate buildings. Forty-seven per cent were housed with the senior high school, and 29 per cent were housed with the elementary school. Of the latter two categories 36 per cent were "grouped in segregated portions of the common building."

With respect to the other criteria set up by the North Central Association, 59 per cent claimed provisions for supervised study, 52 per cent allowed some freedom of choice of subjects or curriculums, 82 per cent promoted by subject, 95 per cent practiced departmentalization, 55 per cent of the teachers taught both in the junior and senior high schools, 44 per cent made special provision for pupils who could not stay to complete the full program, 56 per cent "adjust[ed] school work . . . to the peculiar needs of the sickly," and 52 per cent provided for those who were "inept at book study and who do better with more concrete or vocational studies."

With regard to the pushing down into the seventh and eighth grades of subjects previously offered in the four-year high school, the evidence indicates that the recommendations which began with the Committee of Ten had been well heeded. Algebra, science, and languages were found to be prominent offerings at the seventh- and eighth-grade levels. Many other subjects emphasized by later groups — domestic science, manual training, music, and agriculture — were part of the curriculum of these early grades.

After presenting the above data of the study Davis concludes:

> In general summary, therefore, it may be said that approximately 300 schools in the North Central territory have consciously sought to take steps looking to the modification of the 8-4 plan of organization in harmony with the junior high school idea; that possibly 175, or 60%, of these have already incorporated enough of the commonly accepted characteristics of a Junior High School to be entitled to bear that name; that another group of 75 (approximately 25%) have made good beginnings, but have advanced only a short distance on the road to reform; and that the remaining 43, or approximately 15% of the whole number, are deceiving themselves with names — are mistaking the husk for the kernel.[40]

[40] Calvin O. Davis, "Junior High Schools in the North Central Association Territory, 1917-1918," in the Appendix of *Procedures of the Twenty-Third Annual Meeting* of the North Central Association of Colleges and Secondary Schools, 1918.

Figure 1 indicates the relative emphasis upon certain functions of the junior high school, as expressed by school administrators and other educational leaders, obtained in a study of school documents (usually prepared by school

FIGURE 1

Percentages of Statements in School Documents and of Educational Leaders Concerning Functions of the Junior High School

Peculiar Functions Proposed

Per Cent

0 10 20 30 40 50 60 70 80 90 100

1. Retention of pupils
2. Economy of time
3. Recognition of individual differences
4. Providing conditions for better teaching
5. Improving the disciplinary situation and socializing opportunities
6. Exploration and guidance
7. Beginnings of vocational education
8. Recognizing the nature of the child at adolescence
9. Securing better scholarship
10. Effecting financial economy
11. Relieving the building situation

School documents
Educational leaders

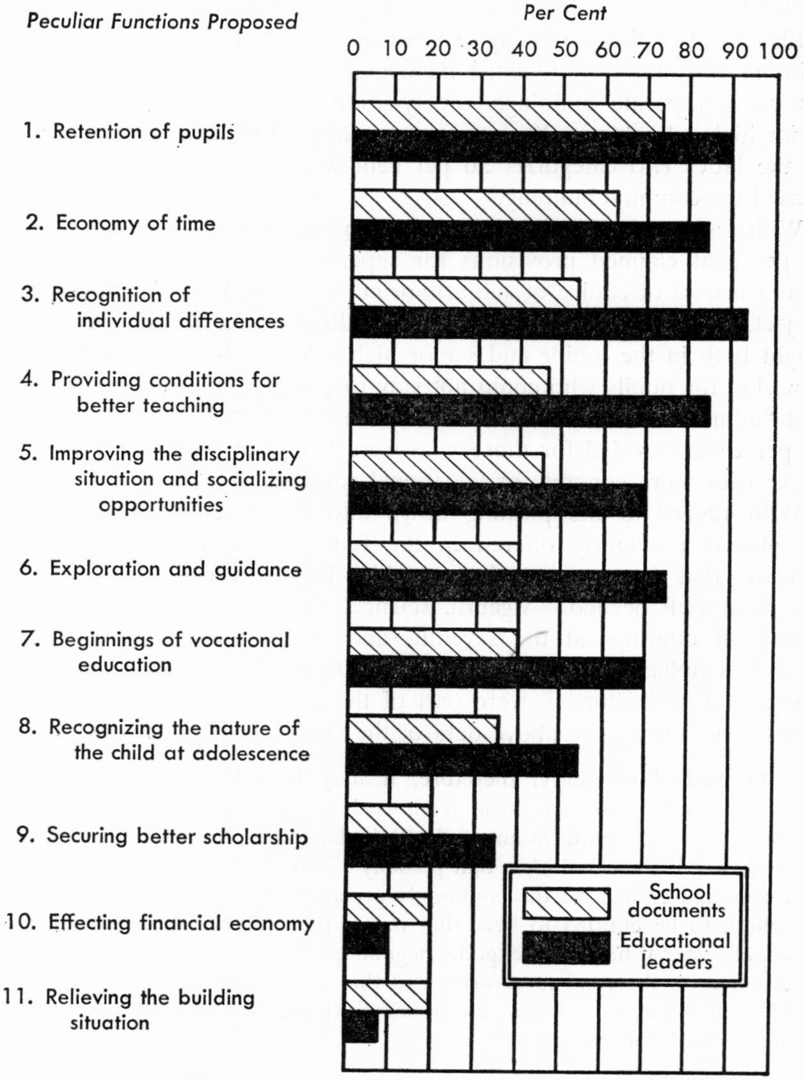

Redrawn with permission from a chart appearing in *The Junior High School* by Leonard V. Koos, published by Ginn and Company, owners of the copyright.

superintendents and principals) and the published statements of educational specialists largely during the period 1910-1916.

Another significant summary of current educational thinking on the functions of the junior high school of approximately 1920 is given by Davis from his study of existing practices and contemporary educational writings:

> What is a junior high school? — It may be said that a junior high school is a school that comprehends the following factors:
>
> 1. A separate organization of the seventh, eighth, and ninth grades, or at least, two of these grades.
> 2. A separate building in which to house the grades.
> 3. A separate staff of teachers and supervisory officers to administer the work of these grades.
> 4. A program of studies differing greatly from the course of study to be found in the like-numbered grades of the traditional school in America.
> 5. A partial or complete departmental organization of subject matter and teaching.
> 6. The organization of a limited number of curricula, each containing groups of constant and of variable courses.
> 7. A definite, effective plan of educational and vocational guidance, definitely and effectively administered.
> 8. Certain elective studies, to be chosen by pupils under guidance.
> 9. Socialized recitation periods.
> 10. Supervised study periods.
> 11. Promotion by subject.
> 12. Methods of instruction, differing notably from the methods employed in the grades above and the grades below.
> 13. The organization and administration of student activities in accordance with the needs and interests of adolescent pupils, regardless of the practices prevailing in the grades above or below.
> 14. The organization of the school year, the school week, the school day, and the school hour in such a manner as to produce a school discipline, a school spirit, and a school accomplishment that finds justification in and through the principles of psychology, physiology, sociology, and pedagogy, regardless of the bias of tradition, the demands of particularized life callings, and the requirements of the senior high school and colleges.
> 15. The admission of pupils to the school on the basis of what is best for each individual, without undue regard to the conventional school work he has mastered.
> 16. The recognition of individual differences in capacities, tastes, and purposes in the organization and conduct of class work.
> 17. A new name.[41]

At the close of the third decade of accelerated attention to the junior high school years which began with the concern of the Committee of Ten in 1893

[41] Calvin O. Davis, *Junior High School Education* (Yonkers, N.Y.: World Book Company, 1924), pp. 13-14.

for the articulation of the work of Grades 7 and 8 with that of the high school, it may be concluded that the major ideas of this committee had now been accepted by a significant segment of our schools. Even some features distinctly emphasized only since 1900 are now accepted generally in theory and to a considerable extent in practice, such as vocational training, aspects of individual differences, and exploration and guidance.

It is well to note, however, that recognition of the uniqueness of early adolescence, stressed by such eminent leaders as Nicholas Murray Butler, John Dewey, and G. Stanley Hall, had little influence on the development of the junior high school prior to 1920, as may be seen from the figure above by Koos and the statement of accepted functions by Davis. Dewey had characterized Grades 1-6 as the school of childhood — the elementary school — and the junior high school grades as the school of early adolescence. The two schools had distinct functions related in part to the biological maturity of each age group. These men were concerned primarily with relating the basic functions of the junior high school to emerging adolescent needs, not with the organizational patterns of the school. Yet the latter are what seem to have caught the imagination of those who established or sponsored junior high schools, such as the influential North Central Association, whose 1918 and 1919 characterizations of the junior high school center upon organization rather than upon the needs of early adolescence. Out of four surveys of opinions of educational leaders as to what should be the characteristics and functions of the junior high school, only one mentioned provision for adolescent needs, and it was low on the list.[42]

Nevertheless, the developments made in this new school, strongly encouraged by educational leaders and organizations like the North Central Association, marked an important advance in the evolution of this phase of secondary education.

8. *What were the developments in the junior high school between 1920 and 1960?*

Developments to 1940

In the early twenties Davis, who had been active in the junior high school movement since 1915, said:

> The junior high school may be defined as a school unit developed in the United States within recent years and designed to furnish all pupils, between the ages of twelve and fifteen years approximately, (1) continued common education on high elementary levels, and (2) the beginnings of a differen-

[42] Briggs, *op. cit.*, pp. 49-56.

tiated or secondary education adapted to each pupil's individual needs. By providing a program of studies extensive in scope and by making use of methods of instruction and training that are grounded in the contemporary interests and concrete experiences of boys and girls of the early adolescent period, the new school seeks to mediate between strictly elementary school work and methods and the more specialized contents and processes of the senior high school and of the workaday world. To this end the new educational unit endeavors to organize its activities so as to retain a larger proportion of the pupils in the school for a longer period than has been customary in the past; to give them an appreciative notion of the world and its work in all of its diversified forms . . . to assist them to explore their own capacities, interests, and aptitudes, and to choose, at least tentatively, a course of procedure that gives promise of yielding for them the greatest amount of happiness and, for society, the greatest and most effective service; and, finally, to furnish them such a training as will function ultimately in the career of their choice.[43]

In this same paragraph Davis is less exacting about stipulating Grades 7, 8, and 9 as the inflexible organizational pattern of the junior high school. He says, "To accomplish this program the new unit most frequently makes use of grades seven, eight, and nine in the school system."

This is a unique definition when considered against a backdrop of the usual definitions and statements of functions formulated prior to 1920. It emphasizes the purposes and functions of the junior high school in at least seven particulars, which may be summarized as follows:

1. To provide a gradual transition from the elementary school to the secondary school.
2. To exercise a holding power function and reduce dropouts during this period.
3. To help youth understand the nature of the society of which they are a part.
4. To provide an exploration period for youth to discover and understand their "capacities, interests, and aptitudes."
5. To assist pupils to make the fullest adjustments possible for self-realization and service to society.
6. To provide definite vocational career preparation.
7. To recognize the uniqueness of this school to provide for the needs of early adolescence. (This is probably the most significant of the functions emphasized by Davis and pervades every aspect of the definition.)

The advanced conception of the function of the junior high school held by Davis was shared by some educational leaders of the early twenties such as Briggs, Koos, Cox, Smith, and Spaulding.

[43] Davis, *op. cit.*, pp. 8-9.

During the thirties the emphasis upon the uniqueness of the period of early adolescence for the junior high school program steadily gained acceptance. Glass asserted, "The philosophy of the junior high school movement will be sound in proportion as it is founded upon the psychology of early adolescence."[44] Proctor and Ricciardi of Stanford University support this point: "The junior high school is an attempt to reach and serve the individual student in the early adolescent stage."[45] To read the North Central Association *Quarterly* during the thirties is to recognize Charles H. Judd as an outspoken advocate of the junior high school as a distinct school for early adolescence:

> The junior high school period of life is a period of unique intellectual and social demands. Ninth grade pupils are more like pupils in the grades immediately preceding than they are like pupils in the upper years of the high school. . . . Human nature from twelve to fifteen years of age is different from human nature from fifteen to eighteen. Human nature calls for a junior high school which is different from a senior high school.[46]

Another writer of dubious historical accuracy but evidently caught up in the vortex of contemporary thinking declared, "From the first, the junior high school has been organized around the concept of adolescent needs."[47] And the major textbook on the junior high school to appear during the latter part of the fourth decade defined this school as follows:

> The junior high school is an organization of the seventh, eighth, and ninth grades into an administrative unit for the purpose of providing instruction and training suitable to the varied and changing physical, mental, and social natures and needs of immature, maturing, and mature pupils. "Maturity" here means the arrival of adolescence.[48]

A natural corollary of this growing stress upon the centrality of the needs of adolescence in the junior high school period was the emerging emphasis upon "guidance" as an aspect of education at this time. The following statements, originating at the east and west extremes of the country, are typical. From the East: "The faculty of the Benjamin Franklin Junior High School in Uniontown, Pennsylvania, has definitely committed itself to the thesis that the guidance of youth is its major function, and a conscious effort is being made

[44] James M. Glass, "Tested and Acceptable Philosophy of the Junior High School Movement," *Junior-Senior High School Clearing House,* 7:334, February, 1933.

[45] William M. Proctor and Nicholas Ricciardi (eds.), *The Junior High School, Its Organization and Administration* (Berkeley: Stanford University Press, 1930), p. 11.

[46] Quoted in C. O. Davis, "A Distinctive Training Curriculum for Junior High School Teachers," *North Central Association Quarterly* 8:507, April, 1934.

[47] Walter R. Hepner, "The Junior High School," *California Journal of Secondary Education,* 13:459, December, 1938.

[48] Ralph W. Pringle, *The Junior High School* (New York: McGraw-Hill Book Co., Inc., 1937), p. 68.

to make every resource of the school available for this all-important work."[49] From the West: "The major trend in junior high school reorganization is toward a new synthesis of curriculum and administration to the end that the whole of pupils' activities have guidance values and contribute directly to a harmonious and unified outlook on life."[50]

There is no doubt that the period 1920-1940 showed new and changing emphases in the development and purposes of the junior high school. It is also true that these changes were most marked in the thinking of our educational leadership of the time, while educational practice lagged far behind advancing theory. Those impatient with this situation may well remember that social theory is generally at least a generation ahead of social practice. Some careful students of education, however, believe there is an even greater lag between educational theory and educational practice.

The changing emphases in junior high school education during the second twenty years of its developing theory and practice may be summarized thus:

1. Early adolescence became the focal point of attention around which to develop education for this period. The few voices raised at the turn of the century in behalf of the uniqueness of early adolescence for education became a chorus by 1940.

2. The college preparation ideal of the Committee of Ten, so dominant even into the second decade of this century, rapidly gave way to a recognition that the junior high school had a unique function completely independent of that of preparation for college.

3. The exploratory function passed from the limited concern with vocational interests to encompass the total range of the interests, the abilities, and the capacities of the individual, including an understanding of self in interaction with his environment.

4. The "economy of time" emphasis shifted from a means of earlier entrance to college to a better utilization of time in the seventh and eighth grades particularly to deal with the peculiar educational needs of early adolescence.

5. "Retention of pupils," considered of great importance in the first two decades, rapidly decreased in emphasis as enrollments in the junior high school years began to approach saturation by 1940.

6. The emphasis upon individual differences gained momentum in this period but broadened in character and complexity.

7. Departmentalization fell sharply as the demand increased for the self-contained classroom and block-time and core curriculum programs.

8. Along with the de-emphasis upon departmentalization came a new look at the problem of electives, with growing stress upon broader patterns of general education and limited electives.

[49] Harold R. Mauer, "Guidance at Work in a Junior High School," *Junior-Senior High School Clearing House,* 6:547, May, 1932.

[50] Hepner, *op. cit.,* p. 462.

9. Recognition of the unique personal and social problems of early adolescence, and awareness of the experience concept of learning meant that a much larger place was given to pupil activity programs.

10. Vocational guidance gave way to educational guidance, and in the thirties increasingly to personal and social guidance, with the teacher logically accepting more and more responsibility for some aspects of personal and social guidance.

11. Emphasis upon the improvement of the quality of teaching in the junior high school underwent radical reorientation during the late thirties. The old argument had been that departmentalization would bring to these grades more rigorously prepared subject-matter specialists and consequently better qualified teachers. However, the counter emphasis upon the nature of individual differences and the uniqueness of the early adolescent years, the shift in guidance away from vocational-educational to personal-social, the return to the self-contained classroom, and the introduction of block-time and core curriculum teaching led to a new concept of teacher preparation. Greater understanding of the nature of early adolescence, individual differences, the learning process, and guidance was called for, as well as the ability to implement this knowledge in the classroom.

12. That the junior high school idea became firmly established during this period is reflected in the rapid growth of separate three-year schools — from 387 in 1922 to 2372 in 1938 — and of junior-senior high schools — from 1088 in 1922 to 6203 in 1938.

Developments to 1960

Educational thinking. A survey of the educational writings of this period reveals that a sharp shift in the discussion of the junior high school took place between 1920 and 1940. The next twenty years represents largely a further development of the thinking that had gained such impetus by 1940.

This important change in thinking is most clearly marked in the redirection of emphasis — away from organizational pattern and toward educational function. Whereas the North Central Association back in 1918 had defined the junior high school in terms of its inclusive grade combination, toward the end of the last period major attention was given to the educational needs of early adolescence. The two most widely used texts on the junior high school published at the time clearly reveal the different orientation. Smith, Standley, and Hughes did not attempt a formal definition of the junior high school but commented thus: "Definitions of the junior high school in terms of grade organization are found to be inadequate. . . . Today educational emphasis is being directed toward the formulation and implementation of a program of studies suitable to children of junior-high-school age."[51]

[51] Maurice M. Smith, L. L. Standley, and Cecil L. Hughes, *Junior High School Education: Its Principles and Procedures* (New York: McGraw-Hill Book Co., Inc., 1942), pp. 31-32.

Fourteen years later Gruhn and Douglass reflected essentially this same relationship of values: "The junior high school is an educational program which is designed particularly to meet the needs, the interests, and the abilities of boys and girls during early adolescence." And "A school building, grade organization, and certain administrative features are important in the junior high school only to the extent that they have a bearing on that educational program."[52]

In a statement made near the close of this period the Southern Association of Colleges and Secondary Schools spoke quite clearly on this point:

> The junior high school evolved as an institution conceived to meet the unique physical, social, emotional, and intellectual needs of the late pre-adolescent and early adolescent. The true junior high school is vastly more than a grouping of grades; it involves a program keyed to the growth and development of boys and girls in the late stages of childhood and early years of adolescence.[53]

James B. Conant, who completed a study of the seventh and eighth grades in 1959, agreed with the above writers:

> Because of wide diversity in school organization, professional disagreement, and my own observations, I conclude that the place of grade 7, 8, and 9 in the organization of a school system is of less importance than the program provided for adolescent youth.
>
> . . . The educational program in grades 7 and 8 should reflect the transitional nature of these grades. First, parents and teachers are well aware that early adolescence is a very special period physically, emotionally, and socially. It is a crucial age in the transition from childhood to adulthood and often presents many problems.[54]

Also in 1959, the Committee on Junior High School Education of the influential National Association of Secondary-School Principals, concerned that some semiofficial guidance be given the many communities considering new school buildings at this time, prepared a brief statement relative to the organizational pattern of the school to serve the early adolescent period:

> In deciding upon the kind of grade organization, the major consideration should be the educational welfare of children and youth. . . .

[52] William T. Gruhn and Harl R. Douglass, *The Modern Junior High School* (New York: The Ronald Press Company, rev. ed., 1956), p. 4.

[53] *The Junior High School Program* (Atlanta, Ga.: Southern Association of Colleges and Secondary Schools, 1958), p. 5.

[54] James B. Conant, *Recommendations for Education in the Junior High School Years, A Memorandum to School Boards* (Princeton, N.J.: Educational Testing Service, 1960), p. 12.

> Early adolescents differ markedly in characteristics from pre-adolescence and later-adolescent youth. . . . Therefore, our schools should be organized and administered with some regard to the age characteristics of pupils.

After a discussion of the relative merits of different organizational patterns the Committee summarized its recommendations thus:

> 1. That the three-year junior high school, including grades 7, 8, and 9, is the best type of grade organization to provide an educational program for early adolescence.
> 2. That the combined junior-senior high school is desirable in those communities where the enrollment in grades 7-12 is too small to establish separate junior and senior high schools.
> 3. That the two-year junior high school may be justified in those communities where current conditions make it difficult or impossible to have a three-year junior high school.[55]

Growth. Although there has been a healthy shift of primary emphasis during this period from organizational mechanics to educational function, the organizational pattern is still recognized as contributing to the effectiveness of the program of the junior high school years. The steady growth of the various grade patterns in our public secondary schools from 1920 to 1959 is revealed in Table 7.

It is of interest to note that approximately 63 per cent of all public secondary schools are either of the three-year separate junior high school type or the six-year combined secondary school. However, the growth of the three-year junior high school between 1952 and 1959 has shown only a slight gain over the growth of the combined six-year secondary school, in spite of the obvious preference of educators for the separate junior high school.[56]

A recent study by the Research Division of the National Education Association offers a probable explanation of this situation. The separate junior high school is particularly popular in large urban centers. It was found that 82 to 84 per cent of school districts over thirty thousand population have one or more separate junior high schools, whereas only 31 per cent of urban communities under five thousand population have them. The study suggests two possible inferences: First, in the smaller school systems, still predominant in the United States, where enrollments are small, it has not been considered feasible to offer a desirable educational program at the excessive costs involved in maintaining separate small junior high schools; and second, further growth

[55] Reprinted by permission from "Recommended Grade Organization for Junior High School Education," *Bulletin of the National Association of Secondary-School Principals,* 43:40-42, September, 1959. Copyright: Washington, D.C.

[56] "The Junior High School Today," *NEA Research Bulletin,* 39:47-50, May, 1961.

TABLE 7

Number of Various Types of Public High Schools in the United States, 1920-1959

Type	1920		1930		1938		1952		1959	
	Number	Per Cent of Total	Number	Per Cent of Total	Number	Per Cent of Total	Number	Per Cent of Total	Number	Per Cent of Total
Junior high schools	55	.4	1,842	8.3	2,372	9.6	3,227	13.6	4,996	20.6
Junior-senior high schools	828	5.8	3,287	14.8	6,203	25.2	8,591	36.2	10,130	41.9
Senior high schools (6-3-3)	15	.1	648	2.9	959	3.9	1,021	4.3	1,642	6.8
Reorganized four-year high schools (6-2-4)	7	.01					739	3.1	1,396	5.8
All reorganized schools	905	6.3	5,777	26.0	9,534	38.7	13,578	57.2	18,164	75.1
Regular high schools (8-4)	13,421	93.7	16,460	74.0	15,056	61.3	10,168	42.8	6,023	24.9
Total[a]	14,326	100.0	22,237	100.0	24,590	100.0	23,746	100.0	24,187	100.0

[a] Excludes ungraded schools, as follows: 34 in 1938 and 11 in 1952.

Adapted from data in Walter H. Gaumnitz and J. Dan Hull, "Junior High School Versus the Traditional (8-4) High School Organization," *The Bulletin of the National Association of Secondary-School Principals,* 38:118, March, 1954, Table 2; and U.S. Office of Education, "Advance Release for December 2, 1960," p. 3.

FIGURE 2

Relative Enrollments in Various Types of Public Secondary Schools in the United States, 1920, 1952, and 1959

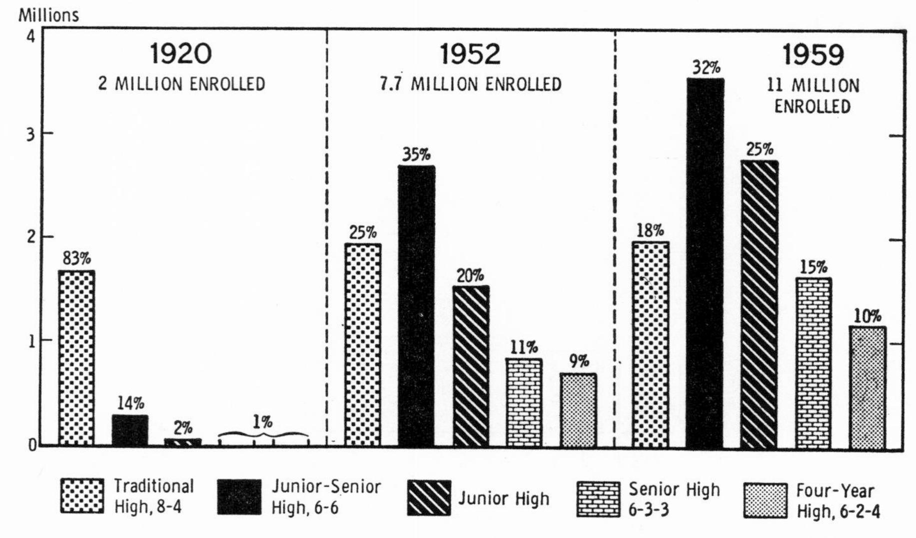

From "Organizational Pattern of the Nation's Public Secondary Schools," *School Life,* May, 1960, p. 3.

of the separate junior high school will be governed in part by the rapidity with which small school districts can be eliminated.

An index of the real growth of the junior high school movement is more accurately observed in the enrollments in the reorganized secondary schools than in the number of separate junior high schools. This is graphically shown in Figure 2, which reveals the rapid shift of enrollment away from the traditional 8-4 pattern to some form of reorganized public secondary school in 1920, 1952, and 1959. Eighty-two per cent of all public secondary school pupils in 1959 were in reorganized secondary schools, compared to less than 17 per cent in 1920.

SELECTED BIBLIOGRAPHY

Ayres, Leonard P. *Laggards in Our Schools.* New York: Russel Sage Foundation, 1909.

Baker, James H. *Economy of Time in Education.* Report of the Committee of the National Council. Washington: U.S. Bureau of Education, Bulletin No. 38, 1913.

Bennett, G. Vernon. *The Junior High School.* Baltimore: Warwick and York, 1919. Chaps. 2, 4.

Bossing, Nelson L. *Principles of Secondary Education.* Englewood Cliffs, N.J.: Prentice-Hall, Inc., rev. ed., 1955. Chap. 2.

Briggs, Thomas H. *The Junior High School.* Boston: Houghton Mifflin Company, 1920. Chaps. 2, 4.

Bunker, Frank F. *Reorganization of the Public School System.* Washington: U.S. Bureau of Education, Bulletin No. 8, 1916.

———. *The Junior High School Movement — Its Beginnings.* Washington: W. F. Roberts Company, 1935. Chaps. 1-7.

Butler, Nicholas Murray. "The Scope and Function of Secondary Education," *Educational Review,* 16:15-27, June, 1898.

Cardinal Principles of Secondary Education. Report of the Commission on the Reorganization of Secondary Education, National Education Association. Washington: U.S. Bureau of Education, Bulletin No. 35, 1918.

Cubberley, Ellwood P. *Public Education in the United States.* Boston: Houghton Mifflin Company, 1919.

Davis, Calvin O. *Junior High School Education.* Yonkers, N.Y.: World Book Company, 1924. Chap. 2.

———. *A History of the North Central Association of Colleges and Secondary Schools, 1895-1945.* Ann Arbor, Michigan: The North Central Association of Colleges and Secondary Schools, 1945.

Dewey, John. "Current Problems in Secondary Education," *School Review,* 10:13-28, January, 1902.

———. "Shortening the Years of the Elementary School," *School Review,* 11:17-20, January, 1903.

Douglass, Aubrey A. *The Junior High School.* Fifteenth Yearbook of the National Society for the Study of Education, Part III. Bloomington, Ill.: Public School Publishing Company, 1917.

"Editorial," *The School Review,* 47:564-566, October, 1939.

Eliot, Charles W. *Educational Reform: Essays and Addresses.* New York: The Century Company, 1901.

Ford, Edmund A. 'Organization of the Nation's Public Secondary Schools," *School Life,* 42:10-12, May, 1960.

——— and Virgil R. Walker. *Number of Public Secondary Schools: Statistics of Education in the United States, 1958-59 Series.* Washington: U.S. Office of Education, 1961.

Gruhn, William T., and Harl R. Douglass. *The Modern Junior High School.* New York: The Ronald Press Company, rev. ed., 1956. Chap. 1.

Hall, G. Stanley. *Adolescence* (2 vols.). New York: Appleton Company, 1904.

Hanus, P. H. "A Six Year High School Program," *Educational Review,* 25:455-463, May, 1903.

Heironomus, N. C. "Is This the Earliest Known Junior High School?" *The Clearing House,* 14:518-519, May, 1940.

Koos, Leonard V. *The Junior High School.* New York: Harcourt, Brace and Howe, 1920. Chap. 1.

Lytle, E. W. "Should the Twelve-Year Course of Study Be Equally Divided Between the Elementary School and the Secondary School?" National Education Association *Journal of Proceedings and Addresses,* 1905, pp. 428-433.

Monroe, Paul. *Founding of the American Public School System.* New York: The Macmillan Company, 1940.

National Education Association. "Report of the Committee on College Entrance Requirements," *Journal of Proceedings and Addresses,* 1899, pp. 659-660.

———. "Report of the Committee on Equal Division of the Twelve Years in the Public Schools Between the District and High Schools," *Journal of Proceedings and Addresses,* 1907, pp. 705-710.

———. *Report of the Committee of Fifteen on Elementary Education.* New York: American Book Company, 1895. See also *Journal of Proceedings and Addresses,* 1895, pp. 232-237.

———. "Report of the Committee on Six-Year Course of Study," *Journal of Proceedings and Addresses,* 1908, pp. 625-628.

———. *Report of the Committee of Ten on Secondary School Studies.* New York: American Book Company, 1894.

———. "Third Report of the Committee on Six-Year Course of Study," *Journal of Proceedings and Addresses,* 1909, pp. 498-503.

Pringle, Ralph W. *The Junior High School.* New York: McGraw-Hill Book Co., Inc., 1937. Chap. 1.

Smith, Maurice M., L. L. Standley, and C. L. Hughes. *Junior High School Education: Its Principles and Procedures.* New York: McGraw-Hill Book Co., Inc., 1942. Chap. 1.

Snedden, D. S. "The Six Year High School," *Educational Review,* 26:525-529, December, 1903.

Strayer, George D. *Age and Grade Census of Schools and Colleges: A Study of Retardation and Elimination.* Washington: U.S. Bureau of Education, Bulletin No. 5, 1911.

Thorndike, Edward L. *The Elimination of Pupils from School.* Washington: U.S. Bureau of Education, Bulletin No. 4, 1907.

Woodward, C. W. "At What Age Do Pupils Withdraw from the Public Schools?" *Report of the U.S. Commissioner of Education,* 1894-1895. Vol. 2, Chap. XXIV.

———. "When and Why Pupils Leave School?" *Report of the U.S. Commissioner of Education,* 1899-1900. Vol. 2, pp. 1366-1367.

2

Philosophy, Purposes, and Functions

A listing of brief quotations from educational literature is illustrative of the scope of misconception attending the philosophy, purposes, and functions of education in the junior high school:

> An overgrown elementary school.
> A school in which the age of the students defies analysis.
> A miniature senior high school.
> Copy cat of the four year high school.
> Sort of step child in the educational organization.
> Another school curriculum out of touch with the real nature and problems of early adolescents in a democratic society.
> The present program of most junior high schools — obsolete!
> The typical junior high school, imitation of senior high school.
> The junior high school, a mistake or landmark.
> A kind of No Man's Land between elementary and senior high school.
> Junior high school, kind of buffer between elementary and high school.
> Junior high school is bad to the extent that it simply imitates either the school for early childhood or the school for mature adults.
> The forgotten teaching area.
> Another school, another gap to disturb youth in climbing the twelve rounds of the ladder of public education.

This degree of confusion attests to the sustained discontent with existing educational programs offered in the junior high school. Dissatisfaction is frequently expressed by professional educators in colleges, by junior high school administrators, and by teachers.

Although early in the establishment of the junior high school there was concern about the philosophical basis of this school as distinct from that of the school divisions above and below, only within recent years have its peculiar functions and purposes been generally recognized. Even now there are those who see the junior high school as essentially a smaller image of the traditional high school, but organized administratively so as to realize more easily the purposes handed down in the now well publicized *Report of the Committee of Ten* of 1893.

1. What is the basis of a philosophy of education?

One of the difficulties in stating a philosophy, for the junior high school or for any aspect of education, is the fact that virtually every teacher and administrator has an operative philosophy of education, whether it is clearly or vaguely understood, and however inconsistent it may be with actual practice.

It is important that the school staff, from the administrator and the teacher to the janitor and the clerical worker, have a common viewpoint with respect to the purposes of the junior high school, as well as its relation to the total educational system, and their particular part in the realization of these purposes.

The relevance of this philosophy to the larger purposes of the American democratic ideal must be clearly understood. Further, the implications for its practical implementation must be perceived by all. The school personnel must always be conscious of the school's relationship to the larger society of which it is but a part, albeit an important part. The school as an institution is the instrument of a society for the perpetuation of itself and in the philosophy of American democracy carries an additional responsibility for the constant exploration of ways and means of expanding and implementing the basic concepts of democracy.

Equally important, administrators, teachers, and all others in contact with pupils, including parents, should be fully aware that historically much of educational theory and practice in America has borne the stamp of the authoritarian spirit and method of European education in which our forefathers were trained. Unfortunately, the authoritarianism of the older European education is still all too prevalent in American schoolrooms.

In accordance with the general philosophy of American democratic society, education in the ideals and practices of the democratic way of life becomes the responsibility of all associated with the school. The enormity and scope of this responsibility are evident and of special significance to all who understand the influence of social change upon the educational task. The tremendous technological advances of our time have led to social changes, necessitating modifications in the preparation required for healthful, productive living. The current educational program quite clearly must look toward today's and tomorrow's requirements as well as toward yesterday's accomplishments or failures.

All educational philosophy must be framed within the foregoing basic concepts before individual or collective professional tenets may be considered sound or applicable. Consequently, all prospective teachers and administrators must be offered opportunities to examine their own educational beliefs and have access to resources which they may utilize to clarify, broaden, and modify them. This self-analysis and study should provide each with a well-formulated social and educational philosophy with which to help early youth to acquire the ideals and behavioral competencies so essential to future citizens in a democratic society.

The way in which the democratic ideal should guide the education of American youth has been succinctly stated by the Commission on the Reorganization of Secondary Education in the famous document *Cardinal Principles of Secondary Education* thus:

> Education in the United States should be guided by a clear conception of the meaning of democracy. It is the ideal of democracy that the individual and society may find fulfillment each in the other. Democracy sanctions neither the exploitation of the individual by society, nor the disregard of the interests of society by the individual. More explicitly —
>
> The purpose of democracy is so to organize society that each member may develop his personality primarily through activities designed for the well-being of his fellow members and of society as a whole.
>
> . . . .
>
> Consequently, education in a democracy, both within and without the school, should develop in each individual the knowledge, interests, ideals, habits, and powers whereby he will find his place and use that place to shape both himself and society toward ever nobler ends.[1]

It is not feasible for school staff members to compose effective purposes and functions implemental to sound educational programs within school units before mutually acknowledging and formulating a conclusive philosophy of education. Participation in appropriate school staff councils addressed to the study and discussion of educational problems, demands, and goals may be viewed as an additional requisite in the development of school administrators, curriculum planners, consulting specialists, and other staff members.

The unique nature of early adolescents, as distinguished from the younger and older groups of the public school population, must be seen as a foundational element in their educational programming. Their developmental features are discernible evidences of special learning needs which logically require special educational instruments to accommodate them.

[1] Commission on the Reorganization of Secondary Education, National Education Association, *Cardinal Principles of Secondary Education* (Washington: U.S. Bureau of Education, Bulletin No. 35, 1918), p. 9.

Since the junior high school is an integral part of the state and local school system, statements of philosophy devised and implemented by junior high school staffs must be reconcilable with the tenets etsablished by the state department of education and the educational planning council of the local *school* system. However, the junior high school staff must firmly express its individual convictions while inculcating high standards of procedure in the instructional program.

The authors of this book propose their educational philosophy as a suggestion to others who are endeavoring to frame their own:

1. Belief in the dignity and worth of each student as a person with inherent rights to the fulfillment of his intellectual, social, and physical capacities for himself and the common good.
2. Belief that every normal student should be able to complete successfully the work of the secondary school, if the program of this school is realistically and responsibly developed in accordance with the ideals and needs of our democratic society.
3. Belief that the growth patterns of the early adolescent are predictive, and different from those of older and younger students. Thus a separate school environment and instructional orientation are essential.
4. Belief that the junior high school is a unique institution with the specific and critical responsibility of offering learning opportunities to early youth which will stimulate learning for personal fulfillment, rather than learning that is for protection against fear, punishment, and/or disapproval.
5. Belief that all educators in the junior high school program must participate in the task of evolving, for all students, adequate learning opportunities which are broad enough in scope to assure them of successful learning achievements. Rewarding experiences in learning at this particular stage of growth are of great import in forming constructive learning attitudes and character structures congruent with the values of a democratic society.
6. Belief that progression in learning is dynamic when the instructional approach encompasses the students in the planning of purposeful activities focused upon their needs and current functioning abilities.
7. Belief that all youth have the potential for learning progression during the early adolescent phase but demand more intensive guidance and nurture at this time.
8. Belief that junior high school educators have a direct responsibility to consider all available information in their attempt to understand and redirect student responses toward learning opportunities. This involves recognition of the multiple influences of extra-school life situations which are potential stress areas experienced by all youth to some degree.
9. Belief that a primary requisite for all junior high school staff members is an understanding of the early adolescent growth and developmental

process and its impact upon learning. Above all, they must have a genuine liking and concern for their students.

A representative illustration of a purposeful educational philosophy is the "Basic Philosophy" of Highland Park Junior High School, St. Paul, Minnesota, formulated by the school faculty after consultation with parents and staff members from the elementary and senior high schools located in the Highland Park district:

Highland Park Junior High School
St. Paul, Minnesota

Our Basic Philosophy

We Believe:

1. That each child in this school has the right to the educational experiences which are best suited to his abilities and his needs, and has a responsibility to take full advantage of these experiences.
2. That each child is worthy of respect as an individual in a democratic society.
3. That each child deserves the opportunity to develop self-discipline and responsibility.
4. That self-discipline and responsibility must be developed in harmony with the stage of maturity which the child has attained. He must be challenged by being given many opportunities to exercise responsibility. At the same time, he must not be asked to accept responsibilities beyond what is reasonable for one of his stage of maturity. In such areas, he must have the counsel and supervision of adults.
5. That children learn best when they participate in worthwhile activities and when they recognize and accept the purpose of the activities.
6. That children learn at different rates and have different abilities. That teachers must consider this fact when planning educational experiences for children.
7. That educational experiences for children should be carefully planned, systematically developed, and designed to enable them to develop to the maximum extent which is consistent with their abilities. These educational experiences will include such essentials as:
   (a) Command of the fundamental skills of communication and thought
   (b) Cooperative habits and attitudes of living
   (c) Creative interests and skills
   (d) Understanding of the physical and cultural work around them
   (e) Skills and knowledge for citizenship, home living, work, and further training.

2. What purposes of education are needed?

The educational philosophies formulated by junior high school staff members and approved by their local and state school systems should contain the ultimate purposes of education for early youth. The purposes specific to this school unit and evolved by individual educators, national educational organizations, and local school staffs are important to examine when considering educational beliefs.

The introduction of the junior high school organization into the public school system appears to have occasioned numerous reformulations of the general purposes of education. Many had national recognition and acceptance and were perceived as providing guidelines for better meeting the educational needs of all youth. These alterations were in part responses to the inevitable changes which occur in a dynamic and expanding democratic society, requiring new equipment to cope with new complexities.

Consider the impact of the world-wide economic depression upon public education in this country. Immediately after the onset of this socioeconomic upheaval, the Educational Policies Commission reformulated educational purposes for all elementary and secondary schools under these rather general but realistic headings: (1) The Objectives of Self-Realization, (2) The Objectives of Human Relationship, (3) The Objectives of Economic Efficiency, and (4) The Objectives of Civic Responsibility.[2]

These purposes, prepared by educators, ignored the junior high school's rationale, namely, to provide distinctive educational programming as the best possible resource for the late preadolescent and early adolescent school population, whose learning needs have been repeatedly demonstrated to be unique. This middle school unit is also the mediator for the transitional experiences of the student as he passes from elementary school to senior high school.

A group of junior high school principals from California, in collaboration with the National Association of Secondary-School Principals, framed and published the first compilation of objectives incorporating the "Imperative Needs of Junior High School Youth." These are presented here to emphasize the proclivity toward broadening the junior high school's educational responsibilities:

1. All junior high school-youth need to explore their own aptitudes and to have experiences basic to occupational proficiency.
2. All junior high school-youth need to develop and maintain abundant physical and mental health.
3. All junior high school-youth need to be participating citizens of their school and community, with increasing orientation to adult citizenship.
4. All junior high school-youth need experiences and understandings, appropriate to their age and development, which are the foundation of successful home and family life.

[2] Educational Policies Commission, *The Purposes of Education in American Democracy* (Washington: National Education Association and American Association of School Administrators, 1938), pp. 50, 72, 90, and 108.

5. All junior high school-youth need to develop a sense of the values of material things and the rights of ownership.

6. All junior high school-youth need to learn about the natural and physical environment and its effect on life and to have opportunities for using the scientific approach in the solution of problems.

7. All junior high school-youth need the enriched living which comes from appreciation of and expression in the arts and from experiencing the beauty and wonder of the world around them.

8. All junior high school-youth need to have a variety of socially acceptable and personally satisfying leisure-time experiences which contribute either to their personal growth or to their development in wholesome group relationships, or to both.

9. All junior high school-youth need experiences in group living which contribute to personality and character development; they need to develop respect for other persons and their rights and to grow in ethical insights.

10. All junior high school-youth need to grow in their ability to observe, listen, read, think, speak, and write with purpose and appreciation.[3]

The preceding material is believed to offer significant guidelines to junior high school staff members, parents, and school board members in their respective attempts to design and implement educational programming which is fully equipped to afford the early adolescent progression in learning in relation to his educational development.

A major conceptual modification is a de-emphasis upon subject matter as the singular orientation applied in the realization of purposes. Subject matter may best be viewed as an essential component of the learning process and as having a vehicular relationship to student learning and growth. It must be treated as a means to an end, as the student is always the "end." Subject content exists and must be applied *for the student,* not the student for the subject matter. This concept is again reflective of the value of the individual in a democracy. All sound educational objectives must sustain a congruent relationship to this most significant democratic principle, which embodies the educator's knowledge of and concern for each student he desires to teach.

Koos, a well-known authority on junior high school matters, believes the foremost requisite of the junior high school program is a clear understanding of the characteristics of early adolescent boys and girls, so that their imperative needs may effectively be accommodated. His position on the purposes of junior high school education is as follows:

> . . . Clearly, the only purpose, whatever may have been formerly claimed, peculiar to the *level* [of the junior high school] is that pertaining to the nature of the child during early adolescence. The others, like guidance or provision

[3] Reprinted by permission from M. E. Herriott, "Organizing the Junior High Shool," *The Bulletin of the National Association of Secondary-School Principals,* 35:15-19, December, 1951.

for individual differences, because they are corollary, also share in some degree in distinctiveness, but they are at the same time applicable to school levels above and below. This is not to say that the junior high school has not rendered an estimable service to all levels of education by being the leaven by means of which these other purposes have been popularized, and thus encouraged in application to other school levels.[4]

If the reorganized junior high school is to fully realize the "all pervasive purpose of recognizing the nature of youth during early adolescence," as proposed by Koos, and its other distinctive purposes as an intermediate school, numerous and varied functional aids will be required by contemporary educators.

A conclusive statement of educational purposes has not yet been devised which is considered adequate to all educational groups, partly, perhaps, because of the increased demand that educators broaden and deepen their concepts and skills. The higher expectations are related to the increased comprehension of the unique nature of the early adolescent, which has been developed from research in education, psychology, biology, sociology, and other behavioral and physical sciences. The search for and growth of knowledge by the multidisciplinary approach has been markedly beneficial to junior high school staffs in their struggles to better understand their students and their program purposes.

To stimulate junior high school educators in their evolvement of valid general and special educational purposes for early secondary school programs, the authors of this book offer their suggested list of ultimate objectives:

1. To develop within students their abilities to observe, listen, read, calculate, think, speak, and write with purpose and comprehension.
2. To offer assistance and direction to students in the resolution of their problems so they may effectively cope with their fears, anxieties, and frustrations.
3. To create learning opportunities which will permit the intellectual capacity of the early adolescent to grow and develop to its maximum.
4. To plan situations and activities that will provide typical experiences for students which best accommodate their social and emotional needs.
5. To expand and enrich the progression of learning begun within the general educational framework of the elementary school.
6. To institute learning situations which will assist early adolescents in the healthful advancement from childhood orientation to one of later adolescence or beginning adulthood.
7. To make available sufficient personal interest explorations to initiate a clear understanding of the industry and culture of the adult world.

[4] Leonard V. Koos, *Junior High School Trends* (New York: Harper & Brothers, 1955), p. 30.

8. To provide experiences designed to develop appropriate attitudes and values necessary for living in a democracy as an individual member and as a contributor to the common good.
9. To establish effective resources for developing the health and physical fitness of all students.
10. To organize experience opportunities which will assure a smoother transition from the elementary school to the junior high school, and on to the senior high school.

3. *What educational functions are needed?*

The functions of early secondary education are being modified as educational programs are extended. Program planners require more comprehensive guides, which should include both *general* and *specific* functions, to attain the special purposes so essential to the early adolescent's developmental well-being. What functions should be developed?

Meeting unique needs and individual differences of early adolescents

All boys and girls bring many general and specific needs to the elementary, junior, and senior high school. However, those brought by the junior high school students are specifically related to a *new* and most critical developmental phase of growth, which necessitates special and differential attention from school staffs. The functions most often recognized by junior high school staff members are listed and briefly discussed to illustrate the school personnel's heightened sensitivity to and insight regarding the unique requirements of the early adolescent and the educationally oriented instruments available for their accommodation.

The junior high school student needs opportunities to freely experience gratification of his desires for independence and dependence, frequently experienced at the same time. School programs, therefore, must provide considerable group work in regular classes, social activities in the homeroom, direction and guidance in the constructive use of all mass media, opportunities to participate in devising codes of conduct with appropriate teacher consultation, and opportunities for planning and managing school activities.

Growth in student readiness for independent functioning and responsible self-management is often a result of consistent guidance and emotional support from school personnel during stress or crisis. Such psychological support is essential, during this phase of life, to the development of inner security. When dependency requirements are adequately met, the student's own resources grow and are available for coping more independently with future stress encounters.

Assisting the students in finding resolutions for personal problems is another function of junior high school programming. Boys and girls are typically confronted with difficulties involving personal appearance, adapting to new life interests, devising new codes of conduct to control maturational impulses, and lessened availability of personal learning equipment, which provoke more "plateaus" in mental growth than at any other period.

The staffs of the junior high schools in St. Paul, Minnesota, perceived the following unique personal problems of their students:

> Growth and development sometimes becomes a matter of concern and worry to young teenagers. Physical changes may frighten some children and be a source of pride to others. In some cases, children try to cover up embarrassment by being noisy and boisterous. A few have worries that never come to the attention of an adult.
>
> Mentally, the adolescent is inquisitive and curious. He wants the answers to thousands of questions, though he may be restless to seek them over long sustained periods of time. He needs a variety of activities. His growing interests may range through science, comic books, the arts, television, literature, baseball, government, hot rods, biography, and camp craft. He may spend long periods of time at activities that two years earlier could hold him for only a few minutes and that two years from now would prove thoroughly boring. At other times, he may be a day-dreamer.[5]

Social activities encouraging appropriate boy-girl relationships involve cooperative planning between the school and other social institutions in the community. They may include (1) instruction and practice in dancing, socially approved conduct, sports; (2) informal group activities in regular classes and participation in all-student social activities; (3) appropriate instruction in sexual development and associative behavior in health and physical education classes, and in cooperation with parents; and (4) participation in the various character-building and recreational organizations available in the school and the community.[6]

Teachers are obliged to help the early adolescent appraise himself realistically by joining in the planning and discussion with other adolescents in the school, home, and community. This specific function is often obscure in junior high school instruction.

The use or misuse of the teacher-student relationship has many ramifications. Keen awareness and insight of the teacher are essential in making it a healthy motivational force for the *student's* independent growth.

The early adolescent's typical inclination to emulate a teacher often indicates that his own self-esteem has been enhanced. The searching for and reaching out to an "ideal" identification model may guide the student into a constructive growth experience as he temporarily borrows strength from this

[5] *An Exploration of the Junior High School Program* (St. Paul, Minn.: St. Paul Public Schools, 1957), pp. 4-5. Pamphlet.

[6] See *Basic Purposes for the Reorganization of the Junior High School Program* (Cedar Rapids, Iowa: Public Schools, 1958). Pamphlet.

source. He frequently feels a fervent loyalty toward a particular faculty member and may engage in minor misconduct to "test" the teacher's friendship. In reality, he is demanding corrective direction from the idealized figure. The discerning teacher will be warmly responsive, but firm, in providing appropriate correction. The teacher's misuse of this model role for the purpose of self-aggrandizement will negate the constructive nature of his influence.

The existent educational purposes attending the introduction of the junior high school as a component of the public school system were essentially incongruent with those envisioned by the proponents of this revolutionary concept of learning for early adolescent youth. Society's limited perception of educational needs contributed to the conflict, and formal learning opportunities were available to only approximately one-half of the early youth group. These circumstances were directly related to our society's rejection of the obligation to identify and provide universal formal education for all children as a basic preparatory requisite for growing up in a democratic society. (See discussion in Chapter 1.)

The implementation by most states of free universal public education through the sixteenth year brought many benefits. Some were immediately realizable, such as the concept of individualization; others were contingent upon the further development and application of instructional purposes and functions. It became apparent that one of the basic responsibilities of educators was to initiate effective means in the junior high school for accommodating the individual *differences* of the students. Most contemporary educators accept the concept of individualization and design their instructional programs accordingly.

The multiformity of individual differences is easily understandable when one considers how differently families feel about child-rearing practices, socialization, education, money, culture, religion, community activities, physical well-being, and countless other matters directly affecting student responsiveness. If junior high school teachers realize that each student reacts differently to the various components of his individual situation, they will be better able to offer learning opportunities that can circumvent the obstacles in the way of student progress.

Heterogeneous grouping of students is preferred when present class enrollments of thirty to thirty-five are reduced one-third since there rarely exist psychological or educational reasons to justify other classification systems. The marked variances in student abilities, aptitudes, and interests are typically manifested in proportion to the reduction in class enrollment.

In a study by Lounsbury, twenty-four junior high school possible purposes and functions were listed and ranked according to importance to curriculum and instruction by education specialists.[7] "To provide for homogeneous or

[7] John H. Lounsbury, "The Role and Status of the Junior High School," unpublished doctoral dissertation, George Peabody College for Teachers, 1954, pp. 217-218.

ability grouping" received next to the *lowest rank* of validity in instructional programs for early adolescents. It is evident that "Grouping of itself is meaningless unless the teaching utilizes the kind of group provided to fulfill the purposes of general or specialized education."[8]

Developing basic learning skills

All junior high school students need to experience progression in the development of their thinking and reasoning skills. Accurate, effective discussions of issues in all areas of human experience afford a productive way to meet this basic learning requirement. As teachers plan and work with their students, collecting, organizing, and evaluating information and presenting their approaches to problem solving as represented in their instructional work units, the ability to think and act logically will increase.

To reason logically one must be able to read and listen with comprehension; express ideas clearly in oral and written communication; and calculate, observe, and analyze effectively in learning situations, in and out of the instructional setting. In recent years, increased emphasis has been placed on educational research and practice to improve the functional relationship of the basic learning skills — "the three R's." All major schools have benefited but special effort has been directed toward elementary and junior high schools.

The quantity of research in teaching reading is enormous: "Well over 3000 studies have been made."[9] The data indicate that the level of reading ability is a basic educational factor in Grades 7, 8, and 9 of the junior high school. This important skill includes remedial, recreational, and functional reading, in an adequate school library program as well as in language arts, social studies, and all other learning areas. Every teacher is now a reading teacher in the junior high school because "any increase in the basic skill to read reflects an increase in scholastic achievement."[10]

In his report *Recommendations for Education in the Junior High School Years,* Conant says:

> Instruction in the basic skills begun in the elementary school should be continued as long as pupils can gain from the instruction. This statement applies particularly to reading and arithmetic.
>
> Pupils with average ability should read at or above grade level; superior pupils considerably above grade level. By the end of grade 9 even the poorest readers (except the mentally retarded) should read at least at sixth-grade level.
>
> . . . .
>
> I especially stress reading because pupils will not succeed in high school

[8] Kimball Wiles and Franklin Patterson, *The High School We Need* (Washington: Association for Supervision and Curriculum Development, National Education Association, 1959), p. 25. Report from the ASCD Commission on the Education of Adolescents.

[9] C. W. Hunnicutt and William J. Iverson, *Research in the Three R's* (New York: Harper & Brothers, 1958), p. 1.

[10] *Ibid.,* p. 108.

unless they can read at least at the sixth-grade level. The ability to read is imperative in secondary school. I have been in schools in which practically no one in the ninth grade was reading as low as grade 6, and I have been in schools in which from 35 to 50 percent of the ninth graders were reading at the sixth grade level or below. In every case, the overriding consideration appeared to be the nature of the community and the educational expectations of the parents. The success of the elementary schools in teaching the basic skills and the consequent need for special provisions in grades 7, 8, and 9 are largely determined by these factors. Many communities, however, need to recognize the seriousness of the reading problem and to attempt to upgrade their reading programs. I have been impressed by efforts now being made in certain of the large cities.[11]

During the past decade, significant changes have occurred in teaching fundamental skills which are of concern in elementary and secondary schools. These modifications are directed toward (1) broadening and refining the content of the learning tools, affording students opportunities in which they will "no more be forced to drill first and learn meaning later";[12] (2) accepting the concept of differentiality in readiness for and learning progression in the three R's; and (3) accepting the psychological principles of readiness, purpose, and meaning as basic to learning the three R's.

The challenge to teachers in the junior high school is to make proficiency in fundamental learning skills more attractive, meaningful, and functional for the students, as recommended in "Does Student Culture Discourage Scholarship?" by Simpson:

> In the public school, there are two significant social systems in operation: the formal educational system with expectations set forth by the administration and the informal social system with its set of expectations called student culture. The real question is: "Is it possible to have student culture reinforce and support the educational goals of the school administrator?" It *is* possible, and to achieve this goal is both a staggering challenge and a glorious opportunity. Every social situation is a potential source of gratification and frustration. The more gratifying a situation or activity, the more competition there will be to share in it. The two social systems in the public schools will come to support and reinforce each other in direct proportion to the extent that academic achievement is made more interesting, attractive, and rewarding. This is the challenge to educators today.[13]

[11] James Bryant Conant, *Recommendations for Education in the Junior High School Years, A Memorandum to School Boards* (Princeton, N.J.: Educational Testing Service, 1960), pp. 20-21.

[12] Paul Hanna, "The Three R's," *The School Executive,* 70:77, October, 1950.

[13] Ansel P. Simpson, "Does Student Culture Discourage Scholarship?" *School and Community,* 47:7, January, 1961. Report of a Study in Which 9,000 High Schools Indicate Group Acceptance More Important than Academic Accomplishments, by Ansel P. Simpson, Instructor, Department of Sociology and Anthropology, University of Missouri.

According to educational research and successful practice, it is important for the junior high school educator to be acquainted with each student's achievement level in the basic learning skills, in order to help him attain maximum progression in his ability to read, write, speak, calculate, analyze, think, observe, and listen. Programs directed to this end have been initiated in the elementary school and will soon become imperative in senior high school.

Preparing to live in a democracy

In a maturing democracy such as the United States, the educational institutions and programs are established and exist for the youth, not the youth for the institutions. Therefore, all possible opportunities should be given the junior high school student to develop attitudes and beliefs that will enable him to engage in conduct that gives him all the rights and privileges of full membership in a democratic society. Such conduct can best be summarized as actions, verbal or physical, that reflect faith in the worth of all men. "The improvement of students' behavior is the end-product of general education."[14] It is the final measure of effective teaching and learning.

Principles of conduct of responsible citizenship. One of the most critical stages in growing up occurs during the junior high school years. Throughout the last quarter-century, research reports have tended to dispel the belief that early adolescents inevitably pass through a period of disturbance, frustration, and misbehavior. If the school, as well as the home, church, and community, directs, nurtures, and guides early adolescents to understand and appreciate the heritage of their democracy and to dedicate themselves to practice, in and out of school, the conduct of constructive and productive citizens, most youth will safely proceed through this critical period of growing up. "It is estimated that approximately nine-tenths of adolescents pass through this period without permanent emotional disturbance."[15] The conservation of all early youth is a real challenge to educational workers in junior high schools.

When a school community has a high degree of juvenile delinquency, it is considered socially ill. The teaching and practicing of responsible citizenship is the responsibility not only of the school but also of the home, church, and community — of local, state, and national governments and community health and welfare agencies. A reduction in juvenile delinquency requires the constant cooperative efforts of junior high school staffs, parent-teacher asso-

[14] See Will French, "Behavioral Goals of General Education in High Schools," *The Bulletin of the National Association of Secondary-School Principals,* 41:7-9, December, 1957. See also Will French and others, *Behavioral Goals of Education in High School* (New York: Russell Sage Foundation, 1957).

[15] Ruth Strang, *The Adolescent Views Himself, A Psychology of Adolescence* (New York: McGraw-Hill Book Co., Inc., 1957), p. 133.

ciations, community council, and youth character-building organizations in the school and in the community.

An effective citizenship program in a junior high school permeates the total educational system. It has been identified in the Minneapolis junior high schools as one of their nine major school functions:

> *To gain an understanding of our own form of government, a knowledge of the history of our nation, and to accept the obligations of good citizenship:* To develop loyal American citizens who will accept the obligation of citizenship in the home, the community, the nation, and the world is one of the aims of our schools. While boys and girls have been learning these principles and ideals since kindergarten days, they approach them from a more mature point of view in junior high school. Social studies courses are aimed directly toward helping young people face their obligations as citizens more intelligently. However, every class, every club, and in fact the whole junior high school is a laboratory where good citizenship is being learned and practiced.[16]

Advanced junior high school practices provide students with opportunities to experience a sense of belonging, pleasure, self-mastery, and progress from planning and working in partnership *with* their teachers and peers. Achievement that results from submission to the teacher's demands typically affords students only feelings of retreat and intensifies their fears of failure. Democratic procedures prevail in the election of class officers, special groups, and student councils. Study of the function and structure of government is related to current issues on local, state, national, and international levels. Instructional trips and class committee surveys acquaint students with school and community problems, and resolutions are drawn up which point out the responsibilities of citizenship. The acceptance of citizenship values within a democratic society requires communication of organized subject material and democratic practices and attitudes.

Preparation for family living. One of the imperative needs of students in the early and later secondary schools is to perceive the significance of the family to the individual and to society, and to acquire the attitudes and values conducive to successful family living. To supply this need is considered a major function of education since most of us are members of family groups most of our lives. The importance of family living education to those entering junior high school is indicated by the following:

> Nobody, not even the most unprogressive, questions the suitability of a family and sex education program for the seventh-grade pupils who come into junior high school. The look, the sound, the feel of them cry out for everything which this study supplies — their physical growth changes, their sexual

[16] Rufus A. Putnam, *Educational Program, Minneapolis Junior High School* (Minneapolis: Public Schools, Bulletin 1956-1957), pp. 8-9.

maturation, their social heterosexual drives, their self-awareness — their need for education in all these channels of development is pressing hard on them. The program calls for changes in form, content, and class membership beyond the elementary level.[17]

An examination of the programs for home life and family living education reveals marked variation. The difficulties in realizing this objective are striking. The present trends prophesy that the junior high school may assume increased responsibility for teaching (1) family solidarity and the mutual responsibilities of father, mother, daughters, and sons; (2) appropriate information about feeding, clothing, and caring for children, and about budgeting and home decorating; (3) the aesthetic standards of family life; (4) the unique obligations assigned to sexual roles; and (5) healthful development of heterosexual relationships.

Within the framework of family life education in the junior high school program all girls should have learning experiences in homemaking at least in Grades 7 and 8, and an opportunity to elect them in Grade 9.

Appreciation of moral and ethical principles. The program of education in all schools subscribes to the moral and ethical values of democracy in the United States. Students in junior high schools benefit from opportunities to perceive and evaluate all points of view in relation to the common good, as evidenced by cooperative planning and working together in achieving group decisions, individual achievement which gains recognition from others, development of socially responsible self-direction, and contributions from group learning.

The importance of this major educational function was emphasized by the Educational Policies Commission in 1951 in a declaration that moral and ethical values hold the highest priority among the many claims made upon the time and energy of teachers in public schools. This priority evolves from the following aims:

1. Defining as goals the accepted moral and spiritual values in our society;
2. Encouraging and helping the individual teacher;
3. Giving attention to moral and spiritual values in teacher education;
4. Teaching these morals and spiritual values at every opportunity;
5. Utilizing all the school's resources;
6. Devoting sufficient time and staff to wholesome personal relationships;
7. Assuming an attitude of friendly sympathy toward the religious beliefs and practices of students;

[17] Reprinted by permission from "Framework for Family Life Education," *The Bulletin of the National Association of Secondary-School Principals,* 39:97-98, December, 1955. Copyright: Washington, D.C.

8. Promoting religious tolerance actively;
9. Teaching about religion as an important fact in our culture.[18]

Conservation of natural resources. Conservation means wise use of natural resources and concerns all people living in a democratic society in many different ways, as stated by Jim Jackson, education adviser, Missouri Conservation Commission:

> . . . To a farmer it means preventing soil erosion and maintaining soil fertility. To a forester it means fire prevention and the idea of managing trees as a crop. To a sportsman it means observing game laws and promoting wildlife with a proper environment.
>
> To a teacher conservation might mean wise use of a different sort: to teach youngsters to make the best possible use of their time, talents, and energies.
>
> Each of these seeks to improve our well-being in a never ending effort. Because of the rapidly expanding population, the need for effort is growing in the field of conservation as well as in education.[19]

If population growth continues at its present rate, there will be nearly 225 million people in the United States by 1975, and over 300 million by the year 2000. A majority of junior high school students will then be confronted with limited opportunities to engage in the healthful and pleasurable activities connected with open land and water. The obvious import of such anticipated realities to contemporary junior high school educators is that they should communicate to their students a "conservation consciousness" in the use of all natural resources, not as another subject, but as a vital part of the total school program.

Participation in our economic system. The multiple difficulties associated with buying and selling of goods and services in our complicated and fast-changing markets directly affect early youth. "Consumer education" has become one of the newer facets of education for all youth in order "to develop a sense of value of material things and the rights of ownership."[20]

Students of junior high school age are anxious to learn how to manage their personal financial affairs, know the values that consumers should receive, and successfully find their own place in the economic system of a democracy.

The achievement of the goal of consumer education in the junior high school program is implemented by a great diversity of means, from exploratory courses in business education to a consideration of consumer mathematics

[18] Educational Policies Commission, *Moral and Spiritual Values in the Public Schools* (Washington: National Education Association and American Association of School Administrators, February, 1951), p. 80.

[19] Jim Jackson, "Conservation — Why Be Concerned," *School and Community,* 47:10, January, 1961.

[20] Herriott, *op. cit.,* p. 18.

and problems in general mathematics. This goal also may be achieved through study of community resources, instructional trips, class and personal interviews of business and professional people, and especially work experience for part of the school day.

An intelligent understanding of the basic economic concepts is gaining acceptance as a responsibility of the schools in the United States, for the sake of the well-being of the students and the survival of a free and democratic society.

Providing for personal interests and creative experiences

The student's natural curiosity during early adolescence is marked by changes in interests, aptitudes, talents, and abilities. Administrators and teachers thus have a challenging task in programming to best direct and nurture what is a valuable human asset: curiosity about the world.

A block-time period of two or more regular class periods is required to afford adequate instruction in art, music, industrial arts, homemaking, foreign language, science, business or personal typing; and personal interest programs and clubs permit expansion of interests in any of these areas. Participation gives the student experiences in decision making, leadership, social interaction, and appreciation of beauty in literature, art, music, and nature. "An enthusiasm for learning" and "an awareness of and a sensitivity to beauty" are essential in junior high school education.[21] Opportunities to develop them can help students to appreciate beauty, to be creative, to want to learn, and to live abundantly.

The benefits of a personal interest program are multiple; most significant are the fact that the adolescent's natural curiosity is directed toward constructive productivity, which is satisfying to both student and society, and the fact that he is motivated to learn and to prepare to make a wise program selection in senior high school. This major function provides ample opportunity for exploration and discovery, essential in both junior and senior high school programs. The activities offered should have sufficient breadth to adequately accommodate student interests and needs.

Developing mental and physical fitness

"To provide experiences which will help late preadolescents and early adolescents meet the health and physical needs with which they will be confronted" is a basic part of the junior high program of education.[22] Boys and girls experience their most acute growth and developmental changes during their junior high school years. They are not up to the fitness pro-

[21] Helen F. Storen, "Junior High School Priorities," *The Clearing House,* October, 1960, p. 68.

[22] *The Junior High School Program* (Atlanta, Ga.: Southern Association of Colleges and Secondary Schools, 1958), p. 26.

grams carried on in the senior high school. They need systematic instruction in physiology, health, and safety, and in mental hygiene; health services; a physical education program geared to the stamina of students who are growing rapidly and irregularly; and a comprehensive intramural program, available to all students demanding less strenuous physical activity and lower emotional stress than are called for in interscholastic athletics.

Junior high school educators must be responsibly concerned and aware of all resources allowing their students to evolve and sustain the highest level of emotional and physical health. Breakdown risks, both emotional and physical, must not be disregarded. The well-being of early youth has a significant relationship to constructive health practices.

Providing for guidance–counseling

Guidance is recognized as a primary function of junior high school programming. When the curriculum was subject centered and *completely* departmentalized, guidance typically received minimal time, usually the fifteen to thirty minutes devoted to homeroom activities. At that point it was perceived as something quite separate from the fundamental subjects — language arts, social sciences, and mathematics — the usual all-student requisites.

Effective guidance necessitates clear insight into the problem of how students may best utilize junior high school educational opportunities in their learning progression. Noar points out that guidance is not a subject, project, or activity to be taught and learned separately from the instructional program:

> It is a process by which one person, the advisor-teacher, helps the other, the pupil, to move in the direction of solving a problem, or of meeting a need, or of making an adjustment. The process can be accomplished only when the people involved know each other, care for each other, and have confidence in each other. It requires teacher-time as well as knowledge about children and the possession of good will on both sides.[23]

Developing articulation between school units

Making the transition of students from the elementary to the senior high school smooth is a unique function of the junior high school. The principals, counselors, and teachers of both the sending and the receiving schools need to consider these factors in orienting youth to new schools: "(1) maintaining a security balance from the old and familiar to the new and strange; (2) developing continuity for the child as an individual and continuity for the whole group of youth; and (3) improving human relations in the school through appropriate administrative procedures (and guidance)."[24] As stu-

[23] Gertrude Noar, *The Junior High School, Today and Tomorrow* (Englewood Cliffs, N.J.: Prentice-Hall, Inc., rev. ed., 1961), p. 8.

[24] Association for Supervision and Curriculum Development, National Education Association, *A Look at Continuity in the School Program,* 1958 Yearbook (Washington: The Association, 1958), p. 196.

dents enter junior high school in Grade 7 and senior high school in Grade 10, different guidance programs are necessary to facilitate "moving up" to each school. Effective articulation requires a staff oriented to and prepared in junior high school programming, who understand the nature of the students and the program of education offered in both elementary and senior high schools.

Providing integration in teaching and learning

As boys and girls have moved through the kindergarten and the six grades of the elementary school, the majority of their experiences have been with one teacher in a self-contained classroom in a unified program of education. Attitudes, ideals, understandings, and command of basic skills and knowledge were, hopefully, coordinated and integrated, so that each child grew and learned to the limits of his capacity and was seldom, if ever, held back. The sudden change from one to several teachers in junior high school tends to disrupt this unified program of integrated teaching unless a part of the school day is kept free of departmentalization, as advocated by Ahrens in the following brief discussion:

> The integrative function of the junior high school is a significant and desirable one. It is the responsibility of the junior high school to take pupils where they are in their growth toward objectives of education and to provide opportunities for them to solve problems which are of concern to them, so that they can continue to experience optimum growth. This approach to integration gives purpose to subject matter in that it is related to life situations. Integration cannot adequately be achieved in a highly departmentalized program. Hence the core, or block program, has become a common element in junior high school program design. . . . (For half a day, the teacher better understands the special needs of early adolescents for guidance and integration.)[25]

If the integration so important in the elementary school is continued into the junior high school as the means of serving the multiple needs of early youth in all three grades, it is necessary that a block-time organization be used in the instructional program for at least one-third to one-half of the school day with one teacher who is broadly qualified to guide the student in the coordination of his learning experiences.

The functions of the junior high school enumerated in this chapter could be described here only briefly. They are discussed in greater detail in subsequent chapters.

[25] Maurice R. Ahrens, "The Junior High School Is Not a Step Child," *Educational Leadership,* 14:466, May, 1957.

SELECTED BIBLIOGRAPHY

Administrative Organization of the Modern Junior High School, The. Albany, N.Y.: Council for Administrative Leadership, 1959.

Ahrens, Maurice R. "The Junior High School Is Not a Step Child," *Educational Leadership,* 14:463-467, May, 1957.

American Association of School Administrators, National Education Association. *Conservation Education in American Schools.* Twenty-Ninth Yearbook. Washington: The Association, 1951.

Association for Supervision and Curriculum Development, National Education Association. *A Look at Continuity in the School Program.* Washington: The Association, 1958.

Bossing, Nelson L. *Principles of Secondary Education.* Englewood Cliffs, N.J.: Prentice-Hall, Inc., 2nd ed., 1955.

Commission on the Reorganization of Secondary Education, National Education Association. *Cardinal Principles of Secondary Education.* Washington: U.S. Bureau of Education, Bulletin No. 35, 1918.

Conant, James Bryant. *Recommendations for Education in the Junior High School Years, A Memorandum to School Boards.* Princeton, N.J.: Educational Testing Service, 1960.

Design for Early Secondary Education in New York State, A. Albany: Department of Education, University of the State of New York, 1954.

Dolen, R. A. *And Away They Go.* St. Paul, Minn.: St. Paul Public Schools, 1961.

Educational Policies Commission, National Education Association. *Moral and Spiritual Values in the Public Schools.* Washington: NEA and American Association of School Administrators, February, 1951.

———. *The Purposes of Education in American Democracy.* Washington: NEA and American Association of School Administrators, 1938.

Exploration of the Junior High School Program, An. St. Paul, Minn.: St. Paul Public Schools, 1957.

French, Will, and others. *Behavioral Goals of Education in High School.* New York: Russell Sage Foundation, 1957.

Grant, Lester J. *The Present Status of the Secondary School Curriculum.* Decatur, Ill.: Public Schools, September, 1960. Pp. 1-73.

Gruhn, William T., and Harl R. Douglass. *The Modern Junior High School.* New York: The Ronald Press Company, 2nd ed., 1956.

Herriott, M. E. "Organizing the Junior High School," *The Bulletin of the National Association of Secondary-School Principals,* 35:14-19, December, 1951.

Hunnicutt, C. W., and William J. Iverson. *Research in the Three R's.* New York: Harper & Brothers, 1958.

"Imperative Needs of Youth of Secondary School Age," *The Bulletin of the National Association of Secondary-School Principals,* 31:7-14, March, 1947.

Johnson, Eric W. *How to Live Through Junior High School.* Philadelphia: J. B. Lippincott Co., 1959.

Junior High School Evaluative Criteria. Salt Lake City: Utah State Department of Public Instruction, 1960.

Junior High School Manual. Harrisburg, Pa.: Department of Public Instruction, Bulletin 248, 1956.

Junior High School Program, The. Atlanta, Ga.: Southern Association of Colleges and Secondary Schools, 1958.

Koos, Leonard V. *Junior High School Trends.* New York: Harper & Brothers, 1955.

Lounsbury, John H. "The Role and Status of the Junior High School," unpublished doctoral dissertation, George Peabody College for Teachers, 1954.

National Education Association. *The Development of the High School Curriculum.* Sixth Yearbook of the Department of Superintendence. Washington: The Association, 1928. Pp. 51-54.

Noar, Gertrude. *The Junior High School, Today and Tomorrow.* Englewood Cliffs, N.J.: Prentice-Hall, Inc., rev. ed., 1961.

Schumaker, Willard G. "Handbook of General Information: School Regulations and Procedures," Kensington, Md., Junior High School, revised, 1961.

Spain, Clarence H. "The Philosophy of Binford Junior High School and Its Implementation," *Bulletin,* The Public Schools, Richmond, Virginia, January, 1959.

Storen, Helen F. "Junior High School Priorities," *The Clearing House,* 35:67-71, October, 1960.

Strang, Ruth. *The Adolescent Views Himself, A Psychology of Adolescence.* New York: McGraw-Hill Book Co., Inc., 1957.

Wright, Grace S., and Edith S. Greer. *The Junior High School, A Survey of Grades 7-8-9 in Junior and Junior-Senior High Schools, 1959-1960.* U.S. Office of Education Bulletin No. 32. Washington: Government Printing Office, 1963.

3

The Nature of Early Adolescence

The impact of the studies by G. Stanley Hall and Edward Thorndike in the early 1900's, on adolescent psychology and individual differences, accelerated the reorganization of public schools into three, instead of two, distinct units. These three units were designed specifically for children from ages five to eleven in elementary school, early youth from twelve to fifteen in junior high school, and later youth from sixteen to eighteen in senior high school, keeping in mind the rate of growth and development of each group.

Since the junior high school has been in operation, educators have gained new insight into the nature of the early adolescent and have begun to recognize his varied and complex needs. Many educators have tended to look outside the school arena for both cause and resolution of problems the early adolescent frequently manifests in his behavior and reaction to school learning demands. But a knowledgeable examination of the stresses inherent in his natural growth and development by junior high school teachers and staff often makes the particular problem presented understandable and thus resolvable within the school setting.

1. How does the junior high school span the years of early adolescence?

The stage of growth and development attained by most youth between their twelfth and fifteenth year of life is usually called *early adolescence.* It is during this critical period of rapid change that the junior high school discharges its responsibilities to youth.

As early as 1940, Smith, Standley, and Hughes reported:

> During each month of the three junior high school years, there is a change in the proportion of prepubescent to pubescent children. In the seventh grade about 70 percent of the boys and about 60 percent of the girls are still prepubescent children. In the ninth grade about 80 percent of the boys and about 90 percent of the girls are mature adolescent youths.[1]

More recent studies on sexual maturity show that students begin puberty between the ages of twelve and fifteen. The results of these studies (Tables 8 and 9) are presented by Cole separately for boys and girls since boys do not reveal any single, objective evidence of sexual maturity, as girls do at first menstruation.

In a study of early adolescent boy-girl relationships, Crow stressed physical growth changes as determinants of certain attitudes held by girls toward group membership and pointed out that "It is folly for us to try to build an effective school system while ignoring the physical and emotional differences between students of early adolescence and those of later adolescence."[2]

After a survey of the results of a half-century of study and research, Corbally, Jensen, and Staub identified and discussed the concepts of flexibility, continuity, and intensification of peer culture during adolescence. They emphasized the necessity for junior high school workers to recognize the rapid and uneven growth and development that begin to occur in early adolescence:

> As far back as biblical times man has recognized the concept of change and the "turning point" that comes at [early] adolescence. Psychologists and physiologists have supplied us with evidence of the nature of this change. So-

TABLE 8

Percentage of Girls Immature and Mature at the Different Junior High School Ages

Chronological Age	Percentage of Girls Immature	Percentage of Girls Mature
12	69	31
13	35	65
14	12	88
15	3	97

Adapated from Luella Cole, *Psychology of Adolescence* (New York: Rinehart and Company, 5th ed., 1959), Fig. 45, p. 69.

[1] Maurice M. Smith, L. A. Standley, and Cecil L. Hughes, *Junior High School Education: Its Principles and Procedures* (New York: McGraw-Hill Book Co., Inc., 1942), pp. 55-56.

[2] Lester D. Crow, "Teenage Traits, Interests and Worries," *Educational Forum,* 20:423-428, May, 1956.

TABLE 9

Percentage of Boys Prepubescent, Pubescent, or in the Process of Becoming Early Adolescent, and Postpubescent

Chronological Age	Percentage Prepubescent	Percentage Pubescent	Percentage Postpubescent
12	62	23	15
13	46	24	30
14	17	23	60
15	4	12	84

Adapted from Luella Cole, *Psychology of Adolescence* (New York: Rinehart and Company, 5th ed., 1959), Fig. 46, p. 70.

ciologists have described the cultural changes that take place at the junior high school age. This growth process is continuous, but there are certain modal points readily recognizable.[3]

Information obtained and validated from the research of many investigators regarding the nature and patterns of sexual maturation confirms the premise that the seventh, eighth, and ninth grades *span the years of early adolescence.* There are a few slow-growing children who do not reach physical maturity by the end of Grade 9 or during the summer prior to their entering Grade 10. However, more students experience the onset of adolescence during their three grades of regular junior high school than in any other three-grade sequence within the standard school program of twelve years or more.

2. *What physical growth is experienced by early youth?*

Physical growth is understood to be an increase in the size and proportions of the various structures of the body from conception to maturity. The first rapid physical growth occurs during the prenatal months and in the first six months after birth. The second surge occurs at puberty, when changes take place in height and weight, vital organs, and in varying degrees the entire biological system; it is experienced in its most intense form in Grades 7, 8, and 9.

Height and weight

Growth in height and weight is related to chronological age and pubescence, but the onset of puberty is a major factor in the pronounced height and weight increase. Although the growth rates of many boys and girls are rapid

[3] John E. Corbally, Jr., T. J. Jensen, and Frederick Staub, *Educational Administration: The Secondary School* (Boston: Allyn and Bacon, Inc., 1961), p. 257.

or slow, most boys mature at age fourteen to fourteen and a half years (in Grades 8 and 9), and most girls, at age twelve and a half to thirteen (in Grades 7 and 8).

Maximum growth in height is attained by boys between seventeen and twenty years of age and by girls between fifteen and sixteen years of age, since physical maturity occurs earlier in girls than in boys. Girls usually experience an acceleration in weight gain in early adolescence. "Girls gain on an average more than 30 pounds during the three year period in which they achieve puberty. Although boys achieve their weight spurt later than girls, it extends over a longer period of time and they gain about 40 pounds during the pubertal period."[4]

There is thus a wide variation in height and weight of students of the same age in the junior high school, due chiefly to the onset of adolescence. It is strikingly illustrated in Figure 3.

FIGURE 3

Variations in Physical Growth for Four Twelve-Year-Olds

Courtesy of the Southern Association of Colleges and Schools from *Four Twelve-Year-Olds,* Personnel Press, Inc.

[4] *The Junior High School Program* (Atlanta, Ga.: Southern Association of Colleges and Secondary Schools, 1958), p. 6.

Physical development

Recognition by teachers of the meaning and ramifications of the surges in height and weight experienced by early adolescents may enable them to help their students cope more effectively with the following frequently associated problems: low fatigue tolerance, personal grooming anxieties, poor motor co-ordination, restlessness and irritability, and negative or indifferent attitudes toward school tasks. Still other typical biophysiologic alterations that mark entrance into adolescence are well described in *The Junior High School Program,* a publication of the Southern Association of Colleges and Secondary Schools (now the Southern Association of Colleges and Schools):

> The bones grow very fast while the muscles grow much slower. Most girls experience a growth spurt of the internal sex organs before bone structure expands adequately to accommodate them thus producing the adolescent "tummy," often a source of embarrassment. Boys often acquire fat around the nipples, abdomen, hips, thighs, cheek, neck and jaw, before the large muscles develop sufficiently to bring proportions into balance. The girls sometimes develop fat in those places considered most inappropriate — the abdomen and hips. In both sexes hands and feet mature before the arms and legs, making the extremities seem disproportionately large. Moreover, the legs and arms tend to grow proportionately more rapidly than the trunk. At the onset of puberty there is a rapid lengthening of the upper leg bone, a two-inch growth in one year not being unusual. Through stimulation by the sex hormone at puberty, the cartilage at the end of the long bones is converted to bone thus accounting for the rapid increase in arm and leg length. When the bones of the trunk lengthen there is a better body proportion but internal organs, notably the heart and lungs, must adjust to their increased and elongated area. During this adjustment there will be periods of sluggishness and ineptness when fatigue comes quickly.[5]

Early adolescents are understandably extremely vulnerable at this stage of maturation since they are required to deal with such a variety of emotionally laden biophysiological changes. Because their individual assets are less available to meet internal and external demands, requirements for guidance from external sources are actually stronger than at any other time in their elementary or secondary school experience.

In our society the most appropriate and effective resource for helping the adolescent handle this stressful period is a dynamic school program that affords him multiple opportunities to perform learning tasks successfully. These opportunities must be based on understanding of the *changeableness* of the early adolescent's learning patterns. If the school program does not accommodate his need to achieve socially approved reality goals, he is likely to feel that his loss of or inability to develop control over his infantile

[5] *Ibid.,* p. 7.

drives and impulses has been confirmed. Such experiences may be looked upon as major determinants in the development of antisocial behavior patterns and attitudes.

The uneven growth of different parts of the body during early adolescence affects body proportions. Teachers should be aware that many students who demonstrate poor posture, lack of muscular coordination, feelings of discomfort, anxiety about facial appearance, and an attitude of sluggishness are temporarily reacting to surges of physical growth.

Biological changes

During early adolescence the larynx enlarges and voice tones are altered, particularly in boys, a change that is of special concern to music and speech teachers. The nervous system, including the brain, has already reached maturity. The heart has its most rapid growth during adolescence, expanding approximately twice as fast as it did during preadolescence. Thus, blood pressure and blood circulation are increased considerably. The stomach doubles in size and rapid growth takes place throughout the digestive system. This accelerated development of the circulatory and digestive systems necessitates the following specific programs in the junior high school:

Well-balanced school lunches must be available to *all* students, and students should be encouraged to continue good dietary practices at home.

A comprehensive health program should be planned with emphasis on appropriate information regarding the growth and development process of early youth. Identification and correction of physical defects, including oral hygiene, and programs oriented to early identification and prevention of mental and physical health problems are important.

The physical education program should be geared to the individual student's physical capacities, rather than to his chronological age, grade, or size. Too often palpitations of the heart, fainting spells, and headaches result from physical exertion not in conformity with individual growth patterns.

Of the multiple physical growth changes experienced at this time, sex organ growth is by and large the most significant and essential to the development of self-identity. The importance of the attainment of sexual maturity is stated by Cole:

> . . . The outstanding change is the establishment of sexual maturity, which is evidenced by both primary and secondary changes. . . . Members of both sexes display a variety of attitudes toward changes in their bodily functions, and these attitudes influence their personalities, their school work, and their general adjustment to life. Of all the developments that take place during [early] adolescence, the coming of sexual maturity is the most profound and the most significant in its influence upon the behavior and interests of boys and girls.[6]

[6] Luella Cole, *Psychology of Adolescence* (New York: Rinehart & Co., 5th ed. 1959), p. 84.

3. *How does social growth influence the education of early youth?*

Rapid biophysiologic growth is often reflected in the social behavior patterns of adolescents and late preadolescents. Awareness and understanding of the social needs and problems that confront students evolve from collaborative efforts of the home, school, church, state, and industry.

Social growth in late preadolescence

The majority of students in Grades 7 and 8, especially the boys, are in the late preadolescent phase of development. Even though *not experiencing drastic physical growth,* they are going through social growth that is an important preparation for early adolescence. The junior high schools afford the best opportunity and assurance that this preparation will be adequate.

The social growth patterns of preadolescent boys and girls are not characterized by the stability of early childhood or by the multiplicity of changes of early adolescence, but they are unique to this phase of development — best described as "in waiting" or the "lull before the storm." Peer groups of the same sex, age, and size search for more freedom than they had experienced in early childhood, when they were overtly more dependent on the care and love of their parents and teachers. As the preadolescent youth becomes interested in knowing more about his own sex, fathers gain in popularity with boys while mothers are more admired by girls. The boys tend to form closely organized gangs and are aggressive, noisy, unkempt, and bold; the girls, who are less well organized, are friendly, tidy, and shy in their peer interaction. Generally, the boys engage in more serious acts of misconduct, annoying others in school, stubbornly rejecting direction from adults, and engaging in hyperactive behavior. Girls are more talkative, hysterical, interested in making good grades in school, and become aggressive in teasing boys for their attention.

Redl explains the personality shake-up of preadolescents, extending even to age thirteen or Grade 8, thus: "During pre-adolescence the well-knit pattern of a child's personality is broken up or loosened, so that adolescent changes can be built into it and so that it can be modified into the personality of an adult."[7] If an individual is unable to have this experience, growth is evidenced only by physical change — the child becomes an "oversized child" or a primitive adult. The change from a preadolescent into an adolescent and adult is a process not of growing bigger and better but of leaving behind or discarding some of what has occupied childhood.

Redl goes on to note why the gang comes into the scene in late preadolescence: "During pre-adolescence it is normal for youngsters to drop

[7] Fritz Redl, *Pre-Adolescents — What Makes Them Tick* (New York: Child Study Association of America, rev. ed., 1959), p. 12.

their identification with adult society and establish a strong identification with a group of their peers."[8] They will seek advice and authority from their pals on a peer code basis but still need and want the advice and love of parents and teachers in making important decisions.

A survey of the literature pertaining to the education of preadolescent youth indicates that they are still "a neglected group" of youngsters, who need more consideration in the schools and in other social institutions. According to Blair and Burton, more serious behavior problems and more delinquency originate during preadolescence than during early adolescence.[9] And Redl reports that "Most referrals to child guidance clinics occur around this [preadolescent] age."[10] When preadolescent youth are more effectively taught and guided in Grades 5 and 6, as described by Loomis in her book *The Preadolescent,* social problems will be fewer during late preadolescence and early adolescence in the junior high school.[11]

Social problems of early adolescence

The social problems that confront most early adolescents are again viewed as by-products of this critical stage of development marked by trying, selecting, and sorting out multiple devices that will test new physical powers and socialization skills. More times than not, the devices selected are not in accord with those of adult society, in which the youth is striving to find a place but rarely succeeding. Since sustaining and controlling his new developmental equipment demands most of his energy, he must look outside himself for directional controls that will enable him to utilize his new powers in acceptable ways. A junior high school program must help him learn appropriate independent functioning, give him opportunities to develop and enhance his socialization skills within his peer group, and offer him relationships with authority figures that are warm, but firm and dependable.

Gaining independence. As early adolescents continue the struggle of late preadolescence for more independence from parents and teachers, they shift from peer groups of their own sex to those of the opposite sex. They also become more secretive. Their goals now are associating with youth who have similar growing problems, conversing and sharing new experiences, increasing self-reliance, establishing self-esteem, seeking personal and social approval of peers, acquiring more freedom of social action, and gaining sympathy and guidance from parents and teachers.

Early adolescent boys and girls face the dangers of antisocial or unethical

[8] *Ibid.,* p. 15.

[9] Arthur S. Blair and William H. Burton, *Growth and Development of the Preadolescent* (New York: Appleton-Century-Crofts, Inc., 1951), pp. 61-63.

[10] Redl, *op. cit.,* p. 1.

[11] Mary Jane Loomis, *The Preadolescent: Three Major Concerns* (New York: Appleton-Century-Crofts, Inc., 1959).

leadership in their peer groups, which may disturb socially approved growth, unless the home, school, church, and community cooperatively plan with youth to provide and maintain social resources that will assure their social well-being in the school and community. Since early adolescents display at times instability, resentment toward being treated like a child, insecurity in class or school, indifference, hysteria, impudence, laziness, aggressiveness, antagonism, shyness, and sensitivity, it is most essential that adequate counseling be provided and that class structure be flexible enough so that teachers may give their students effective personal and group guidance when these disturbances are manifested. Peer-group leadership and action that are socially destructive to the individual and society will then be more effectively counteracted.

Two different communities were surveyed to determine how junior high school students felt about gaining independence from adult control. Students were given free rein as to content of their compositions. Table 10 shows the results of this inquiry.

In their written compositions on "How It Feels to Be Growing Up," fewer students living in homes of lower socioeconomic status expressed satisfaction in gaining independence than did students living in average homes. The educational program of junior high schools must be varied in accordance with the needs and sociocultural climate of the individual communities. Although the junior high school is not the total community, it has the potential to play a vital role in enabling students in any type of community to experience social

TABLE 10

Number and Per Cent of Students in Two Communities Who Expressed Satisfaction in Gaining Independence in Written Compositions, "How It Feels to Be Growing Up"

Type of Community	Number of Compositions	Number Expressing Satisfaction in Independence	Per Cent
Sample 1. Schools in average communities	185	68	37.0
Sample 2. Schools in the county, generally of low socioeconomic status representing a variety of family backgrounds	503	88	17.5

Adapted from Ruth Strang, *The Adolescent Views Himself, A Psychology of Adolescence* (New York: McGraw-Hill Book Co., Inc., 1957), Sample 1 for Grades 7, 8, and 9, but omitting Grades 10, 11 and 12, Table 6, p. 141; Sample 2 for Grades 7, 8, and 9, but omitting Grades 10, 11, and 12, Table 7, p. 142.

growth that is constructive and supports the positive value of American democracy.

Making and holding friends. The development of socialization skills that win and sustain friends usually is cherished by human beings throughout life. There appears to be more need to develop these skills during junior high school than at any other time or in any other school. The rapid physical and social growth of early adolescents intensifies their desire to experience appropriate boy-girl relationships, belongingness in their peer groups, prestige as young people with both their own and the opposite sex, social contacts in the school and in homes "frequently above their social status," confidence in "talking it out" with close friends, and acceptable conduct judgment from healthy friendships in and out of school.

The most desirable and gratifying friendships are usually formed around common interests and hobbies or through participation in group experiences in the classroom, activity programs of the school, and service organizations in churches or other community institutions.

Boy-girl relationships. If a youth has experienced effective personal and group guidance during preadolescence in the home, the school, and the church, his intense interest in the opposite sex will be part of the usual growing-up process and include positive attitudes and expectations toward his anticipated adult social role. Imperative in the junior high school, then, are opportunities to develop and practice socialization skills that will facilitate the formation of healthy, satisfying boy-girl relationships, experiences that will enhance the growth of positive attitudes and a sense of adequacy toward sexual roles, and the chance to develop a personal system of ethical standards and values that will equip students to effectively cope with their present and future life situations.

In the study by Strang already mentioned, boy-girl relationships, development of independence and self-esteem, concern about vocation in the future, concern with social relations, and concern with marriage and raising a family were identified by more than fifteen hundred students in junior and senior high schools as problems that they considered most important, as shown in Table 11.

Strang comments, "They [students] welcome responsibility. Many items in this table represent a combination of the desire to be independent and a willingness to assume responsibility. Certainly adolescents' own statements do not bear out the popular impression of adolescent irresponsibility."

A study by Remmers and Radler for the Purdue Opinion Poll presented a three-hundred-item list to more than fifteen thousand youth in Grades 9, 10, 11, and 12 which covered problems of concern to their particular age group.[12]

[12] See H. H. Remmers and D. H. Radler, *The American Teenager* (Indianapolis: The Bobbs-Merrill Company, Inc., 1957), pp. 80-85.

TABLE 11

Social Problems Most Frequently Mentioned in Written Compositions, "How It Feels to Be Growing Up" by Adolescents

Rank	Category	Per Cent[a]
1.	Concern with boy-girl relations	33.4
2.	Feeling of increasing independence and self-direction	27.6
3.	Concern about vocation or the future	26.4
4.	Concern with social relationships	25.6
5.	Concern with marriage and raising a family	23.1
6.	Awareness of increased responsibilities	19.9
7.	Feelings about religion or morality	17.6
8.	Concern about school success or grades	17.5
9.	Problems of sibling relationships	14.9
10.	Dissatisfaction with school experiences	12.9
11.	Interest in sports	12.3
12.	Concern with larger social problems (national and international)	10.5
13.	Concern with clothes or appearance	10.3
14.	"Feels good," it is "fun," it is a "nice" time of life	9.4
15.	Feeling of frustration that independence is not recognized	8.4
16.	Viewpoint that adults do not "understand" adolescents	6.1
17.	Problems about money	6.1
18.	Suggestions of reluctance to lose dependence	4.4
19.	Awareness of increasing acceptance in the adult world	4.1
20.	Concern with military service	3.6

[a] Figures are relative percentage frequencies — the number of times a given category occurred divided by the number of compositions.

Adapted from Ruth Strang, *The Adolescent Views Himself, A Psychology of Adolescence* (New York: McGraw-Hill Book Co., Inc., 1957), Table 5, p. 138.

Responses from Grade 9, the ending grade-level in junior high school, revealed 104 problems which were especially troubling.

Virtually all of the problems that occurred most frequently in this list involve boy-girl relationships and the art of winning and holding friends, and these are also the most frequently mentioned social problems of students in all grades of the junior and senior high schools, in Table 11. Thus, the program of the junior high school should be geared to helping students feel secure in adjusting to the opposite sex by (1) providing the opportunity for boys and girls to interact together in dramatics, music, art, sports, homemaking, industrial arts, creative writing, and many other areas of learning; (2) assisting them to develop social poise during class and school parties; (3) making arrangements for boys and girls to participate in dancing, playing games of mutual interest in physical education classes and intramural sports; (4) providing interactional experiences between boys and girls in science and social studies class groups; encouraging reading and reporting on library books in small groups in language arts or block-time classes; (5) scheduling regular activity programs of personal interest, and clubs selected by the boys and girls; (6) providing considerable group work, committee investigations and reports, and teacher-student planning in regular classes; and (7) enlisting parents to collaborate with teachers in offering appropriate opportunities to learn socialization skills that are focused around small dinner parties at home and/or school, or similar purposeful activities. In health and physiology, "Classes that are devoted to specific sex instruction, however, should be segregated because in the junior high school the pupils are not ready to discuss, in mixed groups, the sexual side of life."[13]

Aspirations for social goals and standards. In a research project on the aspirations of students in Grades 8 and 9, Urell asked 398 students in an experimental school (which reported a high rate of delinquency) and 232 students in a control school (which claimed an average or above average behavior) to answer the following questions without signing their names: "If you could become any kind of person you want to be, what kind would you choose to be? Why?" Table 12 shows the relative percentage frequencies — the number of times a given occupational or personality category occurred in the written answers to the two questions divided by 398 students in the experimental school and by 232 students in the control school.

Thus 16.6 per cent of the students in the experimental school and 44.8 per cent of those in the control school aspired to professional careers; 11.1 per cent of the students in the experimental school wanted to be nurses as compared to 2.6 per cent of those in the control group. In the experimental group 25.9 per cent and in the control group only 10.3 per cent identified as desirable the personal traits of obedience, respect, and orderliness. To become a good family person and have a happy home appealed to only 4.8 per cent of the students in the experimental school compared with 12.5 per cent of the students in the control school. Since there are notable differences in the social aspirations of the students from the two school neighborhoods, the programs of education must be varied to accommodate the needs in each type of neighborhood.

Urell also reported on 345 experimental school students from a neighborhood of high youth delinquency and 215 control school students in an average or slightly above average neighborhood, in Grades 8 and 9, who were asked, "Who is the most successful person that you know? Why?" Table 13 presents relative percentage frequencies — the number of times a given successful person was mentioned in the written (but unsigned) answers divided by 345 students in the experimental school and 215 students in the control school.

Parents and other relatives were more often considered more successful than any other persons by 37.1 per cent of the experimental school students

[13] Gertrude Noar, *The Junior High School, Today and Tomorrow* (Englewood Cliffs, N.J.: Prentice-Hall, Inc., 2nd ed., 1961), p. 43.

TABLE 12

Aspirations Mentioned by 630 Pupils in Grades 8 and 9

Category	Experimental School (N = 398)		Control School (N = 232)	
	Number	Per Cent	Number	Per Cent
Occupational				
Professional	66	16.6	104	44.8
Skilled labor	52	13.1	29	12.5
Nurse	44	11.1	6	2.6
Theatrical, entertainment	25	6.3	17	7.3
Athlete	18	4.5	6	2.6
Policeman (policewoman), detective	11	2.8	5	2.1
Military	9	2.3	8	3.4
Service occupation	8	2.0	9	3.9
Miscellaneous	24	6.0	9	3.9
Total	257		193	
Personality				
Kind, understanding	75	18.8	40	17.2
Good citizen, obedient, respectful, clean[a]	103	25.9	24	10.3
Good family person, have happy home[a]	19	4.8	29	12.5
Stereotype	34	8.5	25	10.8
Myself	12	3.0	6	2.6
Self-reliant, intelligent, well-educated	38	9.5	26	11.2
Miscellaneous	19	4.8	46	19.8
Total	300		196	
Grand total	557		389	
Average number choices	1.35		1.67	

[a] Differences significant beyond the .01 level of confidence.

Adapted from Catherine Urell, "What Do They Want Out of Life?" *Teachers College Record,* 61:320, March, 1960, Table 1.

and 24.7 per cent in the control group, which finding offers school staff members clues to the nature of the family life of each student, regardless of the kind of neighborhoods. Fully a third of the students in both schools designated a wide range of persons classified as miscellaneous, indicating a broad social acquaintance and admiration. Entertainers are more popular with the less privileged students in the experimental school than with those in the control school. Only 4.3 per cent of the students in the high-delinquency

TABLE 13

Ideals of the Successful Person Mentioned by 560 Pupils in Grades 8 and 9

Category	Experimental School (N = 345)		Control School (N = 215)	
	Number	Per Cent	Number	Per Cent
Parent or other relative[a]	128	37.1	53	24.7
Specific singer, actress, entertainer[a]	42	12.2	2	0.9
Specific schoolmate, friend[a]	33	9.6	5	2.3
Person unidentified (unknown to research team)	31	9.0	8	3.7
Person having desirable personal characteristics	29	8.4	26	12.1
Specific athlete[a]	24	7.0	2	0.9
President Eisenhower	15	4.3	12	5.6
One of his or her teachers[a]	15	4.3	47	21.9
Abraham Lincoln	9	2.6	4	1.9
Specific Negro leader	8	2.3	1	0.5
Specific teen-age "name" singer	7	2.0	1	0.5
Myself	6	1.7	4	1.9
Miscellaneous	120	34.8	73	34.0
Total number choices	467		238	
Average number choices	1.4		1.1	

[a] Differences significant beyond the .01 level of confidence.

Adapted from Catherine Urell, "What Do They Want Out of Life?" *Teachers College Record,* 61:324, March, 1960, Table 2.

neighborhood considered a teacher their ideal of a successful person, but 21.9 per cent of those from the middle-class neighborhood selected a teacher as a successful person.

In Urell's view, some of the goals and values identified by adolescents through their aspirations and perceptions of successful persons are important in planning an effective program of *socialization* and *prevocational* training in the junior high school. Since higher values and goals are generally maintained in the middle-class neighborhoods, socialization needs will vary within the same school district. Regardless of neighborhood, however, students evidence awareness of socially approved conduct. When their school programs adequately meet and reflect their needs, modification in their social standards may be anticipated.

Parents, other relatives, teachers, and community leaders have a strong influence upon early adolescents. By and large, the persons perceived as acceptable models are not far removed from themselves in status and ability, and many students reflect a good self-image, which is a factor that correlates with non-delinquency. Socially approved interests were frequently mentioned, as were all school and religious groups.[14]

The role of social institutions

In order that the early adolescent may learn and effectively apply socially acceptable resolutions for his social problems, the five basic institutions (home, school, church, state, and industry) found in a democratic society must afford him perceptions that are consistent with the values and ethical standards of the society. One of the major purposes of these institutions is to provide youth with a full range of resources through which they may meet their needs and thereby make full use of their personal capacities.

The school is organized to do those things which the home, state, church, and industry do not, or cannot, do as well as the school. It is not a substitute for the home and the other social institutions. However, when these institutins fail to provide adequate education for all youth, the school and its staff must correct their deficiencies so that this democracy will not be threatened as a result of an inadequately educated citizenry.

As the junior high school discharges this broader mission of education in cooperation with the other social institutions, its staff members need observational skills and a knowledgeable framework in order to assess (nature of problems), understand (where located), and bring about positive modifications or resolutions (resolution plans) of the social problems confronting early adolescents and their families.

A comprehensive cumulative record system may be viewed as the nerve center of such a framework when the following data are included and utilized: a brief description of family members; occupational roles; educational levels attained; religious affiliations, active or inactive; cultural orientation; family values and attitudes toward education; and whether these attitudes are in accord with those of the larger community or neighborhood. Information of great import is that regarding environmental stresses, such as acute or chronic financial stress, death or illness of family members, natural disasters, and others beyond the individual family's control.

The development of observational abilities by all school staff members is crucial, for they have many windows through which to observe the early adolescent in his struggle to attain the socialization skills essential to the mastery of his own impulses.

In order to effectively assess, understand, and plan how to handle the early adolescent's social problems, it is essential to involve his parents to whatever degree appears appropriate and realistic. This action often communicates

[14] Catherine Urell, "What Do They Want Out of Life?" *Teachers College Record,* 61:329-330, March, 1960.

to parents the fact that they *do* have something to offer their children, who during this phase of development are engaging in behavior that frequently indicates the opposite, thereby negating a vital need, that of parental love and guidance.[15]

A study of the family pattern of the students who are brought together for the first time in a secondary school yields important information for teachers. The students come to the junior high school from more heterogeneous residential sections than do those in the elementary school, with wide variations in racial and national stock, socioeconomic status, size of families, occupation, and employment. In the different types of communities represented — "across the railroad tracks," "near the river," and "on the hill" — both high and low youth delinquency exists. How can the junior high school be the first important "melting pot" of early youth without a careful exploration of the character of the family of each boy and girl in school? An example of a study of the family background of students in a junior high school is given in the following report, made in 1959, by the principal and teachers of the D. S. Keith Junior High School, Altoona, Pennsylvania:

Character of Family Pattern
(1244 students reporting)

	Number	*Per Cent*
I. Student lives with:		
1. Both parents	1041	83
2. One parent	173	14
3. Neither parent	30	3
II. Parents:		
1. Separated, divorced, or remarried	126	10
2. Deceased:		
a. Father	60	5
b. Mother	17	2
III. Family employment and income:		
1. Father has regular work	920	78
2. Father has part-time work	58	5
3. Father doesn't work:		
a. No job available	117	10
b. Physically unable	35	3
c. Retired	13	1
4. Mother has regular work	274	22
5. Mother has part-time work	135	11
IV. Desire to graduate from high school	1195	96
V. Desire to continue education beyond high school	634	50

[15] See Margaret Bennett, *Guidance in Groups* (New York: McGraw-Hill Book Co., Inc., 1953), pp. 114-116, 182-183, and 288.

A study of the number of students who live with both parents, one parent, and neither parent, made in West Junior High School, Kansas City, Missouri, revealed that only one-half of the seven hundred students lived with *two* parents. The other half of the students lived with one parent, grandparents, other relatives, or acquaintances. The amazing facts on the instability of the families of students in this school caused all staff members to take a more positive approach to the evolvement of activities and units of work necessary to compensate for the deficiencies of the substitute "family" in this downtown neighborhood.

The church has always provided spiritual and moral guidance in helping early adolescent youth assume the responsibilities for social privileges, as discussed by Bossing:

> . . . The importance of the adolescent age as a time of genuine moral interest and commitment has been recognized by the agencies of religion from time immemorial. Institutional religions in our western civilization have always placed great stress upon the early adolescent years. These years have been looked upon as a time of special moral awakening and of ready commitment to ideals and to religious devotion. From Jewish tradition through the long history of the Christian church, age 12 or thereabouts has been regarded as the age to bring youth into the life of the church. Modern psychological knowledge confirms the wisdom of these groups.[16]

As educational workers achieve skill in implementing the concepts and techniques presented in this chapter, which will enable them to know the early adolescent student and his needs and how best to meet them, there will be a "true junior high school," with a dynamic program endowed with its own singular philosophy, purpose, organization, and curriculum.

4. *What are the psychological aspects of rapid growth and development?*

The physical and social growth patterns of early adolescent boys and girls are closely interwoven with their psychological development. Modern psychology assumes that human beings can be molded and developed, which process is the fundamental purpose of education. In the junior high school, the molding of the behavior of early youth requires that staff members understand the psychological aspects of "the learner, the learning process, and the learning situation."[17] In the junior high school, the learner is an early

[16] Nelson L. Bossing, *Principles of Secondary Education,* 2nd edition. © 1955, by permission of Prentice-Hall, Inc., Englewood Cliffs, N.J. P. 127.

[17] Henry Clay Lindgren, *Educational Psychology in the Classroom* (New York: John Wiley & Sons, Inc., 1956), p. 4.

adolescent; the learning processes are those that are most effectively utilized by rapidly growing boys and girls, within the limits of their capacities; and the learning situations consist of a flexible secondary school organization, suitable classrooms, adequate facilities, interested parents, and qualified teachers, who are the key forces in this complex enterprise.

Some of the characteristics of psychological development that are of importance to the junior high school program are the rate of mental growth, mental cycles of growth, and developmental tasks in child growth and development.

Rate of mental growth

The most rapid growth usually occurs between the ages of nine and twelve years and becomes evident much earlier than the surges in physical and social growth. However, boys and girls whose physiological development occurs early will demonstrate a correspondingly rapid rate of mental growth, and those who physiologically mature later will have a slower rate of mental development. There is more variability in learning rates during early adolescence than in childhood.

Psychological development is frequently delayed by difficult social and emotional problems. At puberty, early adolescents take a new interest in life and its wonders, and the gratification of their imperative needs has a profound influence on their rate of intellectual growth.

Mental growth takes place as individual and group purposes and experiences expand in the environment of school and community. A challenging school program, cooperatively planned by the teacher and her students, tends to stimulate mental growth; but a dull, monotonous, fragmented school program tends to retard mental growth.

Teaching motivated by a sincere interest in the adventurous and active early adolescent stimulates effort, critical thinking, and concentration; assures comprehension and retention; makes problem solving possible; and fosters effective ways of learning. It encourages intellectual growth, for "With interest, just as with any keen-edged tool, for those who know not how to use it, there are dangers; but without it only bungling work can be done — no masterpiece of teaching is possible."[18]

Mental cycles of growth

Psychological and educational research studies consistently show that mental growth occurs at a rather constant rate until the onset of early adolescence, when the complex physical, social, and emotional stresses of these years begin to be felt. As early as 1942, Smith, Standley, and Hughes stated, "Although these data are not crucial, they suggest that the complex physical and emo-

[18] William H. Kilpatrick, *Foundations of Method* (New York: The Macmillan Company, 1925), p. 159.

tional factors associated with pubescence may have an influence upon the constancy of mental growth during these ages (12 to 15)."[19]

In a study by the New York State Division of Research including over one thousand individual curves of growth in mental age, three-fourths of the boys and girls passed through a period of two to four years, coinciding with adolescent growth changes, with almost *no growth in mental age.* These "plateaus" need to be fully understood by teachers so that they can identify the students who are at this stage and vary their assignments and requirements of achievement accordingly:

> Mental growth is now recognized as a pattern of cycles. Childhood cycles have been more clearly indicated than adolescent cycles. . . . It is consistent with accumulating evidence about other aspects of growth to suppose that there is an adolescent cycle of mental growth. . . . The most striking feature of this pattern is what appears to be a "plateau" during early adolescent years.
>
> Upon those who seem to be "marking time" mentally, the effect of the pressure of increasingly difficult academic work in the early secondary grades may be serious. Perhaps this explains why some experience a lapse of interest in future education, resulting in their dropping out of school before their potentialities can be realized. But whether he leaves school or not, the individual is likely to be seriously affected. It is difficult to estimate the degree of emotional tension created in children who have moved with relative ease through elementary school if they find upon reaching the secondary grades that more is expected of them than they can do. It is especially important in the early adolescent years, therefore, to help children who are making little or no progress to retain confidence in themselves.[20]

Figure 4 illustrates the variations in mental growth of the one thousand early adolescents twelve to fifteen years old who experienced periods of little or no mental growth while in the junior high school.

The rate of mental growth of children in the elementary school is more constant than it is among early adolescent students. The variability is increased and a greater demand is made for more differentiated teachings in the junior high school, for the range of mental age is approximately eight to nine years in each grade.

Developmental tasks of adolescents

During their physical, social, and psychological growth period there are important developmental tasks in which boys and girls need to experience successful achievement. According to Havighurst:

[19] Smith, Standley, and Hughes, *op. cit.,* p. 86.

[20] *A Design for Early Secondary Education* (Albany: University of the State of New York, State Department of Education, 1954), pp. 10, 11.

FIGURE 4

Schematic Curves on Mental Growth, Illustrating Typical Individual Patterns Deviating from Usual Concept of "Normal" Increase

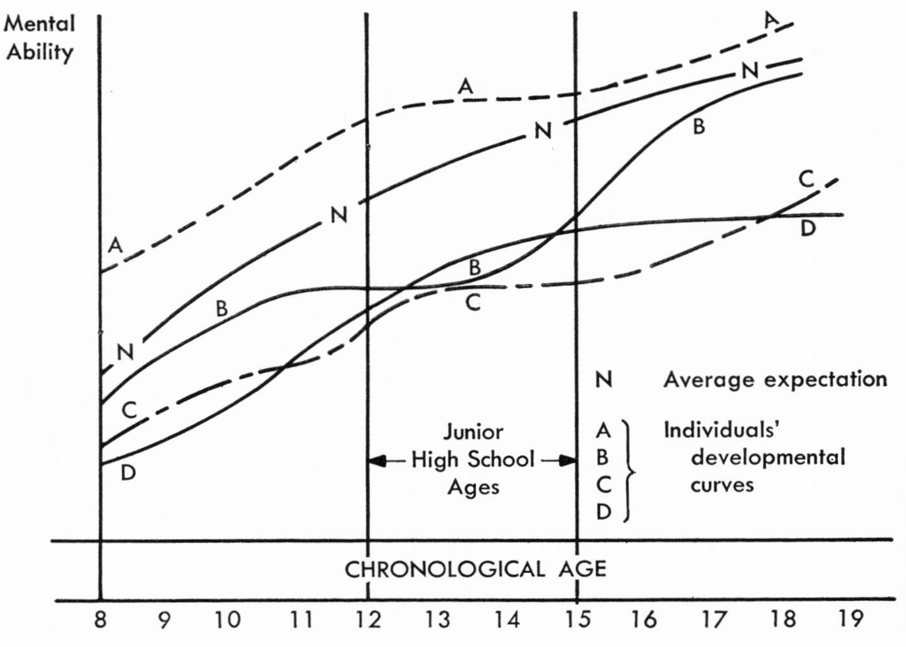

From *A Design for Early Secondary Education* (Albany: University of the State of New York, State Department of Education, 1954), p. 10.

> A developmental task is a task which arises at or about a certain period in the life of the individual, successful achievement of which leads to his happiness and to success with later tasks while failure leads to unhappiness in the individual, disapproval by society, and difficulty with later tasks.[21]

The ten developmental tasks of adolescents listed by Havighurst are as follows:

1. Achieving new and more mature relations with age-mates of both sexes.
2. Achieving a masculine or feminine social role.
3. Accepting one's physique and using the body effectively.
4. Achieving emotional independence of parents and other adults.
5. Achieving assurance of economic independence.
6. Selecting and preparing for an occupation.
7. Preparing for marriage and family life.
8. Developing intellectual skills and concepts necessary for civic competence.

[21] Robert J. Havighurst, *Developmental Tasks and Education* (New York: Longmans, Green & Co., Inc., 2nd ed., 1952), p. 2.

9. Desiring and achieving socially responsible behavior.
10. Acquiring a set of values and an ethical system as a guide to behavior.[22]

While tasks 5, 6, and 7 are chiefly those of later adolescents in senior high school, the other seven are applicable to late preadolescent and early adolescent students. Table 14 shows the developmental tasks of boys and girls of junior high school age in ten categories of behavior. These tasks are impor-

TABLE 14

The Tasks of Two Stages of Development in Categories of Behavior

Categories of Behavior	Late Childhood	Early Adolescence
I. Achieving an appropriate dependence-independence pattern	1. Freeing oneself from primary identification with adults	1. Establishing one's independence from adults in all areas of behavior
II. Achieving an appropriate giving-receiving pattern of affection	1. Learning to give as much love as one receives; forming friendships with peers	1. Accepting oneself as a worthwhile person, really worthy of love
III. Relating to changing social groups[a]	1. Clarifying the adult world as over against the child's world 2. Establishing peer groupness and learning to belong	1. Behaving according to a shifting peer code
IV. Developing a conscience	1. Learning more rules and developing more true morality	
V. Learning one's psycho-socio-biological sex role	1. Beginning to identify with one's social contemporaries of the same sex	1. Strongly identifying with one's own sex-mates 2. Learning one's role in heterosexual relationships

[22] *Ibid.,* Chap. 5. Courtesy of David McKay Company, Inc.

TABLE 14, Continued

Categories of Behavior	Late Childhood	Early Adolescence
VI. Accepting and adjusting to a changing body		1. Reorganizing one's thoughts and feelings about oneself in the face of significant bodily changes and their concomitants
		2. Accepting the reality of one's appearance
VII. Managing a changing body and learning new motor patterns	1. Refining and elaborating skill in the use of small muscles	1. Controlling and using a "new" body
VIII. Learning to understand and control the physical world	1. Learning more realistic ways of studying and controlling the physical world	
IX. Developing an appropriate symbol system and conceptual abilities	1. Learning to use language actually to exchange ideas or to influence one's hearers 2. Beginning understanding of real causal relations 3. Making finer conceptual distinctions and thinking reflectively	1. Using language to express and to clarify more complex concepts 2. Moving from the concrete to the abstract and applying general principles to the particular
X. Relating one's self to the cosmos	1. Developing a scientific approach	

[a] We have not dealt here with the developmental tasks of relating to "secondary" social groups. As the child grows he must relate to groups other than the family and his peers — to school, community, nation, world. There are not yet sufficient data to enable us to delineate the specific developmental tasks in this area.

Adapted from "Table of Tasks of Development in Categories of Behavior," in Association for Supervision and Curriculum Development, National Education Association, *Fostering Mental Health in Our Schools,* 1950 Yearbook (Washington: The Association, 1950), pp. 84-87. This table includes tasks in five stages of development — infancy, early childhood, late childhood, early adolescence, and later adolescence. Since the junior high school deals with boys and girls in their late childhood and early adolescence, only those stages are presented here.

tant to junior high school staff members for the following reasons: The purposes and functions of the junior high school can be more accurately identified and realized, they afford teachers more specific information as to when the individual student can take on a specific developmental task, and achievement of developmental tasks at such points of readiness assists in the selection of interesting units of work, activities, and other learning experiences.

Psychological development during early adolescence means a greater variance in available learning abilities than at younger or older ages. Some of these wide ranges in mental ability are due to rapid changes in physical, social and psychological growth; irregular mental growth beyond eleven or twelve years of age; the fact that girls mature physically and socially one to two years ahead of boys; problems in the attainment of social maturity; constitutional personality traits; and motivational influences from school, home, and community environments.

It is very important that administrators and teachers do not ignore or try to repress the late preadolescent's preparation and approach to early adolescence. The junior high school organization of classes, especially in Grade 7, should emulate that of the elementary school for at least a portion of the school day, but teacher-student planning and group classwork should be emphasized.

The innate complexities of the early adolescent demand a program of education that is fully integrated and geared to the individual differences of the students. They cannot grasp the total venture if instructors make subject matter the nucleus of the entire program and ignore the imperative needs of the individual at this most critical period. It is fallacious to assume that education can be "poured into" a child's mind, although there has been a great deal of "pitcher filling in junior high schools."[23] Subject matter, properly presented, with sincere and sympathetic understanding of adolescence, will focus all effort on goals and standards so intrinsic to his needs that each student will "soak up more basic skills and fundamental subject matter like a sponge."[24] Emphasizing subject matter, increasing the work load with more and more rigid demands for homework assignments, and holding intractable attitudes toward the early adolescent and his needs will inevitably eclipse the basic intent of the junior high school program to be progressive and completely satisfying for every adolescent and teacher.

[23] Helen Heffernan and Maxine Smith, "The Young Adolescent," *California Journal of Elementary Education,* 28:70, November, 1959.

[24] *Ibid.,* p. 71.

SELECTED BIBLIOGRAPHY

Association for Supervision and Curriculum Development, National Education Association. *Fostering Mental Health in Our Schools.* 1950 Yearbook. Washington: The Association, 1950. Pp. 84-97.

Ausubel, David P. *Theory and Problems of Adolescent Development.* New York: Grune & Stratton, Inc., 1954.

Bennett, Margaret. *Guidance in Groups.* New York: McGraw-Hill Book Co., Inc., 1953.

Blair, Arthur Witt, and William H. Burton. *Growth and Development of the Preadolescent.* New York: Appleton-Century-Crofts, Inc., 1951.

Bossing, Nelson L. *Principles of Secondary Education.* Englewood Cliffs, N.J.: Prentice-Hall, Inc., 2nd ed., 1955.

Cole, Luella. *Psychology of Adolescence.* New York: Rinehart & Co., 5th ed., 1959.

Corbally, John E., Jr., T. J. Jensen, and Frederick Staub. *Educational Administration: The Secondary School.* Boston: Allyn and Bacon, Inc., 1961. Chap. 10, "Unique Tasks of the Junior High School."

Crow, Lester D. "Teenage Traits, Interests, and Worries," *Educational Forum,* 20:423-428, May, 1956.

Design for Early Secondary Education, A. Albany: University of the State of New York, State Department of Education, 1954.

Faunce, Roland C., and Morrel J. Clute. *Teaching and Learning in the Junior High School.* San Francisco: Wadsworth Publishing Company, 1961. Chap. 2, "Characteristics and Needs of the Early Adolescent."

Gallagher, J. R., and H. I. Harris. *Emotional Problems of Adolescents.* New York: Oxford University Press, 1958.

Gesell, Arnold L., Frances C. Ilg, and Louise B. Ames. *Youth: The Years from Ten to Sixteen.* New York: Harper & Brothers, 1956.

Gran, John H. *How to Understand and Teach Teenagers.* Minneapolis: T. S. Denison and Company, 1958.

Havighurst, Robert J. *Developmental Tasks and Education.* New York: Longmans, Green & Co., Inc., 2nd ed., 1952.

Heffernan, Helen, and Maxine Smith. "The Young Adolescent," *California Journal of Elementary Education,* 28:69-79, November, 1959.

Junior High School Evaluative Criteria. Salt Lake City: State of Utah, Department of Public Instruction, 1960. Section B, "Characteristics of Junior High School Students."

Junior High School Program, The. Atlanta, Ga.: Southern Association of Colleges and Secondary Schools, 1958.

Kilpatrick, William H. *Foundations of Methods.* New York: The Macmillan Company, 1925.

Koos, Leonard V. *Junior High School Trends.* New York: Harper & Brothers, 1955.

Lindgren, Henry Clay. *Educational Psychology in the Classroom.* New York: John Wiley & Sons, Inc., 1956.

Loomis, Mary Jane. *The Preadolescent: Three Major Concerns.* New York: Appleton-Century-Crofts, Inc., 1959.

Noar, Gertrude. *The Junior High School, Today and Tomorrow.* Englewood Cliffs, N.J.: Prentice-Hall, Inc., 2nd ed., 1961.

Redl, Fritz. *Pre-Adolescents — What Makes Them Tick.* New York: Child Study Association of America, rev. ed., 1959.

Remmers, H. H., and D. H. Radler. *The American Teenager.* Indianapolis: The Bobbs-Merrill Company, Inc., 1957.

Smith, Maurice M., L. L. Standley, and Cecil L. Hughes. *Junior High School Education: Its Principles and Procedures.* New York: McGraw-Hill Book Co., Inc., 1942.

Strang, Ruth. *The Adolescent Views Himself, A Psychology of Adolescence.* New York: McGraw-Hill Book Co., Inc., 1957.

Taba, Hilda, Elizabeth Hall Brady, John T. Robinson, and William E. Vickery. *Diagnosing Human Relations Needs: Studies in Intergroup Relations.* Center for Intergroup Education, The University of Chicago. Washington: American Council on Education, 1951.

Tompkins, Ellsworth, and Virginia Roe. "The Two-Year Junior High School," *The Bulletin of the National Association of Secondary-School Principals,* 41:27-44, September, 1957.

Urell, Catherine. "What Do They Want Out of Life?" *Teachers College Record,* 61:318-330, March, 1960.

Van Til, William, Gordon F. Vars, and John H. Lounsbury. *Modern Education for the Junior High School Years.* Indianapolis: The Bobbs-Merrill Company, Inc., 1961. Chap. 7, "The Personal-Social Needs of Early Adolescents Influence the Junior High School Program."

Wattenberg, W. W. *The Adolescent Years.* New York: Harcourt, Brace & Co., 1955.

Wilson, William E. *The Junior High School.* Report Prepared by The Indiana Association of Junior and Senior High School Principals. Bloomington: State of Indiana Department of Public Instruction, Bulletin No. 246, 1961. Chap. 2, "Characteristics of Adolescents."

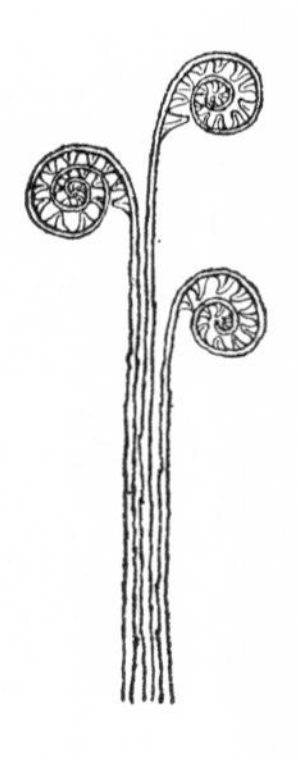

Part Two

CURRICULUM AND INSTRUCTION

4

The Influence of Learning Theories on the Curriculum

The vital relationship of the psychological theory of learning to the curriculum is now commonly accepted. No competent writer in the field of the curriculum today would attempt a serious discussion of curricular problems without indicating clearly the psychological basis upon which the curriculum was being considered.

It is recognized that principles of learning psychology apply to all ages, inasmuch as the learning organism functions in essentially the same way at all age levels. However, at certain periods in his life the individual is under more stress, and more emphasis needs to be placed on the psychological aspects of the learning process at these times. This necessity has a definite bearing on the nature and organization of the curriculum.

It seems desirable, therefore, to make clear the psychological concepts that must guide the junior high school in particular, though they have general applicability, with varying degrees of emphasis at different age levels.

1. How do changing conceptions of learning affect the curriculum?

General conceptions of learning

Many theories of the nature of learning have evolved over the years, but most of them are of relatively late origin, as recent man has begun to subject time-encrusted ideas to critical examination, based increasingly upon the findings of extensive research.[1]

Some theories of learning have tremendous implications for the curriculum while others have greater meaning for teaching processes. In this chapter the three major theories of learning that have great potential for the school curriculum will be considered. Two of them have become outmoded in theory but not in practice; the third, as it gains acceptance, holds much possible significance for the schools of today and tomorrow, particularly for the junior high school.

Mind storage theory. In the *mind reservoir* or *mind storage* theory of learning, the mind, thought to be centered in the brain, was considered an unleakable vessel in which could be stored unlimited amounts of knowledge for possible future use. By some process never satisfactorily explained all this knowledge or information was supposed to be constantly available, and whenever an occasion arose in which any part of it was needed it would instantly be brought to recall.

In practical parlance learning became simply a matter of acquiring vast quantities of information stored in memory. Memorization became the chief means of transferring the mass outside to the inside of the mind. This has often been referred to as a pouring-in process. The purpose of education was simply to fill the mind with as much information as possible. To be a walking encyclopedia thus became the ideal, the supreme evidence that one was an educated person. T.V. programs of a few years ago idealizing the "Quiz Kids," and the plethora of contests featuring adult paragons of encyclopedic information represent an extreme carry-over of this educational idea. The value of the theory may be judged by the fact that with few exceptions the adult participants in these contests had not distinguished themselves highly in their vocations. In fact, they represented a distinctly mediocre level in their vocational success patterns.

Naturally the curriculum became centered in the quantities of information which man had acquired over the centuries. As this mass of information rapidly expanded, the immediate task of curriculum making became one of organizing it into some classification system that would bring related materials together for convenience of reference and study. Thus arose, in antiquity, the beginnings of our present subject-matter classifications.

The mind storage theory of learning declined under the questioning spirit

[1] For a general discussion of different schools of psychology see R. S. Woodworth, *Contemporary Schools of Psychology* (New York: The Ronald Press Company, rev. ed., 1948). For a more specific discussion of learning see E. R. Hilgard, *Theories of Learning* (New York: Appleton-Century-Crofts, Inc., rev. ed., 1956); E. C. Tolman, "Theories of Learning," in F. A. Moss (ed.), *Comparative Psychology* (Englewood Cliffs, N.J.: Prentice-Hall, Inc., 1934); and H. L. Kingsley and Ralph Garry, *The Nature and Conditions of Learning* (Englewood Cliffs, N.J.: Prentice-Hall, Inc., rev. ed., 1957).

that has characterized the scientific era. Ideas accepted for centuries began to be subjected to careful scrutiny and testing. Many studies made in the early 1900's led to an examination of the very foundations of this theory. The data gathered on the question of memory retention and forgetting were devastating to it. It was discovered that man did not retain all the information memorized, but tended to forget rapidly. For example, 60 per cent of materials memorized that had little meaning to the learner, such as nonsense syllables, would be forgotten within twenty-four hours, and 80 per cent would be forgotten within one month. Even meaningful material which was memorized but not used tended to be forgotten rapidly — on the average 50 per cent was forgotten within six months to a year, and within two years upwards of 80 per cent was forgotten. Investigation thus revealed that the mind was more comparable to a sieve than an unleakable vessel. These and other studies have made belief in the mind storage theory untenable.

Mental discipline — faculties of the mind theory. The theory of *mental discipline* or *faculty psychology* had long held sway in educational thinking simultaneously with the *mind storage* theory of learning. Not uncommonly those who professed to believe in both were unaware of the obvious contradiction between them. In America the *mental discipline* or *faculty psychology* theory of learning became popular about the middle of the nineteenth century and had a tremendous influence upon curriculum development until shortly after the beginning of the twentieth century, when this theory came into question. Except among those well grounded in psychological and educational theory, the idea still persists, as does the mind storage theory, and its effect may still be seen in the curriculum practices of our schools.

The mental discipline or faculty psychology theory is based upon the belief that the mind is made up of many functions, among which are memory, reasoning, judgment, imagination, discrimination. These functions were supposed to have definite locations in the brain and to be distinct from each other. They were often characterized as muscles of the mind which could be exercised to develop them. As any function was exercised it became stronger and consequently more useful. Commitment to this theory is well expressed by one proponent: "No means are known whereby the faculties of the mind can be developed but by exercising them. By the potent spell of the magic word exercise, is evoked all human power." This theory assumed a generalized function for each faculty of the brain. Therefore, if the faculty of reason or judgment was strengthened, by whatever means, the general power of reason or judgment could be uniformly applied to any field of human activity. The power of reason developed by extensive exercise in mathematical study was supposed to be equally effective in solving problems involving mathematics, business, politics, social life, philosophy, religion, or romance. It was a distinct virtue of this theory that as these functional areas were developed they did not lose their levels of efficiency.

Phrenology was an extreme offshoot of the faculty theory. It held that the areas of function of the mind literally expanded physiologically as the faculty was developed. Such development would lead to pressure on the skull and produce a slight or noticeable protuberance, a bump, above the site of this function. Likewise the underdevelopment of a faculty would result in a depressed spot in the skull above the function. An earlier period of psychology thus became identified with the use of calipers in connection with the indirect measurement of brain functioning. Phrenology assumed such importance in some psychological circles that the famous psychologist, Jastrow, then of the University of Wisconsin, was reported to have set up a tent on the Midway in Chicago during the World's Fair of 1903 where he charged ten cents for each head read phrenologically — this in the interest of psychological research.

The more serious acceptance of faculty pyschology did have far-reaching effects upon the school curriculum. The theories of mind storage and mental discipline were actually incompatible. Instead of setting up a different type of curriculum the proponents of mental discipline simply took over the general subject-matter curriculum, selected from it and reorganized it to conform to this new theory of learning. No longer concerned about the utility of content, they centered attention upon the organizational form of the subject matter to better develop given mental functions. Not what was learned but how it was learned now became important. A subject was judged primarily by its worth as a means of developing mental functions. As A. S. Welch stated in the preface to his *Analysis of the English Sentence, Designed for Advanced Classes in English Grammar* (1862), "The systematic analysis of the English sentence should hold a prominent rank merely as a means of mental development."

Because of their highly inflected nature, Latin and Greek were naturals for developing the function of discrimination, and mathematics was assumed to be valuable for developing the function of reasoning. Little attempt was made by the teachers or proponents of these subjects to argue their practical worth; they rested their case on the *mental discipline* derived from studying them.

Difficulty became a first criterion in the selection of what was to be studied since this obviously contributed in major degree to mental development. Minutely organized materials became the prized curricular content. The pupil's interest in the subject was of little importance. Indeed, the extremist partisans of this theory considered pupil interest or pleasure in study a liability. As Mr. Dooley, the humorist of the time, observed, "It don't matter now what you study, just so it is hard and ain't liked." And Harold Rugg, in reference to this period, said, "The entire school curriculum was under the sway of a mythical faith in mental discipline. The current point of view was that learning, to be effective, must be hard and disagreeable."[2]

The same spirit of inquiry and challenge that brought the mind storage theory into disrepute also caused the rejection of the theory of mental discipline and faculty psychology. Studies by such men as James, Thorndike, Lashley, Koffka, and others raised doubts about the existence of distinct areas of the brain, each devoted to its own specialized function.

These two theories of learning, extant at the same time, had conflicting influences upon the curriculum. The mind storage theory naturally tended to encourage the expansion of the school curriculum, to the end that the mind might amass all the knowledge possible. The secondary school particularly felt this urge to make new knowledge available; the academy introduced scores of new subjects. On the other hand, the theory of mental discipline prescribed barring new courses until they gave promise of rigorous internal organization. Consequently, many practical subjects which forced their way into the secondary school curriculum between 1800 and 1875, under the growing pressure of the demand for the respectability of the mental discipline theory by its proponents, steadily sacrificed their practicality for rigorousness in organization.

It would be a serious mistake to assume that these disproved theories of learning have been completely abandoned and that the curriculum is now free of their influences. The curriculum patterns and prescriptions found in a majority of our secondary schools are basically those of the latter part of the last century and, indeed, are often justified by the same claims of mind storage or mental discipline learning values. For example, in a recent publication Mortimer Smith, a spokesman for the Council for Basic Education, asserts that "the school's task is primarily transmission of factual knowledge in the basic subjects."[3] It is difficult, for example, to read Conant's *The American High School Today* without sensing the tremendous impact of the mental discipline concept on his curriculum recommendations. The same may be said for many of the contemporary pronouncements of mathematicians and scientists as they attempt to justify more rigorous academic courses for the secondary school — and even for the elementary school. A similar example of the persistence of these outmoded theories of learning among large numbers of academicians is found in the interesting *Report of the San Francisco Curriculum Survey Committee*. The committee consisted of eight academicians from the liberal arts divisions of Stanford University and the University of California, Berkeley. The opening statement of their report says, "We be-

[2] *The Foundations and Technique of Curriculum Construction,* Twenty-Sixth Yearbook of the National Society for the Study of Education, Part I (Bloomington, Ill.: Public School Publishing Company, 1926), p. 24.

[3] Mortimer Smith, *A Citizen's Manual for Public Schools* (Washington: Council for Basic Education, 1959), p. 7.

lieve that the purpose of education is to inform the mind and develop the intellect."[4] References to "easy courses," the stress on academic subjects, depreciation of the public school emphasis upon "education for life in a democracy," "emphasis . . . on a few subjects thoroughly learned" throughout the report indicate clearly the adherence of this group to outmoded theories of learning.

Experience learning theory. A theory of learning that has come into general acceptance among educational leaders, but to date has been exemplified cautiously in school curriculum and instructional practice, holds that *learning is the change or modification of behavior through experience.* According to this theory learning results in changed behavior, and the acid test of whether learning has taken place is the evidence of change in behavior. No change in behavior, no learning.

It should be pointed out at the very beginning of the discussion of this theory of learning that basically the idea of changing behavior through learning has characterized all theories of learning. In the mind storage theory it was assumed that stored-up knowledge would be used to guide one's actions. Proponents of mental discipline believed that the development of the many faculties would result in better control of a person's activities. These were implied assumptions and indirect goals of either form of learning. However, learning itself was immediately concerned with ways and means of storing knowledge in the brain or with the development of the mental faculties.

The theory that learning is change in behavior which comes through experience places primary emphasis upon the outcomes of learning in a behavioral milieu. It focuses attention first upon the nature of the behavior to be learned and then upon the process by which that learning takes place. The same mistake should not be made here that characterized some aspects of the "activity movement" in the late twenties and early thirties. Some devotees of this movement, mistaking the superficial for the essence, identified activity learning as in evidence only when physical motion of a pronounced type was taking place. For them violent forms of physical expression were the indices of much learning. There are various forms of learning that find expression in different degrees of observable behavioral change. For example, a typist exhibits definite observable changes in behavior as effective physical coordination is achieved in striking the correct keys. More subtle behavioral changes take place in appreciational or attitudinal learning. If one professes to have learned to appreciate good music but persists in listening to low-quality music, or if one claims to have changed his attitude from dislike to warm liking of certain persons but continues to avoid them, it is taken for granted that the lack of change in behavior indicates a lack of learning in these respects.

[4] William C. Bark, *et al., Report of the San Francisco Curriculum Survey Committee* (San Francisco: San Francisco Unified School District, 1960), p. 7.

Figure 5 presents *experience* learning graphically. The learner is under the pressure of biological and other drives that create tensions and dissatisfactions. As these drives crystallize into recognized needs and wants and become identified with goals which if attained would bring definite satisfactions and thus relieve unpleasant inner tension, the purpose or motive for learning is established. The learner confronts many problem situations as he seeks to realize the desired goal. The efforts to overcome these difficulties lead to modifications of his behavior in ways that make for reduced effort through more effective behavior in future similar situations. Psychologists tend to define learning in terms of the acquisition of ways of attaining goals and satisfying desires. One psychologist has emphasized the process of this theory of learning by calling learning "activity under tension toward a goal."

Although the theory under discussion is important for all age groups, it is of special significance to the early adolescent period. When the boy or girl is trying to find the answers to many questions of a personal, social, or societal nature, a curriculum organized around the basic needs of this age group and in harmony with this principle of learning is essential for the junior high school.

More specific aspects of the learning process

The experience concept of learning embraces most of the aspects of learning generally accepted by educational psychologists and leaders in curriculum and instruction.

Learning as change in behavior. Whereas in the theories of learning previously discussed attention was focused upon cramming the mind with masses of factual material or ways of developing the mental faculties, in experience learning primary concern is with the behavior of the learner. What behavior competencies are essential to effective living in our democratic society, and how do they find expression in the appropriate actions of the learner? Does he show increased awareness of his responsibility to others? Is he better at getting along with others? Has he made progress in achieving muscular coordination skills? Is he steadily improving in all phases of communication

FIGURE 5

Interactional Situation in Learning

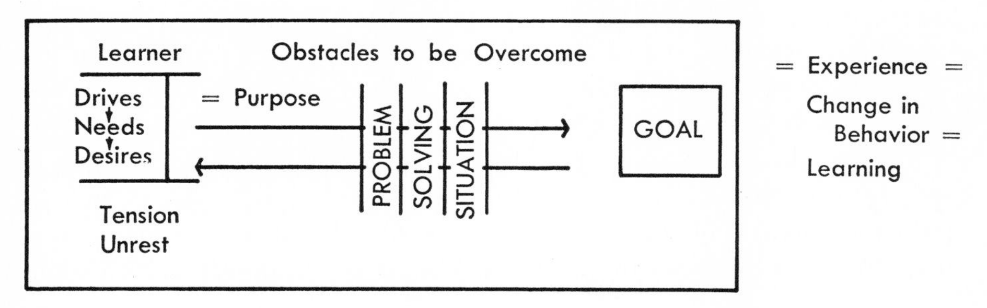

skills? To repeat, the acid test of learning is the extent to which there is evidence of changed behavior. A pupil may have a high score on a pencil-paper test on communication or social verbal information, but if there is no translation into observable behavior skills it is assumed that no learning has taken place. This is not to infer that behavior is developed in a vacuum. There must be a basis for intelligent behavior patterns in fact and understanding. But information per se is not enough. *Intelligent behavior is bona fide evidence that the learner possesses the needed facts, understands their relevance, and transmits that understanding into appropriate activity.*

It is this control aspect of the experience theory of learning that needs continual emphasis, for it involves a radical change in the curriculum and has particular relevance for the junior high school period. Now, attention must be focused upon what kind of behavioral competencies boys and girls should develop from the school learning experiences. Most of the behavioral competencies needed for successful living as children and adolescents, in school, home, and community, are those needed also in adulthood. Since the curriculum embodies the learning situations in which these competencies can be developed, it is most important for early adolescents.

Learning through experience. That change in behavior comes through or is the result of experience is the second major facet of this theory of learning and distinguishes it from all previous learning theories. One has an experience when he interacts with an environmental situation as he seeks to attain a specific goal. The conscious efforts of the learner to overcome all obstacles blocking his attainment of an objective involve a gradual modification of his behavior patterns as he develops effective ways of reacting to a situation and so moving toward his goal. This total interacting process — this experience — in turn results in highly desirable behavioral changes that insure more effective and expeditious ways of overcoming similar difficulties in the future.

Learning as the reaction of the total organism. A careful look at Figure 5 and the foregoing description of experience learning should make clear the total involvement of the learner in any given learning situation. Behavior learning requires the integrated response of all elements of the body: brain, nervous system, muscular system, circulatory system, and all bodily senses. Some may play a more important part than others, but the whole organism is involved. Research brings greater and greater realization of the extremely complex and sensitive nature of learning, and more and more understanding that the learner reacts as a total person to a learning situation.

Learning through activity. John Dewey, one of the early educators of this century, coined the well-known sentence, "We learn by doing." Hilgard gives full approval of this idea, even in the higher realms of thinking, in a quotation from another writer: "The thinker is physically active even while sitting at a desk. . . . complete relaxation and thinking are incompatible; when our muscles are completely relaxed, we go to sleep and cannot think at all."[5] Under the old concepts of learning and the curriculum we had what was called "passive" and "active" learning. The mind could be filled with information via the lecture or telling route even though the learner maintained an attitude of passiveness. But long before experience learning became a well-developed theory, Dewey and others recognized that learning requires the active attention of the learner. Early in this chapter mention was made of those who misconstrued the idea to infer that any kind of activity was synonymous with learning. On the contrary, to contribute to learning, activity must be meaningful and goal directed.

Motivation essential to learning. Educational psychologists have long emphasized the importance of motivation to effective learning. Unless one has a definite purpose in learning there is little incentive for it. Experience learning maintains that motivation results from the learner's identification of his basic needs and desires with specific attainable goals. When he is able to relate his particular felt needs with goals that appear feasible, there is aroused within him a determination — purpose — to attain the goals in question. And unless such purpose is aroused, no goal seeking will take place. "No purpose, no learning" is a phrase that expresses the centrality of purpose to learning in the experience learning theory.

Thus it is supremely important for the school, particularly the junior high school, to set up a curriculum that is centered in the personal and social needs of boys and girls. At this age personal and social problems are of paramount importance. Too, goals are more immediate and imperative. Obviously, purpose is much more easily aroused by the teacher when the pupil can immediately identify learning goals with needs clearly recognized. This does not mean that the learning situation is determined by the superficially understood needs and desires of the immature boy or girl. But much that is basic in desirable behavioral patterns can be learned in the environment natural to the life of the learner. The wise teacher can utilize the immediate purposes of the learner to develop behavioral patterns that satisfy immediate personal and social needs and at the same time will serve him in adulthood. Further, a good teacher is alive to the use of the immediate goal seeking of the pupil to help him realize distant goals understood best by the teacher. The pleasure purposes of pupils in play can be used to lead them to engage in group activities that not only satisfy their current interests but develop desirable social behavior and individual physical coordination skills — educational goals probably recognized only by the teacher. While he understands that the adult goals of education and the objectives of children and youth are likely to differ, it is his responsibility to help the maturing learner

[5] Ernest R. Hilgard, *Introduction to Psychology* (New York: Harcourt, Brace & Co., 1953), p. 311.

to identify his goals and purposes increasingly with those of adult society. By the time the pupil has reached the latter part of his secondary school period, and even earlier for many pupils, under the guidance of wise teachers he should begin to replace immediate goals by more remote ones as he works out his hierarchy of values.

Learning dependent on understanding. In the old mind storage theory learning did not depend upon understanding. As a high school teacher irritably remarked to a pupil who was having difficulty with the concepts of liability and assets, "Well, if you don't understand it, learn it anyway!" One of the authors recalls the frequent comment of his English teachers when they urged memorization of subtle but famous lines from Shakespeare and others: "You may not understand it now but learn it." These teachers regarded learning and memorization as synonyms. For years students of the learning process have at least insisted that understanding facilitated learning, and in recent decades they have taken the position that understanding is essential to learning.

That learning depends upon understanding has been a *sine qua non* of the experience learning theory. Figure 5, "Interactional Situation in Learning," presented on page 101, clarifies the relationship between learning and understanding. As an understanding of the relationship or significance of the goal to the needs of the individual is necessary before effort will be put forth to achieve the goal ("No purpose, no learning"), so modern education is based on the principle that learning can take place only where there is understanding. The old adage "You cannot put an old head on young shoulders" particularly applies to the junior high school period, where the curriculum and teaching methods too long have reflected adult rather than early adolescent levels of understanding.

Problem solving central in learning. Goal seeking as the means of satisfying needs and desires is at the heart of experience learning. As the learner, reaching out toward a desired goal, finds obstacles in his way, he is plunged into problem-solving situations. There are few goal-seeking situations, if any, that do not involve effort to overcome or set aside whatever stands between the learner and his goal. This means careful study and analysis of the situation, identification of the obstacles, and decision on what is necessary to overcome them and whether a frontal or oblique attack is best — time, effort, and the probability of success considered. Not all goals, however desirable, are readily, if at all, achieved. Realization of this fact adds to the complexity of the problem situation. If careful study indicates that attainment of a given goal appears to be impractical, the learner must re-examine his needs and determine whether other goals might hold out promise of satisfying his needs, in full or in part, and which ones seem most feasible.

From the cradle to the grave, we are enmeshed in constant problem-solving situations as we seek to fulfill our needs and desires. As the world changes at an accelerated rate and the tempo of living is correspondingly stepped up it can be assumed that we can call less and less upon the structures of the past to supply the answer to the needs of the future. Problem-solving activities will undoubtedly become the principal concern of learning. In fact, many contemporary thinkers, seeing little in our world of kaleidoscopic change but problems, feel that the development of problem-solving skills has first claim on education.

Recently the reality of this situation was presented forcibly by an air force general speaking to a group of educators:

> In the past it has been the practice of the military to give primary attention to the study of previous military campaign strategies in the training of its officers for future war. Now at the close of World War II we have become painfully aware that such dependence on the past nearly cost us victory in this war, and to continue such dependence on the past in the future will be suicidal. The present world of scientific and technological development is moving so fast that to prepare for the future we must largely scrap our dependence upon past ways of doing things and train our officers to plan new war strategy, day by day incorporating into our war plans the latest scientific developments. Our air battle strategy of the recent war is already obsolete as a result of new postwar scientific knowledge and developments. A war of the future will be won by that nation which has most imaginatively utilized in its war plans the very latest developments in science. Our problem in the air force is to devise educational methods that will train our men to constantly look ahead, and to develop mental habits of continually examining new developments in science for their possible implications for the modification of air-war strategy.

What is true for the education of those responsible for the protection of our nation is equally applicable to the education of other intelligent citizens.

Reflective or critical thinking an essential aspect of learning. When the school becomes concerned with the development of problem-solving skills it becomes concerned also with a corollary responsibility, namely, the development of reflective or critical thinking. All problem solving involves thinking, although sometimes it is of an elemental nature. Over fifty years ago John Dewey recognized this fact when he described the activities of the child as he tries to grapple with the problem of simple adjustment to his surroundings: "These operations of conscious selection and arrangement constitute thinking, although of a rudimentary type."[6] Dewey went on to classify thinking into four levels, the highest of which, "reflective thought" or critical thinking, he characterized in these words: "Active, persistent, and careful consideration of any belief or supposed form of knowledge in the light of the grounds that

[6] John Dewey, *How We Think* (Boston: D. C. Heath & Company, 1910), pp. 157-158.

support it, and the further conclusions to which it tends, constitutes reflective thought."[7]

A present-day psychologist distinguishes between a simple form of problem solving which does not result in the abstraction of principles and that type of reflective or critical thinking about problems which leads to the development of principles or generalizations that may guide future problem solution. Characterizing reflective thinking, Hilgard observes:

> When the thinker uses his past experience, he uses it selectively, choosing only those details that seem related to the problem. In other words, he has some sort of theory or hypothesis that makes those details of his past experience relevant . . . the end point in thinking is a recognition of the *fit* between the conclusion and the requirements of the problem. . . . Thinking requires alertness to new possibilities, and to the possibility of doing things differently from the ways in which they were done before.[8]

Critical thinking, then, means seeing relationships between problem situations, their similarities and differences, and applying generalizations abstracted from previous problems solved to new problem situations. When the learner is able to see clearly the relationship between a specific problem faced and problems previously solved, he can more intelligently decide how to attack the problem at hand. At the same time, he must be alert to new ways of meeting problems, for no two problem situations are exactly alike. The ability to do a high order of reflective or critical thinking is the hallmark of the educated person.

Although the theory of experience learning fits admirably with the goal of developing reflective or critical thinking, it does not follow that such thinking is automatic. Research indicates that critical thinking must be specifically taught; problem-solving skills learned in one situation do not automatically transfer to another.

At least three major theories of transfer of training have been developed, two since the turn of the century. The venerable mental discipline theory has already been considered. It held that the training of the faculty of memory, for example, by whatever means would carry over into any situation where memory was a factor of learning. The philosopher-psychologist William James first questioned this theory through his experiments. It is now discredited.

Thorndike is usually identified with the theory of transfer through identity of elements. In this theory of transfer Thorndike maintained that the learner could take advantage of similar elements found in two learning situations. If the student used a slide rule in one course in mathematics he would be able to

[7] *Ibid.*, pp. 2-6.

[8] Hilgard, *Introduction to Psychology*, pp. 323-324. See also revised edition, 1957, Chap. 13.

use it in a second course also. A pupil who had learned the four fundamental operations in arithmetic would be able to apply them in algebra. This theory of transfer was so direct that its helpfulness has been questioned.

Judd's theory of transfer through generalizations or principles suggests that transfer takes place through the application to a new learning situation of generalizations or principles learned in a previous problem situation. An experiment used to illustrate his theory involved two groups of boys who shot arrows at an object submerged in water. When they had become proficient at hitting the object at a certain depth, its depth was changed. The boys who had been taught the principle of refraction developed skill in adjusting to different depths much more quickly than the boys who had not been so taught.[9] It is this concept of transfer of training that is now generally accepted.

Practice necessary in learning. Repetition has been a feature of every theory of learning. In memoriter learning or the fixing of skills, repetition has always been considered necessary. In the stimulus-response (S-R) theory of learning it became the key to mastery. Since experience learning involves behavioral change, emphasis is still placed upon repetitive aspects of learning, particularly where so-called mechanical skills are concerned.

However, concepts of the nature of repetition and the method of its employment are vastly different. Learning by fixing of skills or memory was achieved by repeatedly stimulating the proper sensory neuron until the proper neural pathways (so-called) had been established in the nervous system. The word familiarly associated with this process was *drill.* The pupil drilled on multiplication tables, spelling lists, writing form, typing, or whatever was to be fixed in the neural pathways so that automatic response resulted. It was customary to hear teachers adjure their pupils to get to work and drill until they had mastered the skill in question.

In experience learning repetition is recognized as essential, but the acts of repetition take on an altogether different meaning. The entire organism responds to a learning situation, and each effort to respond effectively modifies the total behavioral pattern of the organism to some degree. Consequently, every response is different from the preceding one. This means that intelligent learning involves a critical reassessment, after each attempt to attain a goal, focused on the extent of achievement or failure, and the reasons for it. Thus the next effort to reach the goal — acquire the coveted skill — should take place from a new vantage point of modified behavior and involve a modifica-

[9] C. H. Judd, "The Relation of Special Training to General Intelligence," *Educational Review,* 36:28-42, June, 1908. Also G. Hendrickson and W. H. Schroeder, "Transfer of Training in Learning to Hit a Submerged Target," *Journal of Educational Psychology,* 32:205-213, March, 1941. See further discussion in Hilgard, *Introduction to Psychology,* rev. ed., Chap. 11, and A. N. Fransen, *Educational Psychology: The Principles of Learning and Teaching* (New York: McGraw-Hill Book Co., Inc., 1961), Chap. 10.

tion of the total pattern of the reaction purposefully determined. The teacher's instruction to a pupil, "Just drill or practice till you get it," is based on a misconception of the nature of experience learning. Teacher and pupil should study every effort put forth in goal seeking, carefully analyzing it in order to determine what modified pattern of behavioral reaction should characterize the next attempt to achieve the goal. Practice, not drill, is essential in learning.

Individual differences a keystone in experience learning. Possibly no aspect of the nature of the learner and learning has received more lip service in education for over a half-century than that of individual differences. Since the publication of Thorndike's monumental work in 1914 entitled *Mental Work and Fatigue and Individual Differences and Their Causes,* there has been a growing recognition of the complexity of the subject of individual differences by psychologists and educators. Unfortunately the old quip "Everybody is talking about the weather but nobody is doing anything about it" might well refer to our putting into effect what we know about individual differences.[10]

We know that no two people are alike. Here is one with an I.Q. of 140 who gets top grades in all his work; seated next to him is a pupil with an I.Q. of 95 who gets low grades. However, another pupil, with an I.Q. of 100, is a plodding hard worker who gets high grades while still another classmate, with an I.Q. of 150, does mediocre work because he is not motivated and dislikes school. He likes mechanics and would be much happier tinkering around with an old car. One pupil demonstrates outstanding ability in painting; another shows real talent in playing the violin. Joe is a leader, while Tom is retiring, never giving voice to an idea. Some students come from homes of culture and refinement where good books and magazines are present in quantity, where radio, television, and hi-fi with stacks of classical and popular music of quality are to be found, where art is in evidence in furniture, ceramics, and paintings, where the home atmosphere is one of education and the children are accustomed to hearing stimulating conversation by persons of varied cultural interests. Others come from homes of underprivilege, where the parents are uneducated and the environment is culturally barren.

Schools continue to operate on the fiction of grade classification although it has been known for years that there is no such thing as homogeneous grouping on a grade basis. Children in the same class vary widely in their achievements, and individuals are at different levels of achievement in various subjects. A study made of the achievement differences of a group of thirty-two fifth-grade pupils revealed a spread in chronological age from nine

[10] Since Thorndike's pioneer publication many books have been written on the subject. Perhaps the foremost present-day authority on individual differences is Anne Anastasi, *Differential Psychology: Individual and Group Differences in Behavior* (New York: The Macmillan Company, 3rd ed., 1958).

years ten months to eleven years six months, and an I.Q. range from 79 to 143. Variations in class achievements ranged from fourth to sixth grade in arithmetic, third to tenth grade in science, second to ninth grade in spelling, second to eleventh grade in reading, and fourth to eleventh grade in geography. In any sixth-grade class or above it is normal to find a spread of four grades above and below the standard class grade norm. A teacher gave a basic skills test to her fourth-grade class of thirty-six pupils with the following results:[11]

Test	*Grade Spread*
Reading comprehension	5 years 8 months
Reading vocabulary	6 " 5 "
Map reading	3 " 2 "
Use of references	8 " 5 "
Use of index	7 " 6 "
Use of dictionary	7 " 0 "
Punctuation	4 " 0 "
Capitalization	4 " 2 "
Correct usage	8 " 2 "
Spelling	7 " 1 "

A standardized achievement test given to a sixth grade revealed startling variations in individual pupil attainments as well. Typical of the class was the range in subject achievement of one pupil. In spelling and composition this boy was at the fourth-grade level, in arithmetic at the sixth-grade level, in geography at the eighth-grade level, and in literature, social studies, and science he was above the norms for the junior high school.

It is quite clear that the maintenance of grade placement in our schools is unrealistic, and the attempt to maintain a uniform curriculum for a grade level, still so widespread in school practice, is an educational travesty. Particularly is this true at the junior high school level, where each individual should receive special attention.

Another important aspect of individual differences in learning quite generally overlooked in the classroom and in curriculum planning is the perceptual differences with which students approach a learning situation. Explicit in the theory of experience learning is the recognition that each learner reacts to a new situation in terms of his perceptual development, which depends on his background of previous experiences. A class exposed to a new learning situation may be expected to interpret it in as many ways as there are members of the class. It is the task of the teacher to insure some common understanding among the members of the class with respect to a learning situation, although he remains aware that identical perceptual understandings are im-

[11] Adapted from data in *A Guide for Better Instruction in Minnesota Schools,* Curriculum Bulletin No. 1 (St. Paul: State Department of Education, 1946), p. 128.

possible. The problem becomes one of communication and clarity in the exchange of ideas.

In a study of perceptual experience in relation to the measurement of intelligence, Davis has shown the importance of language symbols. He maintains that language symbols used in standard intelligence tests are based upon the perceptions of pupils of above average socioeconomic experiential background and do not fit the perceptual basis of the experience background of those who live "across the tracks" in slum or notably impoverished areas of the community.[12] Considerable attention is now being given to the complex problem of perceptual differences, and important new aspects of perception are being discovered.[13]

Learning a continuous process. The theory of experienec learning differs sharply from older theories in asserting that learning is continuous. The earlier theories of learning assumed that, aside from picking up bits of information in normal out-of-school activities, the pupil would come to school in the morning with his knowledge of the subject to be taught or the mental faculties to be trained in exactly the same condition as when he left school the previous day, unless home study had been prescribed. Not so in experience learning, for according to this theory the learner is continuously reacting to situations, and his behavior patterns are constantly being modified. The school, therefore, cannot be indifferent to the pupil's experiences outside school hours in the home and in the community. The six or seven hours spent in school environment may not be as potent for learning as the seventeen or eighteen hours spent outside of school. The school curriculum has been too closely identified only with what takes place in the classroom.

Intelligence — multifactor rather than unitary. A growing concern with quality or excellence in education as well as an insistence upon greater attention to those thought to have superior ability has led to a more critical attitude toward what is meant by the term "intelligence." Thurstone was one of the earlier psychologists to question the unitary nature of intelligence in his proposed concept of general-special factors of intelligence. Probably few, if any, psychologists today accept the old Binet-Terman simple concept of general brightness as intelligence. In 1951 French came to the conclusion

[12] Allison Davis, *Social Class Influence upon Learning,* Inglis Lectures (Cambridge, Mass.: Harvard University Press, 1948).

[13] For further data on this subject, particularly as it relates to education, consult the studies of Arthur W. Combs and E. Paul Torrance. Attention is called to Arthur W. Combs and Donald Snygg, *Individual Behavior: A Perceptual Approach to Behavior* (New York: Harper & Brothers, rev. ed., 1959); E. Paul Torrance, "Teacher Attitude and Pupil Perception," *Journal of Teacher Education,* 11:97-102, March, 1960; C. M. Solly, *Development of the Perceptual World* (New York: Basic Books, 1960); Ruth C. Wylie, *The Self Concept* (Lincoln: University of Nebraska Press, 1961); and Association for Supervision and Curriculum Development, National Education Association, *Perceiving, Behaving, Becoming,* 1962 Yearbook (Washington: The Association, 1962).

that there were at least a dozen and a half factors of mental activity that could be classified as intellectual.[14] In 1956 Guilford, who has devoted much study to this problem, stated that there may be many factors of intelligence not yet identified, but he concluded, "Of approximately 40 such factors, seven are memory factors and the remaining ones have to do with thinking."[15] Three years later Guilford made this interesting comment:

> With about fifty intellectual factors already known, we may say that there are at least fifty ways of being intelligent. . . . The structure of intellect is a theoretical model that predicts as many as 120 distinct abilities, if every cell of the model contains a factor. . . . Since the model was first conceived, twelve factors predicted by it have found places in it. There is consequently hope of filling many of the other vacancies, and we may eventually end up with more than 120 abilities.[16]

A special factor of intelligence that has received much attention in recent years is that of creativity. It is generally recognized that the contribution of so-called genius to every phase of society is in the area of creativity — the creative person is able to imaginatively develop new ideas and devise new ways of doing things to implement them. Kant, Descartes, Laplace, Galileo, Einstein, Edison, Leonardo da Vinci, Michelangelo, Mozart, Handel, Lorado Taft, Goethe, Emerson, John Stuart Mill, Napoleon, Disraeli, Jefferson, and Lincoln are a few of the geniuses who by their varied creative talents have enriched living and determined the course of humankind. It is of the utmost importance that society find ways to discover potential geniuses early and to encourage the development of their creative talent. The search should begin in the elementary and junior high schools.

What factors, intellectual and otherwise, operate to produce the gifted painter, sculptor, musician, dancer, dramatist, scientist, and military, political, or social leader? The conviction is growing among psychologists and educators that, whatever intellectual attributes may be common to all the gifted, there are distinctive traits that sharply differentiate the varied expressions of creative talent. Unfortunately, the indices of creative talent have not yet been clearly determined, nor have the instruments been devised by which to identify its presence.

It is a grave disservice, especially to the more non-academically talented, that so little research is being done in this area, and that in most schools there

[14] J. W. French, "The Description of Aptitude and Achievement Tests in Terms of Rotated Factors," *Psychometric Monograph,* No. 5, 1951.

[15] J. P. Guilford, "The Structure of Intellect," *Psychological Bulletin,* No. 53, July, 1956, p. 292.

[16] J. P. Guilford, "Three Faces of Intellect," *American Psychologist,* 14:477, August, 1959. For further discussion of this problem see *Personality* (New York: McGraw-Hill Book Co., Inc., 1959), by the same author.

is a naïve dependence upon intelligence tests to distinguish giftedness. Guilford, in speaking of intelligence tests, has declared that "The average test of this character is usually limited to not more than ten of the intellectual factors, none of which is among the more creative, divergent thinking group."[17] He refers to the Jones-Davis analysis of the Stanford-Binet Test of Intelligence, measuring only ten, and the Wechsler-Bellevue Scale, covering possibly six of the fifty or more factors which Guilford identifies as the minimum factors of intelligence at present identified.[18] He is more explicit when he asserts that "Verbal comprehension is the overwhelmingly dominant component of verbal-intelligence tests. A good vocabulary test would often serve as well as an entire battery of tests, most of which are verbal."[19] Recent studies have indicated that the upper 20 per cent of those who took an I.Q. test will include few persons of high creative talent. Creativity and verbal intelligence appear to involve different patterns of ability. If these studies are even approximately correct they have far-reaching implications for the school curriculum.[20]

Intelligence the product of both nature and nurture. Terman and most early students of intelligence testing were convinced that intelligence was purely a matter of inheritance. Terman insisted that the variations found in intelligence test scores given pupils over several years were due not to education but solely to the inadequacy of the measuring instrument; that it had not been possible to develop tests of sufficient precision to avoid some small fluctuation in test results.

Those concerned with curriculum problems must recognize what a formidable array of research data has revealed: that so-called intelligence can be improved through education. Intelligence is now generally admitted to be the product of both nature and nurture. The area of controversy is centered upon the extent to which intelligence can be modified through the media of the educational environment. This controversy is further enlivened by the present challenge to the older limited concept of intelligence previously discussed. As educators have long realized, many learners unable to cope with highly

[17] J. P. Guilford, "The Relation of Intellectual Factors to Creative Thinking in Science," *Research Conference on the Identification of Creative Science Talent, University of Utah, 1955* (Salt Lake City: University of Utah Press, 1956), p. 71.

[18] Guilford, "The Structure of Intellect," *op. cit.*

[19] Guilford, "The Relation of Intellectual Factors to Creative Thinking in Science," *op. cit.*

[20] For further data on this problem see E. Paul Torrance, *Guiding Creative Talent* (Englewood Cliffs, N.J.: Prentice-Hall, Inc., 1962); Jacob W. Getzels and Philip W. Jackson, *Creativity and Intelligence: Explorations with Gifted Children* (New York: John Wiley & Sons, Inc., 1962); and Calvin W. Taylor and Frank Barron (eds.), *Scientific Creativity: Its Recognition and Development* (New York: John Wiley & Sons, Inc., 1963).

verbal-abstract concepts exhibit superior ability in the solution of problems cast in a more concrete setting.[21]

SELECTED BIBLIOGRAPHY

Anastasi, Anne. *Differential Psychology: Individual Group Differences in Behavior.* New York: The Macmillan Company, 3rd ed., 1958.

Association for Supervision and Curriculum Development, National Education Association. *Perceiving, Behaving, Becoming.* 1962 Yearbook. Washington: The Association, 1962.

Baller, Warren R. *The Psychology of Human Growth and Development.* New York: Holt, Rinehart and Winston, Inc., 1961.

Broadbent, Donald E. *Perception and Communication.* New York: Pergamon Press, 1958.

Combs, Arthur W., and Donald Snygg. *Individual Behavior: A Perceptual Approach to Behavior.* New York: Harper & Brothers, rev. ed., 1959.

DeCecco, John P. *Human Learning in the School.* New York: Holt, Rinehart and Winston, Inc., 1963.

Frandsen, A. N. *Educational Psychology: The Principles of Learning and Teaching.* New York: McGraw-Hill Book Co., Inc., 1961.

Getzels, Jacob, and Philip W. Jackson. *Creativity and Intelligence: Explorations with Gifted Children.* New York: John Wiley & Sons, Inc., 1962.

Guilford, J. P. "The Structure of Intellect," *Psychological Bulletin,* No. 53, July, 1956, pp. 267-293.

———. "Three Faces of Intellect," *American Psychologist,* 14:469-479, August, 1959.

Hall, C. W., and G. Lindzey. *Theories of Personality.* New York: John Wiley & Sons, Inc., 1957.

Hilgard, Ernest R. *Theories of Learning.* New York: Appleton-Century-Crofts, Inc., rev. ed., 1956.

——— (ed). *Theories of Education and Instruction.* Sixty-Third Yearbook of the National Society for the Study of Education. Chicago: The Society (distributed by the University of Chicago Press), 1964.

Kingsley, H. L., and R. Garry. *The Nature and Conditions of Learning.* Englewood Cliffs, N.J.: Prentice-Hall, Inc., rev. ed., 1957.

Mowrer, O. H. *Learning Theory and Behavior.* New York: John Wiley & Sons, Inc., 1960.

[21] For further discussion see Hilgard, *Introduction to Psychology,* rev. ed., 1957, Chaps. 18, 19; J. M. Sawyer and C. W. Telford, *Educational Psychology* (Boston: Allyn and Bacon, Inc., 1958), Chap. 7; Warren R. Baller, *The Psychology of Human Growth and Development* (New York: Holt, Rinehart and Winston, Inc., 1961), Chap. 10; and Ernest R. Hilgard (ed.), *Theories of Education and Instruction,* The Sixty-Third Yearbook, The National Society for the Study of Education (Chicago: The Society [distributed by the University of Chicago Press], 1964).

Sawrey, J. M., and C. W. Telford. *Educational Psychology*. Boston: Allyn and Bacon, Inc., 1958.

Solly, C. M. *Development of the Perceptual World.* New York: Basic Books, 1960.

Taylor, Calvin W., and Frank Barron (eds.). *Scientific Creativity: Its Recognition and Development.* New York: John Wiley & Sons, Inc., 1963.

Torrance, E. P. *Guiding Creative Talent.* Englewood Cliffs, N.J.: Prentice-Hall, Inc., 1962.

———, *et al. Explorations in Creative Thinking in Early School Years; I.Q. Achievement and Creativity in School Achievement.* Minneapolis: Bureau of Educational Research, University of Minnesota, 1959.

Wylie, Ruth C. *The Self Concept.* Lincoln: University of Nebraska Press, 1961.

5

Development of the Curriculum

1. What problems are related to the origin of the curriculum?

It is a truism to say that the present is the product of its past. The past explains why we are what we are and gives validity to the old statement that the business of the school is "the transmission of the cultural heritage from one generation to another." In our contemporary world this is, of course, a half-truth, and it becomes less true as changes in the world accelerate. In many phases of life the present becomes increasingly related predominantly to the immediate past; antiquity has little to contribute to an understanding of our world in transition. Students of education, however, recognize that many of the problems of the junior high school, particularly curriculum problems, are intensified by the carry-over into the present of ideas and practices from the distant past.

Influence of the college preparatory function

There can be no doubt that in the chain reaction of historical events the recommendations of the Committee of Ten, reinforced by similar recommendations of other educational committees, profoundly influenced the development of junior high schools. Today, these recommendations are still evidenced in the practices of a large number of these schools.

Chapter 1 detailed the ideas of the Committee of Ten. It is sufficient here to recall briefly their impact on the junior high school curriculum. The Committee originated in the desire of college and university leaders to gain earlier admission for college students. It recognized the school curriculum as the major obstacle to earlier admission. Lengthening of elementary education generally to eight years, with the continuance of the curricular emphasis of the elementary school, left insufficient time in high school for college-oriented students to master the range of subjects required for college admission. Colleges and universities were thus under pressure to offer these subjects as subfreshman courses, necessarily delaying the students' admission to regular college courses.

The Committee of Ten made several recommendations of vital importance to the curriculum of the seventh and eighth grades, now accepted as part of the junior high school period. First, it recommended that many subjects offered in the high school be transferred to Grades 7 and 8 and that a few be shifted to as low as Grade 5. This change would make room for the subfreshman courses offered in college to be given in the regular high school. Second, it recommended that the subjects transferred to Grades 7 and 8 be taught by specialists, as was done in the high school, thus leading to the departmentalization of the curriculum of these grades. A third recommendation was that the methods of instruction used in the high school, which were patterned after those of the colleges and universities, be substituted for the methods then prevalent in the elementary school. To insure the effectiveness of these recommendations it was proposed that Grades 7 and 8 be separated from the elementary school and set up as a separate two-year school recognized as part of secondary education and closely following the high school in purpose, organization, curriculum, and methods.

In spite of the efforts of educators to introduce modern curriculum thinking and practices into the junior high school, these recommendations are still extensively followed.

Extended elementary school period

After the turn of the nineteenth century the elementary school began to develop rapidly. Some educators began to question whether its expansion to eight and even nine years did not allow more time than was necessary to acquire the so-called fundamentals. As pointed out in Chapter 1, President Eliot of Harvard University insisted that the basic arithmetic needed, as well as other elementary school subjects, could be mastered in six years. In this he was supported by many contemporary educators. Butler, Dewey, and Harper at the opening of the twentieth century vigorously maintained that the foundations of elementary education could be acquired readily in a six-year period. A number of national educational committees began to support a shorter elementary school. In 1903 Superintendent James M. Greenwood, on the basis of his experience with the Kansas City, Missouri, 7-4 plan, was convinced that at least seven years was ample time for elementary education.[1] Much later, in 1927, the evidence from a national survey of elementary education indicated that six years was sufficient time in which to master basic elementary education. The study revealed that in practice the seventh and eighth grades were largely devoted to a review of the materials taught in the first six grades.

2. *How does the age period affect the curriculum?*

The writings of educational leaders in the 1880's and 1890's reveal a growing awareness, although vaguely understood, that the seventh-grade age group needed a different educational emphasis from that provided in the elementary school. Some sensed that a major change was taking place in the nature and interest of boys and girls at this time. Some believed there was a direct relationship between the heavy dropout tendency of this age level and the school curriculum. Some associated this problem with the approach of adolescence. At the turn of the century adolescence became a major educational concern of such leaders as Butler, Dewey, and Hall. From that time to the present there has been a steadily accelerating interest in the nature of adolescence and its curriculum needs.

The nature of preadolescence and early adolescence

The accumulating evidence of the nature of preadolescence and early adolescence, as shown in the data presented in Chapter 3 of this book, indicates clearly the uniqueness of this period of development. It is now recognized that the biological changes in process at this time profoundly affect thinking and social behavior.

The fact that biological development, although apparently rapid, is nonetheless relatively gradual creates problems for educational programs. Schools must realize that even in the period immediately preceding the onset of puberty, the reactions of boys and girls are changing, and the educational program must be changed accordingly.

Uneven development of adolescence

The problem of providing a differentiated educational program tailor-made to meet the needs of preadolescence and early adolescence is further complicated by the extreme unevenness of the approach to puberty. Studies of the

[1] James M. Greenwood, "Seven-Year Course for Ward School Pupils," National Education Association, *Journal of Proceedings and Addresses,* 1903, p. 258. It is well to note that at this time the seven-year elementary school was common throughout the South.

development of puberty show that prepubescent, pubescent, and postpubescent pupils are included in all three of Grades 7 to 9. Although most youth have reached adolescent development, a few stragglers still enter the senior high school sexually immature. Boys are generally one to two years behind girls in sex maturation. Thus the school has a most difficult curriculum problem in trying to meet the widely divergent intellectual and social interests and needs of these unevenly maturing groups as well as in coping with the uneven growth within each sex.

Another serious problem grows out of the fact that for many pupils, particularly girls, pubescence begins in elementary school. Recent studies indicate that adolescent development is gradually appearing at an earlier age in the United States, so that in the future larger numbers of pupils may be expected to begin puberty in the sixth and even the fifth grade. The junior high school will then include a larger number who have entered the early stages of adolescence. If this tendency should continue, it will emphasize a problem already confronting the junior high school in its functional relationship to the elementary school. It must raise such questions as: Should the junior high school assume that an educational program for early adolescence is to be the complete responsibility of Grades 7, 8, and 9 as a school unit? Or should the junior high school and the elementary school develop a flexible relationship so that pupils who have reached adolescence will transfer to the junior high school, and preadolescents, regardless of age, will remain in the elementary school until the beginning of pubescence? Or should the junior high school be reorganized so as to include from one-half year to a full year of the present sixth grade of the elementary school?

Closely associated with biologically uneven maturation is the natural concomitant of uneven physical growth, most noticeable to the observer in wide differences in height and weight at a given age level. These differences are of great significance to the pupil and must vitally affect the curriculum, particularly in its social and physical phases. Some recent research seems to suggest definite intelligence growth plateaus during the period of most rapid adolescent development. Here again is a serious curriculum concern of the junior high school years. In fact, all of these aspects of marked individual and group differences in adolescent development taken together present a formidable task for the junior high school as it tries to work out a completely functional curriculum program for all early adolescents.

Educators recognize that a highly academic curriculum is not suited to the needs of this transition period. The curriculum must become more personalized and concerned with the myriad personal and social problems that confront boys and girls at this time, as they try to discover themselves, their relationships with others, especially their heterosexual relationships in the scheme of life, and their emerging sense of independence with reference to their families and to the adult world. A heavy emphasis on problem situations in the school program designed to enable these youth to discover themselves and to develop a rationale that can guide them in their relations with others should be the essential characteristic of the junior high school curriculum.

3. *What are the implications of cultural change for the curriculum?*

Cultural change always profoundly affects the school curriculum. In a democracy, where each citizen is equally responsible with his neighbor for major decisions determining the policies that will govern his community and nation, it is of the utmost importance that he be fully aware of changes that do and are likely to take place. The school that would make intelligent citizens of its pupils, sensitive to the meaning of change, must mirror the awareness of change in its curriculum.

Drucker has emphasized the fact of change and its possible significance, as follows:

> The past is going fast. If there is one thing we can predict, it is change. The coming years will be years of rapid change in our vision, the direction of our efforts, the tasks we tackle and their priorities, and the yardsticks by which we measure success or failure. . . . We thus live in an age of transition, an age of overlap, in which the old "modern" of yesterday no longer acts effectively . . . while the new, the "post-modern" still lacks definition, expression and tools.[2]

A noted writer has observed that we now live in the first period of human history in which it is not possible for one generation to assume that the conditions governing its living can be transmitted unchanged to the next generation.[3]

Nature of change

Within the limitations of one chapter it is possible to indicate only a few areas of change, briefly touching upon their relation to the curriculum problems with which the school, and particularly the junior high school, is confronted.

Change in the status of knowledge. At least two aspects of this problem are of major concern to the school curriculum. The first has to do with the unprecedented increase of knowledge. Only a few centuries ago knowledge had slowly expanded to the point where it was deemed desirable to clas-

[2] Peter F. Drucker, *Landmarks of Tomorrow* (New York: Harper & Brothers, 1959), pp. x, 269.

[3] Alfred North Whitehead, *Adventures of Ideas* (New York: The Macmillan Company, 1933), p. 117.

sify it into broad subject areas. By now each such division has become so minutely subdivided (and further subdivision continues with accelerated tempo) that specialists in subdivisions can hardly understand one another — as former Chancellor Hutchins is reported to have said, "Even the anatomists at the University of Chicago could not speak intelligently to each other unless they were working on the same parts of the body." In the early decades of this century we had word lists such as "The One Thousand Most Commonly Used Words," the Thorndike and Horn lists of "Five . . ." and "Ten Thousand Most Commonly Used Words," and spellers that were regarded as sufficiently exhaustive which included under five thousand words for use in the elementary school. Seashore's studies made in the early 1940's of the vocabularies of college students revealed that the average student used 60,000 common words, 95,000 derived words, and 1500 technical or rare words. At the time, Van Wagenen, studying high school students, found their vocabulary usage only slightly smaller than that of Seashore's college students.

A half-century ago a major university offered such a range of courses that a student carrying a normal academic load would need 110 years to complete it. In 1941 the offerings of another major university were found to be so extensive that it would require 504 years for a hypothetical student carrying a normal load to cover them all. A speaker before an educational group in 1960 made the statement that in the previous year 3,500,000 items of knowledge had been added to the Library of Congress, estimated to be equivalent to the addition of 225 books and pamphlets. If even approximately correct, these facts add up to an almost insoluble problem for those committed to the concept of learning as the acquisition of factual knowledge. "What Knowledge Is of Most Worth?" asked by Herbert Spencer over a hundred years ago, has increasing pertinence for today.

A second consideration of an even more serious nature concerns the rapid obsolescence of so-called knowledge. What we accept today as reliable facts may be proved wrong tomorrow. As the late Charles F. Kettering is reported to have said shortly before his death when discussing certain engineering developments, "Forty years ago everything about fuel engines was in a row of books 18 inches long. Today not one word of that is true, because it was not true then."

Change in transportation and communication. Within the century we have seen the passing of the oxcart and the emergence of the train, the automobile, and now the astrojet plane, which can cruise at well over six hundred miles per hour, in contrast to the three miles per hour of the oxcart. A recent advertisement by Douglas Aircraft suggests, "Trisonic jets that would land you in Los Angeles 1½ hours earlier than your take-off in New York . . . could be operational by the early 1970's." As this is written the X-15 experimental plane is being flown in test flights considerably in excess of four thousand miles per hour. To cross the continent a century ago required week of tiresome travel; now, by plane in luxurious comfort, the same trip can be made between breakfast and lunch. This is to say nothing of the ease and speed of travel by the slower streamliner, or by the more than eighty-five million high-powered automobiles which move along the ribbons of concrete crisscrossing the country.

No less significant are the advances in communication. So standard has the use of the telegraph, telephone, radio, and television become that it is difficult for anyone under forty to appreciate the recency of these media of communication. The telegraph is a little over a century old, the telephone less than a century old. Radio has been transformed from the feeble crystal set into the modern electronic type with world-wide reception within a generation, while color television is still in its infancy. And Telstar has made its appearance with a promise of a revolution in visual communication for tomorrow.

A shrinking world. The advances in transportation and communication have revolutionized the thinking and activities of the people. The provincialism that characterized large sections of our country a generation ago has largely disappeared. The convenience of transportation has encouraged the intermingling of peoples from every walk of life and from every section of the country. The press, radio, and television chronicle events of importance as well as the ideas of individuals and groups from all parts of the nation. This closer interrelation among the people brings about a sense of common understanding, interests, and mutual interdependence.

Further, it is now possible to reach any part of the globe within a few hours, and seconds only separate us from contact with others in faroff places, or from a knowledge of events vast distances away. We are rapidly moving toward the realization of the vision of the late Wendell Willkie expressed in his book *One World.*

These changing conditions — local, national, and international — create many problems for the school curriculum as well as definite responsibilities. We no longer live in isolation, nor is isolation possible even if desired. It is the school's tremendous task to provide opportunities through its curriculum for boys and girls to become fully aware of what is happening in our country and the world as a result of the advances in transportation and communication. They must understand the implications of all this for present and future living within our country and future relations with other nations.

Change from rural to urban life. The difference between an urban population of 5 per cent in 1790 and one of approximately 75 per cent in 1960 indicates a sweeping change in the living status of the American people. But this is not the complete picture. In 1790 the rural population was indeed rural in both its living and its thinking. Isolation through absence of means of communication and primitive modes of travel separated the rural group from the urban in a sense almost incomprehensible to the rural or urban dweller of 1960. Now it is customary for large numbers of people to live in incorporated villages or on small tracts of land as much as fifty miles from their place of work, commuting daily to and from their place of business in the city. For these people the center of interest is likely to be urban, and often much, if not all, of their social life is urban oriented. The tendency of rural farm people to identify themselves more and more with urban centers for business, entertainment, and church activities is rapidly changing America into a city-conscious people. For some rural dwellers concern for farm production is the principal and sometimes only rural interest.

Change from agricultural to complex industrial life. A part of the shift from rural to urban living has been due to the inexorable shift from an agricultural to an industrial economy. In 1820, 71.8 per cent of America's labor force was engaged in agricultural pursuits; in 1960 the proportion had been reduced to 4.6 per cent. This too is the age of the financial colossus in American business. In 1956 there were twenty-two billion-dollar corporations in the United States, and in 1963 there were seventy-eight corporations, each with assets in excess of a billion dollars. In addition there are many near-billion-dollar corporations. The financial size of these firms does not tell the full story. Most of them have numerous subsidiary organizations which in turn are major corporations and in many instances control vast resources not indicated in the assets of the parent firm. The political and social power of these huge aggregations for good or ill almost staggers the imagination.

From the lone producer so characteristic of the farm of yesterday we have moved to mass production in large factories where the individual worker's identity is largely lost in a number or a station. The former face-to-face relationship between employer and worker, typical of the small business, is now impossible. To negotiate his wage and employment rights it has become necessary for the worker to meet power with power through the organization of labor unions whose officers represent him in such negotiation.

Since the large industries, particularly, tend to bring hundreds and even thousands of workers together in one plant, many employees live long distances from their work. This situation militates against the solidarity of family life, and parental contact with the children becomes more tenuous as larger numbers of married women follow their husbands into gainful employment.

Automation and specialization. Further problems associated with industrialization arise from the extreme forms of automation and specialization now developing. Automation has progressively committed to the machine more and more tasks previously performed by human labor. The mechanical ditchdigger has largely replaced the human ditchdigger, the white-gloved push-button operator has superseded the grimy coal stokers in factory and on ship, and the thousands of laborious, time-consuming calculations yesterday made by man are today performed by Univac in minutes. Increasingly human labor has been taken over by robots.

Labor replacement by machines has created serious unemployment, and efforts to equate the economic advantages accruing through the use of mechanical developments have led to featherbedding and similar practices in lieu of more socially intelligent solutions to the complex problems thus created. A higher level of technical skill, and in some instances greater intelligence, will be required for the operation of complex semiautomatic machines.

Further, to offset the extremes of specialization demanded in modern production practices, the curriculum of the school must be designed to acquaint the learner early with the need for and the means of developing a diversity of leisure-time interests.

Implications for change in the curriculum

Curriculum continuously changing. In a world of constant and accelerating change it is illogical to expect the curriculum to remain static. Yet in many schools today the curriculum remains essentially unchanged on the naïve assumption that life will be lived tomorrow as it was lived yesterday. But as we have seen, the knowledge that seemed adequate to meet the conditions of past generations is no longer sufficient for our present and future needs. What is worse, man is continually discovering that many of the so-called facts of yesterday upon which he based his structure of living are not true, or are irrelevant in his strange new world. To the sensitive observer it is crystal clear that in the world of tomorrow there must be a constant restructuring of contemporary knowledge and behavioral patterns to meet new situations.

Reconstruction of curriculum organization. In the past it was thought sufficient to organize the curriculum into broad divisions — mathematics, history, science, language, and literature — the mastery of which would enable the learner to meet the problems of living. This was the essence of the mind storage theory of learning.

This curriculum pattern, which seemed suitable for a relatively static form of society, and the concept of learning appropriate to it, now seems inadequate to meet the conditions of living created by a rapidly changing world. Instead of attempting to amass large quantities of factual data likely to be found incorrect or obsolete for use tomorrow, it would seem more fitting to develop problem-solving skills. If there is one competency youth needs in a world of change it is how to face the unknown, how to attack the new situations that confront him daily, and that will become even more complex and demanding in the future.

A curriculum organized to develop problem-solving skills cannot well be fitted into the traditional subject-matter patterns. Vital life problems have a way of overflowing neatly devised subject-matter divisions and formal classrooms. Normally their solution draws upon many areas and requires data found beyond the classroom, often in the community environment. Furthermore, the traditional fifty-minute classroom period is not well adapted to the demands of problem-solving learning. Large blocks of time of two to four hours have been found to provide the flexibility essential to good problem-solving conditions and use of library and community facilities.

Change in methods. A curriculum reorganized around the development of problem-solving skills requires a radical change in methods of teaching. The older lecture and recitation methods must be largely replaced by unit teaching. Since the unit is organized around a problem situation, it focuses attention upon recognized methods used in problem solving.

4. *What curriculum patterns are now used?*

Many variations in curriculum patterns have evolved in recent years. All of them have found some degree of acceptance in the junior high school. However, these patterns may be classified under two broad types, depending upon the basic orientation of the curriculum concept.

Subject-matter type

Complete isolation of subjects. The curriculum organizational pattern hoary with age and still widely used is the completely separated or departmentalized subject plan. Each subject is taught in isolation from others, and ideally by teachers highly specialized in one subject.

Correlation. In this pattern of curriculum organization each subject maintains its separate identity, but an effort is made to give it internal articulation with one or more other subjects. Within recent decades educators began to realize that subjects did not necessarily stand in isolation, that classification according to subjects was principally for their own convenience. Attempts were made to interrelate the content of one or more subjects where such correlation would lead to enriched understanding by the learner. For example, when a history teacher was considering the early colonial period, the life of the people and historical events were made more vivid by the English teacher, who might have the same students study in her class stories of the rugged life of the frontier families portrayed in such novels as *Leatherstocking Tales,* or by the geography teacher, who might take up the geography of the Atlantic seaboard to deepen understanding of this early period.

A more ambitious effort at correlation might involve the focus of the various subjects upon the colonial period at the same time at a given grade level. The literature classes would study the poetry and novels of that period.

In composition, the themes would be on colonial topics, or reports written in the history class could form the basis for compositional training. The art classes would study colonial art and architecture, the home economics classes the food and clothing of the period, and the music classes the music of the day. Correlation takes many forms but does maintain the separation of the subjects.

Fusion. Fusion is a more radical attempt to secure correlation between two or three subjects by breaking down the divisions that separate them. There are two broad approaches to fusion. The less radical takes large blocks of subject matter from two or three subjects and places them in juxtaposition. Along with teaching the history of the colonial period in New England it would be natural to teach also the geography of that section. A second form of fusion organizes two or more subjects around themes or problems that bring out the essential relationships of these subjects. For example, a teacher of physics and chemistry, deciding to fuse his subjects, would analyze beginning high school courses in each to discover their common principles. Then he would set up problems to illustrate the contribution of principles from each subject to their solution: "How can comfort be increased by air conditioning?" "What's wrong with this photograph?" "What should one look for in buying an automobile?"

A form of curriculum organization which may be classified under fusion is popularly called "unified studies." Often it is but an advanced form of correlation with some slight breaking down of subject-matter lines. Much of the time "unified studies" represent a form of fusion wherein problem units become the center of orientation. At the opposite extreme "unified studies" may best be included with the second, more advanced form of fusion described above.

Broad fields. The broad-fields approach is simply a more inclusive integration of many subjects, as contrasted with fusion, which usually attempts to break down departmental lines between two subjects or three at the most. An early broad-fields organization brought together all high school science offerings in two major science courses. Zoology, botany, biology, and physiology became one survey course labeled life sciences. Chemistry, physics, astronomy, geology, and physical geography were combined into a course called natural sciences. A more typical organization follows this pattern:

(1) Language arts
(2) Social studies
(3) Science and mathematics
(4) Health and physical education
(5) Fine arts and music

Another type of broad-fields curriculum groups the subject areas under more functional headings as follows:[4]

(1) Health and physical fitness
(2) Leisure time
(3) Vocational activities
(4) Social relationships

Still another broad-fields approach is often known as general education. In practice it may represent a more extreme form of the second classification above, wherein the emphasis moves farther from a subject-matter basis of organization toward a completely functional curriculum built around broad problems or needs.

At this point it may be difficult to ascertain when broad-fields or general education deserts the subject-matter orientation and is more accurately identified as a form of the experience type of curriculum.

Experience type

In recent years there have been attempts to organize a curriculum pattern based upon the experience concept of learning. Thus far only the *core curriculum* pattern has evolved.

The core curriculum completely departs from any subject-matter form of organization. It is based upon the psychological theory that learning is change in behavior resulting from experience. The development of behavioral competencies thus becomes the prime curriculum concern. Personal, social, and societal problems are the focal point of orientation, and the interaction between the learner and the environmental matrix in which he has his experiences as he copes with these problems becomes the curriculum. The core curriculum distinguishes between two types of competencies in the organization of the curriculum framework, namely, those which all must achieve to be successful and happy participants in a democratic society, and those peculiar to each learner's needs growing out of his special interests and capacities, which the school is obligated to develop to the greatest extent possible. The concept of the core curriculum will be amplified in considerable detail in a later chapter. This form of the curriculum has been most popular at the junior high school level.

5. What are the characteristics of a good junior high school curriculum?

Basis in the experience learning concept

It has become quite clear that the time-honored subject type of curriculum

[4] Lewis W. Webb, "Ten Years of Curriculum Planning by the North Central Association," *Curriculum Journal,* 8:230-238, October, 1937.

based upon the discredited mind storage theory of learning is now out of harmony with accepted theories of learning. Nonetheless it is still widely used. In education as in other human institutions there is a marked tendency to resist change in favor of the more comfortable status quo. Possibly the persistence of the subject curriculum is accounted for by a recent writer:

> Precious few of the facts of education are retained very long, especially if unused, and fortunate this is. Much of what is regarded as well-established at one time turns out later not to be so firm or turns out to be as true as ever but irrelevant. This is a pity — this reminder that the mastery of facts, of content, is relatively unimportant in true education (and important primarily in quiz shows). It is a pity because teaching facts is so easy. It can be done cheaply and by rather unimaginative people.[5]

Recognition of the nature of preadolescence and early adolescence

Since the junior high school must serve the preadolescent and early adolescent youth, with their unique needs, its curriculum should definitely be oriented around this age group. Unfortunately, the junior high school curriculum has largely ignored the peculiar needs of its students, imitating instead that of the college-oriented senior high school. Reorientation, with the special needs of this transitional period of uneven change from childhood to early adolescence in view, is highly important.

Emphasis upon personal, social, and societal problems

Experience learning is based upon a recognition that learning can be effective only when the pupil has a purpose in learning. He can have such purpose, or motivation, only when he understands why, in a given situation, he should learn. It is generally accepted that genuine motivation for learning must be related to situations in which the learner has an immediate interest, finds a personal significance. The curriculum that considers vital personal and social and related societal concerns will be most likely to challenge the interest of the learner and provide effective learning situations.

Organization around problem situations

Since most vital learning in life has to do with the personal and social problems faced by individuals, it is now commonly agreed that the curriculum should be problem oriented. Not only will such a curriculum naturally spark a dynamic purposing on the part of the learner but it will provide the kind of educational equipment needed by an adult society to cope with a world of accelerating change. The popularization of the organization of units of instruction around problems has been a first step in the development of this kind of curriculum.

[5] Roger W. Heyns, "The Educated Man in Our Times," *The Review,* Indiana University Bulletin, 4:3, November, 1961.

Adjustment to individual differences

It may seem trite to specifically emphasize this curriculum characteristic. For years the literature of education has stressed the nature of individual differences and urged curriculum and school organization to be guided by these differences. Yet large numbers of our schools maintain uniform curriculums, adopting a single textbook for a whole class and using classroom methods adapted to lockstep progress. Using several textbooks for different levels of ability, using the library extensively, teaching by units of instruction, encouraging committee activity in the classroom, and eliminating class grades can do much to offset uniform curriculum practices.

Sensitivity to local environmental learning situations

The average community provides a wealth of resources for vital learning experiences of youth. The utilization of these resources may be of much value in helping to solve the personal and social problems of the learner. The community also represents a microcosm for the study of societal problems. It offers a splendid opportunity to bring what so often are abstract, somewhat meaningless, and therefore dull classroom topics into a natural and meaningful community context.

Recognition of the dynamics of change

The formulation of better curriculum guides is a necessary step toward increasing ease of modification. Loose-leaf guide forms have become the accepted device for those schools that acknowledge the constant need of curriculum change and wish to make necessary changes easily practicable. The school administration that maintains curriculum teacher committees constantly alert to possible modification of curriculum guides and resource materials definitely sets the school curriculum in an atmosphere of expected change.

Recognition of the varying needs for coeducational experiences

The junior high school program is especially complicated by the uneven sex maturation characteristic of junior high pupils. Each sex group shows a wide range in the appearance of pubescence. Some children may reach the early stages of puberty before completion of the elementary school while others are almost at the end of their junior high school years before the approach of puberty. This problem is made more difficult by the fact that boys are usually at least one year behind girls in reaching pubescence.

Thus it is a major problem to set up a realistic school program for early adolescence. When most girls are in the pubertal stage of development, and begin to evince a natural heterosexual interest in association with boys in social activities, the boys are still uninterested in social contacts and may even be hostile to such activities and to the girls. An adequate curriculum should reflect a full awareness of this situation and plan social activities on a progressively coeducational basis as pupils pass through the junior high school years.

Ideal of a unified curriculum for all

Many thoughtful educators today are advocating a unified type of curriculum for the junior high school. The most advanced statement in support of such a curriculum from a major educational organization has come from the Educational Policies Commission, which in *Education for All American Youth: A Further Look* advocated a common curriculum for all in the seventh, eighth, and ninth grades:

> Throughout the junior high-school period, it was agreed, the educational needs of pupils are sufficiently alike to justify a common curriculum for all pupils with ample provision for differentiated treatment of pupils within classes to take account of diversities of interests, aptitudes, and abilities.
>
> . . . .
>
> Beginning in the tenth grade, or thereabouts, young people exhibit differences in certain of these interests and plans which call for a variety of offerings in the curriculum, among which the students, under guidance, may choose.[6]

There are varying degrees of agreement with this statement. Numerous voices have been raised in support of a completely unified school program for the seventh grade, partly because they believe that at this age it is too early for rigorous differentiation in the curriculum, and also because they feel that in the transition from elementary to junior high school the self-contained classroom should be continued. Some maintain that pupils in the eighth grade are still too immature to begin differentiation through departmentalization. Still others would begin cautiously with some curriculum departmentalization in the ninth grade.

There appears to be little justification for a departmentalized junior high school. Many have allowed themselves to be caught up in the college preparatory hysteria of the times, and the accompanying often unspoken but assumed continuance of antiquated curriculum lockstep organization and methods of instruction provides them a spurious justification for a departmentalized curricular program at this age level. The personal and social needs of junior high school youth are, as the Educational Policies Commission has pointed out, sufficiently alike so that some curriculum differentiation within a class situation can satisfy the demands of individual differences.

[6] Educational Policies Commission, National Education Association, *Education for All American Youth: A Further Look* (Washington: The Association, rev. ed., 1952), p. 220. Also the 1944 edition, p. 230.

SELECTED BIBLIOGRAPHY

Alberty, Harold B., and Elsie J. Alberty. *Reorganizing the High School Curriculum.* New York: The Macmillan Company, 3rd ed., 1962.

Allen, Frederick L. *The Big Change.* New York: Harper & Brothers, 1952.

Anderson, Vernon E. *Principles and Procedures of Curriculum Improvement.* New York: The Ronald Press Company, 1956.

Association for Supervision and Curriculum Development, National Education Association. *New Insights and the Curriculum.* 1963 Yearbook. Washington: The Association, 1963.

———. *Perceiving, Behaving, Becoming.* 1962 Yearbook. Washington: The Association, 1962.

Bark, W. C., *et al. Report of the San Francisco Curriculum Survey Committee.* San Francisco: San Francisco Unified School District, 1960.

Bossing, Nelson L. *Principles of Secondary Education.* Englewood Cliffs, N.J.: Prentice-Hall, Inc., rev. ed., 1955.

Broadbent, Donald E. *Perception and Communication.* New York: Pergamon Press, 1958.

Drucker, Peter F. *Landmarks of Tomorrow.* New York: Harper & Brothers, 1959.

Educational Policies Commission, National Education Association. *Education for All American Youth: A Further Look.* Washington: The Association, rev. ed., 1952.

Evans, Luther H., and George E. Arnstein. *Automation and the Challenge to Education.* National Education Association Project on the Educational Implications of Automation. Washington: The Association, 1962.

Getzels, Jacob, and Philip W. Jackson. *Creativity and Intelligence: Explorations with Gifted Children.* New York: John Wiley & Sons, Inc., 1962.

Gwynn, J. Minor. *Curriculum, Principles and Social Trends.* New York: The Macmillan Company, rev. ed., 1960.

Junior High School Program, The. Atlanta, Ga.: Southern Association of Colleges and Secondary Schools, 1958.

Leese, Joseph, Kenneth Frasure, and Mauritz Johnson, Jr. *The Teacher in Curriculum Making.* New York: Harper & Brothers, 1961.

Parker, J. Cecil, T. B. Edwards, and W. H. Stegeman. *Curriculum in America.* New York: Thomas Y. Crowell Company, 1962.

Taba, Hilda. *Curriculum Development: Theory and Practice.* New York: Harcourt, Brace & World, Inc., 1962.

Taylor, Calvin W., and Frank Barron (eds.), *Scientific Creativity: Its Recognition and Development.* New York: John Wiley & Sons, Inc., 1963.

Torrance, E. P. *Guiding Creative Talent.* Englewood Cliffs, N.J.: Prentice-Hall, Inc., 1962.

Wiles, Kimball. *The Changing Curriculum of the American High School.* Englewood Cliffs, N.J.: Prentice-Hall, Inc., 1963.

Wright, Grace S. *The Core Program: Unpublished Research,* 1956-1962. U.S. Office of Education Circular 713. Washington: Government Printing Office, 1963.

Wylie, Ruth C. *The Self Concept.* Lincoln: University of Nebraska Press, 1961.

Zapf, Rosalind M. *Democratic Processes in the Secondary Classroom.* Englewood Cliffs, N.J.: Prentice-Hall, Inc., 1959.

6

Block-Time Class Organization

This chapter will present some of the specific and general components of block-time class organization in the junior high school. Since knowledge of the theoretical concepts is essential to the comprehension and application of the plan, we shall lead off with our definition of block-time organization.

Block-time class organization is deemed to exist (1) when one teacher is scheduled to meet regularly with a class of seventh-, eighth-, or ninth-grade students for two or more consecutive class periods; (2) when the instruction covers material from two or more subject-content areas, required of all students, which would otherwise be presented in single class periods; (3) when the instructional approach is such as to develop and encourage the application of the fundamental learning skills; and (4) when flexibility in presentation is the rule and the curriculum is guided primarily by the learner's needs and responses rather than rigid adherence to separate subjects.

1. How have block-time classes grown and developed?

The significance and value of block-time classes may best be understood by an examination of the factors involved in their development.

The major impetus for such a class structure, as applied in contemporary junior high school instruction, was the educators' increased awareness of the early adolescent's responses to sudden changes in his learning environment. There appeared a renewed recognition of individualization as a significant concept in the evolvement of *learner-centered,* as distinguished from *subject-*

centered, instruction. This and associated insights served to arouse interest in achieving a clearer understanding of learners' individual differences and their implications for effective junior high school instructional practices:

> Departmentalization . . . is out of harmony with what we know about development [of early adolescent youth]. Junior youth do not possess the adjustment possibilities for quickly changing from guidance of one person to the assignments of five or more shifting from a unified emphasis to a specialized interest.[1]

Doubts arose about the soundness of scheduling a separate subject for each class period. The value of departmentalization was questioned by prominent educators in secondary education as early as 1920. Briggs, in discussing articulation between elementary and junior high schools, stated:

> Certainly any bad effects of sudden departmentalization at the beginning of the ninth grade are likely to be worse if introduced two years earlier. The conclusion is upon us that departmentalization in junior high school like other changes in teaching should be gradual.[2]

By 1940 the literature was replete with questions regarding the use of complete departmental instructional programs and with pleas for a gradual transition from the one-teacher plan to the departmental plan in secondary education. In 1955 Koos urged "the better wisdom of moving gradually from the one-teacher regimen of preceding grades, inuring the pupil by degrees to the responsibilities and exigencies involved."[3]

Partial retreat from departmental instruction has been recommended by leaders in early secondary education. It is felt that the sudden change from unified instruction, with one teacher in one classroom in the elementary school, to a specialized, fragmented instructional system, with a different teacher and classroom for each of six or more subjects, must markedly limit the learner's opportunities to experience stability in his learning situation.

Extent of use

Many studies have tried to measure the prevalence of block-time classes in junior high schools. One of the initial studies, reported in 1949, found that "9.7 percent of all junior and junior-senior high schools had block-time classes."[4] A more comprehensive investigation was reported in 1956 by the

[1] J. Paul Leonard, "Frontiers in Junior High School Education," *The Bulletin of the National Association of Secondary-School Principals,* 24:112-119, February, 1940.

[2] Thomas H. Briggs, *The Junior High School* (Boston: Houghton Mifflin Company, 1920), p. 110.

[3] Leonard V. Koos, *Junior High School Trends* (New York: Harper & Brothers, 1955), p. 77.

[4] Grace S. Wright, *Block-Time Classes and the Core Program in the Junior High School,* U.S. Office of Education Bulletin No. 6 (Washington: Government Printing Office, 1958), p. 1.

Committee on Junior High School Education of the National Association of Secondary-School Principals. A questionnaire was mailed to each junior high school principal who was a member of the National Association of Secondary-School Principals. There were two thousand inquiries mailed, and 1170 principals responded to the question "Are there any classes on block-time?" The study group included principals from the District of Columbia and every state except Nevada and Montana. The findings were (1) that 57.3 per cent of the 1170 junior high school principals had block-time classes, and (2) that 72.5 per cent of 358 principals reporting who had over one thousand enrolled in their schools had block-time classes.[5]

State surveys indicate considerable variation in the use of block-time classes by junior high schools throughout the country. A 1955 study by Normington in California reported that 90 per cent of the junior high schools in the study sample used block-time scheduling,[6] and between 1957 and 1961 state-wide surveys were reported by the following six states:[7]

State	*Year*	*Per cent*
Alabama	1957	21.9
Minnesota	1958	32.9
Michigan	1960	("A majority")
New Jersey	1960	56.0
Illinois	1960	61.0
Ohio	1961	53.8

According to both national and state studies, block-time scheduling is most prevalent in the divided junior high schools. However, a survey in New Jersey found 56 per cent of the divided schools and 42 per cent of the undivided schools using block-time periods. Thus, the longer class period was em-

[5] Ellsworth Tompkins: "The Daily Schedule in Junior High Schools," A Study of the Committee on Junior High School Education, *The Bulletin of the National Association of Secondary-School Principals,* 40:177, May, 1956.

[6] Louis W. Normington, "Block of Time Classes in Junior High Schools in California," Ph.D. dissertation, University of California, 1955.

[7] Otto Holloway, "Scope, Trends, and Problems in Core Curriculum in Alabama, 1957" (unpublished), quoted by Nelson L. Bossing in "Trends in Block-Time Classes in Junior High School," *The Bulletin of the National Association of Secondary-School Principals,* 43:34, April, 1959; Nelson L. Bossing and John F. Kaufman, "Block-Time or Core Practices in Minnesota Secondary Schools," *The Clearing House,* 32:532-539, May, 1958; "The Status of Block-Time Programs in Michigan Secondary Schools," *Report of State Committee on Core and General Education,* Bulletin 426 (Lansing: State Superintendent of Public Instruction, 1960) (this study revealed that "a majority of organized junior high schools now have general education within blocks of two or more periods"); New Jersey State Department of Education, "Block-of-Time Programs in Junior High Schools and Six-Year High Schools in New Jersey," *Secondary School Bulletin,* No. 2, March, 1960; *Block-of-Time Scheduling Practices in Illinois Junior High Schools* (Springfield: Office of Public Instruction, 1960), p. 3; Glenn W. Schaller, "A Study of Opinions Concerning the Effectiveness of Block-Time Classes in the Junior High Schools in Ohio," A Research Report for the Degree of Specialist in Education, The University of Michigan, February, 1962, p. 25.

ployed in the six-year undivided high schools in this state almost as frequently as in the divided two- and three-year junior high schools.

Table 15 shows that 7 per cent of the junior high schools with less than two hundred enrolled had adopted block-time scheduling, while 50.3 per cent of those with an enrollment of one thousand or over used block-time classes.[8]

In Illinois, "block-time arrangement is seldom found in schools with an enrollment less than 400," but only thirty-two of the ninety-seven junior high schools reporting block-time classes included Grade 9 in their school organization.[9] Reorganization and expansion of school districts within the various state school systems should markedly reduce the number of junior high schools with enrollments of less than two to three hundred. These modifications may, according to the patterns of use noted above, increase block-time scheduling in junior high school instruction.

Form of introduction

The effectiveness of the block-time organization is usually dependent upon the way in which it is initiated, understood, and supported. Different ad-

TABLE 15

Number and Per Cent of Schools Having Block-Time Classes, by Size of Enrollment in Grades 7-9

Enrollment	Number of Schools Returning Questionnaire	Schools Reporting Block-Time Classes	
		Number	Per Cent
All schools	2517	487	19.3
Less than 200	1185	83	7.0
200 to 400	704	131	18.5
500 to 999	425	165	40.0
1,000 and over	203	108	50.3

[a] For schools failing to report actual enrollments, enrolllments were estimated from data available in the Office of Education.

Adapted from Grace S. Wright, *Block-Time Classes and the Core Program in the Junior High School,* U.S. Office of Education Bulletin No. 6 (Washington: Government Printing Office, 1958), Table 3, p. 6.

[8] See also the comparison of studies made by the U.S. Office of Education showing growth of block-time usage in junior high schools of 15.8 per cent in 1948-1949, 31.4 per cent in 1956-1957, and 40.0 per cent in 1959-1960. Grace S. Wright and Edith S. Greer, *The Junior High School, A Survey of Grades 7-8-9 in Junior and Junior-Senior High Schools, 1959-1960,* U.S. Office of Education Bulletin No. 32 (Washington: Government Printing Office, 1963), p. 20.

[9] *Block-of-Time Scheduling Practices in Illinois Junior High Schools, op. cit.,* p. 33.

ministrative approaches may be taken to change from a completely departmental structure to one that includes block-time classes. The ones most often used are experimentation with block-time organization in one or a few classes; gradual introduction of block-time periods in different junior high schools within a school system; and block-time scheduling in junior high schools when recommended and introduced by state departments of education.

If the block-time structure is adopted by junior high schools, for use in some or all grades for one-third to one-half of the school day, at the rate it has been adopted in the past ten years, within the next decade it will be in evidence in virtually all junior high schools.

Experimental introduction. The following is an illustration of how the block-time plan was introduced in one class on an experimental basis for one school year and three years later was accepted and used by teachers of language arts and social studies in Grades 7, 8, and 9. For the initial year one teacher in Grade 7 volunteered to teach the class. At the beginning of the next school year other teachers in Grade 7 began to request the new organizational pattern. The third year all teachers in Grades 7, 8, and 9 used a two-and-one-half-hour period to develop a common learnings unit integrating language arts, social studies, and homeroom. After the experimental years the common learnings program with the same block-time periods was accepted as part of the regular instructional organization in Grades 7 and 8 in all junior high schools in the city.

Those participating in the experiment attribute their success to the interested and professional attitude of all the school staff toward the common learnings program, the principals' availability to the block-time teachers for individual and group conferences that served to stimulate them in planning and problem solving, the counselors' active participation and contributions, and the consultative assistance given by the original teacher in the experiment. This teacher has since become the supervisor, or helping teacher, to common learnings teachers in all junior high schools in the Kansas City, Missouri, Public School System.

Gradual introduction on a system-wide basis. The introduction of block-time classes in all the junior high schools of the St. Paul, Minnesota, public school system required several years of preparation and planning. The assistant superintendent of schools in charge of secondary education, and a professor of secondary education at the College of Education, University of Minnesota, conducted a workshop with the principals, assistant principals, and counselors in the public secondary schools of St. Paul. The participants in the workshop received college credit in secondary education.

In this workshop of five weeks, a plan was formulated in which language arts and social studies were combined, in Grades 7, 8, and 9, into a block of two instructional periods. Unique in St. Paul's introduction plan was the fact that three new junior high school buildings were planned for completion within three years, one to be ready each year. These buildings were to accommodate a maximum enrollment of twelve hundred; the principals-to-be of the new buildings had one year, during the building construction, to interview teachers within the school system who were interested in teaching block-time classes prior to considering teachers outside the local system. After completion of staff selection by the principal in cooperation with the personnel department of the school system, the supervising principal and his staff planned the program of education within the framework of the general plan as formulated in the college workshop. Block-time classes and all the single-period classes met four, instead of five, days per week during a school term of ten months in order to provide more school time for creative and exploratory learning in the form of assemblies, personal interest activities, and clubs.

The principal, assistant principal, and block-time teachers were assigned *a full-time resource teacher,* two counselors, and a school librarian to aid in improving instruction in the longer class period and in developing a core program. After the three new junior high schools were built, staffed, and equipped, block-time classes for two periods were adopted in Grades 7, 8, and 9 in all junior high schools in the school system, and development of a city-wide core program has now been initiated.

State department of education recommendations. In the criteria designed for junior high schools in Oregon, provision is made whereby students in Grades 7 and 8 are assigned for a block of at least two consecutive periods to one teacher. Such scheduling is acknowledged for the ninth grade but application is more extensive in the seventh and eighth grades, where the two-period minimum is standard. It is believed that the wide divergence in interests and abilities of the students requires some specialized classes and a degree of departmentalization.[10]

The reasons for this rather advanced policy of partial retreat from complete departmentalization and the introduction of block-time classes for two to three consecutive periods have been designated by the Oregon State Department of Education as follows:

> Block-time scheduling can facilitate the implementation of most of the functions of the junior high school. In addition to encouraging integration, it particularly contributes toward guidance. By reducing the number of teachers a student must face and the total number of students a teacher must meet, a much closer student-teacher relationship can be achieved than is possible under a completely departmentalized program. Block-time classes further articulation. Many authorities feel that the child whose education has

[10] See Rex Putnam, *The Organization and Functions of Oregon Junior High Schools* (Salem: Superintendent of Public Instruction, State Department of Education, 1959), p. 15.

been carried on in the self-contained classroom situation of the typical elementary school is not prepared for an abrupt break to a completely departmentalized program. In many schools the block-time classes become the framework for a home room program for activities such as student participation in school management and social affairs, and thus lend themselves to the furtherance of socialization. If they do not specifically further exploration and differentiation, a program of unit teaching within the block may directly contribute to these two functions.[11]

The preceding three examples of administrative procedures employed to initiate block-time classes in the instructional program involved *a large number of staff members.* Wright reported in a study that before 150 junior high schools changed to block-time organization the following groups were oriented most frequently, in this order: "teachers who would be actively involved, such as core teachers, librarian, guidance counselor; entire faculty; faculty and public; and faculty, public and pupils."[12] Ninety-seven junior high schools in Illinois were surveyed in order to better understand their block-time practices, and the following descriptive statement was made: "It appears that usually the driving force for such change comes from the junior high school principal or members of the central administrative staff. However, teachers are ordinarily involved over a rather long period of time in studying and implementing any changeover."[13]

Rate of use at different grade levels

How rapidly has block-time scheduling been adopted in each of the three grades in the three-year junior high school, divided or undivided, since mid-century? In the 130 schools studied by Byers in 1953, 40 per cent of the students in Grade 7 remained with one teacher for more than one period, 35 per cent of those in Grade 8, and 18 per cent of those in Grade 9.[14]

In a selected group of 155 schools McEachen found in 1955 that approximately two-thirds of the schools used block-time organization in Grade 7, 41 per cent in Grade 8, and 22 per cent in Grade 9.[15]

Wright's 1958 survey of 487 junior high schools using block-time class

[11] *Ibid.* See also *The Junior High School in Nebraska* (Lincoln: State Department of Education, 1960), pp. 1-52, and *Junior High Schools for Iowa Youth* (Des Moines: Iowa State Department of Public Instruction, 1960), pp. 1-60.

[12] Wright, *op. cit.*, p. 28.

[13] *Block-of-Time Scheduling Practices in Illinois Junior High Schools, op. cit.*, p. 33.

[14] Richard S. Byers, "Articulation in Junior High School," Ph.D. dissertation, University of Connecticut, 1955.

[15] Howard D. McEachen, "Status and Trends in Organization and Curriculum in Selected Junior High Schools," Ed.D. dissertation, University of Kansas, 1955, reprinted in University of Kansas *Bulletin of Education,* May, 1956, p. 69.

periods found them most often in Grade 7 and least often in Grade 9, as illustrated below:[16]

Grade	*Number of Schools*	*Per Cent*
7	459	94
8	351	72
9	125	26

This consistent distinction in the utilization of block-time classes by grade levels presents an interesting but complex problem. Why has the block-time instructional system grown so rapidly in Grades 7 and 8 but been delayed in Grade 9?

The following benefits accrued from application of block-time classes in all grades, as experienced and formulated by the block-time teachers of West Junior High School, Kansas City, Missouri, are presented in an effort to clarify some facets of this problem.

1. The elimination of the general study hall was considered a learning benefit since study separated from class guidance and instruction is not very effective for the junior high school student. Throughout the school correlation and integration in curriculum instruction was advanced, thereby reducing fragmented learning and grade retardation.
2. Student conduct during class period changes and lunch periods was positively responsive to increased stability and continuity in the situational controls afforded by the block-time class schedules, which place more students and their teachers in the same place at the same time.
3. Guidance needs of ninth-grade students are more observable and effectively met by incorporating homeroom in block-time classes. This benefit seems of marked import since students at this grade level are frequently struggling with conflicting attitudes toward continued education in senior high school. The fact that some of them are not protected by a compulsory school attendance law adds to the significance of this guidance resource.
4. All block-time class teachers have the same regular class period *open in each grade* for cooperative curriculum planning, consultation, team teaching, and student-teacher conferences during the seven-hour school day. The opportunities for teachers to utilize a broader arena of group learning activities within both school and community which serve to stimulate and supplement subject content are definitely enhanced.
5. The application of block-time classes in all three grades is considered essential to prevent the multiple conflicts and disadvantages inherent when

[16] Wright, *op. cit.*, p. 6. (Schools among the 487 not reporting block-time classes in seventh grade (6 per cent) are usually schools not including seventh grade as part of the secondary school organization).

two different kinds of administration, guidance, and instruction are carried on within the framework of one junior high school.

The foregoing benefits have been validated in practice over a period of several years, illustrating the soundness and applicability of block-time class organization in the entire junior high school instructional system.

The low incidence of application of this instructional format at the ninth-grade level as compared to the high one evidenced at the seventh- and eighth-grade levels may be due in part to educators' awareness of the articulation needs of the seventh- and eighth-grade learners. However, the different but realistically more acute articulation problems of ninth-grade students also have to be accurately recognized, understood, and solved. Another discernible explanation for these differences lies in the apparent lag by teacher training institutions in providing preparation that includes effective orientation in the block-time system of instruction in junior high school education.

Improvement in guidance

When two or three regular class periods are combined, guidance becomes an integral part of the teacher's instructional responsibilities, for he is in a position to observe, know, and give meaningful guidance to the learner.

It is rather typical for the school counselor to anticipate a reduction in the demands for his specialized services with the advent of a block-time program. He may assume that the total counseling task will be taken over by the block-time teacher. Initially this is often viewed as a logical assumption, but in actual practice it proves to be invalid. In fact, the demand for the counselor's services significantly increases. As pointed out earlier in this discussion, block-time scheduling allows teachers to become better acquainted with the problems confronting students, and their wider understanding leads to greater utilization of the counselor's specialized help.

The departmental instructional plan tends to reduce the opportunities for teacher and learner to mutually or separately become aware of problems and find their solution through the appropriate guidance resources. When block-time programs are fully implemented the focal point of instruction shifts from an orientation to subject matter to the specific and general needs of the learners. The traditional homeroom, separate from dynamic learning, is becoming vital and useful again in many of the junior high schools as it is incorporated in the block-time class structure.

In a majority of the ninety-seven junior high schools reporting a block-time arrangement in Illinois, "block-of-time teachers and guidance personnel work closely, with the former performing many functions which might fall under the guidance umbrella."[17]

[17] *Block-of-Time Scheduling Practices in Illinois Junior High Schools, op. cit.*, p. 33.

Subjects combined

Junior high schools that adopt block-time scheduling most frequently combine language arts or English and social studies, and sometimes mathematics, science, or both are included. According to Table 16, approximately three-fourths of the block-time classes in 487 junior high schools in 1957 combined English and social studies.

Wright comments on the high incidence of English-social studies combinations:

> First of all, language arts can be taught functionally in developing a unit of work which lies largely in the social studies field. Every unit or problem in a unified studies or core program involves research, writing, discussing, reporting, and the study of needed English skills, as well as the reading of pertinent literature.
>
> In the next place, English and social studies are the subjects of areas most commonly required of all pupils in the three junior high school grades. Furthermore, these are the areas in which units of work relating to the personal-social needs of boys and girls are most often found when the subjects are taught separately. Curriculum guides for both language arts and social studies may

TABLE 16

Subjects Combined in Block-Time Classes in Grades 7, 8, and 9 in 487 Schools

Subjects Combined	Schools with Block-Time Classes				
	Grade			All Grades	
	7	8	9	Number	Per Cent
All Subject Combination	471	355	118	944	100.0
English and social studies	313	265	102	680	72.0
English, social studies, and					
Science	25	15	1	41	4.3
Mathematics	31	11	2	44	4.7
Science and mathematics	30	18		48	5.1
Science and mathematics	40	28	6	74	7.8
Social studies and mathematics	6	3		9	1.0
English and mathematics	5	2	1	8	.9
Social studies and science	8	3	3	14	1.5
English and science	7	4		11	1.2
Other groupings	6	6	3	15	1.5

From Grace S. Wright, *Block-Time Classes and the Core Program in the Junior High School,* U.S. Office of Education Bulletin No. 6 (Washington: Government Printing Office, 1958), Table 6, p. 21.

include such units as orientation to the school, knowing our community, planning for the future, developing leisure-time interests, getting along with others, and family relationships. In this sense, the combination of the two subjects avoids the overlapping that can happen when the subjects are taught separately by different teachers.

And lastly, since so much of American literature helps pupils to understand the history and geography of the United States and of the world and promotes the development of good citizenship, the social studies-English combination provides opportunities for the correlation or fusion of the two areas by the teacher, and can give the pupils integrated learning experiences.[18]

Combining language arts and social studies in at least a two-period block of time encourages the development of dynamic units of work which allow the learner to experience the direct and purposeful application of English tools and to derive pleasure from his efforts to improve his English skills.

The following is a summary of Mott's investigation of a three-year fusion of language arts and social studies at the Alexandria Junior High School in Louisiana:

1. A unit is developed around social studies which involves exploration or colonization. It may be introduced by a film, a lay resource person, or material presented by the teacher.

2. Learners are assigned oral and written reports and library research, which entails the reading of books, magazines, maps, and other appropriate material.

3. New and old English tools are introduced in accordance with the social studies problem or unit of work completion requirements. Various forms of practical application of grammar and composition are included. Developmental reading in a special class is provided students needing extra instruction while the remaining ones continue to improve their reading abilities in their block-time classes. All students are required to read and report in class on at least one book pertinent to each social studies unit and reflecting their level of reading proficiency.

4. The teacher corrects themes and other written work related to social studies and literature, and all students are then required to rewrite material. The slower-learning student is guided to proceed with the tasks on his own work sheet with maximum use of his personal equipment and receives a grade reflecting his abilities, progress, interest, contribution, and workmanship.

Mott discusses the productive aspects of this language arts–social studies fusion in a two-period block of time:

> Experience has shown that working at home is very necessary to complete the unit work. Students are cautioned that this home work must also meet all standards of good composition, and that English tools are for use at all times — not just in English class.

[18] Wright, *op. cit.*, pp. 21-22.

When students become aware of the fact that language arts embraces all that we do in writing, reading, speaking, and even thinking and that they must not think of English as only grammar which is divorced completely from other subjects, then the idea of language arts–social studies becomes meaningful and workable. The introduction of new English tools is then accepted with thanks by the students, as they can apply them in a realistic situation immediately.

By having worked with this situation [as supervising teacher] in which all of the social studies work is done within the framework of the language arts program, the writer feels that fusion on the junior-high-school level is workable and productive of good results. This is substantiated by the fact that a large majority of the students who have gone through this program as outlined here are performing generally above those students who were taught otherwise in our school.

Methods without meaning are sterile. Fusion, according to the procedure herein explained, gives real meaning to the language arts methods which are currently being used. This procedure will produce good results in any junior high-school block period in which the language arts–social studies combination is taught.[19]

During the last decade, while block-time scheduling has become popular in junior high schools, many surveys have reported that language arts and social studies are the most frequently combined basic curriculum areas as they contain the greatest number of interrelated characteristics. They also provide for extensive use of student competencies in music, art, dramatics, and rhythm in a unified program of instruction.

As noted in Table 16, mathematics is usually taught, especially in Grades 8 and 9, in regular class periods. Collaborative planning between teachers of block-time classes or core programs and mathematics teachers will assure more functional instruction in all three curriculum areas. These activities motivate teachers to evolve interesting and practical work units (on, for example, promotion of consistent school attendance patterns; study of the cost of education per student in school; interpretation of standardized tests in reading, language, and arithmetic; etc.), since they usually have the same learners at the same grade level.

The place of science varies markedly. It may be included in block-time classes, combined with mathematics in a double period, or included in a health-science course, and is required for a year or a semester for each grade. Often junior high schools offer science as a *required* personal interest learning area for a semester in all grades except Grade 9, in which, after appropriate guidance, students elect advanced science or biology for two semesters.

[19] Kenneth Mott, "Language Arts–Social Studies Fusion in the Junior High School Block Period." Reprinted by permission from *The Bulletin of the National Association of Secondary-School Principals,* March, 1960. Copyright: Washington, D.C. Pp. 124-131.

Extent of abandonment of block-time system

Ever since mid-century, block-time class organization has been one of the most commonly utilized instructional innovations that have occurred in the junior high school educational program.

In 1958 Wright reported, following a national survey, that 130 of the 2517 junior high schools had abandoned block-time classes. The reasons, reported by the principals, are classified in accordance with Wright's findings:[20]

Reasons	*Number*
Teachers inadequately prepared: Inability to secure qualified teachers; teachers continued to teach subjects and favored their major; untrained teachers and a transiency of teachers; the program was unworkable with our present staff; inability of teachers to make proper use of such time	52
Problems of scheduling: Could not arrange a schedule to include it; scheduling difficulty this session; difficulty in programming	20
Disliked by parents, pupils and/or teachers: Teachers felt they did a better job when teaching in their special fields; protests from parents; teacher, parent, and student objections; teachers feel they do more if they specialize; parental opposition due to bad publicity; public sentiment built up through the years	20
Failed to get desired results from the program: Staff saw no real advantage in it; achieved better academic results without it and equal social adjustment; found a better way — integrative system through teams of teachers; concurrent evaluation plus a follow-up two years later indicated little value for pupils	14
Limitations of space and equipment: School too small; lacked physical plant and aids necessary for success; crowded conditions have necessitated changes; classes too large	14
Not sufficient emphasis on subjects	3
No reason given	7

In this study the primary reason identified for abandonment of block-time classes was the lack of teachers adequately oriented and prepared by teacher training institutions.

[20] Wright, *op. cit.*, pp. 7-8.

2. *What are the educational values of block-time classes?*

Pertinence to fundamental learning skills

Throughout this book the authors hold that the basic learning requirement of early youth is to have experiences that will equip them to meet constructively the demands of the society in which they live. This is the prime objective that all educators at all instructional levels are urged to keep in mind as they evolve, implement, and assess all educational programs for all youth. It is the responsibility of educational workers to provide learners with opportunities that will best facilitate the utilization of the fundamental learning skills that are essential to productive living in today's society.

Block-time scheduling is viewed as a foundation or framework for the whole instructional program in junior high school. It is the best medium through which instruction may effectively engage the late preadolescent and early adolescent learner, and is as important to their desire and availability for learning as is proficiency in the fundamental learning skills.

The longer block-time class period allows teachers and students to apply basic learning skills to subject content as a whole, rather than as fragmented and disconnected elements. It makes it possible for teachers to engage students in the development of cumulative learning by directing them to examine the differing and common features within two or three separate subject areas. Resistance to learning in a specific subject area or to mastering a fundamental learning skill is markedly reduced in this instructional framework. The broader scope of the learning situation permits students more practice with and application of learning tools in different contexts, which in turn strengthens their ability to use these tools. Teachers with several years of practice in block-time teaching frequently state that this system has played a major role in upgrading the quality and quantity of their instruction, both in fundamental learning skills and in subject content.

One of the most significant features of block-time scheduling is the possibility of using more class time for community resources and audio-visual aids. Teachers and students have greater opportunities to study, with appropriate direction, current publications dealing with local and national events; to take field trips; to hear resource speakers by combining a number of classes in the same block-time period; to hear radio and view television education programs; and to participate in other school-community activities.

Students in block-time classes often write news items and feature articles about their class activities for the school paper. This project offers the chance to do creative writing and art work and to interview teachers and student leaders in the single-period subjects and in the personal interest activities and clubs. Another project might be the annual study, revision, and writing of the school handbook, which usually includes a code of citizenship for living in the school and in the community.

In summarizing the values of reporting in class on books read in school, in the library, and at home, Kerr, one of the teachers in block-time classes, says of oral reports,

1. They give the student group experience.
2. They eliminate copying from books for reports or reviews.
3. They stimulate others in the group to read books.
4. The reporting period is enjoyed by all pupils.
5. They save hours of grading written papers.
6. The pupils read more because they have developed a cooperative group spirit.[21]

More effective use of learning resources

Block-time classes increase teachers' opportunities to observe and diagnose both the reading difficulties and the interests of each student, but, of possibly more import, they afford the time to engage the students in activities that are geared to modifying the individual reading problem.

At West Junior High School, Kansas City, Missouri, one reading activity is the "Every Pupil Library Reading Program," which identifies the public library facilities (located in the school building) as an integral component of the curriculum in block-time classes. The teacher and students of block-time classes in Grades 7, 8, and 9 meet regularly in the library for fifty-five minutes every other week, or twice a month. The teacher assumes responsibility for directing and motivating students to select books and use library resources. The librarians present discussions of books, aid students to choose books for both recreational reading and preparation of units of work, and give instruction in the use of the library.

Standardized reading tests, administered at the beginning as well as near the close of the school year, supply teachers and librarians with guidelines to the reading level of each student so that they can more accurately assist him in selecting books and thus finding success and pleasure in reading, rather than frustration.

The Iowa Tests of Educational Development were given to all students when they entered Grade 9 in the Como Park Junior High School, St. Paul, Minnesota, in order to determine their command of basic skills compared with

[21] Marie Kerr, "Do We Teach Reading in the Core Curriculum?" *The Bulletin of the National Association of Secondary-School Principals,* 42:100, February, 1958.

that of students enrolled in other schools of the United States. Table 17 compares eight hundred students tested in 1956 who had completed Grades 7 and 8 in eight-year elementary schools and approximately the same number of students tested in 1958 who had completed Grades 7 and 8 in block-time and other classes in the Como Park Junior High School. The percentile rank of school averages in October, 1956, was lower than that in October, 1958, on all nine tests used except the first one, in which it was slightly higher. Thus, the block-time classes, which combined language arts and social studies in the Como Park Junior High School were more effective in teaching basic skills and knowledge in Grades 7 and 8 than was the traditional method used in the eight-grade elementary schools in the same city school system.

The achievement of 270 students in the common-learnings classes in a block-time structure in some of the junior high schools in Kansas City, Missouri, was measured by administering the California Language, Reading, and Social and Related Sciences tests. The same tests were given to 270 students in non-common-learning block-time classes in junior high schools outside of Kansas City.

The findings in Table 18 are favorable to the block-time structure for common learnings. Means of the scores of the common-learnings students on all three tests were higher than those of the non-common-learning students, and

TABLE 17

Iowa Educational Development Tests and Percentile Rank on School Averages, Como Park Junior High School, St. Paul, Minnesota

Number of Test	Title of Test	Percentile Rank	
		October 1956	October 1958
1	Understanding of Basic Social Concepts	36	34
2	Background in the Natural Sciences	26	55
3	Correctness and Appropriateness of Expression	12	23
4	Ability to Do Quantitative Thinking	70	91
5	Ability to Interpret Reading Materials in the Social Studies	22	68
6	Ability to Interpret Reading Materials in Natural Sciences	14	66
7	Ability to Interpret Literary Materials	16	40
8	General Vocabulary	45	70
9	Uses of Sources of Information	15	47

From "Report of Study of Scores on Iowa Tests of Educational Development in Como Park Junior High School" (St. Paul, Minn.: Office of Secondary and Vocational Education, January 29, 1959), pp. 1-3.

TABLE 18

Summary of the Differences in the Scores of Block-Time and Non-Block-Time Students on the California Language, California Reading, and California Social and Related Sciences

Group	Class	Test	Means
Entire sample	B-T	Reading	107.56
Entire sample	Non-B-T	Reading	104.45
Entire sample	B-T	Language	74.4
Entire sample	Non-B-T	Language	69.9
Entire sample	B-T	Social and Related Sciences	47.6
Entire sample	Non-B-T	Social and Related Sciences	44.1
Average I.Q.	B-T	Reading	103.4
Average I.Q.	Non-B-T	Reading	100.5
Above-average I.Q.	B-T	Reading	118.65
Above-average I.Q.	Non-B-T	Reading	115.65
Average I.Q.	B-T	Language	71.5
Average I.Q.	Non-B-T	Language	69.72
Above-average I.Q.	B-T	Language	79.4
Above-average I.Q.	Non-B-T	Language	76.9
Average I.Q.	B-T	Social and Related Sciences	43.1
Average I.Q.	Non-B-T	Social and Related Sciences	42.1
Above-average I.Q.	B-T	Social and Related Sciences	54.68
Above-average I.Q.	Non-B-T	Social and Related Sciences	50.9

Significant at the 5 per cent level; interpreted from Allen L. Edwards, *Statistical Analysis* (New York: Rinehart and Company, 1958), p. 220. (Significant at the 5 per cent level means that the outcome which has been obtained would occur in 95 out of 100 cases of similar control.) James E. McKnight, teacher of common learnings, Northeast Junior High School, Kansas City, Missouri, "An Evaluation of the Common Learnings Program in Teaching Subject Matter," Seminar and Research Report (unpublished), The University of Kansas City, 1958, pp. 1-31.

in all three cases the differences in the means were significant at the 5 per cent level.

The tests were then classified according to the I.Q. of the students. Those having I.Q.'s ranging from 90 to 100 were called "average." The average I.Q. groups from both the common-learning and the non-common-learning classes were then compared, and in every case the means of the average block-time group were higher than those of the average non-block-time group although the differences were not markedly significant.

The means of the above-average block-time group were all higher than the means of the above-average non-block-time group, and in every case the differences were significant at the 15 per cent level. Neither the block-time nor the non-block-time group contained enough students with below-average intelligence to be compared.

Other values

Values reported by principals. In an evaluative study of curriculum changes in Ohio secondary schools, Knapp asked school administrators having block-time classes whether or not this instructional organization had resulted in an improved educational program. Of the forty-six administrators queried, forty-two, or 91 per cent of the total group, replied that it had. The following three benefits were most often mentioned: It offered a more effective transition from elementary to secondary school; it permitted a closer relationship between teacher and pupil; and it provided increased recognition and accommodation of individual differences.[22] Principals of junior high schools usually report, as in Ohio, that the block-time organization improves programs of education.

Evaluation of block-time practices. In a study of the liabilities and assets of block-time practices, the principals of ninety-seven schools reporting block-time classes were mailed three questionnaires, one for the principal and two for experienced teachers in the block-time classes. A total of 171 usable questionnaires were returned with permission to use the information in evaluating block-time organization in junior high school programs.

The liabilities listed by the principals were the difficulty in obtaining and keeping adequate teaching personnel; the difficulty in scheduling in general, but specifically scheduling time for teacher planning conferences; and the fact that many teachers have strong desires to teach one subject only. The teachers indicated the liabilities to be the shortage of reference and supplementary materials; the shortage of time for preparation and planning; the proclivity of teachers to emphasize one subject at the expense of the other subjects; and inadequate training for teaching block-time classes.

The many assets of the block-time organization as reported by these principals and teachers are summarized below:

1. A student may come to know one teacher well and the teacher easily learns more about a given pupil. Thus, students tend to feel wanted and perhaps more secure.
2. The learning process profits from augmented laboratory experiences, more effective field trips, better use of audio-visual materials, and enhanced opportunities to practice desired skills and develop appropriate attitudes and appreciations.

[22] Dale L. Knapp, "High School Principals Look at Block-Time Classes," *The Bulletin of the National Association of Secondary-School Principals,* 44:53-54, March, 1960.

3. Learners are more inclined to acquire better self-understanding as well as skills in group processes and human relations.

4. Improvement in creative thinking is more likely to advance as the concept of student-teaching planning is explored and implemented.

5. Fruitful guidance opportunities multiply, and students work more readily toward recognition of life goals.

6. Concepts of democratic living come alive as they broaden and become more deeply embedded in the attitudes of students.

7. Integration of learning experiences is enhanced as subject barriers fade away and language arts and reading, for example, in part become important to all teachers.[23]

Although most teacher training institutions in this country are not yet providing sufficient preparation in block-time class instruction, the responses of most practicing block-time teachers are reported to be virtually unanimous in favor of the longer class period for teaching and guiding early adolescent students in junior high schools.

Approval of block-time scheduling by school patrons. If block-time classes are properly introduced, they are generally approved by a majority of the school patrons, as shown in a survey of the patrons from the Shawnee-Mission High School District, Kansas. This school district grew in total enrollment, kindergarten through Grade 12, from 3504 in 1940 to 26,080 in 1959. Six junior high schools were built to accommodate from nine hundred to one thousand students in Grades 7, 8, and 9 in each school. Sufficient classrooms were constructed in each building for block-time classes in Grades 7, 8, and 9. Two periods were utilized for teaching unified studies or core programs with continuous cooperative curriculum planning on a system-wide basis.

In a doctoral study by Wilbur V. Unruh, it was found that 89 per cent of the patrons of the six junior high schools in the Shawnee-Mission High School District favored block-time scheduling for unified studies and core teaching.[24]

Effectiveness of block-time classes. Glenn W. Schaller, Principal of Fassett Junior High School, Oregon, Ohio, formulated and distributed a questionnaire to the 315 junior high school principals in Ohio. Of the 245 principals who returned the questionnaire, 132 or 53.8 per cent had block-time classes, chiefly in Grades 7 and 8, and, as shown in Table 19, an overwhelming percentage of them expressed satisfaction with this type of program. Since 118 out of 132 responding schools, or 89.4 per cent, employing block-time classes are satisfied or well satisfied, and only fourteen indicate dissatisfaction or un-

[23] Summarized from *Block-of-Time Scheduling Practices in Illinois Junior High Schools, op. cit.,* p. 35.

[24] Wilbur V. Unruh, "A Study of Opinion of Parents Concerning Certain Aspects of the Curriculum of the Junior High Schools in the Shawnee-Mission High School District," Ed.D. dissertation, University of Kansas, 1958.

TABLE 19

How Junior High School Principals Feel About Block Programs

Degree of Feeling	Frequency Noted	Percentage of Schools Expressing Degree
Well satisfied	62	46.9
Satisfied	56	42.5
Undecided	7	5.3
Dissatisfied	7	5.3

Adapted from Glenn W. Schaller, "A Study of Opinions Concerning the Effectiveness of Block-Time Classes in the Junior High School in Ohio," A Research Report for the Degree of Specialist in Education, The University of Michigan, February, 1962, Table X, p. 35.

decidedness, there exists a strong endorsement for the block-time program in the junior high schools of Ohio.

In the second phase of this study, 549 teachers in sixty schools identified by the principals as satisfied or well satisfied with block-time classes were mailed a "Teacher Opinionnaire on Junior High Block-Time Classes," designed to evaluate teacher feelings about the block-time program in their schools. Two hundred seventy-six, or 50.2 per cent, of the opinionnaires were returned. Table 20 shows that 78.2 per cent of the teachers were satisfied or well satisfied with the block-time arrangement and only 10.1 per cent indicated dissatisfaction.

Even in the schools described by their principals as dissatisfied with block-time programs 73.3 per cent of the teachers favored and only 26.7 per cent were dissatisfied with this type of instructional arrangement.

The teachers in the satisfied group reacted favorably to most of the thirty-five alleged instructional contributions credited to block-time organization by

TABLE 20

How Teachers Feel About Block-Time Classes

Degree of Feeling	Frequency Noted	Per Cent
Well satisfied	100	36.2
Satisfied	115	42.0
Undecided	27	9.7
Dissatisfied	26	10.1
No response	6	2.0

Adapted from Glenn W. Schaller, "A Study of Opinions Concerning the Effectiveness of Block-Time Classes in the Junior High School," A Research Report for the Degree of Specialist in Education, The University of Michigan, February, 1962, Table XVI, page 41.

its advocates. The following advantages received strong support from these teachers:

> . . . (a) provides better opportunities for unit teaching; (b) provides better opportunities for problem-solving experiences; (c) provides for better correlation, fusion, or integration of subject matter; (d) more convenient to plan class projects which concern welfare of pupils; (e) makes it possible to study problems involving content from more than one subject; (f) cooperative and flexible planning are achieved more easily among teachers and pupils; (g) wider applications of knowledge and skills are possible; (h) provides opportunities to give attention to individual student problems, rather than covering just subject matter material; (i) decreases the number of class changes and thus results in greater security for the pupils; (j) provides for better transition from elementary to junior high school; (k) pupils become better known to teachers because of fewer students; (l) usage of pupil time is more efficient and effectively controlled; (m) more opportunity is given to employ greater use of teacher-pupil planning; (n) permits more effective directed study; (o) encourages greater use of the library; (p) allows for activities requiring larger periods of time; (q) encourages pupils to see relationships between and among fields of knowledge; (r) results in better guidance and counseling to students; (s) provides more opportunities for guidance and counseling; (t) provides for a greater amount of group and work-type procedures within the classroom; and (u) individual differences may be better served.
>
> The teachers reacted less favorably and were inclined to disallow the following alleged contributions credited to the block-time program by its supporters: (a) creates more interest in learning by students; (b) reduces negativism and antagonism toward the school program; (c) pupil attendance, interest and morale is improved; and (d) greater cooperation among teachers is promoted. In other words, the teachers were less sympathetic or favorable to regarding these as contributions resulting from block-time classes.[25]

Generally, the teachers from schools dissatisfied with block-time classes agreed with the alleged contributions credited to block-time scheduling by its advocates and the satisfied teacher group.

A summary of the findings of the principals' opinionnaire follows:

> 1. Approximately 98 percent of the junior high school principals described the organization of the block-time program as consisting of each subject retaining its identity in the block, or where the subjects retained their identity, each subject was correlated whenever possible in the block.
>
> 2. The principals tended to agree with the contentions cited on behalf of block-time programs by its advocates by favorably reacting to the thirty-nine reasons or contributions suggested for block-time classes being utilized in schools. Principals supported the following: (a) provides better opportunities for unit teaching; (b) provides better opportunities for problem-solving experiences; (c) provides for better correlation, fusion, or integration of subject matter; (d) more convenient to plan class projects which concern

[25] Schaller, *op. cit.*, pp. 78-79.

welfare of pupils; (e) opportunity for more effective use of community resources in the curriculum; (f) makes it possible to study problems involving content from more than one subject; (g) cooperative and flexible planning are achieved more easily among teachers and pupils; (h) wider applications of knowledge and skills are possible; (i) more opportunity for supervision and curriculum construction on school time; (j) provides opportunities to give attention to individual student problems, rather than covering just subject matter material;(k) creates more interest in learning by students; (l) brings about greater ease and poise in school by students; (m) presents school life as something not apart from the rest of the world; (n) decreases the number of class changes and thus results in greater security for the pupils; (o) reduces negativism and antagonism toward the school program; (p) provides for better transition from elementary to junior high school; (q) pupils become better known to teachers because of fewer students; (r) usage of pupil time is more efficient and effectively controlled; (s) the student becomes the recipient of improved instruction; (t) pupil attendance, interest, and morale is improved; (u) social adjustment of pupils is improved; (v) more opportunity is given to employ greater use of teacher-pupil planning; (w) permits more effective directed study; (x) encourages greater use of library; (y) provides for pupil-centered approach rather than subject-centered in teaching; (z) allows for activities requiring larger periods of time; (aa) encourages pupils to see relationships between and among fields of knowledge; (bb) provides greater guidance and counseling to students; (cc) results in better guidance and counseling to students; (dd) promotes better home-room guidance services for pupils; (ee) provides more time and better school organization for guidance and adjustment; (ff) provides more opportunities for guidance and counseling; (gg) teachers develop broader outlooks; (hh) provides for greater amount of group and work-type procedures; (ii) individual differences may be better served; (jj) better opportunities are available for cooperative evaluation; (kk) greater cooperation among teachers is promoted; (ll) develops among teachers a better understanding of youth; and (mm) greater enjoyment is derived from teaching.

3. Lack of teachers qualified to teach more than one subject is one of the most significant factors in the continued use of the conventional period approach in junior high schools.

4. The principals believed that the quality of instruction in the block-time period class is as thorough as, or superior to, that provided in the departmental class periods.

5. Problems causing greatest concern to principals were: (a) getting and keeping well-qualified teachers; (b) orienting new teachers to the concept of block-time teaching; and (c) finding time to provide professional leadership to teachers working in the block-time program.

6. Approximately 62 percent of the selected junior high school principals surveyed do not anticipate any further extension or expansion to other grades or other subject combinations of block-time programs in their schools, while 20 percent of the administrators do plan to extend and expand this concept further.[26]

[26] *Ibid.*, pp. 82-85.

Many educational research studies and surveys show that the principals, teachers, and patrons in a majority of the junior high schools are claiming numerous and significant values for the block-time organization. There is also an increased proclivity for state departments of education to recommend block-time scheduling.

Contributions to curriculum development

One of the major contributions of block-time scheduling has been the increase in teacher interest in curriculum and instructional program development.

In a national study of block-time classes and core programs by Wright, data reported by principals of 487 junior high schools which had used block-time organization continuously from 1949 to 1957 revealed (1) that over one-half of the school staffs were consciously doing correlated teaching of two or three combined basic subjects and (2) that one-third of them had advanced to a unified studies program or an experience-centered core program.[27]

Curriculum and Instructional Programs	Number	Per Cent
Teaching subjects separately in block-time period with no consciously planned correlation	51	10.5
Correlated teaching of combined subjects	277	56.9
Fused teaching of combined subjects or unified studies	98	20.1
Experience-centered core teaching, structured and unstructured	61	12.5
Total number of principals of junior high schools reporting	487	100.0

It is quite apparent that the reorganization and improvement of curriculum and instructional programs in the junior high school *first* involve the adoption of block-time scheduling of two or three regular periods. This administrative framework is needed, whether the school staff is emphasizing correlation of fundamental subjects, unified studies, or experience-centered core teaching.

According to Gardner, the experience-centered core curriculum depends on the "large block of time in junior high schools, ranging from about two to three hours in grades 7 and 8, while about two hours are favored in grade 9."[28] The recommendation of block-time organization for core teaching in junior high schools is made by 139 curriculum specialists, 55 of them em-

[27] Wright, *op. cit.*, pp. 9-21.

[28] Gordon A. Gardner, "Conflicting Concepts of the Core Program," summary of Ph.D. dissertation, The University of Washington, in *College of Education Record,* 25:39, March, 1959.

ployed in higher education, 55 by city school systems, and 29 by state departments of education. Geographically, these curriculum specialists were drawn from forty-four states and the District of Columbia.

Of the many values claimed for block-time organization by educational workers, one of the most significant is that it is essential for developing the experience-centered core curriculum, which will be discussed in the next chapter.

SELECTED BIBLIOGRAPHY

Block-of-Time Scheduling Practices in Illinois Junior High Schools. Springfield: Office of Public Instruction, 1960. Pp. 1-35.

Bossing, Nelson L. "Trends in Block-Time Classes in Junior High School," *The Bulletin of the National Association of Secondary-School Principals,* 43:34-36, April, 1959.

———, and John F. Kaufman. "Block-Time or Core Practices in Minnesota Secondary Schools," *The Clearing House,* 32:532-539, May, 1958.

Briggs, Thomas H. *The Junior High School.* Boston: Houghton Mifflin Company, 1920.

Byers, Richard S. *"Articulation in Junior High School,"* Ph.D. dissertation, University of Connecticut, 1955.

Cramer, Roscoe V. "How Effective Is the Core Curriculum in the Junior High School?" *The Bulletin of the National Association of Secondary-School Principals,* 38:172-179, April, 1954.

Dolan, Raymond A. "An Experimental Program," *The Bulletin of the National Association of Secondary-School Principals,* 44:42-43, April, 1960.

Faunce, Roland C., and Morrel J. Clute. *San Francisco: Teaching and Learning in the Junior High School.* San Francisco: Wadsworth Publishing Company, 1961.

Gardner, Gordon A. "Conflicting Concepts of the Core Program," summary of Ph.D. dissertation, The University of Washington, in *College of Education Record,* 25:33-45, March, 1959.

Gibboney, Richard A. "Report on the 1955-1956 Survey of Common Learnings." Harrisburg: Department of Public Instruction, Commonwealth of Pennsylvania, April 15, 1958. (Mimeo.)

Inglis, Alexander. *Principles of Secondary Education.* Boston: Houghton Mifflin Company, 1918.

Junior High School in Nebraska, The. Lincoln: State Department of Education, 1960. Pp. 1-52.

Junior High School Program, The. Atlanta, Ga.: Southern Association of Colleges and Secondary Schools, 1958.

Junior High Schools for Iowa Youth. Des Moines: Iowa State Department of Public Instruction, 1960. Pp. 1-60.

Kerr, Marie. "Do We Teach Reading in the Core Curriculum?" *The Bulletin of the National Association of Secondary-School Principals,* 42:100-101, February, 1958.

Knapp, Dale L. "High School Principals Look at Block-Time Classes," *The Bulletin of the National Association of Secondary-School Principals,* 44:53-54, March, 1960.

Koos, Leonard V. *Junior High School Trends.* New York: Harper & Brothers, 1955.

Leonard, J. Paul. "Frontiers in Junior High School Education," *The Bulletin of the National Association of Secondary-School Principals,* 24:112-119, February, 1940.

McEachen, Howard D. *Status and Trends in Organization and Curriculum in Selected Junior High Schools,"* Ed.D. dissertation, University of Kansas, 1955.

Michelson, John. "What Does Research Say About the Effectiveness of the Core Curriculum?" *The School Review,* 65:144-159, Summer, 1957.

Miller, Helen Rand. "Unified Studies, A History-English Powerhouse," *The Clearing House,* 24:103-105, October, 1949.

Mott, Kenneth. "Language Arts–Social Studies Fusion in the Junior High School Block Period," *The Bulletin of the National Association of Secondary-School Principals,* 44:124-131, March, 1960.

New Jersey State Department of Education. "Block-of-Time Programs in Junior High Schools and Six-Year High Schools in New Jersey," *Secondary School Bulletin,* No. 2, March, 1960.

Normington, Louis W. "Block of Time Classes in Junior High Schools in California," Ph.D. dissertation, University of California, 1955.

"Place of Science and Mathematics in the Comprehensive Secondary School Program, The," *The Bulletin of the National Association of Secondary-School Principals,* 42:9-10, September, 1958.

Planning for American Youth, An Educational Program for Youth of Secondary-School Age. Washington: The National Association of Secondary-School Principals, 1944.

Putnam, Rex. *The Organization and Functions of Oregon Junior High Schools.* Salem: Superintendent of Public Instruction, State Department of Education, 1959.

"Report of Study of Scores on Iowa Tests of Educational Development in Como Junior High School." St. Paul, Minn.: Office of Secondary and Vocational Education, January, 1959.

Schaller, Glenn W. "A Study of Opinions Concerning the Effectiveness of Block-Time Classes in the Junior High Schools in Ohio," A Research Report for the Degree of Specialist in Education, The University of Michigan, 1962, Pp. 1-111.

Schult, Veryl. "Whither Arithmetic in Grades 7 and 8?" *Education,* 79:280-286, January, 1959.

"Status of Block-Time Programs in Michigan Secondary Schools, The," *Report of of State Committee on Core and General Education,* Bulletin 426. Lansing: State Superintendent of Public Instruction, 1960.

Tompkins, Ellsworth. "The Daily Schedule in Junior High Schools," A Study of the Committee on Junior High School Education, *The Bulletin of the National Association of Secondary-School Principals,* 40:177, May, 1956.

Unruh, Wilbur V. "A Study of Opinion of Parents Concerning Certain Aspects of the Curriculum of the Junior High Schools in the Shawnee-Mission High School District," Ed.D. dissertation, University of Kansas, 1958.

Wilson, William E. *The Junior High School: A Report Prepared by the Indiana Association of Junior and Senior High School Principals,* Bulletin No. 246. Bloomington: Indiana Department of Public Instruction, 1961. Pp. 1-116.

Wright, Grace S. *Block-Time Classes and the Core Program in the Junior High School.* U.S. Office of Education Bulletin No. 6. Washington: Government Printing Office, 1958. Pp. 1-70.

———, and Edith S. Greer. *The Junior High School, A Survey of Grades 7-8-9 in Junior and Junior-Senior High Schools, 1959-1960.* U.S. Office of Education Bulletin No. 32. Washington: Government Printing Office, 1963. Pp. 12-23.

7

The Core Curriculum

1. How shall we define core?

Origin of the "core" idea

The core curriculum has experienced rapid development within the past few years. As it has gained in popularity there have arisen many variations in the curriculum patterns labeled "core." At first "core" was applied to a group of subjects all pupils in a school had to study, as distinct from the list of subjects from which the pupil was expected to choose in order to complete his program for the semester or year, or to acquire credits he needed for graduation. The term "core" was used interchangeably with the terms "requireds" and "constants" to distinguish between the "musts" — those subjects the schools considered it essential that all pupils study — and the "electives" or "variables" of the curriculum, which were deemed of particular value to those with special interests or purposes.

In a now famous book, published in 1918 and entitled *Principles of Secondary Education,* Alexander Inglis, a notable leader in secondary education, proposed that the social studies be made the heart of the school curriculum. He emphasized "the integrating values attached to some studies, especially to the social studies and to the mother tongue and its literature."[1] The idea of integration in the curriculum was soon to become of paramount importance in curriculum development.

Chapter 4 gave a brief account of the different devices progressively used

[1] Alexander Inglis, *Principles of Secondary Education* (Boston: Houghton Mifflin Company, 1918), pp. 676, 681-682.

to bring about a more desirable integration of the curriculum, from the hesitant attempts at correlation to the bolder broad-fields and general education patterns, the latter of which, in practice, often has varied from the more advanced form of broad fields to a form to be identified by some with the more completely integrated "core" of the experience-centered curriculum.

Core defined

It needs to be re-emphasized that in this book the basis for recommendations that affect the educational program for the junior high school (and, for that matter, for all phases or levels of education) is the acceptance of the psychological theory that learning consists of the change in behavior that takes place through experience. Consequently, *the term "core" is applied to that phase of the experience curriculum which is concerned with the development of the types of experiences all learners need in order to achieve certain behavior competencies considered essential for effective living in our democratic society.*

That this concept is being generally accepted by specialists in curriculum is evident from their writings. One of the pioneers in the development of the core idea in theory and practice defines core as "a continuous, carefully planned series of experiences which is based on significant personal and social problems and which involves learnings of common concern to all."[2]

Another writer who spent many years developing a core program in the Wells High School of Chicago, states, "The core program consists of the activities of living necessary for *all* as worthy members of our social order."[3]

One of the earlier influential educational organizations to sponsor the core idea was the Educational Policies Commission. In its now famous *Education for All American Youth,* the Commission describes a distinctive curriculum feature which it calls a "Common Learnings" program. Its essential agreement with core is clear in the following quotations:

> What does this title "Common Learnings" mean? It means that this course consists of learning experiences which *everyone* needs to have regardless of what occupation he may expect to follow or where he may happen to live. . . .
>
> Here is a course . . . designed to provide most of the learning experiences which, it is believed, all young people should have *in common* in order to live happily and usefully during the years of youth and grow into the full responsibilities of adult life. . . .
>
> Briefly stated, the distinctive purposes of the course in "Common Learnings" are to help all youth grow in six areas:
>
> 1. Civic responsibility and competence

[2] Hollis L. Caswell and others, *The American High School,* Eighth Yearbook of the John Dewey Society (New York: Harper & Brothers, 1946), p. 143.

[3] Paul R. Pierce, *Developing a High-School Curriculum* (New York: American Book Company, 1942), p. 129.

2. Understanding of the operation of the economic system and of the human relations involved therein
3. Family relations
4. Intelligent action as consumers
5. Appreciation of beauty
6. Proficiency in the use of language.[4]

J. Paul Leonard has defined core in these words:

> The core then, as we are using the term, refers to that part of the curriculum which takes as its major job the development of personal and social responsibility and competency needed by all youth to serve the needs of a democratic society.[5]

Leonard continues by listing five characteristics of core that definitely remove it from a subject-matter basis and give it a personal and social problems orientation.

Krug, in a discussion of the unique nature of core, points up its concept sharply:

> The course of study offerings may be organized primarily either in terms of the logical patterns of human knowledge or in terms of some conception of the needs and problems of children and youth and of society. . . . But the organization of the course of study must choose one basic underlying principle or the other. It is really a rare instance of an "either-or" proposition.[6]

A research study conducted by Gardner attempted to determine what agreement existed among secondary school curriculum specialists as to the meaning of the core program. A checklist "characterized by varied and conflicting concepts of the core curriculum" derived from a careful study of the educational literature on core was prepared and submitted to nineteen curriculum specialists for critical appraisal. The revised checklist was then sent to a jury of 139 curriculum specialists selected as follows: (1) fifty-five professors of secondary school curriculum in higher institutions of learning where the doctor's degree in education was offered; (2) fifty-five secondary school curriculum directors or consultants employed in cities with a population of 100,000 or more; (3) twenty-nine secondary school curriculum directors or

[4] Educational Policies Commission, National Education Association, *Education for All American Youth* (Washington: The Association, 1944), pp. 248-252. See also the 1952 revised edition, pp. 237-241, in which the Commission maintains exactly the same statements.

[5] J. Paul Leonard, *Developing the Secondary School Curriculum* (New York: Rinehart & Co., rev. ed., 1953), pp. 396-397.

[6] Edward A. Krug, *Curriculum Planning* (New York: Harper & Brothers, 1950), pp. 85-86.

consultants employed by state departments of education. In all, forty-four states and the District of Columbia were represented on this panel of judges.

Here are some of the conclusions reached in the study:

1. Although not necessarily limited to the following statements, purposes for a core program should include: (1) helping youth to acquire basic citizenship skills, understandings, and behaviors through a more effective and functional organization of the curriculum than practiced in the conventional approach to general education; (2) helping youth to deal with significant personal-social problems that involve learnings of common concern to all youth; (3) helping youth to understand his own behavior and the behavior of other persons; (4) helping youth to live democratically — thinking critically, working cooperatively with others, respecting the worth of other people; (5) helping youth to deal with guidance problems. . . .

2. At a 92 per cent acceptance level, the jury favored the idea that "learning" should be defined as change in behavior that results from experiencing. . . .

3. Core program patterns should be characterized by broad preplanned problem areas. Within these problem areas, there should be provision for dealing with (1) the interests, concerns, and needs common to all youth in our society; (2) the major areas of living (social functions); (3) the problems of major social significance to all members of our society (societal problems); (4) persistent life situations. . . .

4. Problem solving should be emphasized in a core program. (a 90 per cent jury acceptance level)

5. . . . according to major jury support, the following ideas, in addition to those already indicated, should be made a part of the meaning of a core program: (1) teacher pupil planning should occur, but generally within the preplanned structure for a core program; (2) group dynamics should be used; (3) value judgments (what ought to be) should be sought, as opposed to simply dealing with what is or what was; (4) subject matter should be brought in only if appropriate to the development of a unit; (5) guidance should be one of the major responsibilities of the classroom teacher. . . .

6. At a 97 per cent acceptance level, the jury approved the following statement, "It is important that core program teachers and teachers of special interest areas should plan together to provide youth with related opportunities to learn in these two areas of the curriculum."

7. Jury data clearly indicated the idea that many and varied types of evaluation materials and procedures should be used when evaluating core programs.[7]

In spite of the continued widespread tendency to popularly and superficially give almost anything that represents a little correlation or any use of a multiple-period block of time the name "core," it is clear that curriculum special-

[7] Gordon A. Gardner, "Conflicting Concepts of the Core Program," The University of Washington, in summary of Ph.D. dissertation, *College of Education Record,* 25:33-39, March, 1959.

ists have reached a high degree of unanimity as to the concept of a core program. It may be well here to look at the over-all pattern of core more closely.

Core program and core curriculum

The definition of core given earlier in this chapter referred only to the segment of the experience curriculum concerned with acquiring the competencies needed by all citizens. Because many think no further about the necessity to plan the curriculum to insure the development of these competencies, but feel that providing a teacher with an extended block of time and complete freedom to deal with the problem interests that arise in a group will do the trick, core has been criticized as being largely haphazard and without organization. Where such practices parade under the banner of core, the criticism of disorganization is justified.

It would seem of the utmost importance that, consistent with the essential place of pupil purposing in the concept of experience learning, pupil exposure to experiences most likely to develop these competencies should be carefully planned. The study of the curriculum specialists' conception of good core practice revealed their strong emphasis upon broadly preplanned problem areas. To insure a balanced development of the common competencies for all, an organized program is necessary. *The core program, then, refers to the total organizational activities of that part of the school curriculum devoted to the determination of the personal and social competencies needed by all, and the procedures, materials, and environmental facilities by which the school assures the adequacy of the learning experiences essential to the development of these competencies.*

Unfortunately, there is much confusion over the relationship of the core program to the rest of the curriculum. Many who are ready to accept a definition of core based upon experience learning see no dichotomy or conflict in accepting the mind storage or the mental discipline concept of learning as the basis for the rest of the curriculum. It would seem entirely superfluous to assert that there must be unity in learning, and consequently unity in the curriculum — unity between the common competencies represented by core and the other necessary competencies required by individual differences. This concept of unity between the two phases of experience learning is called the core curriculum. *Thus, the core curriculum refers to a pattern of the experience curriculum organized into a more closely integrated and interrelated whole, in which one division, the core program, is devoted to developing the common competencies needed by all, and the other division emphasizes the development of special competencies based upon the recognition of individual differences in interests, aptitudes, and capacities, the entire curriculum utilizing consistently the same basic principles of learning, teaching methods, and problem organization.*[8]

[8] For a further discussion of the core concept see Nelson L. Bossing, *Principles of Secondary Education* (Englewood Cliffs, N.J.: Prentice-Hall, Inc., 2nd ed., 1955), Chap. XIII.

2. *What are some characteristics of the core curriculum?*

1. The core idea is based upon the fundamental psychological principle that learning involves change in behavior which is brought about through experience, and that the curriculum consists of the learning situations designed to foster those types of learning experiences most likely to produce desirable behavior change.

2. The core is organized around those problems of personal and social concern common to all youth in our democratic society.

3. The core seeks to draw upon a wide range of informational sources, materials, and appropriate activities necessary for the solution of these vital personal and social problems. Whatever in the total environment will contribute to their solution is considered "grist for the mill" by the alert teacher. The core involves a complete disregard of existing subject-matter lines or subject-matter emphasis.

4. The core emphasizes the utilization of genuine problem-solving procedures and techniques in personal and social problem situations.

5. The core involves and provides for much teacher cooperation in curriculum planning. The core curriculum activities must be seen and planned for as a whole, and by all teachers as a group as well as individually. Teachers do not function as "prima donnas" within their own pre-empted areas but work as part of a professional group, contributing their general and special skills to the common goal of helping boys and girls develop in maximal degree those competencies needed for successful living.

6. The core involves the joint planning of pupils and teachers for the solution of vital problems.

7. The core makes individual and group guidance an integral part of teaching, the core teacher accepting as his basic responsibility many of the major functions now assumed by guidance specialists and counselors in the more traditionally organized schools. In the core idea, teaching and guidance become largely synonymous terms.

8. The core idea involves a recognition of the over-all organization of the curriculum into two highly integrated and interrelated divisions: (1) the core program, devoted to the types of problems common to all youth and the competencies all must possess to function successfully in our society, and (2) the section of the curriculum devoted to the development of special concerns of pupils, in which individual interests, aptitudes, and abilities are explored and the requisite skills for each are provided an opportunity for development. Both divisions are based squarely on the same principles of learning, teaching methods, and problem organization.

9. Administratively important to the success of the core idea is the provision of large blocks of time in the day's schedule to facilitate guidance, the

maximum use of problem-solving processes, and the use of community resources.

10. Administratively important to the success of the guidance function of the core idea is the need to provide for longer spans of association between core teachers and pupils in order that teachers may know the pupils better — their environmental backgrounds, their interests, abilities, and learning development. Some schools are experimenting by allowing teachers to remain as advisers to a group for two or more years.[9]

3. *What are some problems of core organization?*

If the core curriculum worker takes experience learning seriously he confronts a major problem as he attempts to develop a curriculum consistent with the implications of this learning theory. He must take a radically different approach to curriculum making from any that has been used in the past.

Determination of the competencies to be developed

In the traditional curriculum the primary task was to select subject-matter materials appropriate for memorization or storage in the mind. The problems that haunted the curriculum worker were at least twofold: First, how was he to be sure that blind spots in the education of the learner would not result from his possible failure to cover adequately the total range of human knowledge? This became all the more serious as knowledge accumulated at an accelerated pace and the human mind found it impossible to grasp more than a small fraction of extant knowledge, or to delve into more than a few of the myriad divisions and subdivisions of that vast array. Second, even if some agreement could be reached on what were the most essential areas to be studied, a still more perplexing question had to be answered: "How much of each area should be mastered?" On both counts the subject-centered curriculum specialists have been getting deeper and deeper into an impossible morass from which there seems to be no possible rescue.

Those concerned with the development of a curriculum based upon experience learning face similar though less difficult problems of covering adequately the scope of human activities in which behavioral competencies will be needed and the further problem of how intensively these competencies should be fostered in the various areas of living.

[9] An adaptation of a list that first appeared in Nelson L. Bossing, "What Is Core?" *The School Review,* 63:212-213, April, 1955. With few changes the same list appears in Bossing, *Principles of Secondary Education,* pp. 409-410. For a similar list see Leonard, *op. cit.,* pp. 397-400. For a statement of what core is not, see Harold Alberty, "A Sound Core Program," *National Education Association Journal,* 45:20-22, January, 1956.

Over the past four decades at least five significant attempts have been made to determine the scope of the experience curriculum. There has been a remarkable degree of agreement among them, both in nomenclature and in the areas of human activity to be covered. Three examples are selected for illustration:

Mississippi — Major Areas of Human Activities

1. Protecting life and health
2. Making a home
3. Conserving and improving material conditions
4. Cooperating in social and civic action
5. Getting a living
6. Securing an education
7. Expressing religious impulses
8. Engaging in recreation
9. Expressing esthetic impulses.[10]

Santa Barbara — Basic Functions of Human Living

1. Developing and conserving personal resources
2. Developing and conserving resources other than personal
3. Producing, distributing and consuming goods and services
4. Communicating
5. Transporting
6. Re-creating and playing
7. Expressing and satisfying spiritual and esthetic needs
8. Organizing and governing [11]

Stratemeyer — Persistent Life Situations

1. The family
2. Civic social activities
3. Work
4. Leisure
5. Spiritual life [12]

The problem of the core curriculum worker thus is to determine the kinds of behavioral competencies needed by youth and adults in each of these major

[10] *Mississippi Program for the Improvement of Instruction, Curriculum Reorganization in the Secondary School, Grades 7-12,* Bulletin No. 7 (Jackson: State Department of Education, 1939), p. 28. A discussion of the Mississippi list is to be found in O. I. Frederick and Lucille Farquer, "Areas of Human Activities," *Journal of Educational Research,* 33:672-679, May, 1937.

[11] *Experimental Curriculum in Santa Barbara City Schools,* Bulletin No. 1, revised (Santa Barbara, Calif.: Santa Barbara City Schools, November, 1941), pp. 22-63.

[12] Florence B. Stratemeyer and others, *Developing a Curriculum for Modern Living* (New York: Bureau of Publications, Teachers College, Columbia University, 1947), p. 99. Some modification of this list appears in the 1957 edition.

areas and the approximate degree of proficiency required for normal living. Then the task becomes one of setting up a wealth of learning situations designed to provide all boys and girls with experiences that will develop a high level of the needed competencies in all areas of living. As the pupils engage in problem solving of various kinds and constantly learn to generalize from their learning experiences to other problem situations, they develop most surely the kind of behavioral skills called for in their contemporary living and most effective in adult life.

To insure that each pupil has an opportunity to become involved in the solution of a wide range of personal and social problems requires careful planning on the part of every core teacher and extensive and constant interplanning between teachers.

Structured versus unstructured core programs

The matter of careful planning to see that pupils in core classes get broad experience in problem-solving situations raises the question of whether a core program should be structured or unstructured. As pointed out earlier, there is a good deal of anarchy in so-called core teaching. Often the teacher, in an effort to honor the principle of pupil purposing in learning, follows the impulse of the moment, wherever it may lead. Any serious discussion of structured versus non-structured core programs is largely a matter of semantics. Among the major writers on core there appears to be no one who advocates complete teacher license to follow the will-o'-the-wisp suggestion of the moment. One who has advocated the largest degree of teacher freedom in utilizing vital pupil purposing in classroom planning, consistent with a balanced curriculum to insure the development of needed pupil competencies, puts it this way:

> In place of predetermined subject matter courses, the modern junior high school teacher uses pupil-teacher planning techniques to explore the areas of their interests and the learning needs that are common to the pupils in the groups. This does not relieve the teacher from his responsibility for also finding out and meeting the specific learning needs of individuals. Modern techniques promote the development of a permissive atmosphere in which creativity, originality, and initiative are encouraged.[13]

The problem of a structured curriculum becomes rather a question of "how much structure." It is possible to so structure the program that no flexibility is left. For example, in a school that professes its adherence to core there are seven units that must be studied by all pupils in the seventh grade. This means in practical terms a completely structured curriculum for the seventh grade. Another school assigned specific units to be studied in each of the

[13] Gertrude Noar, *The Junior High School, Today and Tomorrow*, rev. ed. © 1961, by permission of Prentice-Hall, Inc., Englewood Cliffs, N.J. P. 36.

seventh, eighth, and ninth grades. After some experience with this highly structured curriculum the staff realized that it was as formal and lifeless as the subject curriculum from which they had tried to escape. Recognizing that this rigid curriculum violated what they knew about the psychology of learning, they set up a list of units designed to give a variety of experiences to the pupils covering the areas of competencies they wished to develop. These became guides to the teacher as she planned problem units with the pupils. The teachers constantly checked the growing competencies of their pupils and the type of problem units they had studied against a chart showing a balanced learning program. Thus under the alert and subtle guidance of the teachers there was flexibility and genuine student problem solving, yet always wisely checked against a broadly planned school curriculum. This system provided an over-all structured curriculum yet insured abundant flexibility to capture the personal and social problem-solving purposing of the learner.

4. *What are some educational implications of core?*

Acceptance of guidance responsibilities by core teachers

In the philosophy of the core curriculum guidance is an integral part of teaching. Since the core program is responsible for the development of personal and social competencies of youth and is committed to the organization of the curriculum around personal, social, and societal problems of boys and girls, it places the core teacher directly at the heart of guidance activities. One authority on core in a large high school of which he was principal would not permit face-to-face counseling by the guidance specialists in his school. He held that the unique relationship between teacher and pupil in core made the teacher the key to personal guidance. The trained guidance specialists were to counsel the teachers and give them technical help when guidance problems became complex.[14]

In core the teacher occupies a very different relationship to the pupil from that of the traditional subject-specialist teacher. The latter is expected to give almost exclusive attention to his specialty and to the pupil's mastery of the subject. His attitude is well illustrated in an incident related by a superintendent concerning one of his teachers. A student in the high school approached the teacher early in the week to ask about a possible event the student thought was to take place later in the week. To his inquiry the teacher replied, "You had better check the office on this matter; I am only hired here to teach history." This incident points up sharply the difference between the teacher who conceives his responsibility to be the teaching of his chosen specialty and the one who understands that his primary obligation

[14] Pierce, *op. cit.*

is to help youth develop skills in meeting and solving the vital problems of life that daily confront them. In this concept of function the core teacher recognizes that for all practical considerations "guidance" and "teaching" are synonymous terms.

It is only necessary to check the titles of books and articles on guidance written within the past few years to catch the definite trend toward recognition of the central place of the teacher in guidance. Recent studies of why schools have adopted the multiple-class period reveal a growing awareness on the part of administrators that where teachers have one-half to two-thirds fewer pupils and a longer period of association with the pupils guidance is enhanced.

Student activities an integral part of the curriculum

There has been a long-drawn-out struggle to have so-called extracurricular activities accepted as part of the curriculum on an educational par with all other subjects. In spite of the fact that all we know about learning suggests the equal, if not superior, value of extracurricular activities in the development of mentally healthy, socially competent, and adjusted personalities, the subject vested interests are slow to acknowledge the educational worth of these non-academic areas.

Their resistance is a logical conclusion to a concept of learning that makes mind stuffing the pinnacle of education. There is a necessary dichotomy between amassing facts and taking part in activities whose primary objective is the acquisition of desirable attitudes and wholesome social behavioral competencies. Since the core curriculum is centered in a philosophy of values that makes the betterment of the quality of human relations the goal of education, and the acceptance of experience learning focuses the educational process upon developing the skills to attain such betterment, extracurricular activities ought to be accepted on the same basis as other educational resources in the curriculum. Therefore, in core all that will contribute to desirable social behavior has general curriculum acceptance and must be scheduled as a regular part of the school program.

Replacement of homeroom by core classes

The homeroom is the outgrowth of increasing school enrollments and the commitment to subject-matter instruction. As schools became larger, pupils found themselves isolated within their classrooms and subject departments. More serious, as classes grew, teachers became further isolated from their pupils. Schools took on the features of a factory assembly line. Teachers became responsible for a smaller segment even of their major field and knew less and less about the total activities in the school. Further, large numbers of teachers did not regard the personal problems of pupils as their concern. They were subject specialists.

As a result pupils could not get adequate advice even on which courses to take. Round pegs were more frequently getting into square holes. Pupils in courses they did not like or found too difficult began to fall by the wayside or became discipline problems. Pupil contacts with each other became only incidental and limited.

The homeroom was an attempt to remedy a situation created by a fundamentally wrong approach to education. It was a device created within the framework of a subject curriculum to bring key teachers into contact with pupils in order to provide better counseling in matters of registration. The idea was that pupils could be enrolled in courses more suited to their interests and abilities, and that bringing them together would foster a sense of group cohesion and raise school morale. Much more recently the homeroom has been thought to serve the purpose of guidance.

In actuality few teachers accepted this additional duty graciously. It was contrary to the training of the subject specialist to acknowledge it as a bona fide educational responsibility. Besides, few had any notion of the meaning of guidance or how to undertake it. Having no vital contact with these pupils outside the homeroom, they lacked the basis for true guidance. Many teachers were not informed of the purpose and function of the homeroom. A school superintendent in a major city, evidently anxious to get on the popularity bandwagon when homeroom advocacy became widespread, simply announced that the school system was adopting the homeroom program. Teachers were placed in charge of groups with but the faintest idea of what they were expected to do. After making routine announcements, they turned their room into a study hall for the rest of the period. A study made some years ago revealed that about two-thirds of the homeroom periods were under thirty minutes long; most were ten to twenty minutes in length, with school announcements the principal activity. Neither in the philosophy nor in the structure of the subject curriculum is the homeroom natural. Not surprisingly, therefore, in subject-oriented schools this device is obsolescent.

In the core curriculum the idea of the homeroom *is* natural, its purposes compatible with core classroom activities. Core emphasizes pupil needs and pupil problems as the heart of the curriculum and the primary concern of the teacher. Moreover, the utilization of large blocks of time with the consequent reduction of pupils by at least 50 per cent makes possible personal acquaintance with each pupil. The tendency to extend the core teacher-class relationship for from one to three years provides an ideal environmental situation for guidance. Administrators have been quick to see the core class as the logical place for those activities previously assigned to the homeroom, and the core class as the natural replacement of the educationally artificial homeroom.

5. *How does core fit the junior high school?*

Questioning of core in the junior high school

It may be surprising to some that core should be questioned at the junior high school level. Yet many educators seriously challenge the core idea at this level. They regard the period of transition from childhood to early adolescence as a time when the curriculum should be completely centered on the needs and problems of emerging adolescence. They believe the problems of change and adjustment so unique and all-pervasive at this time as to require a largely undifferentiated curriculum for all. The Educational Policies Commission, one of the early major educational organizations to advocate the core curriculum, was unequivocal in its insistence that a common curriculum for all should be provided at the junior high school level. The Commission set forth its position in these words:

> There was also the question of differentiation of courses in the secondary schools. At what times and in what ways, it was asked, do the interests and educational needs of maturing youth tend to diverge widely enough so that parts of the curriculum should be correspondingly differentiated? And in what respects do the educational needs of youth continue to be common to all and best served through a curriculum followed by all students? . . .
>
> Throughout the junior high school period, it was agreed, the educational needs of pupils are sufficiently alike to justify a common curriculum for all pupils with ample provision for differentiated treatment of pupils within classes to take account of diversities of interests, aptitudes, and abilities.
>
> Beginning at the tenth grade, or thereabouts, young people exhibit differences in certain of their interests and plans which call for a variety of offerings in the curriculum, among which the students, under guidance, may choose.[15]

Since the Educational Policies Commission has been one of the most important national educational organizations to give major emphasis to the core idea, we may well look at its graphic plan for Grades 10 to 14 (see Figure 6). In this plan it should be noted that ideally periods 3-6 should be a part of common learnings or core. The thin lines that separate science and health and physical education from common learnings in this chart, the Commission indicates, are a compromise with the practical limitations of the present extreme specialization of teachers. When teachers are more broadly prepared, science, health, and physical education will properly belong to common learnings. The Commission thus suggests that ideally four of the six periods of the tenth grade should be given over to a common curriculum for all.

[15] Educational Policies Commission, *op. cit.,* pp. 230-231. The same statement appears in the 1952 revised edition, pp. 219-220.

FIGURE 6

Core Curriculum Organization Pattern in American City

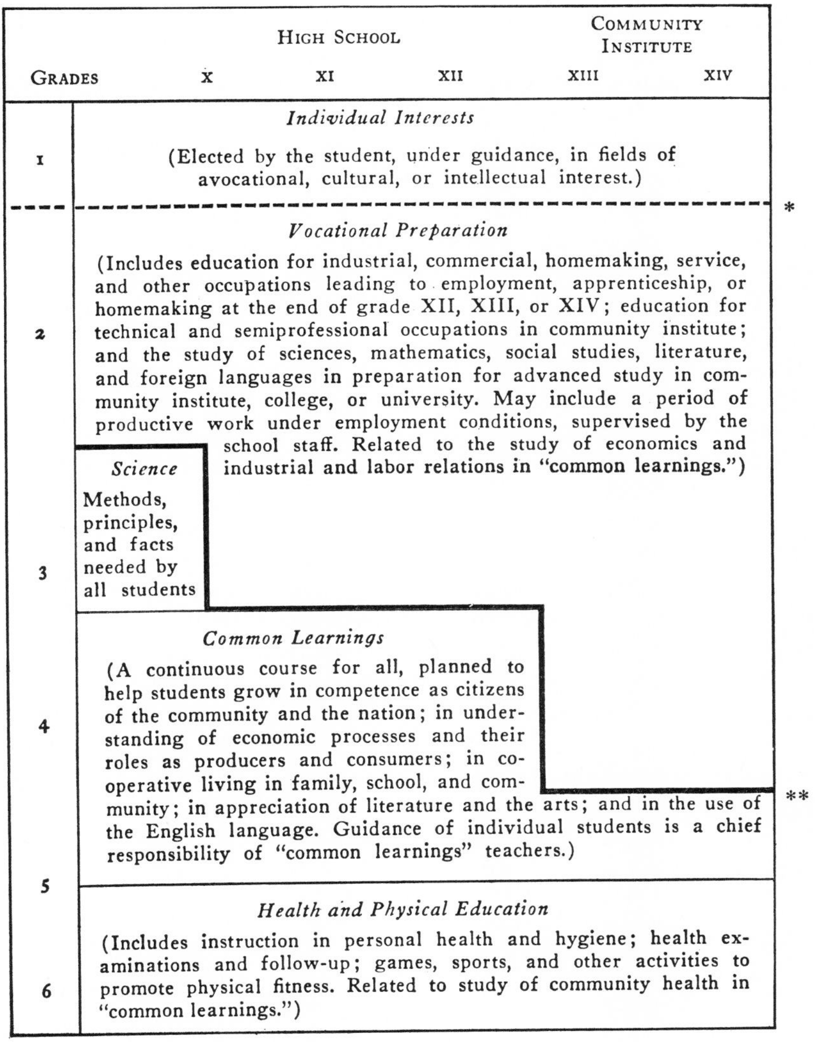

Grades	High School: X	XI	XII	Community Institute: XIII	XIV

Hours (1) — *Individual Interests*

(Elected by the student, under guidance, in fields of avocational, cultural, or intellectual interest.)

\- *

Hours (2–3) — *Vocational Preparation*

(Includes education for industrial, commercial, homemaking, service, and other occupations leading to employment, apprenticeship, or homemaking at the end of grade XII, XIII, or XIV; education for technical and semiprofessional occupations in community institute; and the study of sciences, mathematics, social studies, literature, and foreign languages in preparation for advanced study in community institute, college, or university. May include a period of productive work under employment conditions, supervised by the school staff. Related to the study of economics and industrial and labor relations in "common learnings.")

Science

Methods, principles, and facts needed by all students

Hours (3–5) — *Common Learnings*

(A continuous course for all, planned to help students grow in competence as citizens of the community and the nation; in understanding of economic processes and their roles as producers and consumers; in cooperative living in family, school, and community; in appreciation of literature and the arts; and in the use of the English language. Guidance of individual students is a chief responsibility of "common learnings" teachers.) **

Hours (5–6) — *Health and Physical Education*

(Includes instruction in personal health and hygiene; health examinations and follow-up; games, sports, and other activities to promote physical fitness. Related to study of community health in "common learnings.")

* Broken line indicates flexibility of scheduling.

** Heavy line marks the division between differential studies (above) and common studies (below).

From Educational Policies Commission, National Education Association, *Education for All American Youth* (Washington: The Association, 1944), p. 244.

Core plans suggested and found in junior high schools

The curriculum plan which the authors believe to be educationally sound for the junior high school would vary from the "common curriculum for all" advocated by the Educational Policies Commission in one minor respect. From the seventh through the ninth grades one period each day should be set aside for physical activities and student activities. The major part of the day should be devoted to core. Except for the specific time to be given to health and physical activities, the differentiated part of the curriculum should be devoted to student activities. Such a program is shown in Table 21.

This modified plan recognizes the possible advantage of ease in administering a differentiated student club and activities program in which several core classes could be merged at a given time to offer greater activities diversification. The same advantage holds for the conduct of intramural sports in the health and physical activities period.

Many variations in the core program at the junior high school level are to be found in practice, from the inclusive program suggested in our modification of the total "common learnings program" proposed by the Educational Policies Commission to programs that can only charitably be labeled core.

In a small community junior-senior high school the junior high school was partially organized to take advantage of the total secondary school staff and to merge the pupils for band and other student activities — see Table 22.

A city which has an extensive core program in the junior high school varies the time requirement for core from the seventh grade through the ninth. The distribution of common learnings or core over the three years in relation to additional required and elective courses may be seen in Table 23. There are some unique features of the Winston-Salem curriculum plan which this table does not reveal. In the "Curriculum Bulletin" from which the table was constructed certain premises that give meaning to the curriculum plan are discussed:

TABLE 21

Junior High School Core Curriculum, Seventh Through Ninth Grades

Periods	Monday	Tuesday	Wednesday	Thursday	Friday
2½	Core	Core	Core	Core	Core
1	Health and Physical Activities	Student Activities	Health and Physical Activities	Student Activities	Health and Physical Activities
1	Lunch	Lunch	Lunch	Lunch	Lunch
2½	Core	Core	Core	Core	Core

TABLE 22

Schedule of Small Junior High School, Seventh Through Ninth Grades

Time	Five-Day Schedule
8:45 to 9:25	Band practice, homeroom, and certain special activities (band and certain activities included senior high school students)
9:30 to 10:25	Individual interest studies under guidance of regular junior high school teachers and senior high vocational teachers
10:30 to 12:10	Core
12:15 to 12:55	Lunch
1:00 to 1:55	Individual activities: clubs, intramurals; under supervision of all secondary school teachers
2:00 to 3:55	Core

The first of these is that there are certain learning experiences which every eleven-, twelve-, and thirteen-year old needs. These learning experiences are built around the development of competencies in oral and written communication, the building of worthwhile concepts concerning the society in which one must live, and the development of a realistic and satisfactory self understanding. These basic educational experiences are found in the common learnings class.

Secondly, each junior high school student needs training and experience in using the problem-solving approach. This is important . . . because the young

TABLE 23

Junior High School Curriculum Schedule, Winston-Salem, N.C., 1960

Grade	Common Learnings (Core)	Required	Electives
7th	Hours = 4	Hours = 2	Hours = 0
8th	Hours = 3	Hours = 2	Hours = 1
9th	Hours = 2	Hours = 2	Hours = 2

Adapted from data found in *The Junior High School in the Winston-Salem (North Carolina) City Schools,* A Curriculum Bulletin, Publication 400-1 (Winston-Salem, N.C.: Winston-Salem–Forsyth County Schools, September, 1959), pp. 11-14.

> person today experiences a multitude of problem situations in his daily activities. The degree of success and happiness which he achieves is directly dependent upon the skill he employs in identifying and analyzing these problems, in reaching adequate conclusions based upon the available evidence and in being able to act intelligently on the basis of the conclusions reached.
>
> Third, junior high school youth ought to have the opportunity to study in some detail many broad fields of knowledge. This opportunity is provided through special interest courses. The special interest courses are of two types: (1) basic mathematics, science, and language courses, and (2) exploratory courses. The basic special interest courses meet each day and are so arranged as to allow the student to progress as rapidly as his interest, aptitude, and achievement will allow. . . . The exploratory courses are also designed to provide for the junior high school student an introduction to many broad fields of knowledge. To achieve this aim the exploratory courses are planned to meet on alternating days.[16]

It should be noted that the distinction between required and elective courses is not too clear since there must be electives chosen from the two types of "special interest" courses. Careful safeguards have been set up in balancing electives between the two types to avoid specialization and to insure proper exploration of several fields of knowledge.

Another junior high school core curriculum plan which places even greater stress on exploratory courses is presented in Table 24. It is the most structured of the plans thus far discussed. However, the joint commissions responsible for the chart point out that the average school is not able to start immediately with the following concept of core, which they accept, namely:

TABLE 24

Suggested Time Allotment for Junior High School Program by Grades

<table>
<tr><th>Grade</th><th>60 Min.</th><th>60 Min.</th><th>60 Min.</th><th>40 Min.</th><th>60 Min.</th><th>60 Min.</th><th>60 Min.</th></tr>
<tr><td>7</td><td colspan="3">Core</td><td rowspan="3">L
U
N
C
H</td><td>Explor-
atory</td><td>Math</td><td>Physical
Education</td></tr>
<tr><td>8</td><td colspan="2">Core</td><td>Explor-
atory</td><td>Explor-
atory</td><td>Math</td><td>Physical
Education</td></tr>
<tr><td>9</td><td colspan="2">Core</td><td>Explor-
atory</td><td>Elective</td><td>Math
Elective</td><td>Physical
Education</td></tr>
</table>

Adapted from *The Junior High School Program* (Atlanta, Ga.: Southern Association of Colleges and Secondary Schools, 1958), Fig. 2, p. 82.

[16] *The Junior High School in the Winston-Salem (North Carolina) City Schools,* A Curriculum Bulletin, Publication 400-1 (Winston-Salem, N.C.: Winston-Salem–Forsyth County Schools, September, 1959), pp. 11-12.

TABLE 25

Curriculum Program of the Bryant Junior High School, Flint, Michigan, 1962

Period	1	2	3	4	5[a]	6[a]	7
7	Common Learnings.			L U N C H	Math	P.E. / Fine Arts	Ind. Arts or Home Ec.
8	Common Learnings		Math		Science	P.E. / Fine Arts	Ind. Arts or Home Ec.
9	English	Social Studies	Math		P.E. / Science	Elect one Ind. Arts Home Ec. Science	Elect one Music Art Speech Latin French

This chart indicates the nature, not the order, of the courses as they appear in the actual program schedule.

[a] Physical education alternates with fine arts in seventh and eighth grades and with science in the ninth grade.

> The third approach to determining the content in the core is through basing the curriculum upon common problems, needs, concerns and interests of early adolescents and upon the demands, pressures, and forces of society which impinge upon the daily living of these young people.[17]

To organize a core curriculum to embrace the limited core concept stated above the schedule shown in Table 24 is recommended. A junior high school in Flint, Michigan, utilizes the plan given in Table 25.

Why core is popular in the junior high school

There are at least four major reasons why core is popular in the junior high school. First, since most elementary school pupils are accustomed to a self-contained classroom and one teacher, it is considered in the nature of a traumatic experience to shift them suddenly to a situation of many confusing bells, classrooms, and strange teachers. This factor was recognized long be-

[17] *The Junior High School Program* (Atlanta, Ga.: Southern Association of Colleges and Secondary Schools, 1958), p. 42.

fore the fact of individual differences was confirmed by research studies. Some supporters of this view have maintained that only in the ninth grade should a cautious departmentalized program be introduced. Others have favored partial departmentalization beginning in the eighth grade. Few curriculum authorities look with favor on departmentalization at the seventh grade. Many schools have departmentalized seventh grades mostly because of outside pressures rather than firm conviction.

Second, there is a conviction that junior high pupils are not sufficiently mature for departmentalized instruction. This point of view found most radical support in the position of the Educational Policies Commission, which opposed any break from the self-contained classroom idea. The Commission contended that through the ninth grade needs and interests are so alike that what adjustments have to be made can be cared for in the classroom under a common curriculum for all. It is this conviction on the part of educators that gives greatest validity to the arguments in favor of little, if any, differentiation in the over-all curriculum, at least in the early years of the junior high school.

Third, a general revolt has arisen against aping the senior high school in its highly departmentalized curriculum practices. In part this may be influenced by the previous two reasons discussed. There are those who think early teenagers are too immature physically to participate in strenuous competitive athletics and too immature socially to imitate the sophisticated behavior of the senior high school students.

Giving strength to the reasons thus far suggested against early and rash departmentalization in junior high school is the freedom of this institution from the bugaboo of college entrance requirements that has paralyzed sound curriculum and pedagogical practices in the senior high school. The tendency to determine college entrance on the basis of twelve units instead of sixteen has freed the junior high school to plan its own curriculum without too much concern for college admission requirements. This feeling of release from college and university domination no doubt has much to do with the rapid development of core at the junior high school level.

Unfortunately, many schools are still too much influenced by what they think are the separate course demands of colleges. They overlook the findings of the Eight Year Study and other studies, which show quite clearly that personal-social qualities determine college success far better than any pattern of subjects required for admission to college. In fact, the persistent tendency of colleges and universities to insist on a battery of specific courses as entrance requirements has no justification in research evidence.

Widespread acceptance of core

During the past two decades the core idea has found wide acceptance, as evidenced in at least three respects: (1) the introduction of core into the schools, (2) the increased attention to core in educational writings, and (3) the large place now given to core in institutions devoted to teacher preparation.

Use. The introduction of core, particularly at the junior high school level, has been rapid. Two extensive studies of block-time and core practices in the public schools were reported by Grace S. Wright of the Office of Education, in 1950 and 1958.[18] In 1958 Wright found that 31.4 per cent of the separately organized junior high schools used block-time classes compared with 15.8 per cent reported in 1950. These same studies showed that, of the so-called core courses reported in 1950, 91.9 per cent represented combinations of English and social studies, or these in combination with other subjects, with some correlation attempted. In the remaining 8.1 per cent of schools fusion and a smaller percentage of problem-centered classes were found. In other words, a large percentage of classes claiming to be core represented little more than regular subjects taught in a multiple-period setting.

However, Wright's 1958 study indicated that a tremendous change had taken place. Not only had block-time classes doubled in the junior high schools, but now 68 per cent reported the use of separate subjects, or these subjects in some form of correlation — approximately 84 per cent attempted some correlation. Twenty per cent of the block-time classes had moved to the use of fusion, with the unit method, while 12 per cent had moved to the experience-problem-centered type of instruction, in which the basis of the courses had become the personal and social problems of pupils in a democratic society. The latter type of curriculum organization approaches the concept of good core class practice held by the advocates of the core curriculum.

A large number of state-wide and regional studies have been made since 1950 of curriculum practices in secondary schools. Most of the more recent ones report a greater percentage of block-time class usage, fusion, and core practices in both junior and senior high schools. Of course, for reasons previously given, the major development of core teaching is found in the junior high school.[19]

Emphasis upon core in educational writings. An important index of the interest in any area of education is the prominence given it in the profes-

[18] Grace S. Wright, *Core Curriculum in Public High Schools,* U.S. Office of Education Bulletin No. 5 (Washington: Government Printing Office, 1950), and Grace S. Wright, *Block-Time Classes and the Core Program in the Junior High School,* U.S. Office of Education Bulletin No. 6 (Washington: Government Printing Office, 1958).

[19] For a summary of all but two state-wide studies reported as of January, 1962, see Nelson L. Bossing, "What Are Trends in Providing for Block-Time Classes in Today's Curriculum?" *The Bulletin of the National Association of Secondary-School Principals,* 43:32-37, April, 1959.

sional literature. By 1953 the number of articles appearing in the pro and con discussion of core had reached sufficient volume to justify a separate classification, "Core Program," under the general heading "Curriculum" in *The Educational Index* for that year. From then up to June, 1961, a total of ninety-two articles had been listed in the *Index.* Probably there were as many, if not more, articles on core in publications of less than national circulation.

Of greater significance is the expanding space given to core in books on secondary education. Not a book on general or secondary school curriculum has been published within the past ten years that has not given extended consideration to core. The more recent the publication, the greater the space devoted to core as an important aspect of the present-day curriculum. A number of books have concentrated exclusively on core. The same can be said for books on the junior high school. The two general texts on the junior high school written in the decade 1940-1950 devoted respectively two and three pages to core. Of the major books on the junior high school written since 1950, all give it at least one full chapter and a very new one has given it five chapters. In all these recent books a discussion of core also appears on many pages in other chapters.

Teacher education in core. The ultimate test of the popularity of core is the recognition given to the preparation of core teachers. In a doctoral study completed in 1959, 1100 institutions of learning preparing four- to five-year secondary school teachers were asked whether they were definitely preparing teachers to teach core. Of the 346 replying in the affirmative, 242 responded to an extended questionnaire designed to determine the extent of core teacher preparation in the United States.[20]

When it is realized that in 1950 probably not over a dozen institutions were seriously engaged in the preparation of core teachers, the expansion of such preparation to one-third of all institutions preparing four- to five-year secondary school teachers in 1958 is indeed phenomenal. It is a well-known characteristic of teacher education institutions that they are slow to move into new areas of teacher preparation until assured that the teachers so educated will find positions.

Demand for core teachers. In the study just mentioned, replies to the question "Why did your institution begin the preparation of core teachers?" are significant. There was almost unanimous agreement that it was begun in response to insistent demand for trained core teachers. At a recent state teachers convention where one of the writers was speaking on core, a period

[20] H. Arnold Holtz, "A Study of the Preparation of Core Teachers," Ph.D. thesis, College of Education, University of Minnesota, 1959. See also Paul Lichtman, "Preparation of Core Teachers in Institutions of Higher Learning," *Core Teacher* (Temple University), 12:1-2, January, 1962.

following the address was opened for audience questions. In quick succession an administrator and a teacher asked, "If I begin a core program in my school, what assurance can you give me that I can secure trained teachers?" and "If I prepare to teach core, what assurance can you give me that I can get a position teaching core?" The chairman of the session, who was from an institution well known for its preparation of core teachers, replied: "I am sorry to say that this past year we had 118 calls for core teachers and only a limited number of core teachers available." The speaker then reported that in his institution approximately the same number of calls for core-trained teachers had been received, with an inadequate supply of prepared teachers available. The major problem at the moment is to get the shortage of core teachers to the attention of those beginning their preparation as secondary school teachers. The current impossibility of meeting the demand for prepared core teachers is a nationwide concern.

6. What evidence is there of the value of core?

It may be argued that the discussion of the previous section is in fact evidence of the value of core. Unless school leaders were convinced that core has value, its use would not have become so widespread as it has over the past dozen years, writers in education would not have given it the increasing attention it has received, teacher training institutions would scarcely have focused so much attention upon the preparation of core teachers, and there would be no such demand for core teachers as is now in evidence. More important are the specific evidences of core's educational worth.

Indirect evidence

The Eight-Year Curriculum Study. Core is generally recognized as the fullest expression of the progressive education idea or movement that began to gather momentum in the late 1920's and the 1930's. The now famous Progressive Education Association study of the value of divergent organizational patterns of the curriculum provided significant support for the concepts of learning and curriculum structure now basic to the core idea. In the early 1930's under the auspices of the Progressive Education Association thirty schools were selected to determine what value, if any, high school curriculums oriented toward progressive education might have for the graduates of these schools in their future success in college. Over three hundred outstanding colleges and universities agreed to accept graduates of these high schools on the recommendation of the respective faculties, instead of requiring them to pass an entrance examination or a prescribed set of high school courses. Each school was free to deviate from the traditional curriculum pattern to whatever extent the faculty deemed necessary to satisfy the demands of its ideas of progressive education.

The plan called for a comparative evaluation of the success of students in college from the innovating schools and of similar students from traditional schools who met the standard entrance requirement. The evaluation was made in terms of scholastic success, participation in activities, and broad cultural interests evidenced while in college.

A study was first undertaken of the 1475 matched pairs from the thirty schools and their comparison group. The students from the thirty schools excelled slightly in academic achievement and were noticeably better in their participation in student affairs and in their broad cultural interests. Since some of the thirty schools deviated very little and others very radically from the traditional curriculum pattern, it was decided to compare graduates from the six schools in which the least change had taken place with graduates of the six schools having the most deviation from conventional college preparatory programs.

The results of this investigation have been reported thus:

> The graduates of the most experimental schools were strikingly more successful than their matchees. Differences in their favor were much greater than the differences between the total Thirty Schools and their comparison group. Conversely, there were no large and consistent differences between the least experimental graduates and their comparison group. For these students the differences were smaller and less consistent than for the total Thirty Schools and their comparison group.[21]

Another comment on the results of the study of the six schools at either end of the continuum follows:

> There were 361 students from the least conventional six schools, and 417 from the most conventional schools. It turns out that the students from the least conventional schools excelled their controls by a score that may roughly be expressed as 27 to 7; while the students from the most conventional schools of the Thirty Schools were excelled by their control group by a score that may roughly be expressed as 14 to 16.[22]

Further, the facts of this study were trenchantly commented upon by the College Follow-up Staff:

> If the proof of the pudding lies in these groups, and a good part of it does, then it follows that the colleges got from these most experimental schools a

[21] Dean Chamberlin *et al., Did They Succeed in College?* (New York: Harper & Brothers, 1942), p. 209.

[22] "Report by Herbert E. Hawkes, Dean, Columbia College, Meeting of the Association of American Colleges, Philadelphia — January 10, 1940," quoted in Wilford M. Aikin, *The Story of the Eight-Year Study* (New York: Harper & Brothers, 1942), p. 150.

higher proportion of sound, effective college material than they did from the more conventional schools in similar environments. If colleges want students of sound scholarship with vital interests, students who have developed effective and objective habits of thinking, and who yet maintain a healthy orientation toward their fellows, then they will encourage the already obvious trend away from restrictions which tend to inhibit departures or deviations from the conventional curriculum patterns.[23]

At the risk of repetition, it needs to be emphasized that the curriculum patterns and methods employed in the six schools deviating most from conventional curriculum patterns utilized concepts that are basic in the core curriculum idea.

Collective report of research specialists. Another indirect source of evidence on the core approach is to be found in a collective study of all pertinent research data on the comparative effectiveness of deviations in curriculum and methods in the period immediately before 1940.[24] Again, the type of experimental projects studied represented deviational practices in harmony with the philosophy of core. This study, too, utilized the services of some of the outstanding educational research authorities. Its published findings represent the most exhaustive compilation and evaluation of experimental data with respect to the effectiveness of modern education yet made.

The results of this careful research revealed that (1) in the area of academic facts and skills the schools that developed their curriculums and methods in the direction of more modern educational philosophy and psychology of learning generally had a slightly better record than the conventional schools with which they were compared, (2) in the development of problem-solving skills the modern schools were much superior to the conventional schools, and (3) the experimental programs were much more effective in the development of social ideas and skills.

Direct evidence

Evidence principally of academic and related achievement. That the indirect evidence of the Eight-Year Study discussed above is pertinent in the evaluation of core success is clearly shown in this reference by Tyler, one of those responsible for the appraisal of the results of the study, to those of the thirty experimental schools organized on a core curriculum basis:

[23] Chamberlin, *op. cit.,* pp. 174-175. Those interested in further information about this significant study should read these additional books: H. H. Giles, S. P. McCutchen, and A. N. Zechiel, *Exploring the Curriculum* (New York: Harper & Brothers, 1942); Eugene R. Smith and Ralph W. Tyler, *Appraising and Recording Student Progress* (New York: Harper & Brothers, 1942); *Thirty Schools Tell Their Story* (New York: Harper & Brothers, 1942).

[24] J. Paul Leonard and Alvin Eurich (eds.), *An Evaluation of Modern Education* (New York: Appleton-Century-Crofts, Inc., 1942).

> The students in these core programs made somewhat greater progress, on the average, than matched students in subject courses in ability to interpret data, to apply principles in science and social studies, and to interpret literature; in breadth and maturity of reading interests; and in democratic attitudes. There were no significant differences in reading rate and comprehension, in computational skills, and in the mechanics of English expression. In college, the graduates of the core programs made somewhat better academic records, participated more, on the average, in extracurricular activities and attained a larger proportion of leadership positions.[25]

Numerous studies of the effectiveness of core in academic achievement have been made. Many of them have tried to discover, also, how well core has developed students in the broader values of education particularly stressed by the proponents of core: problem-solving skills, the ability to apply as well as acquire knowledge, social skills, improved behavior, and broad cultural interests.

An early study that may typify this approach to an evaluation of core has been reported by Cyphert in an extended document and by Kelley and Beatty briefly.[26] Based on the data of the Iowa Every-Pupil Achievement Tests of Basic Skills, "The results show that [in]competency in the basic skills . . . the core program exceeded that of the control group in reading and language skills and in total net gain. The average gain in all areas by the core group was equal to or exceeded the national norms." The core group was above average in problem-solving skills and was "slightly better adjusted to their environment than is the general population of comparable age." Culturally, the core students average over one book per student voluntarily withdrawn from the school library per week. "This is approximately 80 per cent above the high school circulation and is without the aid of stringent book report requirements." An important index of interest and social development, frequently noted in other studies, is found in the improvement of class attendance, which rose from 89 to 96 per cent after the inauguration of the core curriculum; student morale also improved, as indicated by a sharp decrease in disciplinary offenses by 67 per cent after core was instituted, "despite a 20 per cent growth in class size"; likewise there was a marked decrease in dropouts and truancy.

Another unique junior high school using the basic concepts of core in its common learnings program found much the same results as appeared in the Penn experiment, reported above. Citizenship ratings in school rose markedly,

[25] Ralph W. Tyler, "The Core Curriculum," *National Education Association Journal,* 42:564, December, 1953.

[26] Frederick R. Cyphert, *A Survey of the Core Curriculum Program of Penn Junior High School,* Penn Township School District, Pittsburgh, Penna., September, 1954 (mimeographed); Arthur C. Kelley and Robert E. Beatty, "Here's Proof That Core Program Students Learn Basic Skills," *The School Executive,* 72:54-55, February, 1953.

attendance improved, truancy almost disappeared, library usage increased 70 per cent, and Malcolm Keck, the principal, reported that "Standardized tests indicate that when students leave Folwell, they are, on the average, accelerated about one year in achievement in fundamental skills."[27]

On the question of basic achievement the many evaluative studies reported leave little room to doubt the equal and even superior effectiveness of core over conventional curriculum patterns. In the areas of citizenship, wider cultural interests, and social participation, those studies that have given attention to these educational products, particularly emphasized in the philosophy of core, make it clear that the more nearly the curriculum approaches the reality of the core idea the greater the effectiveness of core is shown to be over recognized conventional curriculums.[28]

Evidence of special research — library usage. A comparative study of the use of the library by students of a number of core and subject-centered schools by Cyphert has important implications for library usage and the educational advantages obtaining in core schools.[29] Cyphert points out that "Core schools are more likely than subject-centered schools to have a library period as part of a student's regularly assigned schedule, and consequently give one-third more library lessons yearly." He notes additional points in the comparison of core schools with non-core schools:

1. The librarian generally assumes her instructional responsibility is limited to book classification, the card catalogue, and general reference books. The core teacher, on the other hand, assumes it is her responsibility to develop critical thinking skills through helping students compare the validity of conflicting sources, determine assumptions underlying an author's thesis, and draw valid conclusions from a variety of data, while traditionally oriented teachers tend to be satisfied with subject knowledge mastery.

[27] Malcolm B. Keck, "We Get to Know Joe," *National Education Association Journal,* 41:562-563, December, 1952.

[28] Studies purported to be evaluative of core vary greatly in merit. A few of the better ones that indicate general comparative tendencies are listed: R. F. Gale, "Comparative Study of the College Experiences of Graduates of Core and of the Conventional Curricula," *Journal of Experimental Education,* 27:283-296, June, 1959; John M. Mickelson, "What Does Research Say About the Effectiveness of the Core Curriculum?" *The School Review,* 65:144-160, Summer, 1957; L. A. Van Dyke, "How Effective Is the Core Curriculum in the Junior High School?" *The Bulletin of the National Association of Secondary-School Principals,* 38:165-172, April, 1954; B. Swartz, "Investigation of the Effects of a Seventh and Eighth Grade Core Program," *Journal of Educational Research,* 53:149-152, December, 1959; M. Willis and H. L. Coon, *Learning in a Core-Centered Program,* Fifteenth Yearbook of the John Dewey Society (New York: Harper & Brothers, 1961), pp. 164-188; Grace S. Wright, *The Core Program: Abstracts of Unpublished Research, 1946-1955,* U.S. Office of Education Circular No. 485 (Washington: Government Printing Office, June, 1956); Grace S. Wright, *The Core Program: Unpublished Research, 1956-1962,* U.S. Office of Education Circular No. 713 (Washington: Government Printing Office, 1963).

[29] Frederick R. Cyphert, "How Core Affects the Junior High Library," *Library Journal,* 84:7-9, February 15, 1959.

2. Library instruction in core schools is more likely to be taught functionally as needed rather than to grow out of handbooks or some "arbitrary preconceived sequence."

3. "The internal circulation of core libraries is half again as large as that of non-core schools." Cyphert suggests that libraries built for core schools should be twice as large as those in conventional schools.

4. Core and non-core students appear to have different purposes in school library visits. "Non-core visits have as their primary motivation the desire to select a book for pleasure reading outside of the library. Core students, on the other hand, come to the library chiefly for investigative or research purposes."

5. "Core teachers tend to develop classroom materials collections which are more extensive in both size and use than is typical of subject teachers." The usual types of books in the core classroom collection are (a) general reference and textbooks, (b) special reference books for limited periods on a particular problem, and (c) fiction and non-fiction books at various levels of reading skill, for free reading periods.

6. Both types of schools usually provide specific collections of books for slow readers, "but only core schools commonly have similar special collections for superior readers."

7. The tendency is for more teachers in departmental schools to give specific library reading assignments to their students than is true of core teachers. However, the trend is away from specific library assignments by all teachers.

8. "Core teachers are more than twice as likely to ask librarians to visit their classrooms for planning with students than are their traditional colleagues."[30]

Evidence of special research — self-acceptance concepts. There has been a growing awareness of the importance of developing certain personality traits in youth. A recent study at the junior high school level appears to have unusual pertinence for the curriculum. As Shannon, the author of this study, points out, "An individual's perceptions of self and others have been shown to determine, to a considerable extent, what he does and what he believes." Shannon then goes on to indicate more specifically how his study has vital importance for education:

> Persons who accept themselves as worth-while individuals and who perceive others in their peer group as being equally self-accepting have been found to be better leaders, more successful in academic pursuits, more responsible, and with fewer physical complaints. Evidence suggests that self-accepting persons are better able to make the kinds of contributions that are necessary for individuals to make in our society. These persons are best equipped for successful human relations, an essential competency for effective citizenship.

[30] See also, for further data, Fay J. Buttle and June Berry, "Core Curriculum and the Library," *The High School Journal,* 41:9-13, October, 1957.

. . . it becomes evident that research is needed which identifies those school experiences which contribute to the development of self-accepting persons. What is the nature of the school experience that effectively creates a situation where humans will develop positive concepts of themselves and others?

An attempt to provide part of the answer to this question was made in the research herein reported.[31]

Shannon selected junior high schools which utilized three types of curriculum organizations: (1) "a departmentalized structure," (2) "block-departmental pattern," and (3) "the self contained classroom design." In order to obtain self-concept information "a self rating device that measures the self-concept, self-acceptance, and concept of the ideal self" was used along with another that "provides a person's perceptions of peers in these categories." The findings of this study can be most succinctly stated in quotations from the report:

. . . There appears to be a significant relationship between the curriculum organization which junior high-school students experience and the self–others perceptions of those students.

The findings of this research cannot be construed as definitive evidence. However, at the junior high-school level the self-contained classroom appears to be more productive of persons who accept themselves and perceive others to be self-accepting persons than are either the departmental or block-departmental organizations. The departmental design seems to be less successful than either the block-departmental plan or the self-contained classroom types of curriculum organization in producing junior high-school students who possess perceptual qualities.[32]

SELECTED BIBLIOGRAPHY

Adolescence. Forty-Third Yearbook of the National Society for the Study of Education, Part I. Chicago: The Society (distributed by the University of Chicago Press), 1944.

Alberty, Harold. *Reorganizing the High School Curriculum.* New York: The Macmillan Company, rev. ed., 1953. Part II.

Alexander, William M., and J. Galen Saylor. *Modern Secondary Education.* New York: Holt, Rinehart and Winston, 1959. Chaps. 11 and 12.

American Association of School Administrators, National Education Association. *American School Curriculum.* Thirty-First Yearbook. Washington: The Association, 1953. Chap. III.

[31] Robert L. Shannon, "Student Self-Acceptance and Curriculum Organization in the Junior High School." Reprinted by permission from *The Bulletin of the National Association of Secondary-School Principals,* November, 1960. Copyright: Washington, D.C. Pp. 35-38. (Summary of an unpublished doctoral study.)

[32] *Ibid.,* pp. 36-37, 38.

Anderson, Vernon E. *Principles and Procedures of Curriculum Improvement.* New York: The Ronald Press Company, 1956. Part IV.

Association for Supervision and Curriculum Development, National Education Association. *Growing Up in an Anxious Age.* 1952 Yearbook. Washington: The Association, 1952.

———. *Perceiving, Behaving, Becoming.* 1962 Yearbook. Washington: The Association, 1962.

———. *Preparation of Core Teachers for Secondary Schools.* Washington: The Association, 1955.

———. *The Self-Contained Classroom.* Washington: The Association, 1960.

Benjamin, Harold. *The Saber-Tooth Curriculum.* New York: McGraw-Hill Book Co., Inc., paperback edition, 1959. (Originally published in 1939 under the author's pseudonym, "Abner Peddiwell.")

Bernard, Harold W. *Adolescent Development in American Culture.* New York: World Book Company, 1957.

Birkmaier, Emma M. "Core Curriculum: A Promising Pattern for the Education of Adolescents," *The School Review,* 63:330-333, September, 1955.

Blair, Arthur W., and William H. Burton. *Growth and Development of the Preadolescent.* New York: Appleton-Century-Crofts, Inc., 1951.

Bossing, Nelson L. "Core Idea in the Junior High School," *High School Journal,* 43:126-132, January, 1960.

———. *Principles of Secondary Education.* Englewood Cliffs, N.J.: Prentice-Hall, Inc., rev. ed., 1955. Chaps. XII-XIII.

———. "What Are Trends in Providing for Block-Time Classes in Today's Curriculum?" *The Bulletin of the National Association of Secondary-School Principals,* 43:32-37, April, 1959.

———. "What Is Core?" *The School Review,* 63:206-213, April, 1955.

Chamberlin, Dean, *et al. Did They Succeed in College?* New York: Harper & Brothers, 1942.

Cole, Luella. *Psychology of Adolescence.* New York: Rinehart & Co., 5th ed., 1959.

Coleman, James S., and others. *The Adolescent Society; The Social Life of the Teenager and Its Impact on Education.* New York: Free Press of Glencoe, Inc., 1961.

Core Program, The (Film Strip). Bulletin No. 275. Indianapolis: Department of Public Instruction, State of Indiana, 1962.

Cramer, Roscoe V. "Common Learnings Program in the Junior High School," *The Bulletin of the National Association of Secondary-School Principals,* 35:-158-166, April, 1951.

Douglass, Harl R., and others. *The High School Curriculum.* New York: The Ronald Press Company, rev. ed., 1956. Chap. 14.

Educational Policies Commission, National Education Association. *Education for All American Youth: A Further Look.* Washington: The Association, rev. ed., 1952. Chaps. 7 and 8.

Faunce, Roland C., and Nelson L. Bossing. *Developing the Core Curriculum.* Englewood Cliffs, N.J.: Prentice-Hall, Inc., 1958.

———, and Morrel J. Clute. *Teaching and Learning in the Junior High School.* San Francisco: Wadsworth Publishing Company, 1961. Chaps. 2-8.

Gesell, Arnold L., and others. *Youth: The Years from Ten to Sixteen.* New York: Harper & Brothers, 1956.

Gruhn, William T., and Harl R. Douglass. *The Modern Junior High School.* New York: The Ronald Press Company, rev. ed., 1956. Chap. 5.

Hock, Louise E., and Thomas J. Hill. *The General Education Class in the Secondary School.* New York: Holt, Rinehart & Winston, Inc., 1960.

Koos, Leonard V. *Junior High School Trends.* New York: Harper & Brothers, 1955. Chaps. 4 and 5.

Lawler, Marcella R. *Characteristics of a Core Program* (Film). New York: Bureau of Publications, Teachers College, Columbia University, 1960.

Leonard, J. Paul. *Developing the Secondary School Curriculum.* New York: Rinehart & Co., rev. ed., 1953. Chap. 14.

Lurry, Lucile L., and Elsie Alberty. *Developing a High School Core Program.* New York: The Macmillan Company, 1957.

Merry, Frieda K., and Ralph V. Merry. *The First Two Decades of Life.* New York: Harper & Brothers, 2nd ed., 1958.

Noar, Gertrude. *Freedom to Live and Learn.* Philadelphia: Franklin Publishing and Supply Company, 1948.

———. *The Junior High School, Today and Tomorrow.* Englewood Cliffs, N.J.: Prentice-Hall, Inc., rev. ed., 1961. Chap. 9.

Pierce, Paul R. *Developing a High-School Curriculum.* New York: American Book Company, 1942.

Riccio, Anthony C. "Group Guidance: A Step Toward the Core," *Educational Administration and Supervision,* 40:1-9, January, 1958.

Romine, Stephen A. *Building the High School Curriculum.* New York: The Ronald Press Company, 1954. Chap. 12.

Shannon, Robert L. "Student Self-Acceptance and Curriculum Organization in the Junior High School," *The Bulletin of the National Association of Secondary-School Principals,* 44:35-38, November, 1960.

Schneiders, A. A. *Personality Development and Adjustment in Adolescence.* Milwaukee: Bruce Publishing Company, 1960.

Segel, David. *Frustration in Adolescent Youth: Its Development and Implications for the School Program,* U.S. Office of Education Bulletin No. 1. Washington: Government Printing Office, 1951.

Spivak, Monroe L. "The Junior High: Departmentalized or Self-Contained?" *Phi Delta Kappan,* 38:134-135, January, 1957.

Toops, Myrtle D. *A Core Class Tells Its Story* (Film Strip). Muncie, Ind.: Ball State Teachers College Library, 1958.

Van Dyke, Lauren A. "How Effective Is the Core Curriculum in the Junior High School?" *The Bulletin of the National Association of Secondary-School Principals,* 38:165-172, April, 1954.

Van Til, William, Gordon F. Vars, and John J. Lounsbury. *Modern Education for the Junior High School Years.* Indianapolis: The Bobbs-Merrill Company, Inc., 1961. Chaps. 5, 9-13.

Willis, M., and H. L. Coon. *Learning in a Core-Centered Program,* Fifteenth Yearbook of the John Dewey Society. New York: Harper & Brothers, 1961. Pp. 164-168.

Wright, Grace S. *Core Curriculum Development: Problems and Practices.* U.S. Office of Education Bulletin No. 5. Washington: Government Printing Office, 1952.

———. *Core Curriculums in Public High Schools: An Inquiry into Practices, 1949.* U.S. Office of Education Bulletin No. 5. Washington: Government Printing Office, 1950.

———. *The Core Program: Abstracts of Unpublished Research, 1946-1955.* U.S. Office of Education Circular No. 485. Washington: Government Printing Office, June, 1956.

———. *The Core Program: Unpublished Research, 1956-1962.* U.S. Office of Education Circular No. 713. Washington: Government Printing Office, 1963.

———, and Edith S. Greer. *The Junior High School, A Survey of Grades 7-8-9 in Junior-Senior High Schools, 1959-1960.* U.S. Office of Education Bulletin No. 32. Washington: Government Printing Office, 1963. Pp. 21-24.

Zapf, Rosalind M. *A Core Curriculum in Action* (Film Strip). Detroit: College of Education, Wayne State University, 1948.

———. *Democratic Processes in the Secondary Classroom.* Englewood Cliffs, N.J.: Prentice-Hall, Inc., 1959.

8

The Personal Interest Program

One of the characteristics of early adolescence is the conscious movement away from what the youngster considers the limitations imposed by his parental sphere of influence. A concomitant characteristic is interest in the exploration of self and concern about the more immediate world environment. This intense preoccupation with "self" and "self-interests" may be understood as a direct response to acute inner growth activity, which demands much energy and attention. Certainly these characteristics call for more than passing interest from those who attempt to design and implement effective learning programs for early youth.

The specific concern of this chapter is the mutuality of focus of the early adolescent self-interest and the personal interest program offered by the school. The junior high school represents possibly the most potent influence in the young person's environment. It is under obligation to guide him in the selection of constructive goal-fulfilling pursuits by formulating and nurturing personal interest opportunities which are compatible with his inclination and well-being.

1. How have personal interest programs evolved?

Jess W. Miley, State Superintendent of Public Instruction, Topeka, Kansas, reported that many of the "progressive junior high schools" early in the 1920's reorganized their curriculums extensively as they began to recognize individual differences in students both in native abilities and in personal interest areas. Educators initiated various exploratory methods of exposing the early adolescent to new subject-matter and activity programs which would better acquaint him with a wider range of interests:

> Such situations argue for a broad state policy, to the end that those schools desiring to pioneer and experiment may do so without being hampered by a narrow definition of this particular unit of the school system, or by a fixed program which will prevent that pioneer exploration and experimentation which is so desirable in a new educational unit (the junior high school).[1]

Other state departments of education and local school systems experimented with exploratory courses that would contribute to the evolvement of new personal interest learning experiences without requiring the pupil to commit himslf to an occupational choice in junior high school.

The introductory interest programs were very popular with the students and became accepted in most junior high schools by the late 1930's and the early 1940's. Their growth was so universal that in 1944 the National Association of Secondary-School Principals in its publication *Planning for American Youth* recommended that the curriculum for the *early secondary school,* Grades 7, 8, and 9, with six class periods per day, be comprised of three closely related major components: common learnings for two to three class periods (discussed in Chapters 6 and 7), personal interest programs for at least two class periods, and health and physical fitness for one class period. The personal interest areas consisted of "exploration of personal abilities and individual interests; discovery of interests in art, music, science, languages, sports, crafts, home and family problems, and leisure activities,"[2] an organizational plan at present accepted by a majority of junior high schools.

A survey of instructional programs in 400 junior high schools in 10 midwestern states with enrollments ranging from 200 to 1500 indicated that personal interest activities were scheduled for at least two class periods per day. Offered most often and in order of frequency of occurrence were music, industrial arts, homemaking, science, art, business, foreign languages, speech. and work experience. Science, if not also scheduled in combined or double class periods, would have been offered in regular class periods more frequently than fine or practical arts.[3]

An adequate personal interest program has always been considered basic to education in the junior high school: (1) it forces at least a portion of the

[1] *Junior High School Manual* (Topeka, Kan.: State Department of Public Instruction, Jess W. Miley, Superintendent, 1925), p. 20.

[2] National Association of Secondary-School Principals, National Education Associaciation, *Planning for American Youth: An Educational Program for Youth of Secondary-School Age* (a summary of *Education for All American Youth,* a publication of the Educational Policies Commission, NEA). (Washington: The Association, 1944), p. 47.

[3] The instructional programs were reported by superintendents, principals, and teachers of junior high schools who were students in the course "The Junior High School," College of Education, University of Minnesota, summer sessions 1957, 1958, 1959, and 1960.

curriculum to be responsive to the more prominent individual differences of students discernible during early adolescence; (2) it enriches and vitalizes the learning experience of the students in all other areas; (3) it affords electives, particularly in the ninth grade, which become guidelines to aid students in their selection of appropriate areas of experience during senior high school; and (4) it provides students with possible learning experiences in many fields of knowledge and so permits further exploration of career potentials.

Noar supports the offering of certain personal interest or exploratory experiences within the regular junior high school program:

> The modern junior high school curriculum provides for individual differences partly by offering some areas in which subject matter is more highly specialized than it is in the core or combined classes. These are the electives, the courses from among which students choose one or two, depending on the type of organization designed by the faculty and administrators of the school. In some localities there is one elective to be chosen in the eighth year and two in the ninth. More often, in the seventh and eighth year course choices are limited to the choice of the order in which the various kinds of shop, home arts, and fine arts courses are to be taken, with the understanding that eventually every child shall have them all. In most schools, the ninth year electives are directly connected with that curriculum which the individual child thinks he will take in the senior high school, and it, in turn, is connected with preparation for a remote vocational objective. Thus individual differences in abilities, interests, economic backgrounds, motivations, and aspirations serve as screening devices. The guidance staff advisors, core teachers and counselors spend considerable time in and out of class, helping students and their parents to clarify the issues involved and to make wise decisions.[4]

It is increasingly evident that the personal interest program is being assigned an integral role in the junior high school curriculum and is required to be as broad as is feasible for effective accommodation of the needs of all students enrolled. Possibly one-third of the school day should be devoted to it, and it should be the concern not only of the special teachers but of all school staff members, particularly those participating in block-time or core programs.

2. *How are personal interests to be developed and organized?*

Science

To give purposeful direction to a science program in junior high school the following objectives are suggested:[5]

[4] Gertrude Noar, *The Junior High School, Today and Tomorrow.* © 1953, by permission of Prentice-Hall, Inc., Englewood Cliffs, N.J. P. 201. (See also revised edition, 1961, p. 211.)

[5] See Abraham S. Fischler, *Modern Junior High School Science, A Recommended Sequence of Courses* (New York: Bureau of Publications, Teachers College, Columbia University, 1961), p. 3.

1. To develop a better understanding of the natural and physical forces of the world environment.
2. To develop a clearer and accurate comprehension of the process of human growth and development.
3. To acquaint students with the orderly methods of scientific investigation.
4. To develop a familiarity with the practical aspects of science.
5. To recognize and support the evolvement of creative thinking and doing.
6. To offer opportunities for elective individual or group experimental projects which may be continued after formal instruction is completed.

If science instruction is to be consistent with the objectives of personal interest concepts, it must first consider the interests, curiosities, problems, and abilities of young adolescents. Teachers should use the following six procedures and techniques in guiding their students in a meaningful exploration of the many facets in science in order that they may become apprised of and able to apply the scientific approach to learning:

1. All students need to acquire objective information about physical growth and development, the better to understand and cope with the acute growth changes within themselves and their peers.

2. During junior high school, science instruction is most effective when built upon the foundational science experiences afforded at the elementary school level. Thus while progression in learning is provided, instruction will focus upon those science areas that were not extensively dealt with during elementary school. Too often the elementary science material is duplicated in the first science courses in junior high school.

3. Science teachers, supervisors, and counselors in junior and senior high schools should collaborate in planning their science curriculum. Education, government, and business leaders are demanding that all students — slow, average, and fast — be challenged to utilize their individual abilities to the fullest extent in science areas.

4. Good science teaching, when geared to the interest and maturation of the students, benefits from the use of *community resources,* which vary from school to school. In one community having several junior high schools and one senior high school virtually all students were from high socioeconomic families, and more than 90 per cent of the students perceived college as an established educational goal. The science classes in the junior high schools found extensive supplemental instructional materials in these community resources, among others: periodicals, scientific field trips, materials from local firms, pamphlets and charts from industry, outside speakers who were scientists, and senior high school science teachers.

5. Science programs, instead of centering on talking and/or reading about science, must provide "doing" experiences which are appropriate to the developmental abilities of junior high school students. Adequately equipped

science laboratories and materials for experimentation must be readily available. Many a school has a shortage of special science classrooms and laboratory facilities, as pointed out by Howitt, a science teacher in John Wells Junior High School, New York City.[6] "Laboratory experimentation is the essence of science and its value cannot be overestimated in stimulating interest, thus provoking motivation."[7] This is perhaps one of the most neglected segments of science exploration in the junior high school.

6. Exploration in science in junior high schools should afford the students, within the limits of their abilities, opportunity to understand and appreciate materials representing physical science, biological science, earth-in-space science, oceanography, space exploration, and genetics. If students are taught to answer questions of how and why, as well as what, the different sciences contribute to improved living for all humanity, they will be better oriented to their tasks as the innovators and operators of the future.

After nearly half a century of experimentation with general science in the junior high school, it would appear that adequate exploratory science experiences lie somewhere within the "framework of general science," as cited below in the modern general science program developed by the Science Manpower Project for students in junior high schools:

Seventh Grade — The Environment and Human Needs

I. The Earth in Space
II. The Atmosphere
III. Water Resources
IV. Biological Resources

Eighth Grade — Use and Control of Energy

I. Structure of Matter
II. Transformation of Energy
III. Man and Machines
IV. Body and How It Works

Ninth Grade — Frontiers of Science

I. Atomic World
II. Frontiers of the Earth
III. Maintaining Body Health
IV. Science and Change

The general science planned by the Science Manpower Project is intended to be a guide for further planning and adaptation at the local level. Invariably there are local problems and limitations that require special consideration. Students may or may not have had adequate instruction in the

[6] Lillian C. Howitt, "Aids in Science Teaching in the Junior High School," *High Point* (Board of Education of the City of New York), 41:64-69, November, 1959.

[7] See Robert C. Hanes, "The Challenge of Science Teaching in the Junior High Schools," *High School Journal,* 44:177-180, February, 1961.

elementary school; instructional facilities for certain phases of a program may or may not be available. These are only two of many factors that must be dealt with. Moreover, to remain modern, a course of study must undergo constant revision.

In adapting to local circumstances there is need to consider flexibility. If the course content is prescriptive, or if city-wide achievement tests based upon a particular content are the rule, teachers will aim to "cover" rather than "uncover" ideas. Some teachers also tend to neglect certain areas or units, and to stress those for which they have personal liking. We need to avoid pitfalls of this nature, but at the same time we must have flexibility if we are to deal effectively with individual interest and abilities.[8]

Organizing the science program or exploratory experiences in science involves numerous patterns and sequences at the level of Grades 7, 8, and 9, in general science, health science, earth science, and biology.

Fine arts

Music. Exploration in music has traditionally been a priority selection of students in junior high schools. Music is so much a part of all men, regardless of race, creed, color, or economic status, that youth at all age levels have some degree of motivation to partake of the many pleasures afforded through this form of human expression.

It is up to the teacher to help the youngster find the medium through which he may best express himself in music, and to accept and support his choice even if he elects to pursue a non-participant role. The junior high school music program should provide opportunities for dynamic listening as well as active participation. The first responsibility of the program is to effectively minister to the developmental needs of students who are struggling to cope with their individual "growing pains" — physical, social, ethical, and moral.

Music teachers attempt to promote students' emotional and physical well-being through providing experiences in good posture, in correct breathing, in rhythmical body expression and motor and intellectual coordination, in adjustments to voice changes, and experiences which increase self-esteem through accomplishments in musical activities in the school and community.

Boys and girls learn to cope constructively with their rapidly expanding social requirements through one-to-one friendships which evolve from a mutual interest in music; group interaction having a musical focus; developing competencies which permit participation in musical programs, regardless of professionally directed talents; and using abilities which allow spontaneous responses within musically oriented groups.

Music's second responsibility in junior high school education is to enrich

[8] Frederick L. Fitzpatrick (ed.), *Policies for Science Education*, Science Manpower Project Monographs (New York: Bureau of Publications, Teachers College, Columbia University, 1960), pp. 126-127.

the teaching and learning situation. In block-time classes, student competencies in music reinforce other subject units. Instruction in foreign language is often augmented by music. Science uses music to demonstrate the properties of tone and sound. Music and art are often represented in correlative or integrative learning, each finding expression within all curriculum components.

Music activities programmed in response to student interests and needs foster better teaching and learning opportunities. Music may also be a functional socializing influence in class activities, school assemblies, school activity programs, and school-community relationships.[9]

The third responsibility of music programs in junior high schools is to offer choral and instrumental experiences for students who have special interests and/or talents in music as a career potential or for personal pleasure. In general, the elective choral groups are an outgrowth of the required general voice classes, "the heart of the music program." Mixed choral groups are fast becoming regular elective musical activities in the ninth-grade curriculum. Classes in instrumental music are specially arranged in all three grades for one or two semesters with regular school credit in order to accommodate all ranges of student needs, interests, and talents.

Art. The development of a suitable art program in the junior high school includes numerous goals which are congruent with classroom activities. In his *Early Adolescent Art Education* Reed suggests a list of aims for art in junior high school education:

1. To develop a sensitivity to and appreciation of art.
2. To provide opportunities for creative expression.
3. To teach the fundamentals and techniques which will provide the means of achieving art expression.
4. To develop satisfying avocational interests.
5. To seek out the talented and to provide counseling in the choosing of a vocation.
6. To provide a gradual transition from pre-adolescent art training to art education suiting the needs and interests of adolescents.
7. To provide for social experiences and an opportunity to engage in wholesome activities with the opposite sex.
8. To correlate art with other areas of the curriculum.
9. To develop the relationships between contemporary art and daily living.
10. To help in the development of well-integrated personalities.[10]

Through the realization of these aims teachers with well-equipped art classrooms or laboratories available will be better able to engage students in the

[9] See Frances M. Andrews and Joseph L. Leeder, *Guiding Junior-High-School Pupils in Music Experiences* (Englewood Cliffs, N.J.: Prentice-Hall, Inc., 1953), Chaps. 4 and 10.

[10] Carl Reed, *Early Adolescent Art Education* (Peoria, Ill.: Charles A. Bennett and Company, 1957), p. 19.

appreciation of art in everyday living, and in the appropriate application of art in other learning areas.

Students entering junior high school have already acquired certain attitudes and skills in art. The general arts teacher has an opportunity to build upon these foundational experiences by guiding students in further explorations in art appreciation, creative art, or special areas of crafts. A comprehensive exploratory art program for Grades 7, 8, and 9 is practiced in the state of New York, as indicated by the following:

General Art:

Survey of principles of color and design
Application of design principles to various crafts
Provision for creative expression
Study of relation to design principles in daily living
General survey of vocational opportunities in daily living
(In grade 7, art in daily living is emphasized; and in grade 8, survey of major fields of art is made.)

Basic Art:

Fundamentals of design and drawing
Development of skills and facility in various media
Two or three dimensional designs, creative expression
Appreciation of world arts
(In grade 9, this course is elective.)

Creative Art:

Fundamentals of design applied to various materials
Developmental skills in metals, wood, leather, weaving, ceramics
Appreciation of various crafts and materials
(In grade 9, this course is elective for those students who are interested in art as related to work in crafts.)[11]

From the emergence of the junior high school to the present time, most educational workers have considered music and art for every early adolescent and every early adolescent *for* music and art. Broad exposure to these fine art areas is an inherent part of the curriculum in the junior high school.

Practical arts

Industrial arts. Manual training during the early years of the junior high school was frequently a requisite for boys and was perceived as preparation for or introduction to a trade. Before most states had compulsory attendance laws, it was expected that a comparatively large group of students would not continue school beyond the eighth or ninth grades. In many ways these laws

[11] *Art Education, Grades 7, 8, and 9* (Albany, N.Y.: Bureau of Secondary School Curriculum, State Department of Education, 1957), p. 6.

were a response to increased industrialization, which has markedly influenced the instructional focus in some learning areas. Education's responsiveness to social change is evidenced in the transition from the more specialized orientation of manual training to the broader, more flexible and dynamic orientation of industrial arts.

Social and economic modifications have had a significant influence on the evolvement of a diversified industrial arts curriculum to better equip all students for productive living and functioning in the society of today and tomorrow. Their individual needs and interests are often served by offering, for example, "the major *activities of drafting, woodworking, metalworking, power mechanics, electricity, graphic arts, and the industrial crafts.*"[12]

For industrial arts at the junior high school level to be of maximum value in basic education and guidance of all boys and girls, the teacher must begin with comprehension of the unique needs and characteristics of the twelve-to-fifteen-year age group. A guideline to identification of some of these features by grade level is presented:

At the Seventh Grade Level:

1. Highly active
2. Deficiency in fine coordination of skills
3. Short interest retention
4. A social being — likes to work with others
5. Easy to motivate — likes praise
6. Impulsive — acts before he thinks
7. Much more interest in immediate and personal values
8. A wide range of attitudes and unknown abilities
9. Inquisitive

At the Eighth Grade Level: A Direct Comparison with Seventh Grade Students:

1. Activity more purposeful — becoming more aware of his limitations
2. Improvement in muscular coordination dealing with hand skills
3. Longer interest span
4. More selfish in so far as he begins to like to do things by himself and for himself and probably is more self-critical of what he is doing
5. Less easy to stimulate but his competitive spirit higher
6. Improvement in thinking before acting and he is more conscious of shop safety
7. More interest in deferred and projected values
8. Better able to evaluate his and his fellow students' products
9. More stable, responsible, and restrained.

[12] "Industrial Arts in Education, Definition, Unique Contributions, Basic Areas, and Emphasis by Levels," a statement by the Industrial Arts Policy and Planning Committee of the American Vocational Association, 1960, pp. 5-6.

At the Ninth Grade Level:

1. A marked degree beyond the eighth grade student in stature and muscular coordination
2. Noticeable improvement in acquiring skills and applying knowledge
3. Ready to assume a good deal more responsibility in working on projects
4. Ready to assimilate much more related information
5. Physically much larger and is able to handle heavier objects and equipment
6. Sufficient coordination of hand and eye to be able to use power equipment
7. More safety conscious through observing many demonstrations and study of safe working practices.[13]

A moderately well-equipped and functional industrial arts department is essential to a broad and productive program. This may take the form of a *general unit shop,* preferred in the larger schools, or of a *comprehensive general shop,* most often utilized in the smaller schools. The following advantages were claimed for the comprehensive general shop by Newkirk as far back as 1947:

1. It is well adapted to the organization of industrial arts content in the light of the general education, exploration, and guidance aims of the junior high school.
2. It permits students to be treated as individuals with due respect for their differences in interest and capacities.
3. It enables a student to discover his abilities and aptitudes through manipulation of a wide range of materials, tools, and processes that go with them.
4. It offers an economical way to gain experience in many activities.
5. It makes possible an adequate industrial arts program for the small junior high school.
6. It stimulates the setting up of a well-planned shop and a carefully organized teaching content.
7. It increases teacher efficiency.[14]

Definite advantages of having boys and girls learn together (especially in seventh grade) in special industrial arts and homemaking classes in either the *general unit* or the *comprehensive general shop* are being recognized by many

[13] Henry J. Poppenberg, industrial arts teacher, Junior High School, Rochester, Minnesota, and chairman of Committee in the Junior High School Class, College of Education, University of Minnesota, summer session, 1958, which surveyed the needs of late preadolescent and early adolescent students in industrial arts, in three-year junior high schools.

[14] Louis V. Newkirk, *Organizing and Teaching the General Shop* (Peoria, Ill.: The Manual Arts Press, 1947), p. 19.

junior high school educators. Teachers need to be proficient in the arts and knowledgeable about early adolescent growth and developmental processes, as illustrated in these two program examples:

Coeducational classes in Grade 7 in four junior high schools in Sioux Falls, South Dakota, are scheduled for two days per week. Instruction is given in mechanics (including scale drawing, practical home electricity, use of simple hand tools) and in family nutrition and the "Chef Course" for boys and girls, alternating between the industrial shop and the homemaking laboratory.

In the Junior High School of Carl Junction, Colorado, all seventh-grade boys and girls are divided into three groups and alternate in art, industrial arts, and homemaking, spending twelve weeks in each area of exploratory experiences.

Surveys of industrial arts and homemaking in junior high schools indicate that the time allocated to each course may be a fourth, third, or half of a school term. However, there is a tendency to schedule personal interest areas in industrial arts and homemaking for a third or half of the term in order that sufficient time may be available for meaningful learning before rotation to other areas.

Homemaking. The trends in personal interest areas of homemaking are similar to those of industrial arts. As manual training evolved into industrial arts, the skills of cooking and sewing gradually evolved into homemaking. The family emphasis in homemaking education considers first the needs of the students in all phases of family living. In this expansion of the homemaking program the school laboratories are affording a more integrated instructional approach. The separate foods and clothing laboratories are being enlarged to provide adequate space for the equipment necessary to accommodate broader experiences in the area of homemaking.

In the all-purpose laboratories, the subjects covered are family living in modern society; foods and nutrition; home management and decor; health and home nursing; child care; consumer education; and activities presented by organizations such as the Future Homemakers of America.[15]

As teachers plan more individual personal interest experiences in homemaking in the multipurpose or all-purpose laboratories for the students in Grades 7 and 8 and elective ones for those in Grade 9, they need be cognizant of both the homogeneous and the heterogeneous characteristics of their groups. The girls are typically early adolescent and the boys are preadolescent.

[15] See "Family Focus on Homemaking Education" (Jefferson City, Mo.: State Department of Education, Home Economics Section, Vocational Division, 1959), pp. 1-12; and "Homemaking, Grade 8," *Curriculum Bulletin* No. 104, Kansas City, Mo., Public Schools, 1958.

A survey of homemaking practices in thirty-one junior high schools presents an interesting picture of developments:

> 1. Titles are changing. . . . To make courses more acceptable to boys and to create titles different from later school courses, the junior high school classes have been called "Home Living," "Home Arts" and "Home Making," and "Home Economics."
>
> 2. Boys and girls learn together. Where parents and teachers felt that education for worthy home membership was as important for boys as girls, the facilities, staff, and schedules were arranged to offer homemaking instruction in coeducational groups. Classes for boys and girls occurred more often in the *seventh grade* than in the eighth and ninth grades.
>
> 3. Where homemaking became a part of a scheduled block of time two different ways were noted: (1) a block of nine weeks with classes meeting daily; and (2) a block of time during the day to carry out projects. The first pattern was the most common and was found where boys and girls have an exploration experience with many subject-matter fields. One combination of courses was science, shop, and art for nine weeks, each making up a full year's work. Another grouping was home arts and crafts for nine weeks, scheduled with a semester of art. . . .
>
> 4. More schools required . . . homemaking in the seventh grade and eighth grade than offered homemaking as an elective subject. The opposite of this was true in the ninth grade; homemaking was more often scheduled as an elective course than as a required one.
>
> 5. More schools offered homemaking education in all three grades — seven, eight, and nine — than any other combination of grades. All but one of the thirty-one schools reported offering more than one year of homemaking education in the school program.
>
> 6. Approximately half of the reporting seventh grade home and family life classes had enrollments ranging from twenty-eight to thirty-six students.
>
> 7. Another practice which seemed to be emerging in the programs reviewed was one in which parents and students had an opportunity to help plan the home and family life program and the facilities in which boys and girls can have homemaking experiences.[16]

The broader orientation now apparent in homemaking programs as illustrated in the all-purpose homemaking units is reflective of an attempt to help the student identify, express, and develop creative abilities that would otherwise remain dormant and unavailable for present and future life enrichment.

Some research evidence indicates that there has been a misplacement of technical emphasis in homemaking at the junior high school level. It suggests that this aspect of homemaking is more appropriate in senior high school, where girls are more receptive to vocational homemaking knowledge and

[16] Arleen C. Otto, *New Designs in Homemaking Programs in Junior High Schools* (New York: Bureau of Publications, Teachers College, Columbia University, 1958), pp. 56-63.

skills, and that the more exploratory aspects of homemaking instruction be left to the junior high school.

Foreign languages

Foreign languages were offered in Grades 7 and 8 as well as in Grade 9 in the early junior high school curriculum, but by mid-century most schools had shifted foreign languages, including Latin, modern languages, and general language, to Grade 9. In the early 1960's, although there was renewed interest in Spanish, French, German, Italian, and Russian, in the order named, in the junior high schools these languages have not found extensive acceptance.[17]

The claims advanced by advocates of modern foreign language instruction at the junior high school level may be summarized as follows:

1. The teaching–learning of modern foreign languages is redesigned to challenge the interests and abilities of the students with initial emphasis on communicating rather than on grammatical structure, translation and memorization of vocabulary being secondary in importance. Speaking the language; reading the language, grasping the meaning without translation; and writing only what can be said correctly are the general recommended practices.
2. When seventh- and eighth-grade students are exposed to the laboratory and conversational method of teaching foreign languages, they will be better prepared for the selection and mastery of advanced material in the ninth grade and senior high school.
3. The ability to speak, read, and write a modern foreign language proficiently after four to six years of study will enable more citizens in governmental capacities and during personal travel and study abroad to engage in direct communication with peoples of other countries, thereby increasing understanding between peoples and nations.
4. Students with foreign language communicative abilities can make contributions in other areas of their learning, such as social studies, English, and block-time classes or core programs.

Prior to the initiation of modern foreign language study in the early secondary school, it is well to consider some of the suggested disadvantages:

1. Educators have long advocated a well-integrated general education program as essential at the junior high school level, particularly for the seventh and eighth grades. Foreign language represents a highly specialized departmental offering which appears to be incongruent with the developmental needs of students below the ninth grade.
2. Since foreign language is, psychologically, a habit-pattern form of learning, facility is quickly lost without practice. Furthermore, the junior high

[17] See Grace S. Wright and Edith S. Greer, *The Junior High School, A Survey of Grades 7-8-9 in Junior and Junior-Senior High Schools, 1959-1960,* U.S. Office of Education Bulletin No. 32 (Washington: Government Printing Office, 1963), Tables 33 and 34, pp. 55 and 56.

school student's ability to select a foreign language for study and use is considered inadequate. In spite of the fact that the world grows steadily smaller and peoples draw closer in human relationships, many consider it unrealistic that more than a minority of adults will need communication skills in other languages. Consequently, there is serious doubt that the time required for achieving effective language facility is educationally justifiable at the junior high school level.[18]

Business

The development of instruction in business techniques has passed through at least four stages. The first involved shifting typing, bookkeeping, and shorthand from the high school to the junior high school for vocational purposes, but this practice has been almost abandoned in contemporary junior high schools. Shorthand, bookkeeping, and typing, except for personal use, are now primarily offered as separate subjects or basic business courses in the senior high school.

During the second or "practical" stage, subject matter was reorganized for better adaptation to the learning needs of the junior high school student. Attempts were made to modify the traditional academic subjects toward a more practical orientation, but the result was often no more than a changing of names — from history to commercial history, geography to commercial geography, and mathematics to business mathematics.

In the third, or "experimental" stage, curriculum reconstruction was undertaken with the objective of fulfilling the self-discovery, guidance, preview, and prevocational purposes of the junior high school. This was also directed to students remaining in school longer and thus having less immediate need for specific vocational training.

The fourth was the "fusion" stage, in which penmanship, spelling, business arithmetic, and clerical practice were fused with the general business course. The general business course did not interest students in junior high school because it was highly factual, too difficult, and too poorly integrated to appropriately meet their consumer orientations to the economic system.

Many administrators and teachers in junior high schools consider personal interest experiences in business education important but believe they should be geared to units and projects that realistically reflect the needs of early youth. An outline of the "guiding principles" involved in a modern program of business education, as discussed by Price, follows:

1. The trend in basic business courses is away from having students learn a lot of facts that they may never use or at best do not need to know.
2. The knowledge a student acquires should serve as a means to understand his economic problems.

[18] See Noar, *op. cit.*, rev. ed., pp. 212-216, for a critical appraisal of language study in the junior high school.

3. The more closely allied subject matter is to students' present-day experiences, the more meaningful it becomes.

4. However, no approach should be too one-sided, since most of us serve in a multiple capacity as producers and citizens as well as consumers.

5. The old economic theory courses are no longer acceptable in the new secondary education. . . . The individualistic approach to common economic experiences will bring life to what otherwise might be stereotyped, unrealistic classroom exercise.

6. It is reasonable to assume that education to meet an individual's common problems can be attained from a number of different courses and that the needs of each individual will vary as will the outcomes of any general education program.[19]

Surveys of personal interest trends in business techniques found in junior high school programs show the following:

General business is most frequently offered in regular single class periods in Grade 9 and taught as general information, not as a preparation for a specific vocation. Most junior high school programs emphasize banking, money, ways of making payments, communication, filing, buying, budgeting, insurance, transportation, and shipping. For enrichment purposes community resources, appropriate student financial situations, and visual materials are used in the instruction.

The most frequently elected business technique is personal typing. During the school year of 1958-1959 a questionnaire regarding instruction in typing techniques was sent to business education teachers in 4996 separate junior high schools, some undivided junior high schools (6-6), and some traditional high schools (8-4) by the United Business Education Association, a department of the National Education Association. An analysis of the 2061 responses received and tabulated indicated the following findings to be of most significance: 34 per cent offered typing; 97 per cent said that typing was an elective course; and 65 per cent of the students took typing in Grade 9, 27 per cent in Grade 8, and 8 per cent in Grade 7. Typing for personal use was the major reason for this selection by the students. These findings evidence the approval typing receives as an elective personal interest experience in junior high schools.[20]

Speech and dramatics

Junior high school speech activities were originally attempts to imitate the programs offered in senior high school. Speech and dramatic classes stressed

[19] Ray G. Price, "Business Education as General Education." Reprinted by permission from *The Bulletin of the National Association of Secondary-School Principals,* January, 1957. Copyright: Washington, D.C. Pp. 21-22.

[20] See Hollis Guy, Executive Director, United Business Education Association, a department of the National Education Association, "Headquarters Notes UBEA," *Business Education Forum,* 16:43-44, November, 1961.

preparation and selection of the most capable and talented students for debate, oratory, and declamation in interclass and interschool contests.

In more recent years, with the acceptance of language arts as a broad field of learning and block-time classes as a framework for language arts and social studies, unified studies, and core programs, speech activities have become an integral and effective part of regular instruction. Thus more students are prepared for participation in the extracurricular activities.

All students now engage in oral presentation of book reports, various kinds of class discussions and debates, reporting of committee and survey work, panel discussions, radio and television presentations, questions and answers in small and large learning conferences, interviews, preparation of the class or school paper, and class skits and pageants which are presented in assembly programs. Application of speech skills is encouraged in other personal interest activities and clubs.

Speech activities are basic in block-time and core programs where there is sufficient time to afford meaningful student participation. As teachers communicate their approval of students' practicing speech skills, in whatever class, the value of and desire for proficiency in speech will be enhanced. When teachers are consistently aware of their students' speech patterns as manifested in a variety of situations they more accurately perceive those needing specialized speech therapy.

Students demonstrating interest in continuing speech activities are offered specialized units for one or two semesters in Grade 9. Advanced speech classes and dramatics provide additional experiences, as in choral reading, pantomime, poetry, drama, and storytelling.

Work experiences

It is important to evolve criteria which will insure a *student-centered* approach in incorporating part-time work in the learning experiences offered the early adolescent. Such measures include (1) differential assessment of the learner's needs for part-time work in relation to an understanding of his individual growth and development; (2) knowledge of the form and degree of prior and current deprivations directly impinging upon the adolescent emotionally, economically, educationally, and culturally; (3) careful assessment of *who* the adolescent is, and of the realities of his world, his needs, wants, problems, assets, and liabilities; (4) knowledge of what work experiences may be utilized as effective learning resources developed, directed, and guided by the school staff so as to receive similar educational focus and value as are given other learning aggregations; (5) consideration of the parents' attitudes, positive or negative, toward work as a school experience; (6) selection of work experiences which will demand interaction between a school staff member and the student; (7) certainty that the work facilities have the same standards of physical safety and healthful adult influences required of the regular school setting; and (8) caution that part-time work experiences not be perceived or devised as a means of "getting rid of" or "punishing" the adolescent for certain negative conduct.

Within the framework of these criteria, part-time work may afford constructive opportunities for some early adolescents to enhance and continue their learning experiences by modifying the destructive influences of chronic socioeconomic deprivation. By becoming part-time wage earners these students may acquire some of the basic material necessities essential to maintenance of a state of well-being. They may also find relief from the anxiety attendant on not contributing to the support of other dependent family members. The student who can earn something may be saved from dropping out of school when he becomes sixteen years of age and trying to live without the educational equipment essential to productive functioning in our society.

The following are educational values indicated as having evolved from part-time work experiences developed and implemented as an integral part of the personal interest program in West Junior High School, Kansas City, Missouri:

> Many boys and girls begin to lose interest in school in the eighth and ninth grades. Also many need financial aid. To meet this problem a work-job in connection with the school program is often successful.
>
> To be excused from school one or two hours a day to work can give a pupil:
>
> 1. New interest
> 2. Financial aid
> 3. Experience in the field of work
> 4. Sense of personal accomplishment
> 5. Desire to do better school work so that he can hold the job.
>
> The school should require such pupils to maintain good:
>
> 1. School attendance
> 2. School citizenship
> 3. School achievement
> 4. Work records (periodic reports are required from employers).
>
> This work-school program has met with great success at West Junior High School in Kansas City, Missouri, over a period of some thirty years. This school is located in a low socio-economic area. Many former pupils who worked while in school are now in good positions throughout the United States. They have written the school that if they had not had work, they could not have continued in school.
>
> A work program in connection with school may contribute to making life more meaningful and realistic to some early adolescent students.[21]

The success of this program was largely dependent upon the school counselor's consistent collaboration with the businessmen who provided the work

[21] Ruth Baity, Counselor, West Junior High School, Kansas City, Mo., "Work Experience as Part of School Program," December, 1961.

opportunities. The requirement that students maintain adequate performance in other learning areas was a positive influence for both the student and the employer.

The Ford Foundation granted the Kansas City Trusts and Foundations of Missouri $300,000 toward financing a unique six-year work-study program for teen-age boys in the Kansas City public schools. The primary purpose of this project is to reduce the rate of school dropouts by offering work experiences to selected students for one-half of the school day. The program was initiated during the 1961-1962 school year in four junior or pattern high schools with twenty-five eighth-grade boys from each school whose academic performances indicated that their continued school attendance was unlikely. The boys had special classes in social studies, mathematics, English, and science with one teacher for three hours during the morning. For the remaining three hours of structured school time they worked on maintenance of the school buildings and grounds, landscaping, gardening, painting, and repairing school equipment.

Recognizing that economic realities often force students to drop out of school, the board of education authorized money to pay the young workers. Special teachers direct all work activities during the first stage of the project, but as the boys complete this stage at approximately fifteen years of age, and usually in Grade 9, it is anticipated that they will be ready for selected jobs within the business community, as part-time errand boys or helpers in grocery, hardware, drug, and other retail stores. They will continue to carry regular or remedial academic courses in their individual schools on a part-time basis.

When the boys have reached their sixteenth birthday — by this time they will usually be in senior high school — the school employment supervisor will continue to counsel with and assist them in selecting and obtaining regular part-time employment. After they are seventeen the supervisor will be available to guide them in attaining full-time occupations. A certificate compatible with their training and abilities will be offered those finishing the program. At any time they desire the boys may return to regular high school classes.

Havighurst points out the benefits of appropriate work experiences for boys and girls in Grades 8 and 9 who find their school situations incompatible with their individual resources:

> . . . Therefore, the junior high school should have a program for slow learners which is geared to their ability and also gives them a reasonably clear pathway to growth. Work experience and opportunity is an essential for these boys and girls, who can generally get the feeling of successful growing up by earning money and doing usual work, even if their school performance is a source of discouragement to them. In a rural area, the work experience can usually be obtained on a farm or in a farm household. But in towns and

cities, there should be a patient and persistent program of finding jobs and of supervising the program of these people.

. . . The principal things which the society can do directly for youth are two. One is to examine carefully the existing Child Labor laws to find out whether, under present industrial conditions, they may not be unnecessarily limiting the opportunity of boys and girls fourteen and over to get wholesome work experience. The other is to develop and enlarge programs for wholesome recreation of teen-age youth, giving them an opportunity to get excitement and adventure and pleasure under circumstances that do not deprive them.[22]

Development and degree of emphasis on part-time or extra-school work opportunities as an integral part of the junior high school personal interest program should be directly related to the needs of the student group served and should not be perceived as a "shotgun" cure for all problems experienced by early adolescents. Again, it is necessary to *know* the early adolescent before attempting to do him good.

3. How are personal interest programs introduced?

The personal interest program schedules of three junior high schools are described below.

1. The New Clara Bryant Junior High School in Dearborn, Michigan, initiated a unified arts program that included art, industrial arts, and homemaking. A new wing was added to the school building, extending away from the entrance to the auditorium and connected by a corridor. Across the end of this corridor the shop area — general wood, general metal, and power — is located. On either side of the corridor and extending up to the shops are the homemaking and art spaces. The portion of the widened corridor next to the art and homemaking departments is designed as a gallery, to be used by all departments for displaying completed work.

In actual practice, student projects may originate in any department and may involve the use of tools and techniques available in others. The shop student building a table lamp may complete the design of lamp and shade in the art department, make the lamp in the shop, and go to either the homemaking or the art department, or both, depending upon the materials used, for the shade. In a similar manner, the homemaking student may select a certain project requiring a block-print design and use the art department while developing the design, the shop for preparing the block, and the homemaking department to complete the sewing necessary.

[22] Robert J. Havighurst, "Problem Youth in the Junior High School." Reprinted by permission from *The Bulletin of the National Association of Secondary-School Principals,* April, 1958. Copyright: Washington, D.C. P. 372.

Projects are not typically designed to cut across all departments, nor should efforts be made to involve other departments just for the sake of integration. However, when a project requires tools and equipment and instructional direction from other areas, including the music department, that will enhance the quality of experience for the student, they are readily available. All of the Dearborn junior high schools utilize this unified arts program.[23]

2. The Arts Department of University High School, University of Minnesota, offers art, industrial arts, homemaking, and music. The department staffs attempt through unified arts and advanced arts to enable students to participate in activities designed to stimulate their interest and develop their abilities. Because of mutuality of objectives it is feasible to have a single unit of study representative of all areas. The program is offered in seventh, eighth, and ninth grades. During his three years in the junior high school each student spends approximately one-fourth of the school year in each art area.

Classroom and laboratory facilities for art, industrial arts, and homemaking are located in adjoining suites on the ground floor of Peik Hall, and music rehearsal and practice rooms are housed in an adjoining building. This department affords opportunities for College of Education students to observe teaching methods that may be applied in their own research and experimentation projects. The objectives of the program of related arts, "Designed for Living," are as follows:

1. Establishing areas and providing media through which pupils achieve satisfaction in creative and manipulative activities.
2. Providing exploratory, broadening experiences in the arts areas.
3. Stimulating existing interests and developing new interests in creative, manipulative, and informational fields.
4. Extending the pupil's vocational and avocational horizons.
5. Aiding the pupil in formulating and implementing appropriate problem solving techniques.
6. Fostering the appreciation of worthy performance and craftsmanship.
7. Encouraging good consumer values through home related activities.
8. Promoting an understanding of basic procedures and techniques.
9. Developing an understanding and appreciation of harmony between types of materials and their use.[24]

This program strives to accommodate the changing needs and interests of the students and attain closer integration of art, industrial arts, homemaking,

[23] See James A. Lewis and Herschel K. Bennett, "A Unified Arts Program for Junior High Schools," *American School and University Journal,* 26:153-158, 1954-1955.

[24] "Related Arts, Designed for Living," *Bulletin,* University High School, College of Education, University of Minnesota, April, 1955.

and music by making class scheduling flexible and locating classrooms and laboratories in the same area.

3. The Stewart Junior High School, University of Utah, utilizes the following *new* program:

> Through a series of Stewart Staff Curriculum Work Shops, a more integrated curriculum was suggested which moved beyond the "core plus conventional subjects" organization. Specifically it was suggested for grades seven, eight, and nine that:
>
> 1. The core program remain as it had been organized; i.e., the various grade levels would remain intact. There would be a large block of time available for work. The core would consist of fusion of English and social studies. The general method would continue to be unit teaching.
> 2. All of the special interest areas of the curriculum — music, art, home economics, industrial arts, clubs — would consist of six- and twelve-week predetermined units of work (a block of two class periods). Students would have a variety of choices and be able to cross over into other grades; e.g., a unit of work in art, "Landscapes," might draw students from seventh, eighth, and ninth grades.
> 3. The science and mathematics programs would consist of predetermined units and students would not observe grade lines. Algebra was to remain a full-year sequence, primarily for ninth graders, and some science units, e.g., "Reproduction," would be restricted to ninth graders.
> 4. Units in physical education and health would be required of all students. Once again students could cross grade lines, but units of work would not be definitely predetermined.
>
> . . . .
>
> . . . They [essentially the school staff] indicated clearly their stand on such fundamental questions as the social context in which education is to take place, the meaning of democracy for the school, and the nature of learners and the learning process. Stewart staff members believed that they knew what they were trying to do, how they were trying to do it, and that the results would be worthwhile.[25]

The introduction of the program in Stewart Junior High School increased and expanded personal interest experiences for the students, improved learning in fundamental knowledges and skills, and afforded multiple problem-solving opportunities essential to the development of critical and creative thinking. Additional benefits as recognized by Harmer are: better accommodation of individual differences, more productive guidance services, expanded opportunities for personal and social growth, and more dynamic group interactional experiences.

[25] Earl W. Harmer, "A New Program in Junior High School: A School Staff Attempts to Develop an Integrated Program," *Educational Leadership,* 17:509-11, 521, May, 1960. By permission of the copyright © owner, The Association for Supervision and Curriculum Development.

After three years of consistent planning and experimentation with the various facets of an effective integrated program in Stewart Junior High School, the parents, teachers, and students overwhelmingly endorsed the new program. Its continued use is testimony of its worth.

SELECTED BIBLIOGRAPHY

Andrews, Frances M., and Joseph A. Leeder. *Guiding Junior-High-School Pupils in Music Experiences.* Englewood Cliffs, N.J.: Prentice-Hall, Inc., 1953.

Art Education, Grades 7, 8, and 9. Albany, N.Y.: Bureau of Secondary School Curriculum, State Department of Education, 1957.

Faunce, Roland C., and Morrel J. Clute. *Teaching and Learning in the Junior High School.* San Francisco: Wadsworth Publishing Company, 1961.

Fischler, Abraham S. *Modern Junior High School Science, A Recommended Sequence of Courses.* New York: Bureau of Publications, Teachers College, Columbia University, 1961.

Frederick L. Fitzpatrick (ed.). *Policies for Science Education.* Science Manpower Project Monographs. New York: Bureau of Publications, Teachers College, Columbia University, 1960.

Gruhn, William T., and Harl R. Douglass. *The Modern Junior High School.* New York: The Ronald Press Company, 2nd ed., 1956.

Guy, Hollis. "Headquarters Notes UBEA," *Business Education Forum,* 16:42-44, November, 1961. (Published by the United Business Education Association, a department of the National Education Association.)

Harmer, Earl W. "A New Program in Junior High School: A School Staff Attempts to Develop an Integrated Program," *Educational Leadership,* 17:509-521, May, 1960.

Hatcher, Hazel M., and Mildred E. Andrews. *The Teaching of Home Economics.* Boston: Houghton Mifflin Company, 2nd ed., 1963. Chapter 3, "Understanding and Counseling Adolescents."

Havighurst, Robert J. "Problem Youth in the Junior High School," *The Bulletin of the National Association of Secondary-School Principals,* 42:372, April, 1958.

"Homemaking, Grade 8," *Curriculum Bulletin* No. 104, Kansas City, Mo., Public Schools, 1958.

Howitt, Lillian C. "Aids in Science Teaching in the Junior High School," *High Point* (Board of Education of the City of New York), 41:64-69, November, 1959.

"Industrial Arts in Education, Definition, Unique Contributions, Basic Areas, and Emphasis by Levels." A Statement by the Industrial Arts Policy and Planning Committee of the American Vocational Association, 1960.

Junior High School Manual. Topeka, Kans.: State Department of Public Instruction, Jess W. Miley, Superintendent, 1925.

Lally, Ann M. (ed.). *Art Education in the Secondary School.* Washington: National Art Education Association, National Education Association, 1961.

Lewis, James A., and Hershel K. Bennett. "A Unified Arts Program for Junior High Schools," *American School and University Journal,* 26:153-158, 1954-1955.

Monsour, Sally, and Margaret Perry. *A Junior High School Music Handbook.* Englewood Cliffs, N.J.: Prentice-Hall, Inc., 1963.

National Association of Secondary-School Principals, National Education Association. *Planning for American Youth: An Educational Program for Youth of Secondary-School Age* (a summary of *Education for All American Youth,* a publication of the Educational Policies Commission, NEA). Washington: The Association, 1944.

National Education Association. *The Music Curriculum in Secondary Schools: Handbook for Junior and Senior High Schools.* Washington: The Association, 1959.

Newkirk, Louis V. *Organizing and Teaching the General Shop.* Peoria, Ill.: The Manual Arts Press, 1947.

Noar, Gertrude. *The Junior High School, Today and Tomorrow.* Englewood Cliffs, N.J.: Prentice-Hall, Inc., rev. ed., 1961.

Otto, Arleen C. *New Designs in Homemaking Programs in Junior High Schools.* New York: Bureau of Publications, Teachers College, Columbia University, 1958. Pp. 1-100.

Price, Ray G. "Business Education as General Education," *The Bulletin of the National Association of Secondary-School Principals,* 41:21-22, January, 1957.

Reed, Carl. *Early Adolescent Art Education.* Peoria, Ill.: Charles A. Bennett and Company, 1957. Pp. 1-203.

"Related Arts, Designed for Living," *Bulletin,* University High School, College of Education, University of Minnesota, April, 1955.

Smith, Maurice M., L. L. Standley, and Cecil Hughes. *Junior High School Education.* New York: McGraw-Hill Book Co., Inc., 1942. Chap. VII, "The Program of Studies."

Wright, Grace S., and Edith S. Greer. *The Junior High School, A Survey of Grades 7-8-9 in Junior and Junior-Senior High Schools, 1959-1960.* U.S. Office of Education Bulletin No. 32. Washington: Government Printing Office, 1963.

9

Health and Physical Fitness

Educational literature attests to the persistent obstacles that long have hindered the evolvement and implementation of dynamically oriented health and physical fitness programs in the junior high school. Educators seem to be experiencing a new awareness that the acculturation process is essential to the effective development of such programs.

This chapter will endeavor to reidentify the conceptual responses precipitated by these changes in order that appropriate educational rewards may be realized.

As early as 1944, the National Association of Secondary-School Principals, in its *Planning for American Youth,* stated that "Health and Physical Fitness includes games, sports, and other activities to promote fitness, together with a study of individual and community health."[1] It went on to recommend that this area of learning be considered a major part of the curriculum in early secondary education — Grades 7, 8, and 9 — being scheduled for one class period daily in a six-hour school day. Fifteen years later, a survey of 1360 junior and junior-senior high schools, representing 48 contiguous states and the District of Columbia, indicated that in 80 to 96 per cent of the schools surveyed physical education was required for Grades 7, 8, and 9. In more than half of the schools health instruction was required for Grades 7 and 8, and in 40 per cent of them it was required for Grade 9.[2]

[1] National Association of Secondary-School Principals, National Education Association, *Planning for American Youth: An Educational Program for Youth of Secondary-School Age* (a summary of *Education for All American Youth,* a publication of the Educational Policies Commission, NEA). (Washington: The Association, 1944), p. 47.

[2] Grace S. Wright and Edith S. Greer, *The Junior High School, A Survey of Grades 7-8-9 in Junior and Junior-Senior High Schools, 1959-1960,* U.S. Office of Education Bulletin No. 32 (Washington: Government Printing Office, 1963), p. 57.

FIGURE 7

The Part of the School Day Devoted to Teaching and Learning in Health, Physical Education, and Recreation in Junior and Senior High Schools

Adapted from *The Bulletin of the National Association of Secondary-School Principals,* 44:10, May, 1960.

The modifications evident in present-day utilization of health and physical fitness programs in junior high schools indicate a marked transition from a rather narrow, fragmented program to one that is dynamic and student-centered. Figure 7 illustrates the trend toward scheduling regular instruction in health and physical fitness, including recreational and intramural activities, for one daily class period.

The creation of a dynamic health and physical fitness program is primarily contingent on the degree to which instructional formulations reflect and meet the distinctive needs of early adolescent learners. The foundational typology of these needs, as outlined in the American Association for Health, Physical Education, and Recreation publication *Fitness for Secondary School Youth,* is offered here as a guide for junior high school staffs in setting up their programs:

Needs of Junior High-School Youth

Physical fitness needs

1. A balanced and adequate diet for the demands of growth and activity.
2. A safe school, home, and community environment.
3. Sufficient sleep and rest; for some, as much as ten hours daily.
4. Regular dental and health examinations and corrections of remediable defects.
5. Sufficient daily big-muscle activity for normal development; for many, as much as six hours.

6. Experience in an all-round program of health education, physical education, and recreation with enough instruction and experience in skills to be able to participate in a number of socially desirable activities.
7. Participation in selected games and other activities suited to their strengths and appropriate for their developmental needs with adequate guidance.

Emotional fitness needs

1. Emotional security with a sense of being loved and wanted, of having companionship, reasonable freedom from economic worries, and a sharing of every-day problems.
2. Learn how to find release from emotional tension in ways that are personally and socially acceptable.
3. Learn how to face emotional problems with a reasonable degree of success and self-control.
4. Experiences which will develop desirable attitudes of spectatorship and sportsmanship.
5. Achievement of success with recognition.

. . . .

Social fitness needs

1. Participation in many types of group contacts such as co-recreational dances and games, religious groups, and youth clubs.
2. Practice in social skills such as conversation and courtesies while accompanying others, eating, and participating in various social activities with others.
3. A set of social values which is acceptable to society.[3]

1. Why are special programs needed?

The criteria for junior high school learning programs should always be in terms of their particular suitability for the late preadolescent and early adolescent learner. When programs of health and physical fitness are examined from this view it is apparent that they will not evolve as an upward extension of the elementary school program, nor downward from that in the senior high school, but will reflect only the unique and distinctive characteristics of the junior high school student group.

A health and physical fitness program for the junior high school differs from those of the adjacent school groups in a number of ways.

1. The onset of adolescence is typically accompanied by an abrupt change in the student's perceptions of the major external forces of influence. The new forces are his teachers, and the other adults he selects to assist him in understanding himself and the world about him. Consequently, the early

[3] Karl W. Bookwalter and Carolyn W. Bookwalter (eds.), for the American Association for Health, Physical Education, and Recreation, National Education Association, *Fitness for Secondary School Youth* (Washington: The Association, 1956), pp. 25 and 26.

adolescent's effective utilization of parental influence in the resolution of his questions, concerns, and intense feelings about physical, social, and emotional changes is markedly reduced.

2. Twelve- to fifteen-year-olds are much concerned about their "new selves," as is typically manifested in preoccupation with their personal appearance. They actively seek information about foods that will result in weight gains or losses or decrease the possibility of facial skin eruptions, and appropriate exercises, in order to achieve a desirable body image. They are quite responsive to structured appraisals of their physical assets and liabilities and eagerly participate in remedial activities suggested by their teachers. They are most receptive to keeping individual records of their changes in height and weight.

3. Since the onset of adolescence in girls occurs from one to two years earlier than in boys, girls need information and guidance sooner in order to healthfully cope with their increased instability, mood swings, fatigue, and sexual maturation. These needs are often best met by instructional material regarding growth and developmental processes; separate health classes for junior high school boys and girls are thus necessary.

4. The rapid growth experienced by the late preadolescent and early adolescent student necessitates an annual medical review from a qualified doctor of medicine engaged either by the school or by the parents. Findings from such examinations should enter into the formulation of physical fitness activities in accordance with the individual student's growth patterns as well as his grade, age, and size.

5. The late preadolescent stage of development usually takes place during the seventh grade. The accompanying increased awareness of sexual roles stimulates interest in boy-girl relationships. At this time, it is important to offer special coeducational classes in order that physical fitness teachers may help the students learn socialization skills that will positively influence their present and future interactional patterns.

6. The advancement of students from elementary to junior high school physical fitness activities is accompanied by new hygiene situations; personal privacy while showering and changing clothes becomes a thing of the past. Many students approach this change with the anxiety and discomfort characteristic of early adolescence. If not handled effectively by instructors such anxiety may increase to the extent that school attendance is interrupted.

7. In a democratic society the primary family unit is responsible for meeting the dietary needs of children, but when this resource defaults, the school and/or other social institutions of the larger society must supply them.

8. Adequate time should be allocated for teacher-student conferences regarding individual interests that fall within the scope of a dynamic health and physical fitness program. These interests are often accommodated by playing on various sport teams, acting as squad leaders, or refereeing intersquad

games. Such action is considered essential to the development of group membership and leadership skills.

9. During early adolescence, boys and girls are frequently described as inattentive, restless, irresponsible, obstinate, changeable, sensitive, and lazy. These behavior traits usually reflect discomforts, pressures, and concerns stemming from inner turmoil.

Health and physical fitness programs affording multiple opportunities for successful performance are of definite remedial value to these students, but of greater import is the fact that *student-centered* programs, directed by adequately trained teachers, often help to prevent destructive behavioral responses. Programs in this area of learning *must* offer numerous opportunities for all students to earn tangible awards and/or recognition from peers for demonstrated competencies in one or more games, team sports, or individual recreational activities. The accommodation of the student's individual differences is of prime concern to all health and physical fitness programs in early secondary education.

10. Health and physical fitness teachers need adequate preparation in human sciences and professional social relationship skills in order that they may have the competence "for helping early adolescents to understand what is happening to their bodies, and to accept their bodies in this period of rapid change."[4]

11. "The accident rate of the group 12-15 years of age is higher than that of the elementary school pupils of the age group 5-11 years."[5] Again, uneven adolescent growth patterns are one cause. Another is the desire for adventure, but this may be significantly modified and controlled through a "learning in the out-of-doors" program composed of field trips, school camping, angling clubs, and other special outdoor activities, often serving as a foundation for constructive and satisfying recreational experiences in later adolescence and adulthood.[6]

If programs of instruction in health and physical fitness are designed to accommodate the above learning requisites, their inclusion in the educational program of the junior high school should not be challenged.[7]

[4] *The Junior High School Program* (Atlanta, Ga.: Southern Association of Colleges and Secondary Schools, 1958), p. 8.

[5] Research Division, National Education Association, *The Junior High School.* (Washington: The Association, November, 1959), p. 5.

[6] See Julian W. Smith, *Outdoor Education* (Washington: American Association for Health, Physical Education, and Recreation, National Education Association, 1956), pp. 1-32.

[7] See *Missouri's Guide for Physical Education in the Secondary School, Grades Seven-Twelve* (Jefferson City: Hubert Wheeler, Commissioner of Education, January, 1960), Chaps. 3 and 6; and John H. Shaw, "Emphasis and Sequence in Health Teaching," *The Bulletin of the National Association of Secondary-School Principals,* 44:34-38, May, 1960.

2. *How are adequate programs organized and staffed?*

There is a tendency for state curriculum guides to specify that all physical educators in junior high schools be qualified to teach health and safety. The Oregon State Department of Education suggests that physical education and health be combined and made a requisite for two semesters for all students in Grades 7, 8, and 9 in three-year junior high schools, and in Grades 7 and 8 in two-year junior high schools.[8] This pattern of organization applies to the junior high with seven fifty-minute class periods.

The Iowa State Department of Public Instruction recommends, in *Junior High Schools for Iowa Youth,* a combination of physical education and health for six semesters for all students in Grades 7, 8, and 9. This program "provides many opportunities for physical, intellectual, and social development through individual and group participation in athletic recreational activities such as gymnastics, rhythms, sports, and social activities. Provision should be made for formal instruction in health, including both hygiene and physiology."[9]

In some larger junior high schools with multiple classes in health and safety education, the responsibility for development and coordination of the program is centered in one person, who must be qualified to teach health education classes in Grades 7, 8, and 9 for one-third to one-half of a school term. He is also assigned the task of incorporating well-balanced health and safety experiences involving contributions from the classes of the physical educators and from classes in homemaking, from social studies, block-time classes, or core programs.[10]

In order for health to receive its proper emphasis, all junior high school teachers should be encouraged and expected to use health instruction in their classes whenever appropriate and related to a given curriculum area.

A large majority of junior high schools are treating health, physical fitness, and recreation as a combined basic learning area under the direction of one teacher who is certified for instruction in both health and physical fitness.

The purported administrative and instructional rationale offered for this practice includes the following points:

1. The young students in each grade are assured specially prepared men teachers for boys and women teachers for girls in physical fitness, recreation,

[8] Rex Putnam, *The Organization and Function of Oregon Junior High Schools* (Salem: Superintendent of Public Instruction, 1959), "Suggested Schedules," p. 22.

[9] *Junior High Schools for Iowa Youth* (Des Moines: Iowa State Department of Public Instruction, Division of Curriculum, 1960), pp. 16-17.

[10] See Sara Louise Smith, "Characteristics of a Good Secondary School Health Education Program," *The Bulletin of the National Association of Secondary-School Principals,* 44:45-46, May, 1960.

and health science — persons who are knowledgeable about the basic physiological and hygienic facts which are so often of special concern to the early adolescent and can be transmitted *without difficult scheduling problems.* When health teaching is scheduled separately, too often the instruction is only incidentally presented in a short homeroom period.

2. Since health instruction is given in regular classrooms two days per week, or in an equivalent block-of-time class, more *teaching space* is available for physical fitness in gymnasiums, auxiliary playrooms, and swimming pools. Thus, costly building space for teaching physical fitness and recreation becomes less of a problem.

3. By combining health and physical fitness instruction into one regular class period the maximum enrollment of fifty students in physical fitness classes is automatically reduced to *thirty* or *thirty-five,* which correlates with maximum per-class enrollments of other subject areas. This reduction in class size markedly improves the quality of instruction and guidance.

4. With the *same* teachers for health and safety education and physical fitness, including recreation, the teachers are better able to accurately perceive their students' assets, needs, and liabilities. They can thus devise activities suited to the maturity and physical capacities of each student and give teaching and learning a closer and more meaningful association.

5. Mills reported that virtually all separate health teachers also taught other courses.[11] Since health and physical fitness are more interdependent than other curriculum areas and combined scheduling is more convenient, it is obvious why they are integrated in many junior high schools.

6. Collaboration between parent and teacher is often facilitated when boys relate to a man teacher and girls to a woman teacher in a combined health and physical fitness unit. This is important in the area of sex education. The combined structure also lends itself to easy shifting to coeducational classes for special instruction in folk dancing, square dancing, and social dancing and is useful for the presentation of school programs and award assemblies.

The development of a *balanced* instructional program of health and physical fitness in junior high schools, whether offered in a combined unit or in separate units, requires that all of the professional staff involved understand the *scope* of each learning area.

3. *What is the scope of health and safety programs?*

Instruction is focused on enhancing emotional as well as physical well-being and on protection against the environmental hazards of daily living

[11] Caswell Albert Mills, "A Study of Certain Phases of the Health Education Program of Public Secondary Schools of the State of Washington," Ph.D. dissertation, University of Washington, 1960.

(often referred to as safety education). It is difficult to treat these two aspects separately for they are interdependent. Indeed, health education is now most often viewed as total fitness for living — man in a state of physical, emotional, social, and spiritual well-being.[12] This definition has served to delineate four major teaching and guidance tasks for junior high school education: (1) maintenance of a healthful and safe school environment, (2) provision of adequate school health services, (3) provision of meaningful and functional health and safety instruction, (4) use of home and community resources in health education.

A healthful and safe school environment

The maintenance of a healthful and safe school environment requires the consistent attention of the entire school staff with the leadership and guidance of administrators, health coordinators, health teachers, nurse, cafeteria manager, custodial staff, and student council. Many factors contribute to healthful and safe living in a school, but the most significant are the following:

1. Regular scheduled classes in health and safety.
2. A well-organized health center in which a school nurse serves the personal health needs of the students, confers with physicians and health agencies, and works with health teachers and other teachers to maintain a healthy and safe school atmosphere.
3. A clean, hygienic, hazard-free school building and surrounding area.
4. A school equipped with attractive classrooms with correct lighting and color, seating, heating, ventilation, furniture, and equipment.
5. A pleasant, well-managed, and adequately equipped school cafeteria in which foods of high energy are served, with physical space properly allocated to afford the convenient placement of tables (four to eight individual chairs per table) with appointments that are functional but attractive. Such a setting is a major aid in enabling students to learn and to value socially approved manners that are conducive to the development of social poise. The student council and other school organizations may sponsor and/or assign student hosts or hostesses to various areas as part of an effective orientation procedure.
6. A building plan that allows adequate space for a comprehensive program in physical fitness.
7. A weekly schedule of student activities, formulated by the school staff and student council, which best suits the interests, maturity, and capabilities of each student. (This factor is discussed in detail in Chapter 10.)
8. A health committee, composed of student council members, to promote healthful and safe school living. Safety posters and slogans are often utilized and may be combined with art class activities.

[12] See Marjorie L. Craig and Francis U. Everett, "Developing Health Potentialities," *Teachers College Record,* 61:429-430, May, 1960.

9. A safety program that utilizes materials provided by the national, state, and city safety councils, and by local police, fire, and health departments.

The Robert E. Lee Junior High School at Orlando, Florida, has evolved a safety program as an integral part of regular instruction in health and safety classes. The following is a brief description of this program:

> Each morning along with the daily 10-minute devotional exercise given over the intercom to every room in the school, we broadcast a two minute "On the Spot" safety message. "On the Spot" safety messages are just what the term implies. Any special event of the school day is tied in with a safety message and relayed to the students.[13]

Schlichenmaier believes that student participation is essential to effective school safety instruction. He suggests that during health class periods the teacher engage students in writing safety messages regarding current issues for the oratorically talented student to present over the intercom. Having one student address the class, he says, on the subject of safety practices in daily living is an effective force in reducing serious accidents by 25 per cent and minor accidents by 35 per cent.

School health services

One reason for offering health services is to make information readily available that will develop in each student constructive attitudes and values regarding his own health and safety. The scope of adequate health services in junior and senior high schools is indicated by Harnett:

> 1. Health appraisal — the determination of health status by observation; by screening tests of vision and hearing; by medical, dental, and psychological examination; and by measurements of height, weight, and posture.
> 2. Health counseling and follow-through — guidance to pupils and parents in securing medical, dental, and other necessary care.
> 3. Safety and emergency care procedures — provision for protection from injury and for care in case of accident or sudden illness.
> 4. Adjustment to individual pupil needs — a challenging, flexible school program aided by discerning, understanding teachers.
> 5. Communicable disease control and sanitation — emphasis on immunization, exclusion and readmittance, attendance at school, and close observation.[14]

The augmentation of school health services has, in turn, created many new functions for the junior high school nurse. Those of most import are (1) arranging for health appraisals of students by physicians and public

[13] Arthur W. Schlichenmaier, "The Schlichenmaier Method of Safety Education," *School Activities,* 33:212, March, 1962.

[14] Arthur L. Harnett, "The Scope of Health Education." Reprinted by permission from *The Bulletin of the National Association of Secondary-School Principals,* May, 1960. Copyright: Washington, D.C. P. 30.

health agencies; (2) engaging more parents in conferences concerning the health of their children; (3) serving as a consultant to the health, physical fitness, and recreation teachers; and (4) participating in policy formulation and coordination of school health services including teaching demonstration units for the health teacher and other teachers in a health in-service training program.

Responsibility of the entire professional staff

The health and safety of junior high school students are basic to the entire educational program and are therefore of concern to all school staff members. According to Shaw, a program of health education is usually composed of the following organizational instruction patterns:

> . . . incidental health teaching, correlated health teaching, units of health offered in other courses, and direct teaching in specific health courses. All four of these patterns should be included in a school where careful planning for health education has occurred and where the entire school staff has worked under the guidance of an enlightened school administration in trying to create the best possible health education program for a given situation.[15]

Use of home and community resources

Junior high school staffs should engage all appropriate resources to support and enhance the health and physical fitness of all students. The specific resources and methods of engagement will vary according to the needs and characteristics of the student groups served. It is the responsibility of the school staffs to first observe, identify, and understand the health and fitness needs of their individual students in order to initiate remedial and/or preventive programs.

The following paragraphs describe how two junior high schools serving distinctive student groups evolved effective health programs by utilizing home and community resources. The first description is of a small community school system in Minnesota with six hundred students, enrolled in Grades 1 to 12, whose parents were in the upper middle socioeconomic group. The elementary teachers and the health teacher in the high school did not integrate general preventive health instruction in their classes. Little or no emphasis was placed on corrective treatment of physical problems identified and reported by the county physician and public health nurse following the annual physical examination given to all children.

The sole communication between school staff and parents about the health status and needs of their children was a routine health report taken home by the children. Less than one-fourth of the students with diagnosed physical problems received the treatment recommended. The one physician

[15] Shaw, *op. cit.* Reprinted by permission from *The Bulletin of the National Association of Secondary-School Principals,* May, 1960. Copyright: Washington, D.C. Pp. 37-38.

and dentist in the community left because of lack of interest in and awareness of health needs. At this point the school superintendent became alarmed about the number of students experiencing marked learning difficulties, and further investigation revealed that a variety of remediable physical problems existed. A health education program was then initiated. In the space of two years *all* of the children with identified health problems had received appropriate medical care and treatment. A short time after the start of this integrated school health program a physician and a dentist located in the community on a full-time basis.

The second health program using home and community resources has been in operation more than two decades. The school nurse and health teachers of West Junior High School, Kansas City, Missouri, have guided the seven hundred students, enrolled in regular health classes, in making effective use of health care resources of their choice, which include private physicians, community health clinics, and local hospitals. Even though there were only a few private physicians in this old urban residential area of thirty thousand population, the majority of students with remediable physical problems received the necessary correction through the efforts of the school nurse and the cooperation of twenty-five different public and private health agencies.

Dental care within the school was provided for all students unable to obtain it on a private basis. This service was sponsored by the public school district, the local dental association, the Community Council, and the Parent-Teacher Association.

The effectiveness of the health program impressed the physicians who provided the annual physical examinations for students in the physical education classes. They frequently remarked to the school staff that these children had fewer physical defects than were found among students from other high schools.[16]

Health education is increasingly being recognized and utilized as a *basic* area of learning as it expands in all major schools but especially in the junior high school. Here the student-centered health education approach is an excellent answer to the health needs that are so vital among early adolescent youth, regardless of their socioeconomic situations.

4. *What is the scope of physical fitness programs?*

The physical fitness program in the junior high school should be concerned that all boys and girls learn to function skillfully and efficiently without *undue*

[16] See Roscoe V. Cramer and Otto E. Domian, *Administration and Supervision in the Elementary School* (New York: Harper & Brothers, 1960), pp. 205-213, "Health and Safety Program in Switzer Elementary School." (One of the authors of this book has been principal of Switzer Elementary School and West Junior High School, with a similar health program in both schools for more than twenty years.)

fatigue. It should afford multiple experiences in "some 30 or more sport activities and various exercises"[17] geared to guiding students to conduct themselves in a socially approved manner, respect individual differences, cope with victory and defeat in a sportsmanlike way, and practice appropriate self-control during periods of emotional stress.

Since mid-century the following national educational organizations and prominent educators have described their athletic policies for twelve-to-fifteen-year-old boys and girls in four position statements:

1. In 1952 a joint committee of representatives from five major educational organizations (the National Education Association and two NEA departments, the Department of Elementary School Principals and the American Association of Health, Physical Education, and Recreation; the National Council of State Consultants in Elementary Education; and the Society of State Directors of Health, Physical Education, and Recreation) published the following statement: "Interscholastic competition of varsity pattern and similarly organized competition under the auspices of other community agencies are definitely disapproved for children below the ninth grade."[18]

2. Two years later, the Educational Policies Commission of the National Education Association and the American Association of School Administrators recommended, "No junior high school should have a 'school team' that competes with school teams of other junior high schools in organized leagues and tournaments. Varsity-type interscholastics for junior high boys and girls should not be permitted."[19]

3. Conant stated in his *Recommendations for Education in the Junior High School Years* that "Interscholastic athletics and marching bands are to be condemned in junior high schools; there is no sound reason for them and too often they serve merely as public entertainment."[20]

4. The Society of State Directors of Health, Physical Education, and Recreation vigorously emphasized the danger of highly organized athletic programs becoming the "tail that wags the dog." Stressing the importance of protecting the health and welfare of the relatively immature students in junior

[17] Raymond A. Snyder, "The Scope of Physical Education," *The Bulletin of the National Association of Secondary-School Principals,* 44:53, May, 1960.

[18] Louis E. Alley, "Guides for Conducting Junior High School Athletics," *School Activities,* 33:81-85, November, 1961.

[19] Educational Policies Commission, National Education Association, *School Athletics: Problems and Policies* (Washington: NEA and American Association of School Administrators, 1954), p. 36. When 220 physicians were asked to express opinions as to the suitability of eleven sports for interscholastic competition for boys twelve to fifteen years of age, each of the sports was rejected by a substantial majority, the ratio of disapproval in the case of football being 9 to 1, and in the case of basketball 4 to 1.

[20] James B. Conant, *Recommendations for Education in the Junior High School Years, A Memorandum to School Boards* (Princeton, N.J.: Educational Testing Service, 1960), p. 42.

high school athletic programs, it directed that competitive athletic activities must be appropriate to the age level of twelve to fifteen years.[21]

The marked discrepancy existent between these recommendations and present practices of interscholastic athletics for boys in approximately 80 per cent of the junior high schools is disquieting, to say the least.[22] This state of affairs appears to have several causes. The first is the traditional acceptance of the interscholastic athletic program that has been continually maintained in the senior high school. In 1957 a national survey was made by Tompkins and Roe of the extent to which junior high schools utilized interscholastic athletics. Of the 2329 junior high school principals questioned, 80 per cent responded that "the policy of interscholastic athletics had not changed in their schools since 1950."[23] The findings of this survey accentuate the degree to which athletic program practices in junior high schools are without authenticity and are inconsistent with the concept of the distinctive role of the junior high school.

Second, there is a long-standing tradition that the junior high program is the "feeder" of talented boys to athletic teams in senior high school. It is so deep-rooted in parents, students, and other community representatives that local school staffs, more times than not, question the feasibility of instituting changes in this area of their school programs regardless of how much they may intellectually realize the need for and value in such action. Therefore, recommendations from professional organizations and findings of research are frequently quite impotent or subservient to the intense local demand for "entertainment" and glamour which produces a distorted perception of junior high school purposes in relation to athletic programming.

The purposes of physical fitness programs for boys and girls during their junior high school years, "the turbulent years" of early adolescence,[24] are different in many aspects from those for later adolescents in senior high schools. When the concept that the junior high school has a distinct role to perform in physical fitness is accepted, there will be offered (1) a basic program of physical fitness, including special activities for students not physically able to participate in the regular program; and (2) intramurals and recreational programs.

[21] "A Statement of Junior High School Athletics," put out by the Society of State Directors of Health, Physical Education, and Recreation, March 15, 1961, and distributed by George T. Wilkins, State Superintendent of Public Instruction, Springfield, Ill.

[22] See Wright and Greer, *op. cit.*, p. 61, Table 35.

[23] Ellsworth E. Tompkins and Virginia Roe, "A Survey of Interscholastic Athletic Programs in Separately Organized Junior High Schools: A Project of the National Association of Secondary-School Principals Committee on Junior High School Education," *The Bulletin of the National Association of Secondary-School Principals,* 42:4, November, 1958.

[24] Antoinette Lowry, "The Turbulent Years," *Journal of Health, Physical Education, and Recreation,* 32:16-17, February, 1961.

Basic program of physical fitness

Physical fitness or physical education programs are required by state law almost without exception. In general all students engage in them as a fundamental learning area in each junior high school grade.

At the time boys and girls move from the elementary to the junior high school, they demand considerable guidance and patience from teachers as they adapt to their new environments. A trend is evolving to begin the basic program of physical fitness in the elementary school and extend and balance it in sequential order from grade to grade in the junior high school. It is believed that such a scheme may better accommodate new interests and varied physical abilities of early adolescents by affording a wide range of experiences for exploration and orientation in the "movement skills and appreciations." Such a distinct physical fitness program is offered separately for boys and girls in many junior high schools; however, they vary considerably in different, geographical areas. For one thing, physical facilities — swimming pools, playgrounds, and gymnasiums — are not always equal. Another factor is the availability of qualified teachers with classes not larger than the maximum regular class.

The following sports activities and exercises are advocated by physical educators for basic physical fitness programs in the curriculum of the junior high school:

Program for boys.

1. Games: In instructing boys how to play games in Grade 7, emphasis is placed on games of low organization, but in Grades 8 and 9 attention is focused on the fundamental skills and rules of playing regular seasonal group and dual games such as volleyball, soccer, basketball, touch football, softball, aerial darts, table tennis, hand tennis, and badminton. Body-contact games of tackle football, ice hockey, wrestling, and boxing are not included in junior high schools. Socially approved group interaction and group loyalty and spirit are instructional goals in all activities.

2. Track and field: The events offered in this area for all grades are usually broad jump; high jump; dashes, which vary according to grade from 50 to 100 yards; and relays, which vary from 200 to 440 yards. The shot put and sometimes the low hurdles are utilized in Grades 8 and 9.

3. Self-testing activities and gymnastics: In this broad area boys are helped to achieve individual advancement each year in tumbling skills, pyramids, horizontal bar, parallel bars, rope climbing, and stunts. Screening exercises comprised of pull-ups, sit-ups, and squad thrusts are also offered. As boys develop physical skills in these activities and exercises, muscular coordination and arm and shoulder strength, flexibility, abdominal strength, and agility are achieved.

4. Rhythmical activities: The folk, square, social, and mixer dances are usually elective activities for boys, most frequently chosen in Grades 8 and 9

in preparation for participation in coeducational classes in physical fitness, assembly programs, and school social activities.

5. Aquatics: Boys are instructed in the techniques of swimming, which are presented in a regular sequence in Grade 7. As they continue swimming instruction in Grades 8 and 9, increased competency should be shown at the end of each grade level. Opportunities to develop a higher degree of skill in swimming and diving by electing the swimming club are offered.

Program for girls.

1. Games: The group and dual games that are modified to meet the interests and abilities of girls in the junior high school are giant volleyball, dodgeball, aerial darts, hand tennis, table tennis, and speedball. As girls progress from grade to grade, they evidence more ability in teamwork and increased skill in playing the various games.

2. Track and field: The events offered in this area for all grades are the dash, which is limited to 50 yards in all grades, the relay, ranging from 200 yards in Grade 7, 240 yards in Grade 8, and 320 yards in Grade 9, and the high jump.

3. Self-testing activities and gymnastics: The same kinds of physical activities and exercises are utilized for girls as for boys, with some modifications to accommodate physical strength differentials. As girls develop skill in self-testing activities and gymnastics, they improve their physical fitness, which is as essential for girls as for boys.

4. Rhythmical activities: Folk, square, social, and mixer dances are popular with girls in all grades. They execute them with marked skill and appreciation in coeducational physical education classes, social activities in school, and recreational activities in adult life.

5. Aquatics: Girls are as interested and as capable of becoming proficient in swimming as boys. Swimming skill is essential to water safety while boys and girls are sailing, boating, canoeing, and fishing.[25]

With adequate facilities, specially prepared teachers, appropriate and effective guidance in the physical growth process, and emphasis on safety, this broad physical fitness program offers benefits for all junior high school students.

Intramural and recreational programs

The intramural program has become an integral part of regular physical fitness programs in junior high schools. It affords opportunities for voluntary

[25] See *Tentative Basic Curriculum for Boys and Tentative Basic Curriculum for Girls in Physical Education,* Junior High Schools, Health and Physical Education Department, Kansas City, Mo., Public Schools, 1957; *Curriculum Guide and Handbook for Girls' Physical Education, Grades 7-12,* Secondary Curriculum, Bulletin No. 136, Kansas City, Mo., Public Schools, 1963. Also see President Kennedy's Council on Youth Fitness, *Youth Physical Fitness: Suggested Elements of a School-Centered Program, Parts One and Two* (Washington: Government Printing Office, July, 1961), pp. 19-43.

participation by all students, the talented as well as the less skilled, in the various team, dual, and individual sports. The following is a list of the most popular non-competitive and competitive activities that are usually engaged in during different seasons:

TABLE 26

Intramurals for Boys and Girls

Fall	Winter	Spring
Touch or flag football[a]	Basketball	Softball
Soccer	Volleyball	Baseball[a]
Speedball	Table tennis	Tennis
Archery	Badminton	Archery
Swimming	Tumbling	Track and field
Tennis	Horizontal bar	Swimming
Dance clubs	Parallel bars	Dance clubs
Speed-A-Way	Side horse and buck	Golf[a]
Horseshoes	Swimming	Bait casting[a]
	Shuffleboard	School camping
	Aerial darts	Relays
	Dance clubs	
	Ping pong	
	Roller skating	

[a] Boys only.

From Karl W. Bookwalter and Carolyn Bookwalter (eds.), *Fitness for Secondary School Youth* (Washington: Association for Health, Physical Education, and Recreation, National Education Association, 1956), p. 74.

Intramural activities such as informal play, club activities, special events, tournaments, and meets are in actuality an outgrowth of the basic physical fitness classes. They often have been scheduled for interested students during a student activity period and before and after school. The season for any sport should not exceed six to eight weeks in order that all intramural activities desired by junior high school students may be offered during the school term. The teachers must play an active role in guiding students to experience a wide variety of intramural activities. The program should function continuously throughout the school year with facilities equally available to boys and girls.

All popular games and field events may be used in tournaments and meets in the school with the exclusion of the body-contact activities of tackle football, ice hockey, wrestling, and boxing, since these may result in physical and emotional damage during late preadolescence and early adolescence.

An effective intramural program may also be understood to be a recreational program, for all intramural activities are *elective* and each student freely selects what he finds most enjoyable and interesting. Other recreational activities may be offered during any free time of the school day. In communities where recreational facilities are limited the physical fitness equipment in the school may be made available on Saturday mornings for various student groups. A recreational program in the junior high school is essential, for "Education which is not also recreation is maimed, incomplete, and a half-done thing. The recreation which is not also education has no re-creative value."[26]

Numerous school systems, with junior high schools, operate adequate intramural and recreational programs that afford talented and interested students the resources through which they may prepare for future participation in the competitive athletics of senior high school. Such well-directed preparatory experiences protect against the creation of excessive competition in interscholastic programs, which is incongruent with the physical, social, and emotional capacities of early adolescents.

Many school systems have instituted comprehensive intramural and recreational programs and discontinued interscholastic athletics in their junior high schools. Some of these are enumerated by the city of their location: Minneapolis, Minnesota; Baltimore, Maryland; Salt Lake City, Utah; Des Moines, Iowa; Lincoln, Nebraska; Los Angeles, California; and Kansas City, Missouri. Although the format utilized by the different school systems varies markedly, the existence of the "village green," or commonalities, in all these programs effectively meets the physical, social, and emotional needs of junior high school students.

A descriptive guide for junior high school units of the Kansas City, Missouri, public schools is summarized below in order to illustrate the general characteristics of a program that excludes interscholastic athletics:

Recommendations for Boys and Girls in Intramural Activities in Junior High Schools

1. The point system of earning awards continues to be the responsibility of representative committees with the Department of Health and Physical Education. Awards of school letter and pin may be more meaningful to boys and girls and the student body when presented at an all school meeting or assembly.

2. The intramural program is an integral part of physical education. It should include all team and individual sports taught in the class period, where possible, extra-mural activities, such as bowling, skating, and horseback riding, particularly for girls.

3. The administration and supervision of intramural activities are as follows:

a. Each principal should appoint an advisor of the entire program for boys

[26] Lawrence Pearsall Jacks, *Education Through Recreation* (New York: Harper & Brothers, 1932), p. 2.

and girls, preferably a teacher of boys' and a teacher of girls' physical education.

b. Principals are to appoint additional personnel to assist in the intramural program as the need for assistance becomes evident.

c. An instructor, or advisor, who is assigned to one, or more, regular physical education classes shall conduct an intramural program after school two times each week in order to have adequate facilities. Intramural activities for boys are usually scheduled Monday and Wednesday, and for girls, Tuesday and Thursday.

d. Any boy or girl enrolled in school is eligible for intramural participation.

e. Individual and group awards shall be approved to stimulate participation.

f. Physical examinations for participation in intramurals will be the same as the current practice approved by the Board of Education.

g. Participation should be encouraged, but not required.

h. Participants should understand that a grade achieved in physical education classwork is not affected directly by participation in intramurals.

i. There should be an accumulative record showing each boy's and girl's participation in intramurals. When a student transfers to another school this record should be sent to the new school.

j. The administrator in charge of the budget should give consideration to an amount of money sufficient to defray the expense of operating an intramural program.[27]

This program perceives junior high school intramural activities as an outgrowth or prolongation of the regular physical education classes that allows early adolescents to utilize and integrate the physical, motor, and socialization skills derived from their foundational health and physical education learning experiences within the framework of self-elected activities and sports. Through elective experiences students can often build up the sense of adequacy that comes from successful performance, achieved in areas where individual interest and talent are high.

As junior high schools initiate and sustain adequate programs of health and physical fitness with the essential adjunctive intramural and recreational activities, staffed by *qualified* instructors, not only will the conflicts and pressures accompanying interscholastic athletics be reduced, but early adolescents will become more effective learners.

SELECTED BIBLIOGRAPHY

Alley, Louis E. "Guides for Conducting Junior High School Athletics," *School Activities,* 33:81-85, November, 1961.

[27] See *Intramural Activities for Junior and Senior High School Boys* (Kansas City, Mo.: Health and Physical Education Department, Board of Education, 1961), pp. 1-7; and *Intramural Activities for Junior and Senior High School Girls* (Kansas City, Mo.: Health and Physical Education Department, Board of Education, 1961), pp. 1-11.

American Association for Health, Physical Education, and Recreation, National Education Association. *Fitness for Secondary School Youth.* Washington: The Association, 1956. Pp. 1-150.

———. *Youth and Fitness: A Report of the National Conference on Fitness of Secondary School Youth.* Washington: The Association, 1959.

Anderson, Lester M., and Lauren A. Van Dyke. *Secondary School Administration.* Boston: Houghton Mifflin Company, 1963. Chapter 9, "Administration of Major Types of Extraclass Activities," including "Junior High School Athletics."

Beyer, Mary E. "Who Should Teach Health?" *The Bulletin of the National Association of Secondary-School Principals,* 44:38-41, May, 1960.

Bignell, Edward E. "The School's Responsibility for Recreation," *The Bulletin of the National Association of Secondary-School Principals,* 44:143-149, May, 1960.

Brownell, Clifford L. "The Role of Health, Physical Education, and Recreation in the Space Age," *The Bulletin of the National Association of Secondary-School Principals,* 44:3-9, May, 1960.

Conant, James B. *Recommendations for Education in the Junior High School Years, A Memorandum to School Boards.* Princeton, N.J.: Educational Testing Service, 1960.

Craig, Marjorie L., and Francis U. Everett. "Developing Health Potentialities," *Teachers College Record,* 61:429-434, May, 1960.

Cramer, Roscoe V., and Otto E. Domian. *Administration and Supervision in the Elementary School.* New York: Harper & Brothers, 1960.

———, Earl W. Sams, and Robert L. Holloway. "A Forward Look at Junior High-School Education," *The Bulletin of the National Association of Secondary-School Principals,* 40:425-440, April, 1956.

Curriculum Guide and Handbook for Girls' Physical Education, Grades 7-12, Secondary Curriculum, Bulletin No. 136. Kansas City, Mo., Public Schools, 1963.

Danford, Howard C. (ed.). *School Recreation National Conference Report.* Washington: American Association for Health, Physical Education, and Recreation, National Education Association, 1960. Pp. 1-58.

Educational Policies Commission, National Education Association. *The Central Purpose of American Education.* Washington: NEA and American Association of School Administrators, 1961. Pp. 1-21.

———. *School Athletics: Problems and Policies.* Washington: NEA and American Association of School Administrators, 1954.

Harnett, Arthur L. "The Scope of Health Education," *The Bulletin of the National Association of Secondary-School Principals,* 44:29-33, May, 1960.

Intramural Activities for Junior and Senior High School Boys. Kansas City, Mo.: Health and Physical Education Department, Board of Education, 1961.

Intramural Activities for Junior and Senior High School Girls. Kansas City, Mo.: Health and Physical Education Department, Board of Education, 1961.

Junior High Schools for Iowa Youth. Des Moines: Iowa State Department of Public Education, Division of Curriculum, 1960. Pp. 1-59.

LaSalle, Dorothy, and Gladys Greer. *Health Instruction for Today's Schools.*

Englewood Cliffs, N.J.: Prentice-Hall, Inc., 1963. Chapter 4, "Content, Objectives and Learning Experiences — Junior and Senior High Schools."

Lowry, Antoinette. "The Turbulent Years," *Journal of Health, Physical Education and Recreation,* 32:16-17, February, 1961.

Missouri's Guide for Physical Education in the Secondary School, Grades Seven-Twelve. Jefferson City: Hubert Wheeler, Commissioner of Education, January, 1960. Chaps. 3 and 6.

National Association of Secondary-School Principals, National Education Association. *Planning for American Youth: An Educational Program for Youth of Secondary-School Age* (a summary of *Education for All American Youth,* a publication of the Educational Policies Commission, NEA). Washington: The Association, 1944. Pp. 1-63.

President Kennedy's Council on Youth Fitness. *Youth Physical Fitness: Suggested Elements of a School-Centered Program, Parts One and Two.* Washington: Government Printing Office, July, 1961. Pp. 1-111.

Putnam, Rex. *The Organization and Function of Oregon Junior High Schools.* Salem: Superintendent of Public Instruction, 1959. Pp. 1-43.

Reid, Harry E. "What Kind of Control for Junior High-School Interscholastic Athletics?" *The Bulletin of the National Association of Secondary-School Principals,* 45:91-93, April, 1961.

Research Division, National Education Association. *The Junior High School.* Washington: The Association, November, 1959. Pp. 1-7.

Schlichenmaier, Arthur W. "The Schlichenmaier Method of Safety Education," *School Activities,* 33:212, March, 1962.

Shaw, John H. "Emphasis and Sequence in Health Teaching," *The Bulletin of the National Association of Secondary-School Principals,* 44:34-38, May, 1960.

Smith, Julian W. *Outdoor Education.* Washington: American Association for Health, Physical Education, and Recreation, National Education Association, 1956. Pp. 1-32.

Smith, Sara Louise. "Characteristics of a Good Secondary School Health Education Program," *The Bulletin of the National Association of Secondary-School Principals,* 44:45-46, May, 1960.

Snyder, Raymond A. "The Scope of Physical Education," *The Bulletin of the National Association of Secondary-School Principals,* 44:52-57, May, 1960.

"Statement of Junior High School Athletics, A," put out by the Society of State Directors of Health, Physical Education, and Recreation, March 15, 1961, and distributed by George T. Wilkins, State Superintendent of Public Education, Springfield, Ill.

Tentative Basic Curriculum for Boys and Tentative Basic Curriculum for Girls in Physical Education, Junior High School Grades 7, 8, and 9. Kansas City, Mo.: Health and Physical Education Department, Public Schools, April, 1957.

Tompkins, Ellsworth E., and Virginia Roe. "A Survey of Interscholastic Athletic Programs in Separately Organized Junior High Schools," *The Bulletin of the National Association of Secondary-School Principals,* 42:1-47, November, 1958.

Wright, Grace S., and Edith S. Greer. *The Junior High School, A Survey of Grades 7-8-9 in Junior and Junior-Senior High Schools, 1959-1960.* U.S. Office of Education Bulletin No. 32. Washington: Government Printing Office, 1963.

10

Student Activities

Student activities have had an important place in junior high school from its beginning. One of the conditions which influenced the advancement of the junior high school after the late 1920's was the concern of many educators that unique late preadolescent and early adolescent needs and interests were not being adequately met by programs directed primarily to the needs of late adolescents. Educators have continuously sought effective media through which student activities could be a meaningful part of the learning experiences of the late preadolescent and early adolescent student.

With its relative freedom from the technical course requirements imposed by the colleges, universities, and state departments of education upon the senior high schools, the junior high school has been able to make student activities a more integral part of its educational program. In this chapter consideration will be given to the educational significance of student activities as a regular part of the curriculum, and how they may be and are being integrated into the curriculum program of the junior high school.

Student activities have had a long history in the American secondary school, having been introduced from Europe, where they have been traced to the Middle Ages. These activities were so well received in England's public schools that much of the leadership ability of England's famous men, collectively speaking, has been attributed to "the playing fields of Eton."

In spite of the early introduction of student activities into American secondary schools they were not favored by educational officials here until after 1900, as is evidenced in part by the use of the term "extracurricular activities" for these non-academic or less formal classroom activities.

Not until the newer psychological studies began to challenge the assumptions of the older theories of learning, and evidence of the nature of individual differences and the significance of early adolescence came into prominence just prior to and immediately after the turn of the century did the so-called extracurricular activities begin to receive a new appraisal.[1] With it came a rapid shift in attitude toward the values inherent in these activities. From a stance of completely ignoring them, to one of toleration, and finally to one of full acceptance of their importance in the total educational process by the more progressive schools, a complete reversal of position has taken place in less than three decades of this century.

The change in attitude has been reflected in the rapid shift in the new designations given to these activities. The term "extracurricular activities" has not completely disappeared, but it has been largely superseded, cautiously at first by "extraclass activities," "semi-curricular activities," "co-curricular activities," and finally by the term coming rapidly into general use, "student activities," the term used in this book.[2]

The evolution of the activity concept in junior high school programming has placed considerable emphasis on the contemporary curriculum. With the acceptance of guidance and counseling programs, block-time classes, core programs, and broader exploration of personal interest activities, most junior and junior-senior high schools are now scheduling school organizations and student activities in homeroom or activity periods which afford better opportunities for early youth to make appropriate social adjustments with their peers and adult leaders. This new approach provides a wider variety of projects, enables the student to discover and develop abilities or special talents, and enriches the basic areas of learning.

Thus, the former sharp division between student-centered activities and the curriculum of the junior high school is diminishing. The most appropriate designation for the activity concept is "student activities" as it has now become a part of curriculum in most secondary schools.

1. Are student activities integrable in the curriculum?

The value of student activities within educational programs of four-year high schools began to be recognized by many school staffs immediately prior

[1] For a history of the development of student activities in the early American secondary schools see E. D. Grizzell, "Evolution of Student Activities in the Secondary School," *Educational Outlook,* November, 1926, and, by the same author, *The Origin and Development of the High School in New England Before 1865* (New York: The Macmillan Company, 1923). See also P. W. Terry, *Supervising Extra-Curricular Activities* (New York: McGraw-Hill Book Co., Inc., 1930), Chap. I.

[2] Some twenty or more terms have been used to designate these activities. See particularly Harry C. McKown, *Extra-Curricular Activities* (New York: The Macmillan Company, 3rd ed., 1952); Franklin A. Miller, James H. Moyer, and Robert B. Patrick, *Planning Student Activities* (Englewood Cliffs, N.J.: Prentice-Hall, Inc., 1956).

to the advent of the junior high school. The establishment of this school unit, when "extra-class activities were increasingly advocated and accepted as a vital part of the educational program on a par with the curriculum and, in the minds of many persons, a legitimate part of the curriculum itself," was most timely and fortunate.[3]

A survey of the extent and use of club activities in approximately two hundred junior high schools in 1934 revealed them to be well-advanced and highly organized enterprises. A few years later, Pringle stated, "If the concept of education maintained throughout this book is accepted, there would seem to be no sharp line of demarcation between curricular and extracurricular programs; but only time will determine the degree of coalescence that is pedagogically desirable."[4]

Pringle also delineated the distinguishing features of student activities: (1) strong emotional and social appeal to both preadolescent and early adolescent students; (2) many physical and psychological values for rapidly growing youth; (3) socialization opportunities within the schools; (4) broad exploratory resources; (5) encouragement of spontaneous effort, enthusiasm, and satisfactions; and (6) creative and enriching components applicable to the entire educational program.

The educational role of student activities was fairly well established within the junior high school curriculum during the 1940's. This new prominence has brought into vivid focus the as yet unmet need for staff members to perfect methods for guiding students effectively in group and individual activities. Some improvement occurred when teacher training institutions began to offer preparation in the "activity concept" for trainees oriented toward junior high school practice and to initiate specific training activities in sponsorship of student activities which cut across grade lines.

Shortly after mid-century, Tompkins reported, activity periods were included in the daily schedule in almost two-thirds of undivided junior-senior high schools and in more than two-thirds of separate junior and senior high schools.[5] In a study of the organization and curriculum in 155 junior high schools, McEachen found that club activities for all students had become an integral part of the curriculum in all the schools surveyed.[6]

"What kind of activities program for students in junior high schools?" Jonathan Lowe, principal of Beverly Hills Junior High School, Huntington,

[3] Leonard V. Koos, *Junior High School Trends* (New York: Harper & Brothers, 1955), pp. 86-87.

[4] Ralph W. Pringle, *The Junior High School* (New York: McGraw-Hill Book Co., Inc., 1937), p. 303.

[5] See Ellsworth Tompkins, *The Activity Period in Public High Schools,* U.S. Office of Education Bulletin No. 19 (Washington: Government Printing Office, 1951), Table 4, p. 16.

[6] Howard D. McEachen, "Status and Trends in Organization of Selected Junior High Schools," Ed.D. dissertation, University of Kansas, 1955, p. 106.

West Virginia, asked this question of the principals of twenty-five consolidated and city junior high schools in West Virginia with enrollments of 1500. "Twenty-four of the principals endorsed the *valued place* of the student activities program in their schools." It is interesting to note that all but one approved the student activity program because it provided their students "an opportunity to experience new activities, arouse latent interests and abilities, try out new subject areas, learn to do new things, and thus be properly fitted for the gradual transition from preadolescent education to that type of education and specialization suited to the needs of older adolescents."[7]

In another survey of a limited number of junior high schools, Victor Pitkin, consultant in citizenship education in the State Department of Education, Hartford, Connecticut, requested students to respond to the question "What is the most important honor that you ever had?" The student answers were classified into two groups, in accordance with whether these experiences occurred in or out of school. Examples of responses follow:

Out of School

1. When I received my swimming badge at camp.
2. When I was chosen to help serve food at the Blood Mobile.
3. Baby-sitting — taking full responsibility for care of a 1½-year-old child.
4. Junior bridesmaid at my cousin's wedding.
5. Crowning the Blessed Virgin in my church.
6. Chosen to go with a Scout group to Valley Forge Jamboree.
7. When I won a tennis tournament.
8. When I was made a Star Scout.
9. When I received a certificate stating I was a junior life guard.
10. Getting an award from the Connecticut State Vegetable Growers.

In School

1. Being on the honor roll in my school.
2. Being president of my class.
3. Being in the Leader's Club in our gym.
4. Being on the student council.
5. When I was asked to sing a solo for an assembly program.
6. Being president of my club.
7. Being president of the student council.
8. When I took a leading part in the Drama Club.
9. When some of my work in the Art Club was exhibited at a local art show.
10. When a principal wrote me a personal and wonderful letter for something I had done for the school.[8]

[7] Jonathan Y. Lowe, "What Kind of Activities Program for Students in Junior High School?" *The Bulletin of the National Association of Secondary-School Principals,* 43:254, April, 1959.

[8] Victor E. Pitkin, "What Kind of Activities Program for Students in Junior High School?" Reprinted by permission from *The Bulletin of the National Association of Secondary-School Principals,* April, 1959. Copyright: Washington, D.C. Pp. 255-256.

Student activities are both meaningful to and desired by youth attending junior high school. To de-emphasize them in an effort to insure quality of learning "would be as foolish as to require every pupil in the junior high school to take accelerated mathematics, science, and modern foreign language."[9]

Several research studies on student activities in junior high schools, analyzed by Rennicke and Hearn and edited by Eash, indicated the trends in activity programs for early youth:

> . . . (a) the conscious effort to relate objectives of nonclass activities to the general objectives of education; (b) increased attention to the problems of overparticipation and underparticipation; (c) attempts to solve problems of imbalance, whereby some activities were overemphasized to the detriment of the remainder of the program; (d) broadened student participation in school government and more shared responsibility between students and school management; (e) viewing of nonclass activities as part of teacher's regular load, and not as adjunct of the formal curriculum . . . and (f) linking nonclass activities to projects sponsored by local community and civic clubs.[10]

The continuance of student activities as an integral part of the curriculum in junior high schools is clearly evident. They are being assigned as a regular component in the teaching load of all teachers, and the same professional know-how is being utilized to improve their effectiveness as is directed to other areas of the curriculum.

In the Indiana State Department of Education bulletin, *The Junior High School,* Wilson describes the diverse and distinct educational benefits of student activities not available in regular classes or after school:

> These extra class activities (student activities) should reinforce classroom learning through enrichment, variation, and exploration; provide for the learning of the social skills and social adjustment involved in citizenship, democratic processes, and neutral cooperation; provide desirable activities not possible in the regular classroom which will furnish wholesome recreational experiences for adolescent as well as adult life; lead students to broader social and cultural horizons; develop interest in school, thereby building better school morale; and aid in the discovery and identification of special interests and potential abilities.[11]

[9] R. V. Braham, "What Role for Student Activities in the New Emphasis on Quality in Secondary Education?" *The Bulletin of the National Association of Secondary-School Principals,* 44:111, April, 1960.

[10] Maurice J. Eash, "The School Program: Nonclass Experience," *Review of Educational Research,* 30:62, February, 1960.

[11] William E. Wilson, *The Junior High School* (Bloomington, Ind.: State Department of Public Instruction, Bulletin No. 246, 1961), p. 94.

2. *What principles guide the development of student activities?*

The educational assets offered by a well-integrated student activity program are so numerous as to require a set of guiding principles to aid school staffs in evolving their own balanced combination of clubs and activities. These principles may also provide direction for students in their participation in school activities.

Foundational principles must be correlated with a sound philosophy of junior high school education, consistent with the psychology of learning for early adolescent boys and girls. The list of broad principles recommended by Bossing as guidelines to the development of constructive student activities in junior and senior high schools is presented here:

1. Student activities should be an integral part of the total school curriculum.
2. All activities should be scheduled on school time.
3. As far as possible a specific place on the school schedule should be set aside for student activities.
4. Participants should be free of financial obligations for all basic costs of an activity.
5. Student participation in activities should be encouraged and minimal participation should be required.
6. Students should be free under guidance to participate in the activities of their choice.
7. The administration of admission and participation requirements should be democratic.
8. Annually each activity should be functionally evaluated as a basis of its admission or continuance in the program.
9. Credit for participation in student activities should be awarded on the same principles that govern other curriculum offerings.
10. Sponsors should be limited to the school staff.
11. The function of the sponsor should be advisory and guiding in nature.
12. Student activities should be financed by regular budgetary provision of the Board of Education on the same basis as other curricular activities.[12]

When these principles are applied, student activities typically become integrated with the whole educational program and fulfill the purposes of the junior high school.

[12] Nelson L. Bossing, *Principles of Secondary Education,* Second Edition. © 1955, by permission of Prentice-Hall, Inc., Englewood Cliffs, N.J. Pp. 453-454.

3. *What student activities are needed?*

This question is of considerable consequence to junior high schools. Many activities that would be consistent with the student's elective interests and abilities as they are revealed through appropriate counsel with school staff members are not now being offered.

In his book *The Third Curriculum,* Frederick suggests 287 special interest clubs and activities.[13] The state of Virginia's Governor's Commission reported that 210 student activities were either recognized or functioning in the public schools of the state. A commission appointed to study these activities, along with other areas in the curriculum, to determine the interrelationship between class and school activities in the public junior and senior high schools with enrollments from 200 to 1500 students found a minimum of 200 different student activities being offered. The total list of activities used in a study of 400 junior high schools may be included under the major classifications of student activities corresponding to those in current educational literature:[14]

1. The School Assembly
2. School Publications
3. Social Activities
4. The Student Council
5. Special Interest Activities and Service Clubs

There is an increasing tendency to expand student activity opportunities in most junior high school programming. The impetus for this action stems in part from a philosophy of education aimed at accommodating the diverse interests of all students. Programs formulated in the earlier junior high school afforded active participation only to students demonstrating the most talent and skill, thereby limiting activities and clubs to a relatively small number.

Homeroom

One of the initial organizational features of the junior high school was the designation of a homeroom period of approximately thirty minutes of each school day. Its purpose was to give the young student a sense of security and allow the homeroom teacher to help him find his way through the maze of many students, classrooms, and teachers with a minimum of anxiety. This

[13] Robert W. Frederick, *The Third Curriculum: Student Activities in American Education* (New York: Appleton-Century-Crofts, Inc., 1959), Appendix B, "A Classified List of Student Activities," pp. 433-435.

[14] The student activity programs were reported by superintendents, principals, and teachers in junior high schools, who were students in a course in "The Junior High School," College of Education, University of Minnesota, during the Summer Sessions of 1957, 1958, 1959, and 1960.

structure is retained as a pivot or anchor for early youth struggling to adapt to a new and different learning environment.

As student activities expand, contemporary homeroom activities are more reflective of the increased scope and meaning of the learning opportunities being extended to early youth:[15]

Pupil Personnel Administration and Guidance

1. Student welfare
2. Entertainment of parents
3. Social events or parties
4. Individual guidance
5. Group guidance
   Planning educational program of students
   Boy-girl relationships
   Assistance of students in solving their personal-social-educational problems
6. Report cards and parent conferences
7. The cumulative record card, the basic tool for guidance
8. Development and distribution of codes of conduct or citizenship
9. Class meetings of civic and character-building programs
10. Student handbook preparation and distribution

Student Activities

1. A unit for student council representation
2. A place for nominating, campaigning, and voting for officers
3. Planning and promoting student activity program
   Publications, preparation and distribution
   Personal interest activities and clubs
   School service clubs
4. A unit for student council committee to help manage student activity program
5. A unit for student representation in school-community surveys and improvement of recreational programs
6. A unit for intramural competition, unless intramural activities are organized as a part of physical education classes
7. Cooperative planning with the faculty assemblies for recognition or awards of students in honor society, citizenship, intramurals, and special achievements in classrooms and in student activity program
8. Plan student activities with civic and service organizations of the community as Junior Red Cross, Neighborhood Council, Boy and Girl Scouts, 4-H Clubs, etc.

Administrative Routine

1. Announcements for students and parents
2. Explanation of school policies and plans in the handbook
3. Attendance reporting and promotion

[15] See further lists of activities and projects for the homeroom, Frederick, *op. cit.*, p. 327.

4. School banking
5. School fire drills
6. Locker assignments
7. Selling tickets for school programs and activities
8. Distribution of school information to parents

The regular functions assigned to the homeroom have steadily increased, as the foregoing list indicates, and the student program continues to mushroom. Information obtained from a national survey described the ordinary homeroom scheduling practices as not producing the desired results in student activities:

> One of the most controversial activities in the curriculum program is that of the home room. Theoretically, the home room should be the cocurriculum's basic activity; in practice it is often one of the least popular organizations in the program. In many schools, neither students nor faculty are enthusiastic about their home rooms. It is an organizational concept that should work but fails to live up to its potentialities in many schools. As an indication of this problem, the national survey on which this book is based revealed that not one school recommended the home room as worthy of special mention. Of course, one should not infer from this that all home rooms are inferior. Rather, it should be accepted that, in the opinion of those submitting data, there are other organizations more deserving of special commendation.[16]

Perhaps the best scheme applicable to junior high school scheduling of student activities is to combine them with regular block-time classes, except for operational routines which may be more effectively managed during the first or another regular class period of the school day.

The slow pace in which homeroom activities are becoming an integral part of the longer class period is somewhat surprising in view of the fact that one-half or more of all junior high schools, divided and undivided, have block-time classes. In a study of 251 junior high schools, Lounsbury reported that 59 per cent of the schools employed block-time scheduling and 93 per cent retained separate homeroom periods with an average span of twenty-eight minutes.[17]

All homeroom activities, except operational routine, were consolidated with the block-time class schedule of two and one-half periods for all three grade levels in West Junior High School, Kansas City, Missouri, in this manner: the principal (one of the authors of this book), assistant principal, counselor, and thirty-five teachers conferred and agreed to increase by ten minutes the length of all first-period classes to deal with operational routines, which had

[16] Miller, Moyer, and Patrick, *op. cit.*, p. 172. © 1956, by permission of Prentice-Hall, Inc., Englewood Cliffs, N.J.

[17] See John H. Lounsbury, "The Role and Status of the Junior High School," doctoral dissertation, George Peabody College, 1954, p. 134.

formerly been handled in a separate thirty-minute homeroom period. The major activities of two homerooms were combined into two block-time classes for a year. It was anticipated that such a span of time would afford those involved ample opportunity to evaluate the assets and liabilities of the plan. There was some concern that teachers might feel overburdened with a daily total of five class periods which included teaching, guidance, and homeroom during a seven-hour day. However, after one year all block-time teachers recommended that their homerooms be continued as an integral part of their two daily block-time classes.

Student activities were formulated, sustained, and directed in the block-time homeroom classes by scheduling one weekly class period. First and second periods were alternated during the first semester, and sixth and seventh periods during the second semester, without augmenting the standard teaching load.

It is apparent that the quantity and quality of homeroom activities have *really outgrown the short homeroom period* in highly departmentalized junior high schools. The trend of retreating from complete departmentalization to block-time scheduling, including homeroom activities, helps the homeroom accommodate a broader, more dynamic student activities program.

School assembly

The school assembly is one student activity which did *not* have to struggle for a place in the curriculums of either junior or senior high schools. It had an early initiation in secondary schools and has continued to develop through at least three stages of modification in an educational philosophy which now considers early youth and their preparation for life the focal point of education.

During the initial stage religious activities, such as Bible reading, prayer, and devotional exercises, made up the major part of the school assembly. In the second stage the headmaster or principal and faculty planned and implemented the program. The religious emphasis was sustained to stimulate spiritual and moral conduct, but the program was expanded to include announcements of school plans and policies, and entertainment. The headmaster or principal presided and students were engaged only as non-participating spectators. In the third stage "the student-faculty developed assembly" stressed student participation in planning and producing assembly programs, which evidenced many learning benefits, directly and indirectly, referable to regular classes, homerooms, and various other student activities.[18]

Originated in the early secondary schools, the assembly has broadened its purposes and functions to more effectively relate to the educational needs of

[18] The United States Supreme Court's decision and state legislation permitting or denying Bible reading in the schools has influenced the third stage of the development of the school assembly.

early youth in the junior high school. It is not only the oldest but also one of the most valuable of student activities, since it enables students, faculty, and others to work together to provide a variety of rich and rewarding learning experiences.

The programs influence the students in a positive way and permit them to cope more adequately and constructively with the accelerated changes taking place within themselves as well as in their new environment. The latter is marked by the transition from a small elementary school group to membership in a much larger and more diversified junior high school group. It often encourages students to be enthusiastic participants as well as listeners in school assemblies.

Active participation in the assembly program yields satisfying experiences which build self-confidence and help maintain the stability required to adequately meet intellectual, emotional, and social developmental needs. Assemblies may include student council activities; special holiday programs geared to recognition of ethical, moral, and patriotic values; and formal recognition of outstanding academic and creative achievements in all areas of the curriculum.

Practical application of student participation in the assembly activity is well described in the 1961 Handbook of the Callahan Junior High School, Des Moines, Iowa:

> *Assemblies*
>
> Assemblies are scheduled for Friday morning, usually at 8:50. They feature guest speakers, concerts, shows, talent presentations, and special programs prepared and presented by homeroom and class groups. There may be some professional assembly programs each year but we wish especially to encourage *student prepared and produced* assemblies from classes or homerooms, or volunteer groups. Parents are always welcome at any of these programs.

From the time of the early town meeting in New England, freedom of assembly has been viewed as an inherent right and privilege belonging to all citizens of the United States.

The school, one of the most influential social institutions in a democratic society, must guide students to broaden their intellectual, cultural, and spiritual horizons; foster understanding and acceptance of action for the common good; and assimilate values and beliefs that will perpetuate the democratic way of life. The junior high school assembly is an effective medium through which these goals may be attained. Thompson ably treats this concept in her book *Vitalized Assemblies,* as is demonstrated by this excerpt:

> Assembling is part of the American scene. Being a spectator or a passive listener is part of every day life. The audience situation is an educative device

that offers a wide range of possibilities in developing acceptable attitudes and behavior in large gatherings, not only toward those convoked but also toward the performers and the performances. In this era of urbanization and increased leisure time, such experiences should not be denied either city or rural students. The assembly is an essential part of the school's curricular activities.[19]

Technological advances in audio-visual materials and techniques have produced a wide variety of excellent adjunctive reinforcements to regular school assembly programming. For example, via television, regular teachers can watch experts in a specific content area of instruction and thus expand their own knowledge in a given unit of work. Following the assembly presentation the individual teacher and her students immediately adjourn to their classroom to discuss the material viewed and integrate it with the regular unit of study. These adjunctive instructional experiences necessitate prior collaborative planning by different staff members, including making sure of the availability of the physical facilities of an auditorium and audio-visual equipment.

In modern junior high school programs the significant and unique functions of the assembly continue to expand rather than contract. Thus an auditorium ought really to accommodate 100 per cent of the school enrollment at one session. In the larger schools, where each grade or unit of 250-300 students, inclusive of Grades 7-8-9, occupies a different wing of the school building — "three little schools within one big school" — the auditorium or school theater should afford seating for all of the students in one of the "little schools." Space limitations which preclude school assembly attendance by all students usually force the utilization of more rigid and highly departmentalized procedures, which negates dynamic and functional instructional programs.

School publications

After completing a national survey of school publications in junior and senior high schools, Miller, Moyer, and Patrick concluded, "The point should be reaffirmed, that in only one-eighth of the cases reporting marked success with publications do the advisors believe that the administration requested the initiation of a school publication; in over half the cases reporting, the advisors say that the students saw the need and requested beginning it."[20] As the needs and interests of the students are more accurately identified and understood by junior high school staffs, a school paper, magazine, or handbook is usually published. Yearbooks are common, but the benefits to students are not comparable with those of publications put out several times during the school year. The preparation and issuing of mimeographed or printed junior high school papers on current events and school news offer students multiple learning opportunities which accommodate individual dif-

[19] Nellie Zetta Thompson, *Vitalized Assemblies* (New York: E. P. Dutton & Co., Inc., 1952), p. 11.

[20] Miller, Moyer, and Patrick, *op. cit.*, p. 421.

ferences not often available in the regular curriculum — for example, news reporting and writing, interviewing, line drawing, and feature article writing.

The merger of student activities with all other curriculums has not yet been fully realized, as is evident in many junior high school practices. The rather typical custom of assigning the complete responsibility and the opportunities which accompany the publication of a school paper to a few select journalism students illustrates the fragmentation of a specific activity with potentials of affording meaningful learning experiences to many students. These potentials may be realized by focusing publication work in the block-time or core classes, by encouraging maximum student participation, and by using this activity to reinforce language and art instruction.

Major benefits from publication activities are (1) opportunities to gain experience in critical and purposeful thinking; (2) opportunities for creative expression, both in literary and in graphic form; (3) enhancement of individual self-esteem through recognition by peers, faculty, family, and friends; and (4) opportunities to view tangible evidence of achievements.

The school magazine is usually issued twice a year since students require considerable thought and time to compose original ideas. Engagement of all students capable of and intereseted in literary and artistic work is often best accomplished when a school service club, under the direction of a competent faculty adviser, sponsors, edits, and publishes the school magazine. The magazine may include short stories, poems, plays, humorous articles, cartoons, photographs, line drawings, pictures of carvings, feature articles on special events, reports of student achievements, and biographies of special assembly speakers.

A handbook for students is another school publication, either printed or mimeographed, which is a valuable orientation medium. A scrutiny of student handbooks revealed that most are published by the faculty, the student council, and the homerooms, and have broad application in almost all junior high schools, small and large, those in the latter being more comprehensive.[21]

Social activities

Guiding the social growth of boys and girls twelve to fifteen years old is considered a major function of all junior high school programs. This function is often neglected or poorly implemented, primarily owing to lack of understanding of the nature of early adolescents and their intense socialization interests, which are typically marked by demands for change. An adequate school program, designed to teach students to effectively cope with the often uncomfortable requirements of early youth, must offer opportunities to learn and practice social skills in interaction with peers and teachers within the pro-

[21] The student activity programs were reported by superintendents, principals, and teachers in junior high schools, who were students in a course in "The Junior High School," College of Education, University of Minnesota, during the Summer Sessions of 1957, 1958, 1959, and 1960.

tective environs of the regular class groups. Student activities which are integral components of the curriculum are a major requisite in healthful social development. The success of this program is highly dependent upon school staff interest, awareness, and acceptance of the early adolescent's behavior, frequently manifested in confusion of his assets and liabilities and in his complex system of communication.

Communication, either positive or negative, may be expressed verbally, attitudinally, or by direct action. It may be marked by intense frustration associated with the growth and developmental process and may temporarily impede attempts to use successfully both old and new abilities. Student activities, therefore, must be varied, flexible, and purposeful. The teacher's dedication, sincerity, and empathy toward the early adolescent are crucial in all aspects of a student activity program.

In these critical formative years it is vital for the adolescent to acquire acceptable social values and skills which will equip him to handle most social situations. When the program is carefully planned to accommodate the specific needs of young adolescents, and learning the basic social conduct patterns is considered of prime importance in the curriculum areas of music, art, and physical education, education will have positively fulfilled society's commitment to early youth. The instructional focus in regular classes must also be mindful of the *social* as well as the intellectual and physical components of all students. The socioeconomic and cultural background and type of community in which the students reside must be considered in all activity programming.[22]

A broad student activity program in the junior high school is a forceful motivational influence to students in their selection of appropriate social activities. It may be focused in regular school classes or in activities cosponsored by the school and community, such as Hi-Y, 4-H Club, Boy and Girl Scouts, Anglers Club, Allied Youth Club, School Safety Patrol, Junior Red Cross, and others.

Successful socialization within the school environment necessitates cooperative planning with parents, staff members, and student representatives from regular classes, homerooms, and student council. Parental assistance in the selection of social activities and parental acceptance of appropriate responsibility in relation to student participation in social events held within the school building are strongly advocated.

Student council

A study of student councils in 112 junior high schools in Pennsylvania notes that "student councils have become well established in the junior high schools there, with a growth period dating back three decades [and] that

[22] See also "Special interest activities and clubs" in the latter part of this chapter.

student councils were organized and operated in accordance with accepted democratic principles."[23]

When the student council is accorded important status by the principal and teachers, it will not be considered "an operation in a vacuum," "a plaything," or "the tail that wags the dog" but will be recognized as an essential and effective student activity. Student council experiences often aid in the formation of productive attitudes toward authority, including acceptance of majority decisions and the principal's responsibility to veto inappropriate group recommendations. The principal's veto of decisions made by the student council is similar to "a fire extinguisher on the wall," rarely exercised, but readily available when decisive direction is called for to deter destructive actions, typically associated with the impulsiveness of the early adolescent period of development.

An examination of junior high school student council programs reveals a varied pattern in the nature of specific duties undertaken. Most of the councils have the responsibility to manage with appropriate freedom certain school activities: social events, student government or a citizenship program, special interest activities, and service clubs within the student activity program.

Formulation of codes of conduct. An effective and progressive student government program obligates the student council, with consultation from the faculty sponsor, to assist in engaging all students to participate in formulating and implementing their own code of conduct, which is acceptable within the school and community.

Student-formulated conduct codes are considered a causative factor in the improvement of social conduct in many junior high schools, and their value is markedly augmented when parents and school staff are active participants.

The organization of a Parent-Teacher Association-Student Council Code of the Hastings, Nebraska, Junior High School illustrates how parents, student council representatives, and teachers designed a conduct code. The student council representatives discussed in their homerooms the various aspects of a code and obtained approval from the majority of the student body. A committee was then appointed, composed of student officers and faculty sponsors, the principal and assistant principal, the president of the P.T.A., the school social worker, and several parents selected from the community at large. This committee gathered information from schools and communities with similar codes and, after considerable discussion, devised a code to be applied as a guide for parents and students.

The student council officers drew up and distributed a thirty-three-question "opinion poll." The poll results were tabulated and the majority opinions were incorporated in a conduct code, thereby affording students direct partici-

[23] William Leslie Cross, "The Student Council in the Junior High Schools in Pennsylvania (1955)," *The Bulletin of the National Association of Secondary-School Principals,* 46:257-259, February, 1962.

pation in the code contents. A committee was appointed to formulate a draft of the proposed code, which was then printed, with a local men's service club and a local business firm assuming financial responsibility for all printing.

The purpose of the code was stated in the introduction:

> We, the students of Hastings Junior High School and our parents, in a spirit of cooperation and with a sense of responsibility to each other, our home, our school and our community, recognize that our characters and reputations depend upon our good behavior at all times.
>
> Our common purpose is to make the social activities of the Junior High School years as happy and pleasurable as possible to all concerned, and to this end we adopt this Code of Conduct and pledge ourselves to its year-'round observance. In so doing we recognize that parents' authority is at all times the final authority.[24]

This code ascribes responsibility for acceptable conduct to student and parent. Sections of the code include basic criteria for entertaining, appropriate dress and grooming, acceptable hours and conduct for social events, sincere respect for the rights and property of others, responsibility for homework assignments, proper attitudes toward home duties, and constructive use of leisure time.

These authors believe that codes of conduct for junior high school students afford manifold benefits. The benefits increase when parents actively participate, but it is equally important for school staff members to share in code formulation and implementation.

The role of school staff members differs from that of either the student or parent since they function primarily as consultants within the school environs. Student conduct outside the school arena should, however, concern them in direct relation to the impact it may have upon the student body as a whole. Undesirable behavior reflects upon all constituents of home, school, or community. Thus the need for impressing the value and growth potential of socially acceptable conduct upon malleable early youth cannot be overemphasized.

Special interest activities and clubs

Special interest activities often serve to motivate the development of specific skills. Clubs may be oriented to school and community needs and afford students practical service experience. Or they may allow students to participate in group-defined projects which afford experiences in communicating original ideas, attitudinal modification, and contributing to a common goal or benefit. Special interest activities are of extreme value in exposing

[24] Richard L. Cronin, "Our Junior High School P.T.A. Student Council Code," *School Activities,* 32:135, January, 1961.

the student to the satisfactions obtained from completing a self-selected project or task.

Procedures for organizing and implementing special interest activities are discussed here, as utilized in Kensington Junior High School, Kensington, Maryland, and Highland Park Junior High School, St. Paul, Minnesota.

Kensington Junior High School Program. Interest and service clubs in Kensington Junior High School are organized and scheduled within a school day of six class periods of sixty minutes each, inclusive of passing time. Homeroom periods are scheduled from 8:40 to 9:00 A.M. The interest clubs meet the first period on Tuesday and the service clubs the second period on Thursday, with regular classes scheduled four, instead of five, days per week for an enrollment of 1400 students. The two weekly activity periods are not begun until after the regular school organization is completed, approximately October 1.

Each teacher was sponsor for one of the following interest clubs:

Art for instrumental music students
Art for French students
Astronomy club
Audio-visual aids
Automotive club
Biological science club
Blue and White, school newspaper
Bridge club
Cavalier, weekly bulletin of the school
Chef's club, boys
Chess club
Civil defense
Civil War club
Clothing construction club
College bound club
Computers clubs, interested Algebra 2 students
Current events
Dance band
Debating club
Design and development of space craft
Dictionary club
Dramatics club
French choral club
Future nurse club
Future Teachers of America
Glee club
Golf
Hunting and fishing club, boys interested in outdoor life
Knitting club
Library club
The Maskers, students who are dramatically inclined
Model construction
Outdoor education, camping, camp craft, nature study, girls
Seasonal sports, girls
Self improvement club, posture etiquette, and personality improvement, girls
Slide rule club
Soccer, boys
Spanish club
Student council
Tennis
Typing
World Travellers' club
Study hall, but no points awarded for study hall attendance

At least half of these interest clubs were planned for all students; others were available to one or two grade levels.

The following list of service clubs in the Kensington Junior High School, which met weekly during the second period on Thursday, offered the students in all grades the chance to participate in a special interest activity or task of their own selection, as their contribution to school improvement:

- Audio-visual club
- Bulletin board
- *Cavalier,* weekly bulletin of the school
- Future Homemakers
- Host and Hostess, greet visitors coming to class and explain what class is doing
- Indoor patrols
- Leaders, girls learn to assist physical education teachers
- Leadership training to assist in coaching girls' intramurals
- Officials, boys learn to serve as referees, umpires, score-keepers, timers, etc.
- Outdoor patrols
- *Quill,* literary magazine
- Ninth grade officers
- School store
- Science Fair
- String ensemble
- Student council committees
  - Activities
  - Assembly
  - Publicity
  - School spirit
  - Student handbook
- Horticulture
- Landscaping
- Club attendance
- Student council
- Seventh grade social committee
- Resource materials committee
- Bankers, deposit money in Guardian Savings Bank, members from mathematics classes
- Study hall

If different services were indicated during the school year, new clubs were organized and those no longer needed were dropped. Assembly was held during the homeroom period and was frequently extended from twenty to forty minutes.

The educational program of Kensington Junior High School requires a daily load of five class periods per teacher, plus one homeroom period. Block-time classes or core programs are not represented in this school organization.[25]

Highland Park Junior High School Program. Special interest activities are sustained in the Highland Park Junior High School from 2:05 to 3:00 P.M. each Wednesday, with appropriate teacher direction for all 1200 students. Opportunities for broad interest explorations are expanded by the introduction of additional activities three times during the school year. Thus approximately twelve hours of a twelve-week period are allocated to each activity group. Toward the end of the school year all students, including the sixth-graders from elementary schools, receive a list of special interest activities and a brief description of each activity for their parents to review

[25] Willard G. Schumaker, Principal, Kensington Junior High School, Silver Spring, Md., *Student Activity Schedule of Interest Club and Service Club Programs, 1961-1962.*

with them prior to designating the *five special activities* which are of most interest.

This list includes:

- Acrobatics (boys)
- Amateur radio
- Archery
- Bowling (boys and girls)
- Camping
- Chess and checkers
- Chorus, Grades 7 and 8
- Creative writing
- Dancing, one section for each grade
- Debate
- Dressmaking
- Field-stream and outdoor life
- Figurine painting
- Firearms safety, training program for fall and winter
- Fun with Mathematics
- German
- Golf
- Home decorating
- Junior Red Cross
- Knitting
- Leathercraft
- Metalcraft
- Modeling
- Oil painting
- Pen pals
- Posters, Inc.
- Reading for Fun
- Russian
- Seasonal sports (boys)
- Swedish painting
- Swimming
- Tennis for girls

Clubs are scheduled for the third period from 10:30 to 11:35 A.M. on alternate Wednesdays. The week that clubs do not convene all-student assemblies are held in the auditorium. Preliminary enrollment included the ongoing club activities, and after counsel with their parents students made the desired selections from the following list:

- Art
- Audio-visual
- Auto mechanics
- Bridge
- Camera
- Ceramics
- Dramatics
- Future Teachers
- Journalism
- Junior girls' teen discussions and films of interest
- Library
- Madrigal singers
- Model airplanes
- Modern dance
- Nature-conservation
- Needlecraft
- Party cookery
- Penmanship club
- Physical education leaders, girls
- Pre-drivers
- Printing
- Radio
- Rock study
- Science club
- Sculpture club
- Sports, boys
- Stage crew
- Stamp club
- Student council
- Teenage party planning
- Travelogues
- World affairs

Students selecting the student council plan administer all social events, direct all school fund-raising projects, manage the lost and found department, and handle distribution of school supplies and other similar tasks.[26]

4. *How should student activities be administered and evaluated?*

An increasing number of junior high schools are adding to their regular staff complement a coordinator, or director of student activities, who has major administrative responsibility for the activities program. In other schools a faculty member carries on these duties on a part-time basis.

In 1958 a special committee from the New Jersey Secondary School Teachers Association conducted a survey regarding the status and duties of the activity director. "On the average, these coordinators spent 20 percent of their time during the school day on the activities program." The reports from the 113 schools, out of 186 schools polled, indicated the following duties of activity directors:

1. Regulation of a point system for awards and honors
2. Maintaining records of participation
3. Selecting and training sponsors
4. Initiating and scheduling activities
5. Maintaining balance in the program
6. Regulating policies and procedures
7. Coordinating assembly programs
8. Advising the student council
9. Supervising financial policies and reports
10. Processing requests for materials[27]

The soundness of a student activity program is in direct proportion to how much a given activity or group of activities contributes to the attainment of the fundamental purposes of education. Evaluation of the program requires an examination by administrators and teachers and appropriate consultation with the student council. The following questions are a directional guide to be used in such evaluation:

1. How can the effectiveness of the homeroom be strengthened?
2. How large should the auditorium be for scheduling regular "student-faculty developed assemblies" in junior high schools?
3. What school publications are desired and needed in the educational program of junior high schools?
4. How can the potential of the student council be realized in the school?

[26] R. A. Dolen, Principal, Highland Park Junior High School, St. Paul, Minn., *Special Interest Activities and Club Programs, 1961,* pp. 1-11.

[27] See William S. Sterner, "Across the Continent," *California Journal of Secondary Education,* 34:354-358, October, 1959.

5. Does the activity program provide sufficient and suitable social activities for all late preadolescent and early adolescent boys and girls in school?

6. Do all staff members accept and understand the educational value of student activities?

7. Is the listing of special interest activities and clubs in the school broad enough to challenge the interests and participation of all the students?

8. What activities and clubs are not of sufficient educational value to be continued in the activity programs?

9. How can student activities, including athletics be offered during school time so that students who rely on bus transportation, after-school jobs, and chores do not feel left out?

10. Are faculty members assigned to sponsor activities according to their interests and preparation as far as is possible in order to make activities more meaningful?

11. Are the activities scheduled for a long enough time to be of maximum educational value?

12. Does the activity program provide sufficient opportunity for all students to participate in service organizations and democratic practices?

13. Do the areas of the activity program emphasize informal exploratory learnings rather than competitive activities?

14. How can a comprehensive student activity program be offered without increasing the normal teaching load of the sponsors?

15. Is the activity program on school time supported by the parents of the school?

16. Do students receive credit for participation in activities on school records?

17. Are there sufficient staff members designated to administer, supervise, and evaluate the student activity program with a maximum of student participation and leadership?

The incorporation of student activities into the junior high school curriculum requires a comprehensive and continuous evaluation by all faculty members. The activity program must contribute to realization of the general and special purposes of education for early youth, as delineated in Chapter 2. Programming must be flexible enough to accommodate the ever changing interests and needs of the students, and be of sufficient breadth to challenge every student in the application of his fullest capabilities.

An effectual evaluation of student activity programs is essential to the total educational design, as is demonstrated in *Junior High School Evaluative Criteria*[28] and *Criteria for Evaluating Junior High Schools.*[29]

[28] Salt Lake City, Utah: Utah State Department of Education, 1961, Section K, "Student Activities," pp. 445-467.

[29] Texas Junior High School Criteria Study, Research Study No. 37 (Austin, Tex.: Texas Study of Secondary Education, University of Texas, 1963), pp. 127-132.

Student activities, personal interest activities, and health and physical fitness programs may become an integral part of fundamental learning when block-time or core classes are components of the junior high school instructional organization. This approach may be viewed as being between the setup of one teacher in a self-contained classroom (elementary school) and complete departmentalization (senior high school), where teacher assignments are in accordance with subjects taught.

Student activity programs carried on within the block-time or core class system are distinctly congruent with the integrated learning concept when their formulators, implementers, and evaluators are adequately oriented to the nature of twelve-to-fifteen-year-old adolescents. They must also understand and subscribe to "student-centered" learning before the initiation of a student activity program, with the intention of affording junior high school students opportunities to engage in useful learning designed specifically to best accommodate their interest in themselves and the strange, complex, and demanding young adult culture into which they so suddenly have been propelled.

SELECTED BIBLIOGRAPHY

Austin, David B., Will French, and J. Dan Hull. *American High School Administration: Policy and Practice.* New York: Holt, Rinehart & Winston, Inc., 3rd ed., 1963. Chap. 11, "School Activities and Student Organizations."

Bossing, Nelson L. *Principles of Secondary Education.* Englewood Cliffs, N.J.: Prentice-Hall, Inc., 2nd ed., 1955. Chap. 14.

Braham, R. V. "What Role for Student Activities in the New Emphasis on Quality in Secondary Education?" *The Bulletin of the National Association of Secondary-School Principals,* 44:110-111, April, 1960.

Criteria for Evaluating Junior High Schools, Texas Junior High School Study. Austin, Tex.: The Texas Study of Secondary Education, The University of Texas, 1963.

Cronin, Richard L. "Our Junior High School P.T.A.-Student Council Code," *School Activities,* 32:135-137, January, 1961.

Cross, William Leslie. "The Student Council in the Junior High Schools in Pennsylvania (1955)," *The Bulletin of the National Association of Secondary-School Principals,* 46:257-259, February, 1962.

Dolen, R. A. *Special Interest Activities and Club Program,* Highland Park Junior High School, St. Paul, Minn., Bulletin, 1962. Pp. 1-11.

Eash, Maurice J. "The School Program: Nonclass Experience," *Review of Educational Research,* 30:57-63, February 1960. (A review of a number of research studies on student activities in junior high schools.)

Evaluative Criteria for Junior High Schools. Washington: National Study of Secondary School Evaluation, 1963.

Faunce, Roland C., and Morrel J. Clute. *Teaching and Learning in the Junior*

High School. San Francisco: Wadsworth Publishing Company, 1961. Chap. 6, "The Program of Student Activities."

Frederick, Robert W. *The Third Curriculum: Student Activities in American Education.* New York: Appleton-Century-Crofts, Inc., 1959.

Gruhn, William T. "The Administration of Club Activities in the Junior High School," *Elementary School Journal,* 35:114, October, 1934.

———, and Harl R. Douglass. *The Modern Junior High School.* New York: The Ronald Press Company, 2nd ed., 1956. Chap. 13, "Extraclass Activities."

Junior High School Evaluative Criteria. Salt Lake City, Utah: Utah State Department of Public Instruction, 1960.

Junior High School Program, The. Atlanta, Ga.: Southern Association of Colleges and Secondary Schools, 1958. Chap. 4.

Kilzer, Louis R., Harold H. Stephenson, and Orville H. Nordberg. *Allied Activities in the Secondary School.* New York: Harper & Brothers, 1956.

Koos, Leonard V. *Junior High School Trends.* New York: Harper & Brothers, 1955. Chap. 6.

Lounsbury, John H. "The Role and Status of the Junior High School," doctoral dissertation, George Peabody College, 1954.

Lowe, Jonathan Y. "What Kind of Activities Program for Students in Junior High School?" *The Bulletin of the National Association of Secondary-School Principals,* 43:253-255, April, 1959.

Lowndes, Polly Robbins. *Creative Assemblies.* Minneapolis: R. S. Denison and Company, 1961.

McEachen, Howard D. "Status and Trends in Organization and Curriculum of Selected Junior High Schools, Ed.D. dissertation, University of Kansas, 1955.

McKown, Harry C. *Extra-Curricular Activities.* New York: The Macmillan Company, 3rd ed., 1952.

Miller, Franklin A., James H. Moyer, and Robert B. Patrick. *Planning Student Activities.* Englewood Cliffs, N.J.: Prentice-Hall, Inc., 1956.

Pitkin, Victor E. "What Kind of Activities Program for Students in Junior High School?" *The Bulletin of the National Association of Secondary-School Principals,* 43:255-256, April, 1959.

Pringle, Ralph W. *The Junior High School.* New York: McGraw-Hill Book Co., Inc., 1937. Chap. 16.

St. Paul Junior High School Study: The Report of the Consultants. Minneapolis: Bureau of Field Studies and Surveys, College of Education, University of Minnesota, December, 1962.

Schumaker, Willard G. *Interest Club and Service Club Programs,* Student Activity Schedule of 1961-1962, Kensington Junior High School, Silver Spring, Md.

Sterner, William S. "Across the Continent," *California Journal of Secondary Education,* 34:354-358, October, 1959.

Thompson, Nellie Zetta. *Vitalized Assemblies.* New York: E. P. Dutton and Company, 1952. Pp. 1-148.

Tompkins, Ellsworth. *The Activity Period in Public High Schools.* Washington, U.S. Office of Education, Bulletin No. 19, 1951. Table 3, p. 15.

Van Til, William, Gordon F. Vars, and John H. Lounsbury. *Modern Education for the Junior High School Years.* Indianapolis: The Bobbs-Merrill Company, Inc., 1961. Chap. 18, "Developing the Co-Curricular and Activity Program."

Wilson, William E. *The Junior High School.* Bloomington, Ind.: State Department of Public Instruction, Bulletin No. 246, 1961. Pp. 1-107.

Wright, Grace S., and Edith S. Greer. *The Junior High School, A Survey of Grades 7-8-9 in Junior and Junior-Senior High Schools, 1959-1960,* U.S. Office of Education Bulletin No. 32. Washington: Government Printing Office, 1963. Tables 14 and 15, p. 25. (These tables indicate that most junior high schools schedule student organizations and activities in homeroom or activity periods within the regular school program of six or seven class periods.)

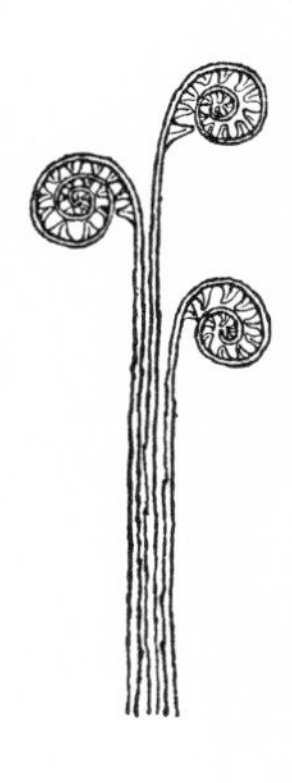

Part Three

STUDENT PERSONNEL ADMINISTRATION

11

Guidance-Counseling

1. Why do we have guidance-counseling in the school?

To appreciate the place of guidance and counseling in the junior high school it is important to understand their relation to education. Guidance-counseling came into being as the early junior high school was becoming firmly established as a separate secondary school.

Emergence of guidance-counseling

Before 1900 relatively few youth were attending the secondary school, and the majority of these were college oriented both in intention and in studies pursued. Since most high school students anticipated a professional career the secondary school emphasized a narrow college preparatory curriculum.

With the turn of the century came a rapid increase in high school enrollments. In fact the influx of students doubled each decade from 1890 through 1930. Thereafter the rate of enrollment growth declined slightly, owing to the draining off of youth for military and industrial service in the 1940 war years, plus the fact that the theoretical point of enrollment saturation was being approached.

Along with this rapid expansion came increasingly diverse types of students. Whereas the few attending high school prior to 1900 were predominantly college bound and professionally oriented, now the high school was suddenly confronted with a growing ratio of students who had no interest in or expectation of college attendance. Many had no clear purpose in view following high school graduation, while others were committed to varied vocational goals which required a kind of preparation much different from that needed by the proportionately decreasing college preparatory students.

In an effort to meet these changing conditions, during the second, third and fourth decades particularly, high schools rapidly widened the range of curricular offerings. The larger the school, the greater its proliferation of courses was likely to be. It is reported that in the early 1920's fifteen distinctly different four-year curriculums and fourteen two-year curriculums were offered within the total Chicago secondary school system, some schools proudly boasting a large number of these curriculums. Sometimes the larger schools offered as many as one hundred to two hundred subjects. It should be pointed out that the junior high school, too, began to ape the senior high school practice of curricular expansion to meet pressing pupil demands.[1]

As course offerings expanded, problems of maladjustment arose. Courses the student thought had certain vocational value were found to fit a different vocational need. Often students found themselves in courses for which they had no interest and which they were unable to handle. This state of affairs led to a serious loss of time for many students, and more serious still were the emotional disturbances, frustrations, and an accelerated rate of dropouts. The entire situation was aggravated by the fact that teachers were trained as subject specialists with little or no knowledge of the nature and purpose of courses outside their field of specialization. Even worse, many teachers had no concern for anything but their specialty. Teachers who did feel a responsibility for the human beings in their charge generally considered themselves untrained and inadequate to help the student in trouble. At this time specially trained personnel capable of assisting students with their educational and vocational problems did not exist.

Beginnings of the guidance movement

It is generally agreed that the first effort to cope with this situation outside of the school was made toward the end of the first decade of this century. In 1908 Frank Parsons, a member of the Boston school staff, began vocational placement counseling to out-of-school youth. At first he was concerned with helping youth find jobs for which they had the requisite abilities, interest, and skills. He urged that schools establish placement offices where students could receive help in accordance with their abilities and technical skills.[2] As a result of the work of Parsons the Boston Vocational Bureau was organized in 1908. The idea quickly caught the imagination of those interested in helping youth. Two years later the first national conference on vocational guidance was held in Boston. Similar conferences followed, in

[1] For a picture of the extensive proliferation of the curriculum prior to 1919 see John E. Stout, *The Development of the High School Curricula in the North Central States From 1860 to 1918* (Chicago: University of Chicago Press, 1921), pp. 46-56.

[2] Parsons died in 1908, but his ideas were preserved in a book written just before his death, *Choosing a Vocation* (Boston: Houghton Mifflin Company, 1909).

1912 in New York, and in 1913 in Grand Rapids, Michigan. It was in Grand Rapids, in 1913, that the National Vocational Guidance Association was organized. Harvard University, as early as 1911, had the distinction of being the first institution of higher learning to offer a course in vocational guidance.

Jesse B. Davis is sometimes called the pioneer school counselor because of his active pupil counseling while at Central High School, Detroit, Michigan, 1898-1907. Then, as principal of the Grand Rapids High School, Grand Rapids, Michigan, in 1907 he undertook to teach educational and vocational guidance through courses in English composition in which students explored their own interests and abilities, the nature and requirements of various vocations in terms of the basic knowledge and skills each required for success, and the possibilities for advancement in each. His educational plan was featured in a small, interesting book entitled *Vocational and Moral Guidance,* published in 1914.

As the guidance movement developed it gradually expanded to give more attention to the educational aspects of guidance. In 1918 the appearance of Brewer's book *Vocational and Educational Guidance* heralded this broader approach and made educational guidance an integral part of the school's educational responsibility. For more than a decade after Parsons and Davis had sparked the guidance movement its emphasis was primarily vocational. The educational aspect of guidance was largely concerned with vocational fitness and training.[3]

2. *What is the modern conception of guidance?*

Changing conceptions of guidance

That the guidance movement and the conception of guidance should undergo change occasions no surprise to present-day educators. Guidance has followed the normal pattern of evolution of other educational movements during this same period.

When the guidance movement began it was at first concerned with the obvious. Youth needed help to secure jobs, particularly in urban centers. Job placement became a natural point at which to start. As the school population increased and the volume of early school leavers mounted, the pressing concern was for placement assistance. As late as 1910 less than half of the elementary school pupils completed the fifth grade, and the heavy dropout ratio in the secondary school gave the placement movement

[3] For a rather complete historical treatment of the early period of the guidance movement the reader is referred to a book written by one of the pioneer leaders of the movement — John M. Brewer, *History of Vocational Guidance* (New York: Harper & Brothers, 1942). Also see Carroll H. Miller, *Foundations of Guidance* (New York: Harper & Brothers, 1961).

a sense of urgency.[4] It was only natural that the placement counseling phase of guidance should first attract the attention of Parsons and others.

Further, at this time only the more superficial aspects of vocations were understood. Years were required for an analysis even of the cruder characteristics of vocations. Careful scientific job analysis of specific occupations with a corresponding determination of the exact skills necessary for success — and, educationally, how these could be developed — came much later. For many years vocational and educational guidance, therefore, was confined largely to the selection of a vocation and the courses thought most likely to contribute to the job skills necessary for success in it.

The results of numerous studies on the nature of the individual which gathered momentum after 1910 had a tremendous impact on the guidance movement. Thorndike's historic volume on *Mental Work and Fatigue and Individual Differences and Their Causes,* published in 1914, brought together a wealth of research on individual differences, before mostly unknown, which has had a profound effect on all phases of education as well as on the problems of guidance. In this connection an earlier monumental two-volume study on adolescence by G. Stanley Hall needs mention.[5] It contributed further to the understanding of individual differences and was the forerunner of a phase of study most pertinent to a major guidance-counseling problem of this book. The growth of research knowledge on the complexity of individual differences has forced upon the guidance movement, as it has upon other phases of education, a continuous reappraisal and modification of its concepts.

A document of major significance was the report of the Commission on the Reorganization of Secondary Education entitled *Cardinal Principles of Secondary Education,* published in 1918. Individual differences and changing conceptions of learning were given a prominent place among other new developments which it was felt should deeply affect the future of American education. With the changing nature of the secondary school population this commission also believed that the time had come to consider a radical change in the purposes and direction of secondary education. It reversed a quarter of a century of educational emphasis and declared the primary function of secondary education to be the preparation of youth for effective civic-social-ethical living in a democratic society. College preparation, which had been the dominant purpose of the secondary school since the pronouncements of the report of the Committee of Ten made to the National Education Association in 1893, became almost an incidental part of secondary education. The report introduced a radically new pattern of thinking with respect to the educational function of the secondary school. The point of view of this commission has been accepted generally by responsible educational

[4] See Chapter 1 for more data on the school elimination problem of this early period.
[5] G. Stanley Hall, *Adolescence* (New York: D. Appleton Company, 1908).

groups. Perhaps the most extensive elaboration of the basic thinking of the Commission on the Reorganization of Secondary Education has been a series of publications by the Educational Policies Commission jointly created by the American Association of School Administrators and the National Education Association. Of particular interest is *Education for All American Youth*, published in 1944 and revised and worked out in greater detail in 1952. Here guidance in the framework of the new educational thinking is given extended treatment.

With the new conceptions of education elaborated in these and other notable pronouncements by thoughtful educational groups since 1918, guidance has taken on new dimensions. The problems of selection of and educational preparation for a vocation have become more complex. But, significantly, guidance is now related to almost every phase of education, every stage in the development of the individual.[6] While the proper vocational adjustment of the learner is still regarded as important, this function has been expanded to include the physical, mental, and social adjustments of the pupil within himself and in his school, his home, his community, and in fact virtually every part of his environment.

This more inclusive conception of guidance-counseling has been expressed by two well-known specialists thus:

> Guidance is assistance made available by personally qualified and adequately trained men and women to an individual of any age to help him manage his own life activities, develop his own points of view, make his own decisions, and carry his own burdens.
>
> . . . .
>
> As now interpreted, guidance touches every aspect of the individual's personality — physical, mental, emotional, and social. It is concerned with all of an individual's attitudes and behavior patterns. It seeks to help the individual integrate all his activities, using his basic potentialities and environmental opportunities.[7]

This concept of guidance is emphasized by the Texas Study of Secondary Education in the succinct declaration that guidance services are "related to all phases of the educational program."[8] In full harmony is the point of view expressed by Cottingham and Hopke in a different way:

[6] It will be of interest to the reader to note the counselor's responsibility for the curriculum of the school as it affects the vocational life of both boys and girls. See C. Gilbert Wrenn, *The Counselor in a Changing World* (Washington: American Personnel and Guidance Association, 1962), pp. 77-78, 95. A reading of this interesting book will give directly and by implication a clear picture of the extended scope of the guidance-counseling function now held by a leading spokesman for the movement.

[7] Lester D. Crow and Alice Crow, *An Introduction to Guidance: Basic Principles and Practices* (New York: American Book Company, 2nd ed., 1960), pp. 14, 15-16.

[8] *Criteria for Evaluating Junior High Schools,* Research Study No. 37 (Austin, Tex.: The University of Texas, 1963), p. 134.

FIGURE 8

Focus and Scope of School Guidance

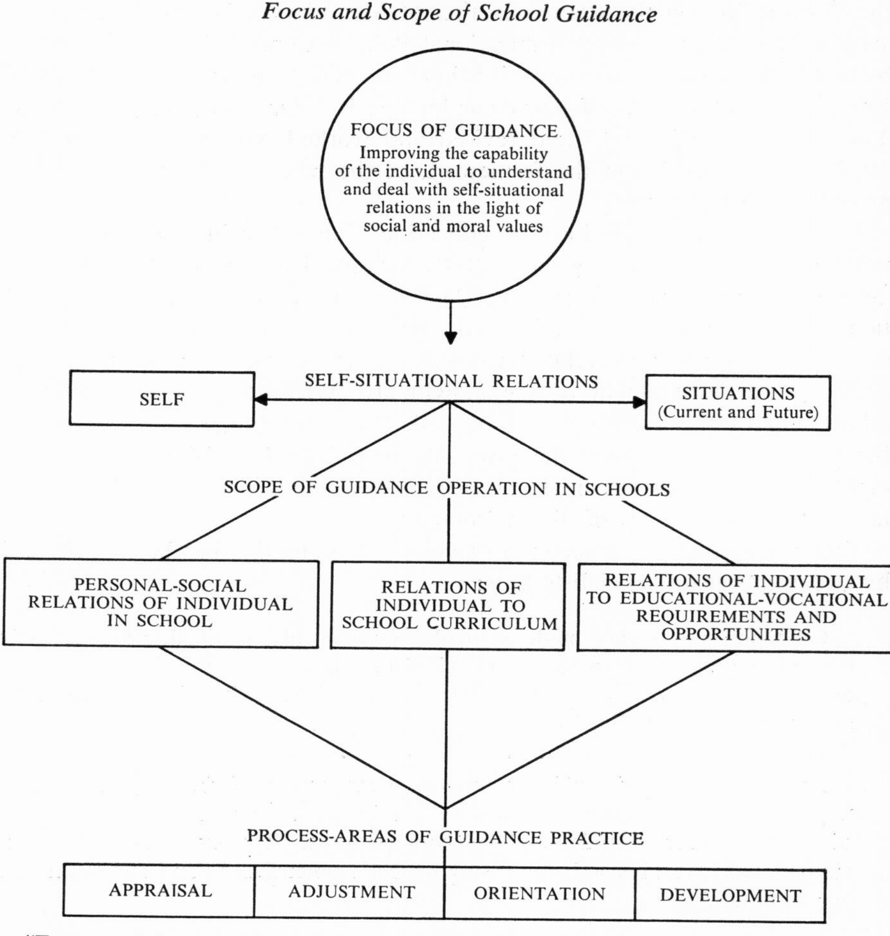

"Focus and Scope of School Guidance" from *Guidance Policy and Practice*, 3rd ed., by Robert Henry Mathewson (Harper & Row, Publishers, Inc., 1962).

> Guidance is the process of helping a person to develop and accept an adequate and integrated picture of himself and his role in the world of everyday living, to test his concept against reality and to convert it into a reality with satisfaction to himself and benefit to society. The guidance process should result in a student being more capable of self-understanding and self-direction in obtaining his needs in a democratic society.[9]

Figure 8 demonstrates the nature and extent of the guidance activity as seen by a specialist in the field.

[9] Harold F. Cottingham and William E. Hopke, *Guidance in the Junior High School* (Bloomington, Ill.: McKnight and McKnight, 1961), p. 42.

There has been a trend toward using a more inclusive term than "guidance" by some workers in this field. The terms "personnel services" or "pupil personnel services" have found growing favor with the proponents of change as including the functions now usually embraced in the terms "guidance" and "counseling," and even more. There appears to be a desire by some specialists to get away from what they feel are the limiting concepts that historically have been associated with the term "guidance." Arbuckle feels that "guidance" has been (and is still being by many) largely associated with the older conception of vocational guidance and counseling, and with "something that is done to a person by another individual."[10]

The idea that "new wine should not be put in old bottles" appears to be the basis for this desire for new terminology. Too, no doubt it represents the natural urge of an emerging group for special professional status. In the brief history of the guidance movement great strides have been taken in the broadened scope of the term "guidance," and in the expanded techniques developed to render services to the pupil. Like every other technical professional service, both in and outside the field of education, there has been a constant effort to discover new terms that more definitively characterize the scope and the refinements of the activities involved.

Judging by the definitions of those proposing changes in the nomenclature that sets this function apart, no basic change has come in the concepts accepted under the term "guidance" in its use by contemporary writers in this field. For example, Johnson and his associates, while concerned with a modification in terms, seem not to differ from modern concepts of guidance in their definition of "pupil personnel services":

> Pupil personnel services are those individualized aspects of the educational program which are designed to enable each student to reach his full potential in the areas of vocational, personal, and emotional development. These services prepare him to assume increasing responsibility for his decisions and grow in his ability to understand and accept the results of his choice.[11]

[10] Dugal S. Arbuckle, *Pupil Personnel Services in American Schools* (Boston: Allyn and Bacon, Inc., 1962). See discussion of the problem in Chap. 3.

[11] Walter F. Johnson, Buford Steffire, and Roy A. Edelfelt, *Pupil Personnel and Guidance Services* (New York: McGraw-Hill Book Co., Inc., 1961), p. 3. It is not the province of this chapter to enter into the discussion now going on in certain quarters of the professional guidance movement as to the interrelation of "guidance" and "pupil personnel services," to make the reader aware of the situation. As Crow and Crow state the case in their text referred to earlier in this chapter, page 18, "There is a difference of opinion, however, concerning the relationship that should exist between guidance and personnel services" (p. 18). They point out that some authorities maintain that "guidance" is the all-inclusive term covering all that is envisaged in pupil personnel services, while others take the reverse position. For a further discussion of this issue the reader is referred to Walter F. Johnson *et al.*, and Crow and Crow, *op. cit.;* also Francis C. Rosecrance and Velma D. Hayden, *School Guidance and Personnel Services* (Boston: Allyn and Bacon, Inc., 1960), Chap. 1, and Arbuckle, *op. cit.*, Chap. 3.

Relation of guidance to education

It would be difficult indeed to distinguish between the function and purposes of guidance in the quotations above and the general definition commonly accepted by leaders in education. Among educators, education has quite generally been considered the process by which boys and girls are helped to understand themselves and their environment, assisting them to develop the competencies to meet successfully the physical, mental, and social problems of a personal and societal nature which every normal, and to some extent every abnormal, person can be expected to encounter in the course of his life. Modern education and psychology recognize more fully than ever that, within the educational framework, the necessity to develop the self-will or motivation to utilize these competencies looms ever more important in our rapidly changing society. This idea has been well expressed as it applies to our democracy by a leading educational organization:

> The central purpose of education is to bring about change in individuals; for learning is change in the skills, knowledge, and understanding possessed by individuals and as individuals change, the society they create inevitably changes. . . . The school that serves individuals and a free society best nurtures this growth by bringing every individual it touches as near as possible to the best he can be.[12]

It would seem quite clear from all that has been said thus far that education and guidance are in essential agreement. They should be. It would be an anomalous situation if those responsible for guidance or personnel services insisted upon being a vital part of the school program, yet separated from it in purpose and function. With this view certainly all but the extremists in guidance and personnel services, and probably they too, would agree.

In the broadening conception of guidance and personnel services these activities may at times be projected outside of the activities usual to some schools, but it is well to note that the constant enlarging of the concept and scope of the educational task is pushing the school's concerns farther and farther beyond the immediate confines of the school grounds, and beyond the limitations of former responsibilities for Grades 1 to possibly 14, always in the direction of the wider obligation of the school to the adult community and beyond. This extension of the educational obligation will become more pronounced with the accelerated change, local and world-wide, that will continue to impinge more strongly upon the school, challenging it to extend its services.[13]

---

[12] American Association of School Administrators, National Education Association, *Inservice Education for School Administrators* (Washington: The Association, 1963), p. 43.

[13] Note the excellent picture of how this change is affecting the task of counseling by Wrenn, *op. cit.* All that Dr. Wrenn has said with respect to the influence of world

No doubt difficulty has arisen owing to lack of a clear understanding that concepts of education, including those of guidance, have undergone radical change, and basically for the same reason that the thinking in the guidance field has. At an earlier period it was natural to think of vocational guidance as a rather extraneous activity of the school when the school was supposed to help the pupil master large blocks of subject matter while the function of guidance was to help him choose a vocation and select the courses appropriate to fit him for that vocation.

Moreover, modern education recognizes that the child is a complex being who must be considered as a total personality. Youth vary widely in abilities, interests, and rate of maturation. No two pupils are alike. Nor do they react alike to the same stimuli. Mass procedures in the classroom must give way to more individualized treatment. One person may have the science ability of an Edison, one the vocal talent of a Caruso, another the literary genius of a Browning. By the same token wide differences in interests may be present without any necessary relation to verbal intelligence. While one may discover his interest in mechanical activities, finding his greatest delight in working with a discarded automobile, another, a lover of nature, is happiest when collecting butterflies or observing the behavior of insects or birds in their natural habitat.

All this is complicated by our present knowledge of the learning process. Consequently, the old idea that education could be carried on exclusively en masse as though the members of the group would respond the same way in a given educational situation, or that the mastery of large segments of subject matter could be equated with education, has long since been abandoned by alert educators, though unfortunately it is still too prevalent in many schools. Education is now quite generally thought of as guidance of the individual pupil in his learning activities in such a way that he will develop those understandings, attitudes, and behavioral skills that will enable him to function as an intelligent, competent member of a democratic society.

Possibly a further confusion has arisen in part from the failure of many guidance people to grasp fully the difference between the over-all function of education and the differentiated responsibilities of its personnel. A hint of the nature of this difficulty is revealed in the thinking of guidance specialists when they suggest that from one point of view guidance includes the whole of education but from another "it is seen as a specialized service whose primary concern is with the individuals."[14]

---

change on the work of the counselor could be paralleled by its effect upon the task of education and its personnel. In this connection the reader might well turn to a similar book written for a larger educational audience — Luther H. Evans and George E. Arnstein (eds.), *Automation and the Challenge to Education,* Project Staff for the Educational Implications of Automation, 1961-1962, National Education Association (Washington: The Association, 1962).

[14] Donald G. Mortensen and Allen M. Schmuller, *Guidance in Today's Schools* (New York: John Wiley & Sons, Inc., 1959), p. 3.

Aside from the teachers, few of the school personnel except the doctor, dentist, or nurse are in contact with the pupil except on rare occasions, and even the health staff members see the pupil seldom, and then for specific and limited reasons. The guidance or pupil personnel service staff, observing that all too many teachers, subject-matter specialists, meet in class from 150 to 200 pupils daily, might readily get the idea that the pupil received little personal help in such a lockstep system. Consequently, those coming into the guidance-counseling field might superficially decide that the regular staff was not primarily concerned with the individual, nor educationally oriented in his direction. Whatever personal attention the pupil received would have to come principally, if not only, from the guidance-counseling staff.

This picture of the educational scene is deceptive. Good teachers commonly *are* concerned with the pupil and his problems. In fact, the average teacher would no doubt say, "Why else are we here?" As reiterated in this book, and in the writings of modern educators, there has been a mounting emphasis upon the individual in the educational process, and upon the many facets of the individual's personality which the teacher should consider his direct responsibility. The performance of our schools, unfortunately, often fails to bring practice into line with accepted educational theory.

Relation of guidance to counseling

As indicated above, the guidance movement has begun to expand its concepts of function and to proliferate and definitize its activities. The concept of counseling as a phase of guidance is a case in point. Even among specialists in the field there is considerable difference of opinion as to the relation of guidance to counseling. However, with a few notable exceptions, it seems to be rather generally agreed that counseling is a phase of the larger function of guidance. Patterson insists that counseling is only a part of "the guidance services of the school," although he regards it as the "major service," and the type of activity which requires the most extensive training.[15] Cottingham and Hopke observe that "Although often used synonymously with guidance, most authorities agree that counseling is one aspect of guidance and that counseling services are part of an over-all guidance service program." They maintain that counseling is a "person-to-person contact" while guidance is carried on by various procedures including person-to-person and group contacts.[16]

While most counselors seem to find their major concern with the face-to-face relationships, it is not that simple. Usually the counselor is the lone professional guidance person and must undertake all the activities that are

[15] C. H. Patterson, *Counseling and Guidance in Schools* (New York: Harper & Brothers, 1962), p. 109.

[16] Cottingham and Hopke, *op. cit.*, p. 54. See also the distinction made by Rosecrance and Hayden, *op. cit.*, pp. 18-19, and E. L. Tolbert, *Introduction to Counseling* (New York: McGraw-Hill Book Co., Inc., 1959), p. 3.

embraced in guidance or pupil personnel services. And, to be realistic, this will probably be the situation for the indefinite future. Wrenn, who has been referred to earlier and to some degree at least represents the professional guidance movement, in a discussion of this problem outlined the "counselor's program responsibilities." These involve (1) both individual and group counseling; (2) consultations with staff and parents; (3) studying student population changes and interpreting their significance to the school administration and curriculum committees; and (4) rendering a liaison service between other school and community counseling resources, making these available to teachers and students.[17] It must be obvious that these duties alone will not leave much time for the coveted, and desirable, face-to-face counseling the counseling specialists would like to do exclusively.[18] Nevertheless, Wrenn continues to point up the associated activities that must necessarily drain away the counselor's time and energy. It was with a sense of realism that a veteran guidance authority on a panel at a gathering of several hundred educators, when asked what he regarded as an ideal ratio of students to guidance personnel in the high school, replied thoughtfully, "One counselor to every seventy-five students so that a minimum of two full one-hour conferences a year could be held with each student."

Importance of the teacher in guidance-counseling

At least three aspects of this problem should be given consideration. The first involves the basic function and responsibility of the teacher in modern education. Throughout this book, as is true in all discussions of modern education, the teaching function is considered to center in personally helping boys and girls, individually and in groups, to understand themselves and their relationships with others and to meet the problems of a personal, social, and societal nature that constantly impinge upon them. This is the central task of education and of the teacher, who must be the personification of education in the direct contact with the learner in a learning situation.

It is a truism that the teacher has always been the focal point of the teaching act, as the pupil has been the center of the learning act. Reduced to its primary terms it has been expressed most vividly in the old picture of the complete teaching act with Mark Hopkins on one end of the log and a student on the other end. Whatever the educational program, historically the teacher always has been the one directly in contact with the pupil, and the one held most responsible for the success or failure of the resultant pupil learning. It

[17] Wrenn, *op. cit.,* pp. 141 ff.

[18] The sense of frustration felt by counselors who chafe at what they regard as extraneous demands made upon them in the school and community, which detract from their ability to devote almost complete time to face-to-face contact counseling, is evidenced in Angelo V. Boy and Gerald J. Pine, *Client-Centered Counseling in the Secondary School* (Boston: Houghton Mifflin Company, 1963), pp. 3-5.

has ever been thus, it is no less true today, and as far as can be foreseen it will be so in the future.

The teacher's education has been projected on the unquestioned assumption that teaching depended implicitly and explicitly on a personal relationship inside and outside of the classroom. Only on occasion, and then usually momentarily, have administrative officials come in contact with pupils for specific educational purposes. Now, with the introduction of many specialized services in the school, the pupil occasionally meets the school nurse, doctor, guidance specialist, etc., but these contacts are rare. The unique relationship of the teacher with the pupil is emphasized in this statement:

> It is the teacher who determines in a large measure the characteristics and quality of the program provided the boys and girls enrolled, for it is he who will work intimately with them in planning and developing learning experiences that promise to contribute most to their education. The role of the teacher is central to the discharge of the responsibilities for which the school was established in the first place.[19]

The logical implication of all that has been said is that guidance-counseling is a natural and inescapable function and responsibility of the teacher. It would appear to be untenable and irrational not to take advantage of a person so strategically placed in the educational milieu. And such is the position taken by two eminent educators:

> *The teacher is the key person in the guidance program in the secondary school.* The significance of this principle cannot be overstressed. A guidance program can be effective only to the extent that it has the enthusiastic and intelligent support of every teacher in the school. . . . It is the teacher, however, who has the intimate contact with pupils which is highly essential in guidance. The teacher meets the pupils daily in homeroom and classes, he has them in clubs and other extra class activities, and he has opportunities with their home and out-of-school backgrounds. . . . The teacher-pupil relationship is the one in school which best lends itself to the personal relationships so essential to effective counseling.[20]

The teacher's place in the guidance function is made clear in the section on "Guidance Services" of the *Evaluative Criteria for Junior High Schools:*

> The complexity, multiplicity, and depth of the personal, social, emotional, and physical problems that early adolescents face make it necessary for all

[19] William M. Alexander and J. Galen Saylor, *Modern Secondary Education: Basic Principles and Practices* (New York: Holt, Rinehart & Winston, Inc., 2nd ed., 1959), p. 3.

[20] Vernon E. Anderson and William T. Gruhn, *Principles and Practices of Secondary Education* (New York: The Ronald Press Company, 2nd ed., 1962), pp. 405-406.

> adults who work closely with them to become deeply concerned with, and actively engaged in, the guidance function. Classroom teachers and parents provide professionally trained counselors with much of the pertinent information needed to complete the student inventory. . . . Counselors, in turn, provide classroom teachers with information and assist them in using it to fulfill the guidance responsibilities teachers must assume.[21]

That the specialists in the field of guidance-counseling recognize the centrality of the teacher in guidance-counseling activities is increasingly evident in their writings. Only the most extreme maintain the thesis that guidance-counseling can be done only by the highly trained guidance specialist. Thoughtful leaders see clearly that the teacher must be the backbone of guidance-counseling for the mass of students in any realistic sense. As one writer declares, "For most pupils, the classroom is the focal point of the school. . . . Thus, the classroom teacher is, to use a military phrase, the first line of defense."[22] Another is much more emphatic: "It is not a question of whether or not teachers can or should counsel — they do it every day. They provide the only sort of counseling that many pupils will receive."[23] An observation that all those who are fully cognizant of what has been going on in teaching over the years at once recognize to be true is that "good teachers have always done counseling."[24]

Possibly the most intelligently thought out reaction to the problem of teacher participation in guidance-counseling and the mutual cooperative relationship that should exist between the guidance specialist and the teacher is revealed in this reflective comment:

> Educational leaders are beginning to discover, during this period of introspection, that proliferation of specialists will never satisfy the need for individualization of education. The teacher serves as the primary instrument by which the vast machine of the school takes care of the unique needs of the child. To perform this vital function the teacher must learn to use the special skills of the pupil personnel worker. These specialists in turn will take over a larger role as consultants to the teacher, supplementing his central skills with their more peripheral understandings.[25]

The second aspect of the problem has been rather extensively discussed in earlier parts of this chapter and alluded to specifically in the last three pages.

[21] *Evaluative Criteria for Junior High Schools* (Washington: National Study of Secondary School Evaluation, 1963), p. 229.

[22] Clifford P. Froehlich, *Guidance Services in the Schools* (New York: McGraw-Hill Book Co., Inc., 2nd ed., 1958), pp. 261-262.

[23] Tolbert, *op. cit.,* p. 36.

[24] Mauritz Johnson, Jr., and others, *Junior High School Guidance* (New York: Harper & Brothers, 1961), p. 101.

[25] Walter F. Johnson *et al., op. cit.,* Preface, p. vii.

It needs little more than a restatement at this point. Practically, it is simply a question of how adequate a job of satisfying the guidance-counseling needs of school youth can reasonably be expected of the counselor. We have shown that there is a serious shortage of even the minimum guidance personnel officially declared desirable. It is equally clear that if it were possible, even within a calculable future, to secure a counselor for every three hundred pupils, over half the secondary schools of this country would be without such specialized assistance.

In a discussion of the shortage of school counselors in the *Parent Teacher Association Magazine,* the following statement was made: "A recent publication of the U.S. Office of Education has this to say about the shortage — 'although one full time counselor to 250-300 high school pupils is generally considered optimum, the current ratio for the nation as a whole is one in 750.' "[26] And the evidence presented indicates that even a far greater ratio of pupil personnel staff to pupils still would leave the needs of students largely unmet because of the physical limitations of time for counselors to see students as frequently as necessary, and the great amount of time that must be devoted to phases of counseling other than face-to-face contacts.

The third aspect of the problem is "What are the alternatives?" The extremists among the counselor group particularly would deny all counseling to other than the highly trained counseling staff. Such an arrangement would make teachers simply lesson-hearing functionaries. It would sentence the majority of schools to being without counseling assistance for an indefinite future, probably far beyond this generation.

The practical and rational alternative would seem to be to accept the educational function of the teacher now in vogue in theory, if not always in practice, and put pressure upon the profession and its preparation institutions to seriously carry forward a system of guidance-counselor education of all school teachers. Thus a highly intelligent and cooperative counseling program could be developed between the teachers and those specifically trained as guidance-counselors. This is in essence the proposal of Johnson and his associates, quoted above, and many others who look at the problem realistically. It seems only feasible to assume that teachers must, under contemporary educational philosophy and purposes, give increasing attention to the problems of youth. To this end their education should be more definitely oriented. And they should be able to look to and receive cooperative assistance from the pupil personnel service specialist.

The plain fact that guidance-counseling must be performed by the teaching staff if large numbers of pupils are to receive any assistance in this area has long been recognized by school leaders as well as by the more realistic leaders of the guidance movement. Some school administrators have gone so far

[26] "All About School Guidance," *Parent Teacher Association Magazine,* 55:29, May, 1961.

as to deny the general practice of face-to-face counseling on the part of guidance specialists in their schools on the theory that (1) it is unrealistic to expect to have a guidance-specialist–pupil ratio low enough to make guidance-counseling adequate; (2) modern educational theory makes teaching essentially a guidance function and therefore renders specialized counseling largely a duplication of the educational function in the school; and (3) at least at the present stage of guidance-counseling, functionally considered, efficiency in the use of a limited number of highly trained guidance-counseling personnel would dictate that they train the teachers in the skills of counseling — that is, serve as resource persons to the teachers, who are in the best position to give direct counseling assistance to the pupils.

It was this general approach to the problem of urgently needed guidance-counseling in a high school of over 2500 pupils that led Dr. Paul R. Pierce, then principal of the Wells High School of Chicago, to assign his personnel specialists in the guidance clinic to the primary task of servicing the teaching staff — both homeroom and classroom. He felt that their value to the school would be much greater in the larger service of the teaching staff than if their energies were largely dissipated in trying to render personalized services to the pupils directly. The members of the clinic, in accordance with their specialized training, gave the teachers necessary information and suggestions about health problems of pupils, provided test data on pupils where needed, with interpretations of the data as the specialist understood them, assistance where psychological understanding was important, essential data on the home and community background of pupils, and such other pertinent assistance as was needed in situations where the busy teacher obviously could not conveniently obtain such background material.[27]

Fortunately, the modern secondary school is incorporating much of the guidance function in its educational program as a central responsibility of the teacher. This development flows naturally from the enlarged concept of the functions of education in a democracy, a more realistic understanding of the nature of children and their educational needs, and a better understanding of the learning process. Increasing emphasis upon guidance-counseling is now being given in the education of teachers. However, in the future there will be an even greater need for the guidance-counseling specialist who is broadly educated to understand not only the pupil but also the peculiar functions of education within our society as the tempo of living becomes more rigorous, and to assist the teacher in his correspondingly more complex educational tasks. It would appear that in the future guidance personnel may render their most effective contribution to the school in the servicing of the teaching staff, who must be the primary face-to-face guidance-counselors in the classroom

[27] Paul R. Pierce, *Developing a High School Curriculum* (New York: American Book Company, 1942). See Chap. 7 for an interesting account of an administrator's ideas on guidance-counseling as developed in the Wells High School, Chicago.

situation. How much face-to-face counseling in the schools of tomorrow will be done by the guidance-counselor specialist must be determined as more effective educational procedures are developed.

3. *Why do we have guidance-counseling in the junior high school?*

Relation of guidance and the junior high school

Guidance-counseling in the junior high school takes on special significance because of the uniqueness of this segment of the educational ladder of our public school system. The importance of guidance in the junior high school has been recognized from its early beginnings. In Smith's words, "Guidance is then the very keystone of the junior high school,"[28] and Briggs, who pioneered as a leader of the junior high school, said, "The importance of guidance, both personal and educational, increases with departmental instruction."[29] Davis, another leader in the formative period of the junior high school, suggests that "With all his tendencies toward individualism and his efforts to discover his own elements of strength and weakness through independent choice and procedures, the adolescent is a being who needs the advice and guidance of sympathetic teachers."[30] Probably the best summary of the position of these early junior high school leaders is given by Pringle:

> In their books on the junior high school, Briggs, Davis and Smith have named exploration and guidance as correlated functions of the junior high school, and Koos finds these mentioned by 75 percent of the leaders in the junior high school movement. Briggs makes it his third objective; Davis thinks it is the most important "of all the functions of the junior high school."[31]

Johnson with equal vigor has stated the case for the present professional guidance movement in these words: "Guidance is a primary concern of the junior high school, which initial stage of secondary education is a crucial one in the guidance of youth."[32] This point of view is strongly backed by Cottingham and Hopke with considerable evidence to support their position.[33]

[28] William A. Smith, *The Junior High School* (New York: The Macmillan Company, 1926), p. 377.

[29] Thomas H. Briggs, *The Junior High School* (Boston: Houghton Mifflin Company, 1920), p. 253.

[30] Calvin O. Davis, *Junior High School Education* (Yonkers, N.Y.: World Book Company, 1924), p. 53.

[31] Ralph W. Pringle, *The Junior High School* (New York: McGraw-Hill Book Co., Inc., 1937), p. 80.

[32] Mauritz Johnson, Jr., and others, *op. cit.*, p. 1.

[33] Cottingham and Hopke, *op. cit.*, Chap. 3, "The Need for Guidance in the Junior High School."

This school stands at the point of transition of boys and girls from the elementary school — the school of childhood — to the first segment of the secondary school — sometimes known as the school of early adolescence. It represents a change from a school of restricted community outlook. The elementary school, for the most part, serves a neighborhood group homogeneous in its cultural background and socioeconomic level and usually of similar racial and religious composition. Many of the children have played together and many others were known casually in the community before going to elementary school.[34]

As children move from the small neighborhood school to the larger junior high school which serves several elementary school communities, they are introduced to new and often strange cultural patterns, differences in socioeconomic levels, frequently different racial stocks, and varied religious outlooks and customs. In addition the larger school brings problems of adjustment to new pupils, teachers, and curriculum patterns, and to enlarged school facilities — libraries, gymnasiums, cafeterias, and shops. Too, several teachers are likely to replace the one-grade teacher, particularly in the more traditionally departmentalized junior high school.

The most significant change, however, is that taking place in the pupil. The approach of adolescence is profoundly affecting his outlook with reference to selfhood and his emerging relationship to society as he becomes a responsible, self-directing person. In this period of personal and social adjustment the child is beginning to assert himself as a person, to discover his own set of guiding values. Feeling unnecessarily restrained by adult controls, he seeks by various means to circumvent these blocks to his freedom and self-expression. He has a tendency to feel misunderstood, and little by little he withdraws from the dependent confidential relationship that had existed between him and his parents. This search for selfhood is clearly recognized by a recent authority in guidance:

> If it is granted that awareness of selfhood is sharpened during adolescence, the correlative need is to discover clearly the nature of that self. In fact, it might not be too greatly amiss to assert that the dominant aim of the junior high school pupil is *self discovery* and that the school's main job is to help him with this process.
>
> . . . .
>
> Guidance is concerned with helping people resolve problems they encounter in their personal lives. Junior high school pupils face problems involving adjustment to the situation in which they find themselves and problems involving planning for the future.[35]

[34] For an extended discussion of the nature of the junior high school the reader's attention is called to the first four chapters of this book.

[35] Mauritz Johnson, Jr., and others, *op. cit.*, pp. 13-14, 21.

Yet the need for someone to confide in and to lean on for counsel still exists. In this environment the teacher has a unique privilege to be the ready listener and confidant of the pupil. Helping boys and girls to make the successful transition from childhood to adolescence; to come to a considered understanding of and acceptance of themselves; to develop an intelligent, wholesome, and constructive point of view toward life, others, and the world in which they live; to develop effective problem-solving skills, and the purpose to utilize those skills daily, not only to further their own achievement but to enrich the lives of their fellow men and promote the ideals of their society — all this is the peculiar function and opportunity of the junior high school teacher.

Guidance in block-time classes

The movement to develop block-time class organization in the secondary school has been most popular in the junior high school. Studies indicate that some form of block-time organization, combining two, three, or four class periods in a single class under one teacher, is used in over 40 per cent of the junior high schools having an enrollment of less than 300 pupils and in over 50 per cent of schools with more than 300 pupils. According to a study of larger junior high schools, 57.3 per cent of 1170 responding schools used some block-time classes while in schools enrolling over 1000 pupils "the percentage using block-time classes is 72.5."[36] Recent studies of block-time classes and core in several states support these findings.

The significance of block-time classes for guidance has been quite generally recognized by administrators. One of the major values attributed to the block-time class organization is its reduction of the teacher-pupil ratio by at least 50 per cent with the corresponding opportunity it gives the teacher to become better acquainted with fewer pupils, and with their personal, social, and educational problems, and often their home backgrounds. Here is a unique opportunity to render effective guidance-counseling service to classroom pupils.

Critics of the idea that the teacher with a daily pupil load of 150-200 can do good guidance-counseling under these conditions have a point. Handling that many pupils in groups of thirty to forty in five or six successive forty-five-to-fifty-minute class periods per day, the teacher can scarcely know much more than the names of pupils, much less become sufficiently acquainted to offer intelligent counsel to them. Even more serious, the educational concept under this factory type of classroom procedure tends to perpetuate the old

[36] "The Daily Schedule in Junior High Schools," *The Bulletin of the National Association of Secondary-School Principals,* 40:176-221, May, 1956. For more detail on the block-time class in the junior high school, see Chapter 6 of this text. For further data, see Grace S. Wright and Edith S. Greer, *The Junior High School, A Survey of Grades 7-8-9 in Junior and Junior-Senior High Schools, 1959-1960,* U.S. Office of Education Bulletin No. 32 (Washington: Government Printing Office, 1963), pp. 18-21.

stereotype of education as the mastery of so much subject matter set-out-to-be-learned, and the appropriate teaching method as that of lecture-recitation-test to insure proper acquisition of this subject matter. Focus thus tends to be away from the learner and toward what is set-out-to-be-learned. Teachers are discouraged from thinking of the pupil and his needs.

The block-time class organization, on the other hand, militates against the monotonous use of the lecture or the recitation. It encourages the use of a variety of methods, and teaching focuses more naturally on the pupil as an individual, a personality. The goals of education become more personalized. Also, under the larger block-time arrangements teachers do not feel under such pressure to cover ground. Consequently they are freer to introduce classroom procedures more in line with modern conceptions of education and learning. This in turn furthers individualization of instruction and guidance-counseling as a part of the classroom activity.

4. How is guidance related to the curriculum?

For many years the importance of the curriculum to guidance has been recognized by discerning educators. That the curriculum is related to course failures, retardation, dropouts, truancy, and delinquency has long been known; it is now substantiated by extensive experimentation in curriculum practice and in learning behavior.

Over thirty years ago a farsighted school administrator set up a guidance program in a new high school. He made this trenchant observation concerning the policies adopted to govern the new program:

> As in the other areas of our program, we early set up basic principles to govern our guidance procedures. First, it was regarded as basic that problems which conventionally call for guidance should be anticipated and eliminated through development of a curriculum fitted to pupils' interests, abilities, and needs. This would care for such matters as subject failures and truancy, which traditionally consume guidance time and efforts. Our principle was thus equivalent to saying that curriculum improvement is the chief vehicle of guidance.[37]

Guidance specialists too are increasingly aware of this twin relationship. In fact there are very few recent writers in the guidance-counseling field who do not see curriculum as a major instrument of guidance. A recent statement on this point is most emphatic:

> The whole rationale of the developmental phases of guidance rests upon the provision of a wide variety of curricular and extra-curricular experiences for students and the evaluation of these by each individual in relation to his own needs and goals. Subject-matter instruction, individual study, cocurricular activi-

[37] Pierce, *op. cit.*, p. 217.

ties, student government, athletics, and other aspects of the school curriculum may affect student development favorably or adversely.[38]

5. *How is guidance related to the core curriculum?*

The core curriculum idea has found its greatest popularity in the junior high school, mainly because the educational and learning concepts have been most congenial to the unique purposes and functions of the junior high school as seen by modern educators. Core presupposes a philsophical educational concept, a point of view with respect to the purposes and functions of education in a democratic society and with respect to the nature of learning. This means full acceptance of guidance-counseling as an integral part of core teaching.[39]

Core is based upon the psychological principle that learning takes place through experience, and its supreme manifestation is a corresponding change in the behavior of the learner. It represents, too, a shift in educational concept from the subject-matter curriculum with its emphasis upon the mastery of factual knowledge to the experience-learning-centered curriculum with its emphasis upon personal, social, and societal problems as the basis of education. The core curriculum, therefore, gives primary attention to the pupil and his needs. Thus it tends to be personalized and flexible in content and organization.

The essential place of guidance in the core curriculum flows from the acceptance of common educational concepts. Guidance is committed to the same educational purposes as core. Guidance is based upon the same psychological principles of individual differences and learning as core. To each the immediate and long-time needs of boys and girls are of first importance, and each stresses the development of wholesome behavioral patterns that will enable the individual to become a competent and responsible member of society. Further, core emphasizes the wholesome teacher-pupil relationship in the educational process, which is at the heart of the person-to-person theory of guidance-counseling. It is these mutually accepted educational concepts that give guidance such an important place in the core curriculum.

As has been previously pointed out in this book, the nature of the core idea implements the activities of guidance.

[38] Robert H. Mathewson, *Guidance Policy and Practice* (New York: Harper & Row, 3rd ed., 1962), p. 289; see also Patterson, *op. cit.*, pp. 3-13, and Mauritz Johnson, Jr., and others, *op. cit.*, pp. 252-253.

[39] For a more complete discussion of core in the junior high school see Chapter 7 of this book. For a comprehensive discussion of the core curriculum itself see Roland C. Faunce and Nelson L. Bossing, *Developing the Core Curriculum* (Englewood Cliffs, N.J.: Prentice-Hall, Inc., 2nd ed., 1958), especially Chaps. 3-5 and 8.

The philosophy of core makes guidance activities essentially a part of the core curriculum idea. The central concept of the core curriculum is that it shall be organized around the personal, social, and societal problems important to youth. Since the classroom activities focus upon these vital problems, the guidance responsibility of the teacher becomes paramount. He must help youth to discover their needs, to recognize the nature of real problems that beset them, and to develop adequate behavioral skills to meet the problems that perplex them now and adapt these skills to new problem situations as they arise. These educational tasks involve basic guidance-counseling skills on the part of the teacher.

Anderson and Gruhn have indicated the place of guidance in core succinctly: "In many secondary schools the functions of the homeroom have been combined with those of the core or block-time class. In these schools the core class therefore becomes the center of the guidance and counseling program."[40]

A leader in the guidance movement has recognized the unique interrelationship of guidance and core in this statement: "When the core curriculum functions most effectively, one teacher serves as both teacher and counselor for the youngsters. In such a position a teacher may shift his role almost imperceptibly to serve whatever function is most appropriate."[41]

The core curriculum emphasizes an extended period made up of two or more class periods. The opportunity which this extended block of time affords for the use of problem solving and other useful methods not feasible in the traditional forty-five-to-fifty-minute class period has been alluded to in the section on block time. The classroom methods appropriate to the solution of personal and social problems are difficult to handle in a regular class period. The interrelated nature of problem-solving procedures requires a longer time in which progression can be satisfactorily made from one phase to another without the interruption of bells. Teacher-pupil planning, individual and group approaches to problem solving, and the most practical use of out-of-school resources, so essential to the core idea, are more easily taken care of in an extended class period. Moreover, this methodology not only provides for teacher guidance in the development of problem-solving skills and productive human relationships but offers the teacher built-in opportunities for personal and group guidance-counseling.

The core curriculum increases the opportunities for guidance-counseling. Many schools with the core curriculum are now extending the time teachers are associated with the same pupils. In the departmentalized plan teachers seldom have a pupil for more than one semester. Under the core concept the advantages the teacher has for guidance-counseling are being multiplied by scheduling core classes for at least a full year. The extension

[40] Anderson and Gruhn, *op. cit.,* p. 415.
[41] Walter F. Johnson and others, *op. cit.,* p. 131.

of the core-class–teacher relationship to the entire span of the junior high school is now advocated by core curriculum workers and is being put into effect in many schools.

The advantages of this longer period of association of pupils with their core teachers are numerous. A much more intimate acquaintance with the pupil is possible. There are important contacts for effective guidance-counseling. Knowing that he will have a class group for several years, a teacher can plan for the curricular needs of his students on an individual basis. The use of a cumulative folder replete with data on the individual and with copious samples of his developmental progress in behavioral competencies, largely assembled by this same teacher during the junior high school career of the learner, should enable the teacher to fit the program to the needs of each pupil. In the perspective of such a long-term relationship the teacher can use flexible and appropriate methods which are more adaptable to the rate of development of numbers of pupils in the class. All this makes possible greater sequential guidance planning and a discriminating program of counseling activities.

SELECTED BIBLIOGRAPHY

Adams, James F. *Problems in Counseling: A Case Study.* New York: The Macmillan Company, 1962.

Anderson, Vernon E., and William T. Gruhn. *Principles and Practices of Secondary Education.* New York: The Ronald Press Company, 2nd ed., 1962. Chap. 16.

Andrew, Dean O., and Roy D. Willey. *Administration and Organization of the Guidance Program.* New York: Harper & Brothers, 1958.

Arbuckle, Dugald S. *Counseling: An Introduction.* Boston: Allyn and Bacon, Inc., 1961.

———. *Pupil Personnel Services in American Schools.* Boston: Allyn and Bacon, Inc., 1962.

"Aspects of Guidance and Counseling," *The Bulletin of the National Association of Secondary-School Principals,* 47:1-100, September, 1963.

Association for Supervision and Curriculum Development, National Education Association. *Guidance in the Curriculum.* 1955 Yearbook. Washington: The Association, 1955.

Boy, Angelo V., and Gerald J. Pine. *Client-Centered Counseling in the Secondary School.* Boston: Houghton Mifflin Company, 1963.

Buchheimer, Arnold, and Sarah C. Balogh. *The Counseling Relationship, a Casebook.* Chicago: Science Research Associates, 1961.

Byrne, Richard H. *The School Counselor.* Boston: Houghton Mifflin Company, 1963.

Cottingham, Harold F., and William E. Hopke. *Guidance in the Junior High School.* Bloomington, Ill.: McKnight and McKnight, 1961.

Cottle, William C., and N. M. Downie. *Procedures and Preparation for Counseling.* Englewood Cliffs, N.J.: Prentice-Hall, Inc., 1960.

Crow, Lester D., and Alice Crow. *An Introduction to Guidance: Basic Principles and Practices.* New York: American Book Company, 2nd ed., 1960.

Evaluative Criteria for Junior High Schools. Washington: National Study of Secondary School Evaluation, 1963.

Foster, Charles R. *Guidance for Today's Schools.* Boston: Ginn & Company, 1957.

Froehlich, Clifford P. *Guidance Services in the Schools.* New York: McGraw-Hill Book Co., Inc., 2nd ed., 1958.

Gordon, Ira J. *The Teacher as a Guidance Worker.* New York: Harper & Brothers, 1956.

"Guidance and Counseling," *Review of Educational Research,* 27:192-202, April, 1957.

"Guidance and Counseling," *Review of Educational Research,* 30:97-183, April, 1960.

"Guidance Practices in the Secondary School," *The Bulletin of the National Association of Secondary-School Principals,* 46: entire issue, November, 1962.

Humphreys, J. A., A. E. Trayler, and R. D. North. *Guidance Services.* Chicago: Science Research Associates, 2nd ed., 1960.

Hutson, Percival W. *The Guidance Function in Education.* New York: Appleton-Century-Crofts, Inc., 1958.

Johnson, Mauritz, Jr., and others. *Junior High School Guidance.* New York: Harper & Brothers, 1961.

Johnson, Walter F., Buford Stefflre, and Roy A. Edelfelt. *Pupil Personnel and Guidance Services.* New York: McGraw-Hill Book Co., Inc., 1961.

Johnston, Edgar G., and others. *The Role of the Teacher in Guidance.* Englewood Cliffs, N.J.: Prentice-Hall, Inc., 1959.

Kelley, Janet A. *Guidance and Curriculum.* Englewood Cliffs, N.J.: Prentice-Hall, Inc., 1955.

Loughary, John W. *Counseling in Secondary Schools: A Frame of Reference.* New York: Harper & Brothers, 1961.

McDaniel, Henry B., and G. A. Shaftel. *Guidance in the Modern School.* New York: Dryden Press, 1956.

McGowan, John F., and Lyle D. Schmidt. *Counseling: Readings in Theory and Practice.* New York: Holt, Rinehart & Winston, Inc., 1962.

Martinson, Ruth, and Harry Smallenburg. *Guidance in Elementary Schools.* Englewood Cliffs, N.J.: Prentice-Hall, Inc., 1958.

Mathewson, Robert H. *Guidance Policy and Practice.* New York: Harper & Row, 3rd ed., 1962. Chap. 11, "Operation of Guidance on Various Levels."

Miller, Carroll H. *Foundations of Guidance.* New York: Harper & Brothers, 1961.

Mortensen, Donald G., and Allen M. Schmuller. *Guidance in Today's Schools.* New York: John Wiley & Sons, Inc., 1959.

Patterson, C. H. *Counseling and Guidance in Schools: A First Course.* New York: Harper & Brothers, 1962.

Peters, Herman J., and Gail F. Farwell. *Guidance, A Developmental Approach.* Chicago: Rand McNally and Company, 1959.

Riccio, Anthony C. "Group Guidance: A Step Toward the Core," *Educational Administration and Supervision,* 40:1-9, January, 1958.

Rosecrance, Francis C., and Velma D. Hayden. *School Guidance and Personnel Services.* Boston: Allyn and Bacon, Inc., 1960.

Stoops, Emery (ed.) *Guidance Services: Organization and Administration.* New York: McGraw-Hill Book Co., Inc., 1959.

Tolbert, E. L. *Introduction to Counseling.* New York: McGraw-Hill Book Co., Inc., 1959.

Willey, R. D., and W. M. Strong. *Group Procedures in Guidance.* New York: Harper & Brothers, 1957.

Wrenn, C. Gilbert. *The Counselor in a Changing World.* The Commission on Guidance in American Schools. Washington: American Personnel and Guidance Association, 1962.

12

Evaluating and Reporting Student Progress

1. Why is evaluation a problem?

An important factor in the creation of the junior high school was a recognized need for greater scope, clarity, and accuracy in evaluating and reporting student progress in all learning areas.

In the early 1900's subject-matter mastery, as shown by standard achievement scores, was the primary determinant of student progress. Studies of the nature and extent of dropouts indicated that less than 50 per cent of those who entered first grade completed fifth grade, and the dropout ratio increased rapidly through the seventh to the ninth grade.[1] These disclosures motivated many educators to explore their respective programs for factors that might be contributing to the high dropout rate in elementary and secondary schools. The investigations aroused marked concern about public school programs. The curriculum was considered a major source of difficulty, and specific questions were raised as to the relationship between evaluating and reporting processes and dropouts. Low marks or failures were regarded by many parents as evidence of inadequate school programs or a distorted view of the learning capabilities of their children; often, indeed, parents were prompted to encourage their children to leave school.

Children typically assimilate the assessments and values ascribed to educational opportunities and their learning capabilities by their parents. When these attitudes and values are negative, and are reinforced by the teachers' reports of student school progress, the desire of the early adolescent to be

[1] See Chapter 1 for more data on school departures.

exposed to learning opportunities and the belief that he is able to effectively meet some of the obstacles inherent in tasks presented undergoes marked changes. Constructive and positive motivational forces are often overpowered by negative ones of fear, anxiety, and hopelessness toward most learning situations.

In consequence the student's impulse is to remove himself from the school, the source of his stress. He may take any of a variety of actions directed toward either a temporary or a permanent departure from the school situation. Inevitably most junior high school students, upon encountering these experiences, will have painful inner responses, but the exact form and degree will depend on their individual makeup and the influence of the home. The effect upon learning progress is predictably destructive. Quitting school and trying to obtain gainful employment frequently fails because opportunities for work are almost non-existent for those without the minimum equipment of a high school education or specific trade skill. Completion of some formal secondary educational program is fast becoming a prerequisite to training in the trade skills.

These obstructions may be perceived as forces influencing early youth to incorporate antisocial values and to participate in antisocial conduct. Such behavior may be understood as their expression of resentment against the society and its social institutions, which are perceived as having denied them acceptance and opportunities for constructive work with the attending satisfaction that comes with achievement.

The school progress reports per se are not nearly so critical as the far-reaching effects upon the students' attitudes, which reflect their images of themselves as inadequate, worthless, and rejected. The disapproval symbolized by the communications and attitudes of parents and teachers toward failing or low marks is often the triggering influence which negates or impedes present and future participation in available learning opportunities. Thus youth's usual anxieties toward their learning capabilities in relation to the demands made upon them are intensified.

Many educators view this situation with increased alarm. They are impressed with the striking connection between withdrawal from learning opportunities and the usual methods of measuring and reporting student progress. Their concern, however, does not forestall the continued application of a single instrument for evaluating and reporting student mastery of subject content: the final examination. This narrow and limited assessment technique neglects the broad scope of subject areas of learning and denies the existence of other vital educational objectives.

Junior high school staffs adhering to this single, mechanistic evaluation procedure administer a "final" examination just prior to issuance of the report-to-parents card. This instrument is supposed to measure the degree of student mastery of subject matter which was introduced during the preceding semester or reporting period. The teacher often rigidly and defensively relies solely on the examination paper as the final and only element to be considered in the appraisal of student growth. Unfortunately, many parents tend to support this procedure without conflict, as it is the same marking and reporting system *they* have experienced.

The highly departmentalized junior high schools tend to use the evaluation and reporting schemes applied in senior high school programs rather than those of the elementary schools. Thus they continue to deny their responsibility to seek the almost universally accepted general and specific objectives of junior high school education.

Correction of the situation, which is considered critical to early youth, may best be achieved when all junior high school staffs modify their approach to evaluating and reporting student progress by an awareness and acceptance of the educational objectives, functions, curriculums, instruction, and guidance responsibilities presented in this book. When this is done it is believed that learning progress will be better understood and learning opportunities can be intelligently modified. This approach also aids the teacher's perception of individual students' assets and liabilities, which is essential to competent and effective instruction in all learning areas.

Considerable research effort is involved in the formulation of junior high school educational purposes and the selection of appropriate learning activities or the development of learning situations suited to their realization. When the school staff has undergone such rigorous anticipatory experiences in educational planning it will have tended both consciously and unconsciously to determine many aspects of the criteria that later will govern the evaluation of pupil learning. Specifically, this consists of critically assessing the correlation between the proposed learning opportunities and the objectives formulated by junior high school professional staffs.

It should be kept clearly in mind, however, that student learning progress may not be fully appraised from the drawing board; abstract and general evaluation procedures cannot accurately anticipate the variables inevitable in the actual teaching–learning process. Individual differences, of both students and teachers, for example, and the unique features in all school organization, preclude rigidity in the utilization of preplanned evaluation and reporting schemes.

A prime requisite of evaluation and reporting is to provide students and parents with a full assessment of learning progress. This necessitates the application of multiple procedures and will not be supplied by one or four report cards issued on completion of various learning units. Student progress requires direction and guidance, a major factor of all effective evaluation and reporting. The instructional benefits that accrue from using reliable instruments to measure student progress are evident in the development and utilization of learning materials that best meet the requirements of a specific student or group. Adequate application in this area will be of marked assistance in the reduction of faulty or misplaced instruction.

2. *What is the teacher's place in evaluation?*

The teacher occupies a primary place in the evaluation of student progress and in making known the results of evaluation to parents. It is the teacher who has been associated most intimately with the student and is therefore best equipped to appraise what progress he has shown in knowledge, understanding, attitudes, and general behavioral skills, both technical and social.

It is the teacher who should know what the broad educational purposes are that govern the total school program, and particularly what objectives have been given primary emphasis in the class and made the basis for evaluation. Consequently, it is the teacher who should be vested with the major responsibility for the development of the evaluative plan and the procedural steps that make it up.

By the same token the teacher has an obligation to be familiar with the generally accepted principles of evaluation and the range of measurement instruments available. Equally important, he should understand the nature and appropriateness of the measuring instruments in relation to all aspects of the evaluation proposed.

Inasmuch as present educational objectives place much stress upon behavioral learning, the teacher needs to be aware of the newer evaluative criteria and procedures that require special approaches to measurement not taken by the older and more commonly used pencil-and-paper tests. He must be doubly alert to current devices by which changes in behavior can be tangibly and accurately assessed.[2]

3. *What are some important aspects of evaluation?*

Assumed areas of objective evaluation

Traditionally it has been assumed that a person's psychological elements or characteristics, such as intelligence, basic aptitudes, and fixed interest patterns, were capable of being measured by pencil-and-paper — so-called objec-

[2] For the purposes of measurement and evaluation discussed above the teacher should have available for ready reference such books as: J. Stanley Ahmann and Marvin D. Glock, *Evaluating Pupil Growth* (Boston: Allyn & Bacon, Inc., 2nd ed., 1963); R. Murray Thomas, *Judging Student Progress* (New York: Longmans, Green & Co., Inc., 2nd ed., 1960); Robert H. Bauernfeind, *Building a School Testing Program* (Boston: Houghton Mifflin Company, 1963); J. Wayne Wrightstone, Joseph Justman, and Irving Robbins, *Evaluation in Modern Education* (New York: American Book Company, 1956); Georgia S. Adams and Theodore L. Torgerson, *Measurement and Evaluation for the Secondary-School Teacher* (New York: The Dryden Press, 1956).

tive — tests. With even greater assurance it has been believed that academic subject-matter knowledge could be measured with a high degree of accuracy by these same instruments. The complex factors in health and physical well-being made measurement somewhat more difficult, but nonetheless these were believed capable of being reasonably well established through the use of pencil-and-paper and oral examinations and by means of highly reliable mechanical instruments.

Further, what could be objectively measured with a high degree of accuracy could with slightly less accuracy be interpreted and evaluated, it was felt, skill in evaluation suffering in dependability roughly in direct ratio to the degree of accuracy of the measuring instrument employed.

Although the instruments of measurement have become more accurate with time, there has been a lessened assurance in evaluating the results of measurement. What seems to be a highly efficient measuring instrument in reality may not produce the completely valid data it was designed to supply. Many aspects of learning once thought to be relatively simple factors to measure are discovered to be complex, whereas the instrument may be measuring only one or a few of the elements of the total learning situation.[3] Even what in the past was thought of as *simple* memory can no longer be considered simple. It is a complex process with many facets. It is not the province of the present chapter to consider at length this important phase of measurement and evaluation. Scores of excellent books are readily available to the teacher concerned with this over-all problem. But certain aspects of measurement and evaluation are of particular significance for the junior high school.

Special techniques of evaluation in the non-academic areas

During the past twenty years educational workers have sought procedures to provide better evaluation and reporting of student achievement in the non-academic areas, which are specifically concerned with physical, personal, and social equipment. These are the elements essential in the development of the student's integrative capacity, a primary feature in all purposive learning. Achievement in these areas affords the early adolescent opportunities for successful application of other knowledges and competencies. The increased confidence and resources so gained allow him to surmount obstacles inherent in the realistic appraisal of his learning progress.

[3] For a discussion of this problem as it affects intelligence measurement see Chapter 4; for a broader consideration of the complex problem of measurement see National Education Association, *Testing, Testing, Testing* (Washington: American Association of School Administrators (NEA), Council of Chief State School Officers, and National Association of Secondary-School Principals (NEA), 1962); also consult current articles critical of the limitations of measuring instruments. Most contemporary texts on measurement and evaluation give consideration to this problem. The teacher may find it of value to read some of the books highly critical of some phases of testing, such as Banesh Hoffman, *The Tyranny of Testing* (New York: The Crowell-Collier Publishing Co., 1962).

The student's wish to achieve the expected learning goals and his fears that they may not be realized are often equalized when the attending anxieties are contained at a level which does not deter or impede his learning. The factors contributing to the effective development of his integrative abilities are derived from multiple learning opportunities which permit the identification of achievements in all growth areas.

A survey of 400 junior high schools with enrollment ranging from 200 to 1500 students revealed that these special criteria were most frequently utilized to evaluate and report the student's personal and social growth patterns:[4]

Work Habits and Effort

Has necessary materials at hand
Follows plans and directions accurately
Makes good use of time and materials
Prepares assignment on time
Turns in neat and well-organized work
Shows initiative
Works quietly
Takes pride in work
Is attentive in class
Participates well in group work
Persistence in overcoming difficulties
Effectiveness in working independently
Is industrious
Shows self-direction
Plans work wisely
Knows when and how to seek help
Gives best effort

Health Habits

Sits, stands, walks correctly
Keeps face, hands, fingernails, and clothing clean
Makes use of handkerchief
Brushes and cares for teeth regularly
Has good habits of selecting foods and eating
Keeps head and hair neat and clean
Observes safety rules of school and community
Takes interest and pride in being healthy and physically fit
Develops various skills for wholesome recreation
Takes active part in individual, dual, and team games

[4] From records of summer graduate school students (superintendents, principals, counselors, and teachers) enrolled in the course "The Junior High School," taught by one of the authors of this book at the University of Minnesota, College of Education, 1957 through 1960.

Citizenship and Conduct

Gets along with others
Takes an active part in group activities
Demonstrates desirable characteristics
Respects authority and school regulations
Takes good care of school materials and equipment
Plays well with others
Is dependable
Does effective school work in group activities on both class and school levels
Is courteous
Is a cooperative worker
Respects the rights and feelings of others
Contributes his share
Shows leadership
Cooperates with officers and sponsor of student council

Social Attitudes

Pays attention when others are speaking
Shows good sportsmanship
Is courteous in speech and manner
Takes responsibility in caring for the appearance of room, building, and grounds
Takes active part in social activities in his homeroom, classes, and school

Social and Emotional Development

Is kind and cooperative
Respects the rights of others
Capable of winning and holding friends
Feels concern for others
Has honor and personal integrity
Is trustworthy
Respects and appreciates teachers
Recognizes the authority of a majority vote in group projects and activities
Accepts constructive social responsibility
Shows growth in self-control
Cooperates with teachers and student officers of social activities
Accepts social responsibility without supervision
Possesses self-esteem
Develops wholesome social leadership

Participation in Student Activities

Listens attentively and takes active part in assemblies
Contributes to school publications
Works effectively for the success of social activities
Is active in student council work
Is interested in special activities of the school
Has a desire to serve his school as member of service clubs

The tendency of many junior high school staffs to appraise and report student progress within a broader curriculum and instructional program provides (1) more learning tasks for all students, leading to additional opportunities for success; (2) more observance and reflection of all evidences of growth and development of early youth within the evaluation process and promotion determinants; (3) increased awareness of personal and social modifications, which allows teachers to be more accurate in assessing student achievements in all regular areas of learning; and (4) the construction of broad, flexible, and reliable measuring instruments for teachers to apply in their evaluation of achievement and growth.

Regardless of procedures and techniques used in evaluating academic skills, there is a definite inclination for teachers to mark and report evidences of student changes in habits, attitudes, and personal and social growth patterns. This is consistent with modern conceptions of the nature of the learning process and the objectives of education.

Many junior high school educators regard the application of several teacher-made written examinations, short in length, and directly related to and immediately following specific class learning experiences, as the best way to appraise the validity of student learning, curriculum, and instruction. These measures often allow for more effective evidence of the marked variabilities and individual responses of adolescent learners. Such procedure also minimizes fears, anxieties, and resentments often triggered by the single final examination.

Adolescent learners are inclined to respond to the traditional objective appraisal instrument with intense feelings. Their attempt to cope with it by "cramming" impedes their efforts to integrate the required knowledge. These responses may not be discerned by the teacher, for high scores are often attained, but sustained and integrated comprehension may not be achieved. The response pattern thus set is frequently continued by students throughout their secondary school experiences and into college. However, the time comes when the cramming mechanism is no longer able even to temporarily satisfy educational demands. Other solutions must then be sought and removal from the demand source by dropping out of school is the typical action.

When educators perceive strong evidences that the junior high school provides an important environment for either constructive or destructive learning attitudes, patterns, and responses, they will more carefully examine and perhaps modify their evaluating and reporting practices.

Importance of guidance and counseling in evaluation

Scores and markings on only certain subject content are not adequate for reporting student progress. A comprehensive evaluation program should include regular and frequent assessments of problem-solving abilities, interests, and attitudes as observed in student-teacher relationships, group interactions, student activity participation, and personal interest areas. Such an evaluation plan is designed to provide reliable indications for modification of the school program, to show where objectives and materials of learning experiences are satisfactory or unsatisfactory, and to help students perceive their learning and growth progression.

The staffs of junior high schools with programs committed to student-centered learning opportunities believe that evaluation means appraising student growth in areas of knowledge, attitudes and behavior, and habits of orderly thinking. This requires that teachers understand basic guidance and counseling principles and practices which will contribute to their ability to help each student understand his liabilities and assets as evidenced in his performance in all learning areas. Guidance may thus not only improve learning but also prevent the student from giving way to the negativistic responses of intense fears, anxieties, and resentments frequently accompanying the usual, limited evaluation procedures.

The daily class instructional activities provide teachers with numerous opportunities to utilize their guidance and counseling techniques as they observe and appraise student progress in specific areas of learning, recognize problem areas, develop corrective measures, and evaluate responses to regular and special guidance and counseling activities. These practices may then be viewed as advancing and evaluating student progress simultaneously, which should be the ideal of all junior high school programs.

The problem of evaluation in block-time and core classes

Teachers in block-time classes and core programs have even more opportunities to observe, recognize, and appraise the associative influences of physical, social, and emotional forces upon student learning progress. They are also in a better position to apply guidance skills in their interactions with students, by devising special conditions in their classes which enhance and motivate productive student discussion, by assuring the students that the instructional purpose of their relationship is to assist them in learning, and by expressing both directly and indirectly the desire to understand them, their thoughts, and their feelings without indicating personal likes or dislikes.

The block-time or core teacher is afforded the time span necessary for continuous student progress appraisals which is essential to their validity. These appraisals are derived from written and verbal tests (teacher-constructed or student-constructed), student-teacher conferences, standardized tests, group interactions and observation of student participation in various learning activities.

The application of many and varied assessments over a considerable time span allows the teacher to recognize more accurately and quickly those students with problems necessitating the specialized services of counselors, school nurses, or other appropriate sources. Thus he can directly assist his students in resolving attitudinal problems which are obstacles to maximum learning.

Core teachers are obliged to design and implement varied techniques to assess and report student progress, as is pointed out by Faunce and Bossing in *Developing the Core Curriculum:*

> . . . He [the teacher] has set himself to the challenging task of helping his students to achieve a more desirable social and vocational adjustment through guidance, of developing well-rounded individuals through correlated learning experiences, and of teaching democratic attitudes and abilities through the provision of a democratic classroom experience. He therefore cannot avoid the implications of these goals when he sets out to evaluate. Since new purposes require new evaluative techniques, the core teacher is challenged by the nature of his assignment to develop procedures for evaluation.[5]

Individual cumulative record and evaluation

Another area in which teachers require preparation is in the construction and utilization of an individual student record system. It must contain all material considered pertinent in the assessment of student progress and growth: (1) standardized tests, (2) performance patterns, (3) learning attitudes, (4) health records, (5) samples of students' work, and (6) observations of developmental growth by the teacher.

Assessments derived exclusively from standardized tests must not be rated above those obtained from other measuring instruments consistent with the criteria outlined in the preceding pages of this chapter. There is marked evidence that standardized tests have not yet been constructed to accommodate the multiplicity of developmental variables present in early adolescence. They are inadequate, too, in providing valid and exact views of individual progress; apparently, even with repeated application, they do not accurately account for the human factors of individual differences. Thus, teachers must perceive any evaluative evidences produced by standardized tests as only one of many determinants to be considered in formulating an *accurate* appraisal of learning progress.

Records of each student's performance patterns in areas of learning, including an appraisal of daily class achievements, show his ability to integrate learning and may reveal the need for modifications of instructional practices and/or materials.

A descriptive comment regarding significant changes in the student's learning attitudes must incorporate the teacher's comprehensive notations on study habits, class participation, attention span, responses to instructional demands, reactions to testing experiences and results, changing behavior patterns, and

[5] Roland C. Faunce and Nelson L. Bossing, *Developing the Core Curriculum,* Second Edition. © 1958, by permission of Prentice-Hall, Inc., Englewood Cliffs, N.J. P. 340. See also Rosalind M. Zapf, *Democratic Processes in the Secondary Classroom* (Englewood Cliffs, N.J.: Prentice-Hall, Inc., 1959), pp. 297-314.

use of extra-class learning aids. Teachers need to have available a cumulative record covering the student's school experiences in their entirety and portraying in orderly fashion his progress and growth.

To summarize, it is essential to recognize the intellectual, physical, emotional, and social components as catalytic agents in all goal-directed human learning. The inclusion of these interacting elements in the cumulative record often affords a dynamic profile of the student's relationship to the aggregation of learning opportunities. When one or more of these factors become dysfunctional, the learner's progress is seriously impeded.

4. What are significant practices in evaluating and reporting student progress?

Some newer marking modifications in relation to class or grade

Evaluating student progress in relation to standing in class or grade has changed considerably, especially in junior high schools with block-time or core programs.

At the time of the adoption of block-time classes at West Junior High School in 1946, the marking system of five letter grades (E — excellent, S — superior, M — average, I — inferior, F — failure) was being utilized by all junior and senior high schools in Kansas City, Missouri. All teachers with homerooms incorporated in a block-time period were concerned. In their opinion the highly departmentalized school organization and the rigid and fragmented marking system were the major forces underlying one-fifth of student failures in learning. They recommended that, prior to any student's retention in a grade or subject, his individual pattern of growth and development be reviewed and carefully appraised. Also, with regular school attendance, his grade level promotion should be consistent in all learning areas. This policy was adopted in spite of current indications from educational research that grade retention is beneficial to instruction and learning within junior high schools.

These special procedures and techniques were designed as guidelines for student progress appraisals that would advance, and not retard, learning:

1. Greater emphasis was placed on the initial recognition and appraisal of variations in individual class learning needs prior to initiating new learning materials.
2. More attention was given to student orientation prior to grade entrance and completion by both teachers and school counselors.
3. The instructional programs in all areas of learning were organized according to abilities, needs, and interests of the students.
4. All teachers offered consistent encouragement to all students to apply maximum effort toward learning progression.

5. Counselors, teachers, principal, and parents conferred at the middle of each reporting period with, or about, students observed as not exerting maximum effort in one or more areas of learning. This conference gave all concerned ample time to obtain special help before completion of the unit of instruction.

6. Students with poor attitudes, from deprived homes, and of low aptitude for regular school work were many times reclassified and given permits, especially in Grades 8 and 9, to seek part-time gainful employment, as described in Chapter 8.

7. There was an unusually large percentage, in this particular student population, with language difficulties, a limited command of academic skills, intellectual liabilities, and lack of parental encouragement toward high school completion. These students were assigned, in groups of fifteen to twenty, to block-time and mathematics classes for half of the school day, with one and sometimes two different teachers, so that they could receive more individualized instruction. During the other half of the day they worked in classes in other areas of learning, including the student activities program.

The constant belief in, and use of, these special procedures for nearly two decades reduced the percentage of retardation from 20 per cent in the 1946-1947 school year to less than 1 per cent of the students enrolled in Grades 7, 8, and 9 in any subsequent school year.

In two junior high schools in Fontana, California, evaluation instruments have been broadened and designed to accommodate better teacher appraisals of learning progression in all areas of the school program. Since the institution of these changes students seldom have to repeat an area of learning:

> During the 1958-59 school year, this program was initiated with eight retained students at Sequoia Junior High School, Fontana, California (approximate enrollment — 830 students). By the end of the school year, five of the retainees had been replaced in their regular grade level and had adjusted successfully to the grade-level program. Three students had developed such a negative attitude toward school and learning that they were unable to re-adjust to school life.
>
> During the 1959-60 school year, the program was continued at Alder Junior High School, Fontana, California (approximate enrollment — 530 students). Five students were involved in the program and all five had returned to their regular grade level by the end of the school year.[6]

At present the technique of marking student performance in relation to class or grade is not as rigidly followed as it was in the early junior high school. By using not one but many evaluative instruments it is possible for

[6] Thomas W. Fine, "Student Retention in the Junior High School." Reprinted by permission from *The Bulletin of the National Association of Secondary-School Principals*, November, 1961. Copyright: Washington, D.C. Pp. 84-85.

teachers to recognize and appraise more evidences of early adolescent learning progression and growth achievements.

Development in early adolescence may be described as acute, fast, temporary, regressed, advanced, static, and fluid; the most outstanding and consistent feature is *instability*. When traditional evaluation and reporting concepts, procedures, and techniques are utilized by teachers in formulating measuring instruments, their appraisals are multitudinous and of broad dimension. But the use of these instruments may have a destructive effect on student learning, not only during adolescence but during the development of a mature life style with its unprecedented demands. Full understanding of these questions will of necessity await further research to validate definitive correlation, but there is enough evidence to arouse immediate consideration.

Many junior high school educators have acknowledged these concerns by devising special techniques aimed toward particularizing measuring instruments to provide for the consistent element of *instability,* so predominant during the preadolescent and early adolescent years. These special procedures are varied, non-specific in form, and considered appropriate when they conform to two major principles: (1) they secure valid evidences of student achievements in line with the educational objectives of the junior high school program; and (2) they further, rather than obstruct, student progress in all areas of learning.

The import of — and the potential destructiveness of — some evaluative techniques and procedures is illustrated in this excerpt from Lichter, Rapien, Seibert, and Sklansky's *The Drop-Outs:*

> School malfunctioning is one of the early signs of personality disturbance. Left on his own the child may adopt nonconstructive, even harmful means to master his fears and anxieties. Gradually, such maladaptations become a way of life. They do keep him from experiencing unpleasant inner feelings, but at the same time they also keep him from achieving a positive kind of happiness in healthy interpersonal relationships. At [early] adolescence, instead of being relatively free to decide what kind of person he wants to be, the die has been cast and his character is already solidifying.
>
> Failure in school, then, may be the first ominous sign of a budding character disorder. Prompt intervention (or modification of a particular marking system), brought about by the school's acuity in perceiving trouble and its readiness to make referral to treatment resources, provides a real service to the individual child and to society.[7]

The thesis that should remain focal throughout the program of junior high school education may best be described as the attempt to center the cor-

[7] Solomon O. Lichter, Elsie B. Rapien, Francis M. Seibert, and Morris A. Sklansky, *The Drop-Outs, A Treatment Study of Intellectually Capable Students Who Drop Out of High School* (Glencoe, Ill.: The Free Press of Glencoe, Inc., 1962), pp. 261-262.

responding components of curriculum, school organization, and instructional processes around the needs and characteristics of the early adolescent learner. Concomitant with this orientation is greater impetus toward individualizing the evaluation and reporting process. Within this frame of reference numerous junior high school teachers have become increasingly cognizant of the necessity for the following three major features in evaluation and reporting practices: (1) integrative application of guidance-counseling concepts and/or services as preventive and remedial to deterrents of student progress; (2) broader and more flexible, purposive utilization of multiple measuring instruments; and (3) a cumulative record for each student, including all information pertinent to the student's progress and growth.

The dual marking system

When student progress is appraised and a report to parents is formulated by correlating the achievement and growth attained, in relation to the student's own abilities and those of his classmates, a dual marking system is in force. It is increasingly being accepted and applied by junior high school educators. When dual marking is used, the kind of achievement attained is rated in one column of the report card in relation to grade standards, and in another column in relation to known ability to achieve. Strang describes how a dual marking system can operate within the framework of traditional grade standards:

> . . . The first estimate may be in the form of a letter grade or in percentage form. The second estimate is usually designated by a number: 1, 2, 3, 4, 5. Thus, Sylvia's mark in social studies in terms of her grade's standards might be a B or an 85. But mental ability tests may show that Sylvia has the ability to do far better work in this field than she is doing. In terms of capacity, then, her work may rate only a 4 or a 5, and her grade would appear as B/4 or B/5 (or 85/4 or 85/5).
>
> Such appraisal of the pupil's individual capacity to achieve makes the bright student aware of unrealized goals. At the same time, it does not discourage the less able student who is doing his best.
>
> . . . .
>
> By the seventh and eighth grades, if pupils have built up a sense of personal worth and an acceptance of individual differences, and if their school experience has helped them set up realistic goals for themselves, they can accept marks as measures of school achievement. They will not be unduly discouraged by a poor mark in a subject in which they have done their best, because they will realize that they cannot excel in everything. Instead, they will turn their attention to things in which they *can* succeed.
>
> On this level, the dual marking system — evaluating achievement in terms of grade standards and appraising it in terms of the child's ability to achieve — is

still valuable. However, even this marking system does not alone accomplish one important purpose of reporting: It does not show specific ways in which the pupil can improve.[8]

The limitations of dual marking are briefly discussed by Thomas:

It is difficult to say for sure who is happiest under such an arrangement as this. But in most cases it probably is the poorer student, for the system gives him more opportunities to receive commendation for his efforts in the form of a saisfactory mark.

In theory at least this method of grading is the best, for it suits the mark to student ability. But in practice its potential advantages are usually reduced somewhat by influences arising from tradition and human nature. For instance, our school systems in the past have been geared to judging the student against his classmates or against the teacher's standard. With this tradition, it is often hard for the bright pupil who may be a bit lazy to accept a lower mark than that received by the slow but diligent classmate who obviously does not know as much as the bright one. The slow student, too, recognizes that he is not nearly so capable as his better endowed classmates, so that he may regard his own high mark with some suspicion.[9]

A dual marking system suggests to parents their child's achievement in comparison to that of other students in his grade and denotes whether his learning progress is considered to be above or below his abilities. This method is perceived by many as effective and beneficial in appraising and reporting progress, when accompanied by regular explanatory parent-teacher conferences. Numerous dual marking report cards are currently being used in junior high school programs. The Simley Junior-Senior High School report-to-parents card is illustrative of this format (see Figure 9).

Another system of dual marking accepted by many junior high school educators uses two different columns to designate the degree of achievement in relation to other members of the class and an assessment of the individual effort expended according to self-comparison. This reporting method is designed to identify learning areas requiring improvement. The Campus School, State University College of Education, Plattsburg, New York, utilizes this card system in intermediate and junior high school grades. The outline below illustrates how the system marks student achievement in relation to effort demonstrated in reading and literature, language speaking and writing, mathematics, science, citizenship education, art, music, homemaking, arts and crafts or industrial arts, physical education, and French:

[8] Ruth Strang, *How to Report Pupil Progress* (Chicago: Science Research Associates, 1955), pp. 19 and 22.

[9] Thomas, *op. cit.,* courtesy of David McKay Company, Inc. P. 342.

FIGURE 9

A Dual-Form Report Card Used at the Simley Junior-Senior High School, Inver Grove–Pine Bend District No. 199, South St. Paul, Minnesota

Office Comments

1. ______________________________
____
2. ______________________________
____
3. ______________________________
____
4. ______________________________
____

Signature of Parent or Guardian

1. ______________________________
2. ______________________________
3. ______________________________

A Report to Parents

from

Simley Junior-Senior High School

Inver Grove-Pine Bend Dist. No. 199

Rt. No. 1, South St. Paul, Minnesota

This report is designed to give parents information in regard to the all-around development of the student by indicating growth in subject progress according to individual ability as well as achievement in subject matter in comparison to the rest of the class.

Karl O. Dahlager..........Superintendent
Vernon S. Larson..........Principal
Robert Brown..........Counselor

FIGURE 9, continued

Office Copy

NAME ______________________ SENIOR HIGH SCHOOL GRADE ______________

QUARTER	1st			2nd			3rd			4th			Final	Final
SUBJECT	Subject Grade	Subject Progress	Conduct	Subject Grade	Subject Progress	Conduct	Subject Grade	Subject Progress	Conduct	Subject Grade	Subject Progress	Conduct	**Test**	**Grade**
ENGLISH														
SOC. STUDIES														
PHY. ED.														
HEALTH														

ATTENDANCE

	1	2	3	4
DAYS ABSENT				
TIMES TARDY				

CONDUCT

Conduct is based upon the student's behavior in or about his classroom of study. It is independent of his subject grade. Average behavior would be "C".

Subject Grades

A Outstanding Work
B Well Above Average
C Average Work for Grade Level
D Below Average
F Failure

Subject Progress (According to individual ability)

O Outstanding
S Satisfactory
U Unsatisfactory

(Reason for unsatisfactory progress)

1 Absence
2 Incomplete Work
3 Poor Work Habits
4 Poor Attitude
5 Parent-Teacher Conference Recommended

Growth in Knowledge and Skills

Achievement Marks — Class Comparison	Effort Marks — Self Comparison
A Excellent	1 Very Good
B Above Average	2 Good
C Average	3 Fair
D Below Average	4 Poor
F Failing	An (X) indicates that your child needs to make improvement

Additionally, progress in the personal and social growth of the student is denoted.

Student progress in correlation with apparent abilities

There is a tendency in school systems utilizing the progress-in-relation-to-abilities method in elementary school units to apply the same system in Grades 7 and 8 and often in Grade 9.

In a survey of 1360 junior and junior-senior high schools in the forty-eight contiguous states and the District of Columbia, Wright and Greer reported more than one-third of these schools as marking students in Grades 7, 8, and 9 in accordance with apparent "pupil ability."[10]

The major educational reason for marking and promoting young adolescents in relation to "pupil ability" rather than on grade or uniform standards is to reduce and/or prevent critical anxiety during this period of growth, already so laden with complexities and concerns about self-worth and identity. Moreover, it appears unrealistic to try to assign valid uniform standards within the framework of the gross and rapid patterns of change so typical of early adolescence.

The marks, or symbols, identifying progress in relation to apparent student abilities varies considerably. The most often applied symbols are

O — Outstanding
Marked superiority according to ability.

S — Satisfactory
Growth is satisfactory according to ability.

U — Unsatisfactory
Growth is not satisfactory according to ability — needs improvement, and parent–teacher conference is recommended.

[10] Grace S. Wright and Edith S. Greer, *The Junior High School, A Survey of Grades 7-8-9 in Junior and Junior-Senior High Schools, 1959-1960,* U.S. Office of Education Bulletin No. 32 (Washington: Government Printing Office, 1963), p. 44, Table 26.

The practices presented in the foregoing pages may be characterized as in harmony with the criteria for appraising and reporting student progress, in both elementary and secondary schools, reported by Mortensen and Schmuller:

1. There is a two-way trend away from and toward systems which compare a pupil's progress with the class. Some schools wish to grade each pupil according to his ability and others grade on a "competitive" basis.

2. There is a widespread movement toward evaluation of personality and character traits in addition to subject-matter achievement.

3. There is marked increase in the use of qualitative and descriptive reports in lieu of single quantitative scores. Letters to the home and parent conferences are typical. This trend seems to have reduced the number of reportings to the home and spread the reporting period over a longer length of time.

4. There is a trend toward increased participation of the parents in the development of the reporting form; in some instances pupils have helped devise forms.

5. There is a trend toward evaluating progress in terms of recognized and acceptable objectives of the school. Thus, if parents participate in developing school policy, this type of reporting has greater meaning and can cover a broader base; for example, health and participation in character-building programs may be evaluated.[11]

Reporting student progress

The numerous modifications and advancements in curriculum and instruction programs in contemporary junior high schools have increasingly identified and stressed individualization as the foundation for evaluating and reporting student progress. Educators continue to design and apply their respective marking and reporting systems as they strive to devise instruments to reflect this new emphasis.

Reporting of student progress is rapidly being expanded to encompass the total development of early youth. Report cards to parents take many different forms and are usually augmented by regular parent-teacher conferences. In 1958-1959 more than three-fourths of the urban school districts in the United States reported pupil progress in elementary schools by means of both parent conferences and report cards. In half of the districts this combination method is used in junior high schools, and in two-fifths, in senior high schools. The trend at all school levels is away from reporting by card only and toward reporting by card plus a conference with the parent.[12]

Another interesting trend in urban school districts concerns the frequency of reporting student progress to parents. Table 27 indicates that 55.7 per cent

[11] Donald G. Mortensen and Allen M. Schmuller, *Guidance in Today's Schools* (New York: John Wiley & Sons, Inc., 1959), pp. 209-210.

[12] See "Report to Parents," *NEA Research Bulletin,* 39:24, February, 1961.

TABLE 27

Frequency of Pupil Progress Reports to Parents, 1958-1959

Frequency	Estimated Number of Urban School Districts Having					
	Elementary Schools		Junior High Schools		Senior High Schools	
	Number	Per Cent	Number	Per Cent	Number	Per Cent
Twice a year	27	0.7	9	0.3	8	0.2
Three times a year	127	3.5	30	0.9	10	0.3
Four times a year	1,642	45.2	1,196	38.3	1,220	35.7
Five times a year	231	6.4	149	4.8	179	5.2
More than five times a year	1,604	44.2	1,740	55.7	2,001	58.6
Total	3,631	100.0	3,124	100.0	3,418	100.0

From "Report to Parents," *NEA Research Bulletin,* 39:25, February, 1961.

of the junior high schools report to parents more than five times a year, and 38.3 per cent four times a year. Thus, while the majority of junior high schools give parents regular reports more than five times a year, there is an increasing inclination to reduce this number to not more than four times a year. This longer time between reporting periods serves (1) to minimize the overemphasis on formal marks; (2) to increase the effectiveness of teacher-parent consultations, affording time for improved student performance to be effected in accordance with the goals formulated by teacher, parent, and student; and (3) to allow time for the student with learning disabilities to use the specialized services available from the school counselor, social worker, and psychologist.

The Stewart Junior High School staff, College of Education, University of Utah, has, since 1959, effectively implemented a report-to-parents procedure derived from correlating achievement with prior formulated learning goals devised by teachers, students, and parents. The educational objectives are drawn from broad areas of learning and various adjunctive subtopics within the block-time and other class activities. The Stewart report-to-parents card is illustrated in Figure 10. It goes to the parents three times a year. Subject-matter content is utilized as an essential means through which students attain their general and specific learning goals. This reporting system has no comparative scores or letter grades. In the four years of its use, teachers, students, and parents of Stewart Junior High School have evidenced a marked degree of satisfaction with their method of reporting student progress.

The purposes of marking and reporting student progress will, in the final analysis, afford structural guidelines for the formulation of all specific systems. These purposes are suggested by Ahmann and Glock thus:

FIGURE 10

A Report Card Designed to Provide Parents with More Complete Data on the Learning Progress of Their Children

PARENT'S SIGNATURE: ______

COMMENTS BY PARENTS: ______

R E P O R T   T O   P A R E N T S

WILLIAM M. STEWART SCHOOL - SALT LAKE CITY, UTAH

Date ______

This report attempts to appraise the individual growth and development of our students. Since no two people grow alike it is felt that comparative scores or letter grades do not adequately report individual progress. We are offering this more comprehensive summary in the place of scores or letter grades.

REPORT OF ______

GRADE ______ 19___, 19______

ASSIGNMENT NEXT YEAR, GRADE ______

TEACHER ______

PRINCIPAL ______

ATTENDANCE RECORD

Days Present	
Days Absent	
Times Tardy	

FIGURE 10, continued

REPORT TO PARENTS
WILLIAM M. STEWART SCHOOL - SALT LAKE CITY, UTAH

Name______________________ Term____________ Year______________

Homeroom Teacher____________________________ Grade ______________

Four large areas are presented in the report, each with various sub-topics. Favorable development in these areas is the goal toward which we are working. Each student will normally move toward these goals at a different rate. The teacher recognizes this and marks accordingly.

Special sections are designated for parent and teacher comments.

When the growth is even, and steady, it is indicated by a [✓]
An unusual spurt of growth following a period of very little growth is shown by a [×]
Where little evidence of growth is seen, we mark [O]
When sufficient evidence is not available to the teacher he uses the symbol [—]

GOALS TOWARD WHICH WE ARE WORKING	Soc. Stud.	English	Mathematics	Science			Art	Home Econ.	Ind. Arts	Music	Phys. Edu.	
	OBSERVATIONS OF TEACHERS											
I. CITIZENSHIP - INDIVIDUAL RESPONSIBILITY:												
a. Accepts personal responsibility for his own actions in halls, rooms, playgrounds, going to and from school												
b. Shows evidence of willingness to serve the entire group in school projects and activities.												
c. Demonstrates respect and care in using public property and consideration for his personal property and that of his classmates.												
d. Demonstrates a growing ability and insight in analyzing situations and facing problems and in reacting appropriately to them.												
e. Shows ability to relate himself to his classmates in a variety of ways; personal friends, participation in games, and committee membership.												
f. Demonstrates ability to accept differences among his classmates and others he comes in contact with.												
g. Shows courtesy, consideration & willingness to accept and act on suggestions from teachers & classmates.												
h. Shows insight into personal hygiene as evidenced by good grooming, appropriate dress and cleanliness.												
i. Shows growth in health knowledge and practices as evidenced by physical condition and control.												
j. Reports to all classes promptly or presents legitimate excuse for absence or tardiness.												

HOMEROOM TEACHER COMMENTS:

II. LEARNING AND STUDY SKILLS:												
a. Uses a variety of resources: people, books, magazines, pamphlets, pictures, etc., for needed information. Organizes this info. wisely for specific use.												
b. Participates constructively in classroom discussions and other school activities.												
c. Accepts responsibility for assignments and completes them promptly.												
d. Shows willingness to work beyond mini. requirements.												
e. Complies with legitimate requests, willingly, and promptly and does not alibi.												
f. Places proper emphasis on accomplishment and is not overly concerned about an immediate reward.												
g. Initiates new activities, presents additional ideas.												
h. Budgets time to given need or program of activities.												
i. Willingly spends extra time to complete work.												
j. Provides the necessary materials to do work with.												
k. Shows a willingness to work experimentally.												
l. Applies previous knowledge, experience to new situa.												
m. Shows increasing ability to work alone or with the group according to need.												
n. Exercises independence to seek extra aid when need.												

HOMEROOM TEACHER COMMENTS:

FIGURE 10, continued

Name ______________________ Term ________ Year ________

III. COMMUNICATIVE SKILLS:
- a. Shows growth in ability to communicate informally with classmates, teachers, and other adults.
- b. Shows growth and ability to phrase a request, to organize ideas, to present a point of view, to relate an experience.
- c. Shows growth in ability and willingness to present ideas in writing.
- d. Keeps records useful for himself and/or for the group.
- e. Shows growth in the mechanical aspects of writing:
  - sentence structure
  - spelling
  - punctuation and capitalization
  - penmanship
- f. Uses graphic material, statistical tables, charts, maps, etc.
- g. Chooses to read in free time; reads a variety of material, much of which he locates independently.
- h. Shows growth in ability to adjust rate of reading to purpose.
- i. Shows growth in effective comprehension of reading.
- j. Shows evidence of understanding and relating sound mathematical and science concepts to everyday life.
- k. Demonstrates ability to recognize the elements of a problem and to use the scientific method in its solution.

HOMEROOM TEACHER COMMENTS:

IV. CREATIVE ASPECTS OF LIVING:
- a. Shows a growing awareness of, and appreciation for, the creative arts such as literature, music, art, design, crafts, homemaking, etc.
- b. Recognizes his own creative abilities, accepts his personal limitations, and consciously develops the capabilities which he does possess.
- c. Seeks to discover new ways of expressing himself, creatively.
- d. Shows recognition and acceptance of the talent and special ability of others.
- e. Recognizes that freedom and a permissive atmosphere are necessary for effective exploration and creativity.

HOMEROOM TEACHER COMMENTS:

"SPECIAL SUBJECT" TEACHER COMMENTS: ______________________

The purposes of marking and reporting can best be defined in terms of those who use them — pupils, parents, teachers, school administrators, and employers. In the final analysis, reports should serve one purpose — to facilitate the educational development of each pupil in relation to his ability. Their effectiveness should be judged in terms of this criterion. Therefore, they succeed to the extent that they improve the likelihood that each pupil will achieve to the degree that his talents allow.[13]

[13] Ahmann and Glock, *op. cit.*, pp. 546-547.

Marks and reporting student progress in core classes

Core instruction requires that teachers perceive learning progression and developmental growth within the context of the individual's functioning, as observed and appraised from the encounters with the multiple learning opportunities afforded him as a class, school, and community member.

Core teachers therefore evolve and implement rather unique ways to appraise, mark, and report the learning goals attained: (1) they direct and guide students in self-assessment; (2) they set up individual conferences between student and teachers, focused on clarification of problems within the curriculum areas; (3) they appraise student learning continuously, through multiple learning situations; and (4) they initiate, plan, and engage parents in a collaborative endeavor to effectively meet the student's general and specific learning needs.

In discussing "What about Marks" (evaluating and reporting student progress in core classes), Faunce and Bossing say:[14]

> Probably no problem has been so vexing to core teachers as that of what to do about school marks. In the first place, it seems clear that the conventional competitive, symbol marks are quite inadequate for reporting the kind of growth that core teachers seek to achieve in their students. Marks not only fail to describe the many aspects of development to which core classes are devoted; they also actually violate certain important purposes of the core curriculum unless their use is carefully guarded. Compare the following list of purposes that have been discussed at various points in this book with the list of attributes that usually characterize the use of symbol marking:

The core class seeks:	Symbol marking tends:
To learn the skills of cooperative planning.	— To encourage competition.
To learn the skills of self and group appraisal.	— To place evaluative responsibility solely upon the teacher.
To help students to adjust more successfully to their peers.	— To erect barriers between peers.
To provide a well-rounded learning experience.	— To place undue emphasis on subject mastery.
To make evaluation continuously, as a part of group planning.	— To emphasize terminal evaluation.
To help students to grow from where they are.	— To force all to meet minimum standards, or quit.
To provide learning experiences deriving from the intrinsic needs and desires of the learner.	— To serve as an extrinsic motivation, thus helping to perpetuate poor teaching.

[14] Faunce and Bossing, *op. cit.* © 1958, by permission of Prentice-Hall, Inc., Englewood Cliffs, N.J. Pp. 360-361.

In *Democratic Processes in the Secondary Classroom* Zapf presents a form designed as a cooperative teacher–student evaluative-marking device in which specific items reflect the educational purposes and student learning behaviors stressed in the core curriculum concept and made functional in the classroom. Opposite these items in one column are self-evaluative marks which the student in a serious appraisal of his work in the classroom over a given period has awarded himself. In the second column, paralleling the first, the teacher has recorded for each item the marks which represent her best judgment of the student. Before filling in her column the teacher has placed a strip of paper over the marks of the student to avoid being influenced by his evaluations.

If there are serious differences in the judgments of student and teacher for any of the items recorded, the teacher calls the student in for a conference, and together they explore the reasons for the discrepancies. The teacher constantly strives to discover pupil merit, if any exists, for the differences in marks. If the student can demonstrate that the teacher has not recognized all the factors in the situation, as is possible particularly in a large class, the teacher adjusts the grade in a third column. In such instances the student's mark may be accepted or even a higher grade may be given if the teacher feels that the evidence presented warrants it. If the teacher is not convinced that she has underestimated the situation, the mark stands. The teacher, of course, must be the final judge. However, this plan provides a basis for the establishment of rapport with the student and a feeling on the student's part that the teacher seeks to be fair. It offers an educational experience for both.

This form is then used as a report to the parents. With its definite characterizations of educational purposes and what is expected of the student it is considered an educational device for the parents in terms of the work of the school, as well as a medium for reporting the learning progress of the student. In the event the parents have questions on any part of the report form it provides an excellent basis for a teacher–parent conference. (See Figure 11.)

The predominant purpose of this chapter is the delineation of concepts within which the process of evaluating and reporting student progress may evolve as a foundational concept of junior high school education.

The authors believe that if evaluative processes are to be reliable and valid, they must be in a positive correlation with junior high school educational objectives and the student's apparent capacities, and with all the attending complexities unique to early adolescence. To accomplish a full realization of these concepts no single appraisal and/or measuring instrument is sufficient; experimentation and a critical analysis of many and varied methods are required. And finally, it is believed that the primary criterion for any and all reporting procedures is that they do not impede learning.

FIGURE 11

A Teacher-Pupil Cooperative Evaluation Form

Progress Toward Class Goals Name: Larry Anderson Date: Nov. 2			
	Pupil	Teacher	Con-ference
I. *Working in groups*			
1. Be responsible for my share of the work.	4	3	4
2. Stick to the work that needs to be done.	3	3	
3. Share information and materials with other members.	4	2	4
II. *Class discussions*			
1. Take active part.	2	2	
2. Be quiet while others are talking.	4	4	
3. Listen to other people's ideas.	4	?	3
4. Be friendly.	4	4	
III. *Working on problems*			
1. Collect information from many sources.	4	4	
2. Select best material that fits the problems.	4	4	
3. Collect enough material to solve the problems.	4	4	
4. Be able to use the card catalog.	3	3	
5. Be able to use the *Readers' Guide.*	2	2	
6. Write notes in own words.	3	3	
IV. *Reporting to the class*			
1. Organize material so that it is smooth.	3	3	
2. Give reports without reading notes or paper.	4	4	
3. Speak clearly.	4	4	
4. Use good English.	4	4	
5. Illustrate the material.	1	4	3
Total points	61		62
Average	$3\frac{7}{18}$		$3\frac{8}{18}$
Key: 5 = A, 4 = B, 3 = C, 2 = D, 1 = E	C+		C+

From Rosalind M. Zapf, *Democratic Processes in the Secondary Classroom.* © 1959, by permission of Prentice-Hall, Inc., Englewood Cliffs, N.J. P. 307.

SELECTED BIBLIOGRAPHY

Ahmann, J. Stanley, and Marvin D. Glock. *Evaluating Pupil Growth.* Boston: Allyn and Bacon, Inc., 2nd ed., 1963.

Bauernfeind, Robert H. *Building a School Testing Program.* Boston: Houghton Mifflin Company, 1963.

Black, Hillel. *They Shall Not Pass.* New York: William Morrow and Company, 1963.

Carter, Harold D. "Over-Achievers and Under-Achievers in Junior High Schools," *California Journal of Educational Research,* 12:51-56, March, 1961.

Chansky, Norman M. "Elementary School Teachers Rate Report Cards," *Journal of Educational Research,* 56:523-528, July-August, 1963.

Conant, James Bryant. *Education in the Junior High School Years.* Princeton, N.J.: Educational Testing Service, 1960.

Daltman, Howard, and Kenneth E. Michael. "What Are Some New Trends in Reporting Student Growth and Achievement to Parents?" *The Bulletin of the National Association of Secondary-School Principals,* 44:146-149, April, 1960.

Devita, Joseph C. "No Homework . . . No Report Card Grades . . . Ungraded," *The Bulletin of the National Association of Secondary-School Principals,* 45:180-184, October, 1961.

Faunce, Roland C., and Nelson L. Bossing. *Developing the Core Curriculum.* Englewood Cliffs, N.J.: Prentice-Hall, Inc., 2nd ed., 1958. Chap. 15, "Evaluating Progress in the Core."

———, and Morrel J. Clute. *Teaching and Learning in the Junior High School.* San Francisco: Wadsworth Publishing Company, 1961. Chap. 13, "Evaluating the Junior High School."

Fine, Thomas W. "Student Retention in the Junior High School," *The Bulletin of the National Association of Secondary-School Principals,* 45:84-85, November, 1961.

French, Will, and associates. *Behavioral Goals of General Education in High School.* New York: Russell Sage Foundation, 1957.

Frymier, Jack R. "Assessing Junior High School Students' Motivation," *The High School Journal* (published by The University of North Carolina Press), 45:302-305, April, 1962.

Gruhn, William T., and Harl R. Douglass. *The Modern Junior High School.* New York: The Ronald Press Company, 2nd ed., 1956. Chap. 17, "Evaluating, Reporting, and Recording Pupil Progress."

Harris, Pearl, and Frank Trotter. "An Experiment with Underachievers," *Education,* 82:347-349, February, 1962.

Hock, Louise E., and Thomas J. Hill. *The General Education Class in the Secondary School.* New York: Holt, Rinehart & Winston, Inc., 1960.

Hull, J. Dan, and Howard H. Cummins. "How Fare American Youth in 1962?" *School Life,* 44:13-17, January-February, 1962.

Johnston, Edgar G., Mildred Peters, and William Evraiff. *The Role of the Teacher in Guidance.* Englewood Cliffs, N.J.: Prentice-Hall, Inc., 1959.

Jones, Mary Cover. "A Comparison of the Attitudes and Interests of Ninth-Grade Students Over Two Decades," *Journal of Educational Psychology,* 51: 175-185, August, 1960.

Lichter, Solomon O., Elsie B. Rapien, Francis M. Seibert, and Morris A. Sklansky. *The Drop-Outs, A Treatment Study of Intellectually Capable Students Who Drop Out of High School.* Glencoe, Ill.: The Free Press of Glencoe, Inc., 1962.

Lurry, Lucile L., and Elsie J. Alberty. *Developing a High School Core Program.* New York: The Macmillan Company, 1957.

Marking and Reporting. Revisions of the Progress Reports and Supplementary Reports to Parents. St. Paul, Minn.: The Office of Assistant Superintendent of Secondary and Vocational Education, St. Paul Public Schools, Bulletin 3, June, 1954.

McKean, Robert C. *Principles and Methods in Secondary Education.* Columbus, Ohio: Charles E. Merrill Books, 1962. Chap. 8, "Grading and Reporting Student Progress."

Maskowitz, Samuel D. "Guide Lines for Marking Procedure," *High Points,* 44:26-30, April, 1962.

Mortensen, Donald G., and Allen M. Schmuller. *Guidance in Today's Schools.* New York: John Wiley & Sons, Inc., 1959. Chap. 6, "Techniques for Understanding the Individual" and Chap. 7, "Techniques for Understanding the Individual (Continued)."

Muessig, Raymond H. "How Do I Grade Thee? Let Me Count the Ways," *The Clearing House,* 36:414-416, March, 1962.

Noar, Gertrude. *The Junior High School, Today and Tomorrow.* Englewood Cliffs, N.J.: Prentice-Hall, Inc., 2nd ed., 1961. Chap. 15, "Meeting the Needs of the Slow and Gifted Pupils," and Chap. 18, "Reports of Classroom Work."

Noll, Victor H. *Introduction to Educational Measurement.* Boston: Houghton Mifflin Company, 1957.

Nordberg, H. Orville, James M. Bradfield, and William C. O'Dell. *Secondary School Teaching.* New York: The Macmillan Company, 1962. Chap. 8, "Evaluating Student Achievement."

Ohles, John F., Margaret Sawkins, and J. Brien Murphy. "The Cumulative Record," *The Clearing House,* 36:531-535, May, 1962.

Pemberton, John H. "Rx for Report Card Blues," *The Clearing House,* 36:75-77, October, 1961. (A self-evaluative system for pupils in science.)

Perdew, Phillip W. *The American Secondary School in Action.* Boston: Allyn and Bacon, Inc., 1959. Chap. 7, "Appraising Pupil Progress."

"Report to Parents," *NEA Research Bulletin,* 39:24-25, February, 1961.

Russel, James W. "The Mark of the Best," *The Bulletin of the National Association of Secondary-School Principals,* 45:112-114, February, 1961.

Strang, Ruth. *How to Report Pupil Progress.* Chicago: Science Research Associates, 1955.

———. *Reporting to Parents.* New York: Bureau of Publications, Teachers College, Columbia University, 1958.

Thomas, R. Murray. *Judging Student Progress.* New York: Longmans, Green & Co., Inc., 2nd ed., 1960.

Van Til, William, Gordon F. Vars, and John H. Lounsbury. *Modern Education for the Junior High School Years.* Indianapolis: The Bobbs-Merrill Company, Inc., 1961. Chap. 21, "Evaluation and Reporting."

Wright, Grace S., and Edith S. Greer. *The Junior High School, A Survey of Grades 7-8-9 in Junior and Junior-Senior High Schools, 1959-1960.* U.S. Office of Education Bulletin No. 32. Washington: Government Printing Office, 1963.

Wrightstone, J. Wayne, Joseph Justman, and Irving Robbins. *Evaluation in Modern Education.* New York: American Book Company, 1956.

Yauch, Wilber A. "School Marks and Their Reporting," *National Education Association Journal,* 50:50 and 58, May, 1961.

Zapf, Rosalind M. *A Core Curriculum in Action* (Film Strip). Detroit: College of Education, Wayne State University, 1948.

———. *Democratic Processes in the Secondary Classroom.* Englewood Cliffs, N.J.: Prentice-Hall, Inc., 1959.

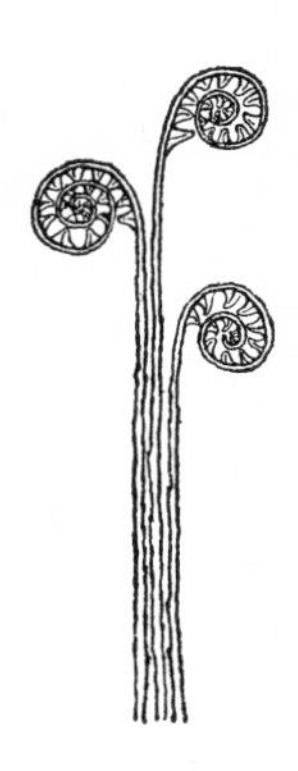

Part Four

STAFF AND FACILITIES

13

Staffing Problems

The junior high school came into being in part to meet the educational needs of students twelve to fifteen years old that are significantly different from those of younger and older children. But the failure of teacher education institutions and state departments of education to provide special programs for the adequate preparation and certification of professional personnel to teach and guide youth during early adolescence has caused major problems in staffing junior high schools with competent principals, consultants, counselors, and teachers.

1. How are adequate staffs to be selected and organized?

The selection and organization of a junior high school staff to administer, supervise, guide, and teach every student in the ways that best meet his educational needs is a difficult and complicated task. To accomplish this task in junior high schools of different sizes it is necessary to (1) de-emphasize the role of the subject-area department chairman, thus avoiding a narrow focus and extreme specialization; and (2) place more emphasis on administrative staff, consultants, and counselors, in order to help teachers understand the nature of the young adolescents, how they learn most effectively, and their home and community situations and backgrounds — the ultimate objective being, of course, the maximum physical, social, and intellectual growth and development of these young people.

One of the primary factors to be considered in staff selection and organization for junior high schools is the size of the school. A study was made in

1959 by the Council for Administrative Leadership, Albany, New York, to determine how to organize adequate junior high school staffs in relation to the teaching, administrative, and guidance loads in schools of different sizes. A questionnaire sent to seventy registered junior high schools in New York State asked each recipient to indicate which staff members performed any or all of the following administrative functions: improving educational opportunity, working with pupils, obtaining and developing personnel, maintaining effective interrelationships with the community, and providing funds and facilities. These functions were representative of the forty-three administrative functions which were identified as vital to the achievement of purposes set up for "the development of students in early adolescence."

After receiving and analyzing usable replies from thirty-nine junior high schools, the Council for Administrative Leadership reported that the median pupil–teacher ratio of 22:1 in the junior high schools of New York was satisfactory; that the principal, to be an effective educational leader in his school, should have the median pupil–administration ratio of 365:1 reduced to 210:1; and that the median pupil–guidance ratio of 470:1 should be reduced to not more than 250:1. In accordance with these recommendations, the Council suggested improvements for staffing junior high schools with enrollments of 500 and 700 to 1000 students.

Schools with enrollments of under 500 pupils

In sparsely populated school districts, there are some junior high schools with 300 students enrolled, but seldom is it necessary to provide extensive staffing in a school with an enrollment under 400 to 500 students, since the advent of enlarged and consolidated school districts. The Council for Administrative Leadership's suggested list of personnel for Smallville Junior High School in New York State, with an enrollment of 500 pupils is summarized as follows:[1]

A full-time principal.
A half-time assistant principal for business and management.
One full-time and one half-time counselor.
One part-time reading consultant.
One part-time nurse.
One part-time librarian and consultant of instructional materials.
A curriculum development council with teacher representatives from each grade level and a teacher released for half-time to serve as chairman and consultant for the teachers.
Advisory council on administrative affairs.
Sufficient teachers for student–teacher ratio of approximately 22:1.

[1] Council for Administrative Leadership, *The Administrative Organization of the Modern Junior High School* (Albany, N.Y.: The Council, 1959), pp. 1-48.

Adequate secretarial and clerical help.
Adequate custodians, matrons, and cafeteria workers.

The relationships and responsibilities of all members of the staff, including an advisory council and curriculum development council, are shown for Smallville Junior High School in Figure 12.

Schools with enrollments from 700 to 1000 pupils

An enrollment of 700 to 1000 students usually permits the most desirable staffing, which positively relates to the rapid increases in the early secondary school population and the development of larger school districts.

FIGURE 12
Smallville Junior High School

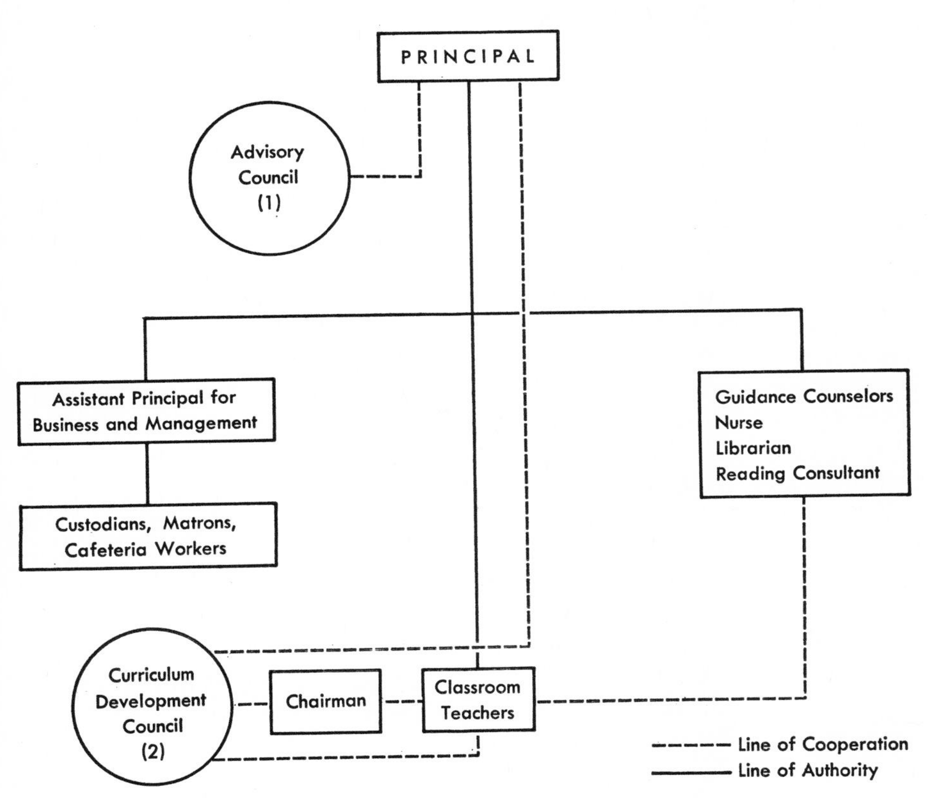

(1) Includes principal, assistant principal and teacher representatives.
(2) Composed of teacher representatives from each grade level with one teacher released halftime to work with this group and serve as consultant and helping teacher.

Adapted from *The Administrative Organization of the Modern Junior High School* (Albany, N.Y.: Council for Administrative Leadership, 1959), Chart IV, p. 43.

The Council for Administrative Leadership's staff for the Ridgeway Junior High School in New York State would be as follows:[2]

Principal.
Two assistant principals.
School nurse.
Part-time or full-time psychologist.
Three guidance counselors.
Part-time or full-time co-ordinator of student activities.
Part-time or full-time co-ordinator of instructional materials and librarian.
Reading consultant.
Speech correctionist.
Two school-wide councils:
Instructional council for instructional planning and curriculum development and improvement — including subject matter area teachers.
Administrative council for determination of school policy and operation in the areas of personnel, management, and school organization.
Sufficient teachers for a student-teacher ratio of approximately 22:1.
A secretary, stenographer, and clerk.
Adequate custodians, matrons, and cafeteria workers.

The Council's recommendations for optimum staffing of Ridgeway Junior High School are graphically illustrated in Figure 13, which demonstrates the relationships and responsibilities of all the staff members in their regular positions and as members of the institutional and administrative councils.

Although general agreement has never been reached on the most desirable size for a junior high school, most educators suggest that an optimum staff is most feasible in schools with an enrollment of 600 to 900 students. The Southern Association of Colleges and Schools (formerly the Southern Association of Colleges and Secondary Schools) recommends an average daily membership of 720 students in the junior high school with 25 to 30 students per class in Grades 7, 8, and 9 and block-time classes or core programs which include language arts, social studies, guidance, mathematics, physical education, exploratory courses, and specialization subjects in the ninth grade.[3]

The staff of a junior high school considers the many special and general needs of each pupil as the *focal point of the curriculum.* Consequently class size must not be excessive but should range from twenty to twenty-five students in regular attendance in order for the classroom teacher to have the opportunity to know the assets and liabilities of each student. This under-

[2] See *ibid.*, pp. 30 and 35-37.

[3] See *The Junior High School Program,* A Joint Study Conducted by the Commission on Secondary Schools and the Commission on Research and Service (Atlanta, Ga.: Southern Association of Colleges and Secondary Schools, 1958), pp. 40, 74; and *The Junior High School Program in Illinois* (Springfield, Ill.: Office of the Superintendent of Public Instruction, 1961), p. 101.

FIGURE 13

Ridgeway Junior High School

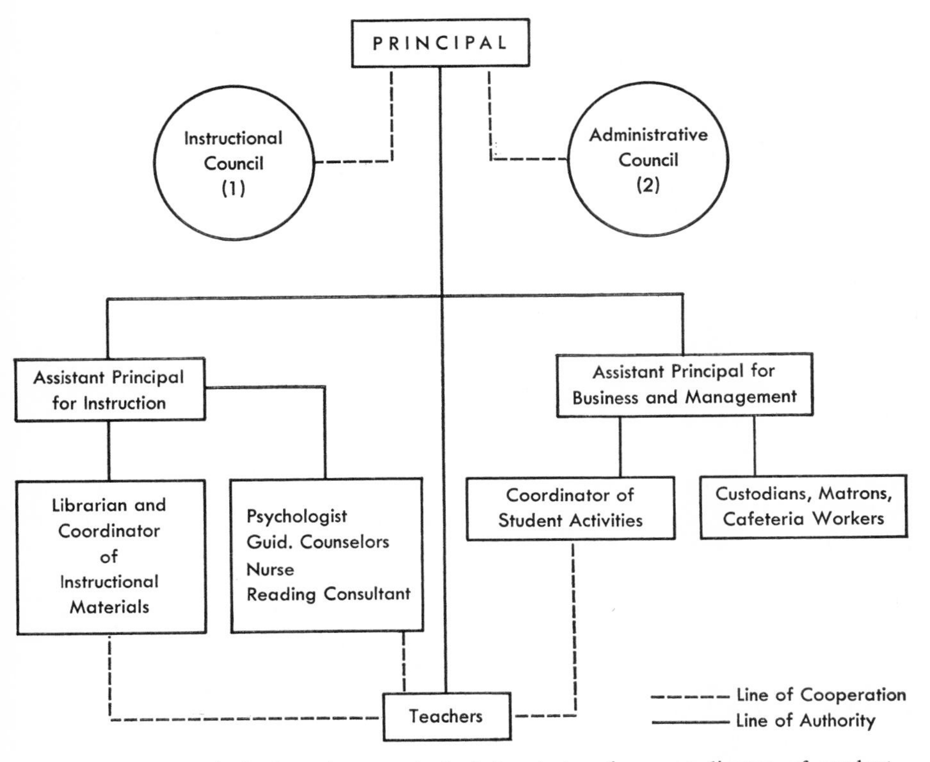

(1) Includes principal, assistant principal for instruction, coordinator of student activities, coordinator of instructional materials, psychologist, guidance counselors, and three teacher representatives from each grade level.

(2) Includes principal, two assistant principals, coordinator of student activities, and coordinator of instructional materials.

Adapted from *The Administrative Organization of the Modern Junior High School* (Albany, N.Y.: Council for Administrative Leadership, 1959), Chart 1, p. 38.

standing is generally considered vital to the early adolescent's learning, for he is having his first experiences with the beginning demands of adulthood. These experiences will mold his patterns and attitudes toward not only his current learning and living but his whole future.

Educational research findings reveal that each student has both unique and general learning needs calling for a broad range of learning opportunities during junior high school, as is detailed in "Characteristics of a Good Junior High School Curriculum" in Chapter 5. In schools of 600 to 900 students more full-time librarians, nurses, assistant administrators, counselors, and consultants will be needed to maintain an adequate program than in schools with enrollments under 500.

Schools with enrollments above 1000 pupils

The most effective administrative procedure in staffing *large* junior high schools is to convert them to smaller schools in separate buildings. To cope with the rapid increases in early secondary school population, this approach should be included in all long-range building and redistricting programs of a school system.

As early as 1919, four junior high schools were in operation in Detroit, where it was believed that a separate school program for Grades 7, 8, and 9 gave early adolescents a better opportunity to apply and develop their abilities. In 1930, twenty-one junior high schools, called "intermediate schools," were in operation with complete departmentalized instruction. Fifteen of these schools were built especially as junior high schools for approximately 1800 students each, with a class size of 35. Six of them had been elementary school buildings, and some were remodeled to provide additional space.

By the middle 1950's the Detroit school system had further expanded its junior high school program, but the larger junior high schools were reduced in size by transferring some of the students to smaller junior high schools located in elementary school buildings where enrollments had declined. The following is a description by H. L. Harrington, First Assistant Superintendent of Detroit Public Schools, of how the very large junior high schools, with complete departmental programs, are being modified in building and population size.

> . . . These junior high schools were smaller than the regular junior high schools, ranging in size from about 300 to 900 pupils, with a median size of about 600. Twenty-two elementary schools have been converted to junior high schools in this way, with others to follow. Altogether about two-thirds of all pupils in grades 7, 8, and 9 are now attending junior high schools.
>
> . . . .
>
> . . . It came to be recognized that principals should be allowed considerable latitude in adjusting programs to their local situations while following the spirit of the program as adopted.
>
> . . . .
>
> A course in general mathematics has been introduced to parallel algebra in the ninth grade. There is also extensive experimentation at present with the newer types of mathematics instruction. Reflecting a change in philosophy, homogeneous grouping with emphasis on the IQ test has been replaced in many schools by grouping based on other criteria. Strict departmentalization in many schools has been partially replaced by the "core" or "block" system of programming, with English and social studies for a group of pupils being taught by one teacher. It is believed that a teacher of a "core" class can know his pupils better and guide and counsel them more effectively than in strictly departmentalized classes. General counseling service in the schools has also been considerably increased. There is extensive experimentation with television teaching. For some years, the salary schedule for junior high school principals and assistant principals has been the same as for those in the senior high

schools. In the planning of new buildings (junior high schools), size is being considerably reduced below the 1800-pupil units erected in the 1920's. While this will reduce the flexibility in schedule making which the larger unit makes possible, it is felt that the smaller unit will enable the school staff to know each pupil better and reduce the impersonality which often attends a large school organization. These changes in policies and practices reflect the thinking, philosophy, and practices generally current in the Detroit junior high schools today.[4]

When the conversion of very large junior high schools to small schools in separate buildings is not feasible, more favorable staffing may be had through application of the concept "little schools within a school," which was adopted in the mid-1940's by the Bass Junior High School in Atlanta, Georgia.[5]

In the early 1960's, many large junior high schools were adopting some type of small-school organization for these educational reasons: (1) It is more reflective of the philosophy, purposes, and functions of the modern junior high school. (2) It enables the school staff to know the students better and reduces the impersonality and teacher–student distance, which is often typical of large school organizations. (3) It has the advantages of optimum staffing and unity of program of the small school, and flexible scheduling. The latter makes it possible to utilize special teachers for instructional services, typical assets of the large school.

In large junior high schools with Grades 7, 8, and 9 the most common pattern for the organization of small schools within a large school is *three* or *more* small schools, each one establishing autonomy by sustaining its own student body, teachers, counselors, instructional consultants or co-ordinators, and administrators.

The Alva T. Stanforth Junior High School in Elmont, New York, uses the three-small-school plan, and the O'Farrell Junior High School in San Diego, California, uses the six-small-school plan. A description of both patterns of organization will illustrate how the faculties of these very large schools have improved their staffing situations. These examples are not considered exclusive but representative of the successful use being made of the three-small-school organization within very large junior high schools throughout the country.

1. When the principal and faculty of the Alva T. Stanforth Junior High School in Elmont, New York, "took a long look" at their school, with 1500 students and growing larger, they desired the advantages that could be gained from both the small and large school organizations. Following considerable

[4] H. L. Harrington, "Detroit Expands Its Junior High School Program." Reprinted by permission from *The Bulletin of the National Association of Secondary-School Principals,* February, 1962. Copyright: Washington, D.C. Pp. 36-38.

[5] See W. Joe Scott, "Nine Schools Make One," *The Bulletin of the National Association of Secondary-School Principals,* 29:78-87, April, 1945.

study, a plan for three schools within a school was developed and recommended to the principal of Central High School District No. 2, Elmont, New York. The proposal was adopted by the Board of Education in June, 1958, and the following plan continues to operate successfully:

> Under our plan of organization, we call each "little school" a *unit* and refer to the plan as the *unit organization.* One of the distinguishing characteristics of our plan is that each unit is a replica of the total school, with its own staff and its own student body composed of grades 7, 8, and 9. The total student body of 1500 is divided into three equal units, each one a school within itself.
>
> For the present school year, 1961-1962, Unit A is composed of six seventh-grade sections, four eighth-grade sections, and six ninth-grade sections. Unit B has five seventh-grade sections, five eighth-grade sections, and six ninth-grade sections. Unit C has six seventh-grade sections, five eighth-grade sections, and five ninth-grade sections. Within each of the units, pupils are placed in ability groups, with above-average, average, and below-average groups in each unit.
>
> A second distinguishing characteristic of our unit plan is the organization and assignment of administrative functions and responsibilities. The principal has responsibility for educational leadership in the entire building, with the assistance of a unit chairman in each unit. Each unit has approximately 500 students, 22 or 23 classroom teachers, and two or three special teachers, all under the leadership of the unit chairman. The unit chairman is responsible for the administration, supervision, and guidance of the teachers and pupils in his unit. Each unit chairman also has school-wide responsibilities in the area of his own particular or special competency.[6]

In this three-unit organization, the administration and faculty of the Alva T. Stanforth School feel that they have solved many of their staffing problems by providing (1) closer relations between administrators, supervisors, counselors, classroom teachers, and students; (2) opportunities for teachers to work together and plan more effective instructional programs; (3) more opportunities for teachers to become acquainted with individual students' needs and interests; (4) better articulation between the small elementary school and the large junior high school; and (5) opportunities for teachers to observe and be aware of peer interaction among students from all three grade levels.

2. The O'Farrell Junior High School, San Diego, California, is an example of a "six-small-school organization" within a school serving a population of 1500 students. The following quotation from W. J. Stone, Principal of the school, briefly describes and evaluates this program:

> A basic part of the organization of the total school program consists of six "small schools" within the school. At each grade level, each half of the stu-

[6] Alton D. Lowe, "Three Schools Within a School." Reprinted by permission from *The Bulletin of the National Association of Secondary-School Principals,* February, 1962. Copyright: Washington, D.C. Pp. 47-49.

dents are programmed to each half of the teachers to form two "small schools" for the grade, or six for the total school. Each has its own student body, faculty, counselors, instructional coordinators, and administrators.

The small school organization aids in the transition from elementary to junior high school by decreasing the number of teacher-student contacts. Through pattern scheduling the student has the same teacher for two periods and is with the same group of students for at least four periods of the school day. If he is enrolled in a fifth class which involves both boys and girls, such as Spanish, music, art, or typing, he might remain with the same group of students for an additional period. In physical education, shop, or home-making, the student remains with all of the students of the same sex in his counseling group, but he also joins pupils at his grade level from other "small schools."

. . . .

A guidance counselor for each of the two small schools in each grade contributes greatly to the guidance program. Each counselor is a regular teacher who is released half time for guidance activities. He has the same preparation as the teachers of the students he advises. Being a member of this preparation group enables the counselor to discuss with the teachers the total guidance program as well as problems of individual students. At O'Farrell, the counselor handles all of the major guidance and discipline referrals of the students in his small school and follows through on each case with the student, the referring teacher, the counseling teacher (block-time teacher), and in many cases, the parent.[7]

Some of the advantages claimed by Stone for staffing small schools of equal size for each grade are (1) closer collaboration among administrators, consultants, counselors, and teachers; (2) more guidance and counseling in the classrooms by the block-time teachers, other teachers, and the counselors of each small school of 250 students; and (3) scheduling of the teachers of each small school for the *same* period, which affords them time to collaborate on guidance and instructional programs for their respective student groups and time during the school day for parent-teacher conferences in which all of the teachers of a student may participate.

Staffing very large junior high schools by adopting the organization of several small schools within a large school is being readily accepted and applied in planning and building new junior high schools which are to accommodate enrollments of 900 or more. For discussion in detail see Chapter 14, "Housing the Junior High School."

Guidelines for school staff organization

1. The enrollment of a single unit school should not exceed 600 to 900 students. In schools of 900 or larger there appears to be a rapidly growing

[7] William Jack Stone, "Communities of Learning in a Large Junior High School." Reprinted by permission from *The Bulletin of the National Association of Secondary-School Principals,* February, 1962. Copyright: Washington, D.C. Pp. 53-54.

conviction that some form of school-within-a-school is highly desirable to permit a functional school staff organization. In fact, the popularity of the school-within-a-school extends to junior high schools of 600 to 900 pupils, because of greater personalizing of teacher–student relationships.

2. One classroom teacher should be assigned to teach twenty to twenty-five students in average daily attendance in each class, depending on the nature of the student's cultural orientation.

3. At least one-third to one-half of all classroom teachers should be scheduled to teach block-time classes or core programs.

4. One principal, the educational leader, contributes and relates to all segments of the program and should have sufficient assistants, consultants, and counselors to provide all the special or unique services that may be needed to fully achieve the instructional and learning goals.

5. The student–total staff ratios should be at least 20:1, depending on the specific and general needs of the student groups. In New York State, "The median [pupil–total staff] ratio among thirty-nine [junior high] schools was 18:1 with the range extending from less than 15:1 to more than 25:1."[8]

2. *What preparation is necessary for principals and teachers?*

Although the knowledge of the unique nature of early adolescent learners has expanded and has been clearly validated since the development of the junior high school in the United States, the colleges and universities have neglected to offer a special program for the preparation of principals and teachers or for those already in positions to develop, organize, and administer programs that will effectively meet the special educational needs of this large segment of the public school population. Until special and separate training and preparational programs are available, as are found for elementry and upper secondary education, the objective of universal education in a democratic society cannot be fully realized.

In discussing the kind of teacher that is required in the junior high school, McGlasson, Manlove, and Weldy at the Junior High School Regional Conference, Indiana University, stated:

> The discussion reports on teacher qualifications reveal that principals are unanimous in their intention to seek specific improvements in the qualifications, training, and certification of junior high-school teachers. The junior high school should be regarded as a separate entity in the educational continuum, and special emphasis should be focused on the educational requirements for teachers in the junior high school. . . .

[8] The Council for Administrative Leadership, *op. cit.*, p. 12, and Table IV, p. 16.

Principals look to the NASSP for leadership in influencing states to provide special certification for junior high-school teachers. While most agree that a special certificate for junior high school is needed, certification alone is not enough. Professional education associations must continue to encourage professional excellence.[9]

Qualifications and preparation of the principal

In "A Study of the Competencies Needed for Junior High-School Principals," Howard C. Rose used the following method and design: (1) A critical survey and analysis of the educational literature was made to establish a comprehensive list of competencies desirable for high school principals. (2) An opinionnaire was then developed from the study of the literature. (3) The opinionnaire was sent to selected principals and superintendents of the geographical area covered by the North Central Association of Colleges and Secondary Schools. (4) The administrators evaluated the relative importance of the competencies to junior and senior high school principals.

An analysis of the data from the opinionnaires pertaining to the relative importance of the selective competencies showed sixteen of them to be more important for junior high school principals than for senior high school principals. Ten of the sixteen that rated much higher for junior high school principals than for senior high school principals are

> . . . (a) Knowledge of child growth and development; (b) Background of successful experience as an elementary teacher; (c) Background of successful experience as a junior high-school teacher; (d) Background of successful experience as elementary-school administrator; (e) Background of successful experience as a junior high-school administrator; (f) Knowledge of development and function of the elementary schools; (g) Knowledge of development and function of junior high schools; (h) Understanding of current issues, problems, and practices of core curriculum; (i) Knowledge and understanding of sound elementary-school curriculum practices; and (j) Knowledge and understanding of effective block-time teaching techniques.[10]

The foregoing ten competencies should be considered integral objectives of a professional educational program for junior high school principals in colleges and universities. Since thirty-five other competencies were rated as *equally* important for junior and senior high school principals, the junior high school administrator should also have a knowledge and understanding of the

[9] Maurice A. McGlasson, Donald C. Manlove, and Gilbert R. Weldy, "Summary of Discussion Groups of the Junior High School Regional Conference — Indiana University." Reprinted by permission from *The Bulletin of the National Association of Secondary-School Principals,* February, 1963. Copyright: Washington, D.C. Pp. 39-40. (Dr. Manlove was Chairman of the Planning and Advisory Committee of this conference.)

[10] Howard C. Rose, "A Study of the Competencies Needed for Junior High-School Principals." Reprinted by permission from *The Bulletin of the National Association of Secondary-School Principals,* February, 1962. Copyright: Washington, D.C. P. 405.

administrative and supervisory functions in the upper, as well as the lower, adjacent school units in order to plan, administer, and supervise a school program intelligently related to the elementary and senior high schools.

The secondary school principals and superintendents of schools in the North Central Association of Colleges and Secondary Schools, in Rose's study, generally agreed with the following special qualifications recommended for junior high school principals by the Southern Association of Colleges and Secondary Schools: He should (1) hold a master's degree in education; (2) have at least five years of recent successful teaching experience including a minimum of two years in junior high schools; (3) evidence a real interest in the education of early adolescents; (4) possess superior skill in human relationships; (5) exhibit personal and social qualities of the highest order; (6) be willing to improve himself continuously in relation to his position of junior high school principal; (7) have at least eighteen semester hours of graduate credit in education based upon adequate prerequisites.

The graduate program for the junior high school principal should emphasize curriculum development and methods of teaching since his major area of responsibility is instructional leadership. It should also include courses in educational leadership, group dynamics, supervision, school administration, history and philosophy, measurement and evaluation, psychological and social foundations, and psychology of learning.[11]

An important function of the junior high school principal and his assistants is to guide their faculties in formulating a statement of philosophy and purposes of education for the early adolescent; direct and stimulate the teachers and specialists to engage in productive research projects; improve the instructional program by classroom visitation and in-service training of teachers; participate in the selection of personnel; and administer and supervise curriculum development, pupil personnel administration and guidance, articulation between grades and school units, relations with home and community, and evaluation of pupil progress and school program. These varied functions require broad qualifications within general education, professional preparation focused upon the program of this "middle school," and a program designed to assure maximum educational growth and development of early youth. The general and professional preparation of a principal should extend beyond a master's degree in education to a minimum of one or more years of graduate work, which is required of administrative specialists in the junior high school.

Preparation of the junior high school teacher

Many competencies needed by junior high school teachers are different from those needed by elementary and senior high school teachers.

[11] See *The Junior High School Program, op. cit.*, pp. 102 and 103.

Additional areas of learning in programs offered by teacher education institutions which would strengthen the junior high school staffs in the Indiana public schools deal with

1. The physical, mental, emotional and social characteristics, and needs of early adolescents.
2. The nature of the learning experience to be provided for direction and learning of the early adolescent.
3. Organization of the junior high school curriculum
   and
4. Organizational pattern which best meets the needs of early adolescents (block-time classes or core programs).[12]

According to surveys of staffing problems experienced by more than half of the junior high school principals in the United States, as discussed in Chapter 6, the most urgent one is finding teachers who are especially prepared in the teacher education institutions to use effectively the following advanced concepts, methods, and techniques of teaching and guidance in block-time classes or core programs:

1. The teacher should have an awareness and understanding of the characteristics, needs, and interests of late preadolescent and early adolescent boys and girls in order to plan with them instructional programs that stimulate, challenge, and motivate them to develop and make maximum use of their individual learning capacities.

2. The teacher's preparation should make possible "teaching with the student" instead of "teaching to the student." When the first concept is utilized in teaching, the student is motivated to participate actively in his learning and to develop positive attitudes toward learning. Teaching according to the second concept stimulates the development of negativistic, resistive, and antisocial attitudes and patterns toward learning and authority that are destructive to living in a democratic society.

In "teaching with students," small student groups from the larger class groups work on separate topics or projects that are parts of the large unit of work. The small groups then prepare and present their findings to the class in oral or written form, or through panel discussions.

3. The teacher should provide opportunities for students to appropriately participate in formulating tests on material covered in units of class work.

4. The teacher should have the knowledge and experience to instruct the same group of students for two or three periods and effectively relate the instruction to two or more subjects or broad fields.

[12] William E. Wilson, State Superintendent of Public Instruction, *The Junior High School,* A Report Prepared by the Indiana Association of Junior and Senior High School Principals (Indianapolis: Indiana Department of Public Instruction, Bulletin No. 246, 1961), p. 100.

5. The teacher should be able to utilize "problem-solving techniques" in student learning from both didactic material and practical problem situations within the classroom, the school, and the community.

6. The teacher should have command of the necessary techniques for identifying and using school and community resources in teaching units of work in two or more basic areas of learning.

7. The teacher should have the ability and desire to recognize and help students resolve their many and varied personal and social problems that may impair their over-all educational experience.[13]

In recognition of the urgent need to provide qualified teachers for school systems inaugurating and developing programs for new junior high schools and for those that are improving established programs, the two commissions of the Southern Association of Colleges and Secondary Schools — the Commission on Secondary Schools and the Commission on Research and Service — suggest that the following discussional guidelines be used in the formulation of distinct and separate preparation programs in colleges and universities for junior high school teachers:

1. A Broad, General Education. Because early adolescence is a period of exploration and widening interests, the junior high school teacher must know "something about everything" and have a broad background of experience. Extreme specialization is not necessary. In the area of language arts, for example, a junior high school teacher must have skills and understanding in written and oral expression, reading, listening and a basic foundation in understanding and appreciation of literature. Expert knowledge of Chaucer or the lesser English poets, although valuable, is not essential. Many junior high school teachers work in a core program where English and social studies are included in a block of time encompassing two or more periods of approximately an hour each. In such a program basic knowledge of history, geography, government, economics and sociology appear to be more important than extensive knowledge in a single subject. The core program and development of large areas of study demand of the teacher considerable knowledge in many fields — the natural and physical sciences as well as the humanities. Moreover, interdisciplinary relationships and the educational value of integrating experiences must be understood and implemented by the teacher. Even more important, the core teacher should be aware of the personal and personal-social problems of early adolescents and of the problems and pressures of society which impinge upon the daily living of these young people. He should be able

[13] Joseph Andrews, "Resistance to Core: Real or Imaginary?" *The Core Teacher,* published by the Curriculum Laboratory, Division of Secondary Education, Temple University, Philadelphia, September, 1962. This study was prepared and conducted by Joseph Andrews, Glendale High School, Glendale, Calif., Wayne Tyra, Belvedere Junior High School, Los Angeles, and Jay Darmstaetter, Stevenson Junior High School, Los Angeles. The project was developed in conjunction with a graduate seminar at Los Angeles State College under the direction of Morris Better.

to use knowledges and skills in the various disciplines in order that he may assist students in the solution of these problems. It is exceedingly important for junior high school teachers working in core programs to use their background of general education in helping students to solve the problems which they have identified as being of concern to them.

In the case of junior high school teachers who are not core teachers but have their major responsibilities in mathematics, science, music, art, physical education, manual arts, etc., more specialization is required, but even so a good foundation in general education is essential. Actually, the general education program for teachers of required subjects, exploratory courses and electives should be the same as the program needed by core teachers. Beyond the general education program, core teachers should elect courses in the social sciences and the language arts while the other teachers should elect courses in their area or areas of specialization.

2. A Program of Professional Education Focused Upon the Junior High School Program. Because the junior high school serves as a bridge to span the gap between the integrated program of the self-contained classroom of the elementary school and the departmentalized program typical of most secondary schools, the junior high school teacher must have some knowledge of both types of programs and mastery of some of the techniques of teaching in each. Specific method courses for junior high school teachers should be provided by teacher education institutions, and those students destined to work in junior high schools be required to take them. The professional education courses to be included should require a minimum of 18 semester hours credit and may well total 27 or more semester hours credit. [These] courses should be . . . designed to give the teacher a broader and deeper understanding of human growth and development and learning; to build competence in junior high school teaching; and to clarify the objectives, functions, scope, organization and administration of the junior high school. A suggested outline which provides leads to a desirable program follows:

Human Growth and Development Learning.

1. Adolescent growth and development with emphasis upon the early adolescent period. This study should include observations, case studies and participation experiences with groups of early adolescents. Particular attention should be given to the implications of what we know about the growth and development of the age-group for the curriculum and teacher–pupil relationships.
2. Educational psychology with stress upon how learning takes place.
3. Group dynamics and group process taught in a laboratory situation.
4. Techniques of group guidance and individual counseling. Related to these experiences should be the development of understandings and insights in recording and interpreting growth data.

The Junior High School Program.

1. The evolution of the junior high school curriculum.
2. The design of the junior high school curriculum.

3. The core curriculum.
4. The required subjects, exploratory experiences and electives.
5. Approaches to the selection of content.
6. Methods of teaching.
7. Providing for individual differences of early adolescents.
8. Evaluation of objectives.
9. Materials and resources.
10. Approaches to curriculum development and improvement.
11. Organizing the school program-grouping (block-time period).
12. Classroom management — discipline, promotion, preplanning, teacher–student planning.
13. Recording and reporting pupil progress.
14. Using services and resources.

The Junior High School in Our Society.

1. The role of the junior high school in our society.
2. The role of the junior high school in the school organization.
3. The philosophy and purposes of junior high school education.
4. The history and the significance of the junior high school movement.
5. The problems and issues of junior high school education.

The Internship. The program for all undergraduates who are preparing for teaching in the junior high school should include a well-planned and organized internship. This should be a full-time experience for students lasting a minimum period of twelve weeks, preferably for a full semester. The directing or cooperating teacher should be carefully chosen. Only the very best teachers should be used. They should be prepared for the experience by the staff of the teacher education institution. Likewise, the students should be carefully prepared through planning with them and through providing participating experiences for them with groups of early adolescents. The college should provide adequate supervision of students during the internship.

3. A Program Designed to Assure Development of Personal Qualities. Many factors have a bearing upon the development of teachers who are able to teach in the junior high school. First in importance is the factor of selection. Teacher education institutions must have high standards of admission to assure that students accepted for education as junior high school teachers are intelligent, emotionally adjusted, academically well grounded, healthy, trustworthy, buoyant, adaptable, in brief, persons whose total impact on young people is wholesome and constructive. All factors should be taken into account in recruiting and selecting young people who are planning to prepare for junior high school work. Even so, errors in selection are likely to be made and once they are discovered the student who shows little promise of becoming a good teacher of early adolescents should be rerouted to other levels in the school system or to other fields of work.

Once a person chooses to become a junior high school teacher or is employed as a teacher, a program of self-improvement should be planned and developed to strengthen desirable personal qualities. Teachers-on-the-job as well as teachers-in-training who show weaknesses in voice, health, poise, posture or social effectiveness should be helped to bring about any improvement needed. During the pre-service period, college courses, student health services, institutional testing services and counseling services are available. For the employed teacher the in-service activities of the school can help, and summer study and other experiences during the vacation periods may be instrumental in strengthening personality.[14]

The great shortage of qualified and permanent teachers in junior high schools today is readily understood. Although teacher education institutions provide special preparation for elementary and senior high school teachers, they have not yet made available special preparation for junior high school teachers.

DeVane, with the assistance of 22 administrators, 213 teachers, and 1212 ninth-grade students from eleven junior high schools, studied the characteristics and qualifications of excellent teachers and finally concluded that "The study suggests a need for research and experimentation designed to develop programs of preparation for junior high school teachers."[15]

In a state study, the "Michigan Teacher Personnel Study," to determine why there is such a turnover of teachers in the junior high school grades, which have been labeled by many as the most difficult grades to teach, Budde arrived at these conclusions:

> The findings of this study would permit the author to agree whole-heartedly with those who have labeled the junior high school as a "dilemma" or a "school without teachers." In comparison to teachers in other grades, seventh-, and eighth-, and ninth-grade teachers were less permanent in teaching and less permanent at their grade level. They were younger; they had fewer years of teaching experience. Many more of them were required to fill available positions in these grades. Many of them taught in the junior high school grades for a few years and then went on to positions in senior high school.[16]

3. What progress is being made in the preparation of professional staff members?

During the late 1950's and the early 1960's, some of the colleges and universities gradually expanded their teacher education programs to include

[14] *The Junior High School Program, op. cit.*, pp. 95-98.

[15] LeRoy Maxwell DeVane, Jr., "The Qualities and Qualifications of the Excellent Junior High School Teacher," *The Bulletin of the National Association of Secondary-School Principals*, 46:379-380, February, 1962. This study was completed at Florida State University, Tallahassee, Fla.

[16] Ray Budde, Principal of East Lansing (Mich.) Junior High School, "A Study of the Performance of Seventh-, Eighth-, and Ninth-Grade Teachers in Michigan." Reprinted by permission from *The Bulletin of the National Association of Secondary-School Principals*, February, 1962. Copyright: Washington, D.C. P. 390.

special professional courses for the preparation of principals and teachers in the junior high school. This change has come about because junior high school principals and teachers have accepted guidance, block-time classes, core programs, exploratory experiences, health and physical fitness, student activities, and articulation between adjacent school units as basic and essential to the modern junior high school curriculum, and their need in turn has motivated the teacher education institutions to develop some courses that equip them to discharge their responsibilities in these areas.

Summer session programs

A survey of the research on teacher education programs available to staffs of junior high schools reveals that one of the most comprehensive studies is being made by the Committee on Junior High School Education of the National Association of Secondary-School Principals. This committee sponsors an annual survey of summer session courses including conferences and workshops directly devoted to the junior high school.

Every year since 1955 the committee has reported and published (1) the number of leading colleges and universities surveyed; (2) the number and names of the institutions offering one or more summer courses in junior high school education or comprehensive courses in secondary education which include junior high school programs; and (3) a list of the junior high school summer courses available at each college and university responding to the survey as offering courses. A summary of the findings obtained from these annual surveys from 1955 to 1963 is given in Table 28.

It is significant that the colleges and universities listing summer courses during this nine-year period increased from 34 to 148, or 435 per cent, and the number of summer courses, conferences, and workshops increased from 49 to 258, or 525 per cent. The percentage distribution of the 258 college and university summer courses of all types offered in 1963 in the major areas of junior high school teacher education are as follows:

Methods of teaching in specific areas		31.2
Language arts including reading courses	14.0	
Social studies	1.1	
Science	3.7	
Mathematics	7.5	
Fine and practical arts	4.5	
Modern foreign language	.4	
The Junior High School (general course including Junior High School Education and Problems)		26.3
Psychology of the Adolescent including Growth and Development of the Early Adolescent		14.0
Curriculum (general for junior high schools)		7.4
Administration, Organization, and Supervision		9.4

Core Curriculum in Block-Time Periods	3.8
Methods and Techniques of Teaching	2.7
Student Observation and Teaching	2.7
Other major areas	2.5
Total percentage for 258 courses offered in 1963	100.0

Regular session programs

One of the problems consistently encountered throughout the country in junior high schools is the lack of teaching internships directed and supervised by professors of education from the colleges' and universities' summer and regular session faculties. Some colleges of education, during their regular sessions, require students interested in secondary education to earn one-half of their observation and applied teaching credits by teaching the junior high school grades in a six-year laboratory high school. However, opportunities for college students to have teaching internships in a regular junior high school, with either straight departmentalized classes with homerooms or block-time

TABLE 28

Number of Colleges and Universities Surveyed and the Number Offering Summer Courses on Junior High School Education, Including the Total Number of Courses Listed for Each Year from 1955 to 1963

Year of Inquiry	Number of Colleges and Universities Surveyed	Number of Colleges and Universities That Offered Summer Courses on Junior High School Education	Total Number of Such Courses Listed by the Colleges and Universities Reporting
1955	250	34	49
1956	250	50	83
1957	250	73	122
1958	250	80	139
1959	250	112	146
1960	300	147	194
1961	300	130	183
1962	300	145	198
1963	300	148	258

Adapted from the Committee on Junior High School Education, National Association of Secondary-School Principals, "Annual Report of Summer Session Courses on Junior High-School Education in Colleges and Universities," *The Bulletin of the National Association of Secondary-School Principals,* 39:87-88, February, and 39:105-106, May, 1955; 40:151-160, March, 1956; 41:69-80, March, 1957; 42:395-414, April, 1958; 43:217-230, March, 1959; 44:140-157, March, 1960; 45:169-183, May, 1961; 46:232-251, April, 1962; and 47:165-189, March, 1963.

classes or core programs which include student activities from one-third to one-half of the school day, are seldom available.

The new program in the Stewart Laboratory Junior High School, College of Education, University of Utah, has for several years offered *two* block-time classes, with two regular periods in each block, in the fusion of English and social studies and in the special interest areas of music, art, homemaking, industrial arts, and clubs, as described in Chapter 8 of this book. Consequently, students of the University of Utah College of Education desiring to teach in junior high schools are given the chance to participate in supervised observation and teaching in this laboratory school's block-time classes and regular classes.

The Glassboro program, "Preparing Teachers for Block-of-Time," was introduced in the regular sessions of the New Jersey State College at Glassboro, under the leadership of President Thomas E. Robinson, Dean Robert D. Bole, and Education Department Chairman Stanton B. Langworthy, in order to reduce the shortage of competent block teachers in New Jersey. This shortage was discovered from a survey by the New Jersey State Department of Education in which forty-eight of the seventy-two junior high schools with block-time classes reported their major staffing problem to be the lack of teachers skilled in block-time teaching.

In New Jersey the state certification for junior high school teachers authorizes teaching majors in social studies, language arts, sciences, and mathematics in any combination, or individually, in junior high schools not employing a block-time program. Consequently, the New Jersey colleges and universities offer two preparational programs for junior high school teachers.

The special Glassboro program is presented in considerable detail because block-time classes are used in more than half of the junior high schools in this country and this program's primary purpose is to prepare teachers to work in block-time classes or core programs:

> In addition to a wide range of required specialized subject-matter courses, junior high school majors are provided with forty-eight credit hours of restricted electives in general education, including choices in the social sciences, humanities, mathematics, and science, and a total of twelve credit hours of free electives, six in the junior year and six in the senior year. The free electives provide each student with the opportunity to broaden his background as a potential core teacher or to strengthen himself in one particular field as he may feel the need to do so. A faculty advisor has been appointed to counsel students in their choice of courses and to clarify alternatives in problems of personal adjustment.
>
> The purposes and procedures of the professional courses, particularly the laboratory experiences, distinguish Glassboro's junior high school program from the programs of other colleges and, in certain respects, from the elementary and secondary curricula at Glassboro. The staff members who teach in the

program strongly agree that a four-year sequence of professional laboratory experiences is essential, and further, that every student in each of his four years, be with a member of the Education Department long enough, and in varied enough experiences, to insure that he receives the personal attention due him as an individual.

Nearly five-hundred hours of professional laboratory experiences are provided for each student throughout the four-year sequence. The Human Behavior and Development course, a six-credit course which is required of freshmen, involves the student in the continual observation of a junior high school pupil in a classroom setting for a minimum of one hour per week for at least twenty-five weeks. Periodically, one hour of college classroom instruction each week is devoted to small-group discussion of observations. In all curricula, over one-hundred-fifty public school classrooms are utilized in this laboratory experience.

In the sophomore year, junior high school majors take their first specialized professional course. This four-credit course, entitled The Junior High School Student, seeks to develop greater insight into the behavior of young adolescents and an understanding of the ways schools are meeting the needs of these adolescents. The utilization of block-of-time scheduling provides the opportunity for periodic visitations to an off-campus junior high school, where time is spent observing pupils in a variety of activities and engaging in some limited participation with them. The junior high school must be one employing a block-of-time schedule and preferably following a core-type program.

Specific focus is placed on methodology in the junior year with junior high school majors taking The Junior High School Curriculum, a four-credit course, followed by the Junior High School Practicum for eight credit hours. The Junior High School Curriculum places special emphasis upon the purposes of general education, the interrelatedness of subject-matter, the core curriculum and unified studies, the problems approach, teacher-pupil planning, and the unit method of teaching. Students develop teaching units and resource units which are applicable to junior high school block-of-time teaching and provide for the development of study skills and critical thinking. A premium is placed upon each student's ability to state objectives behaviorally in terms of desired understandings, skills, attitudes and appreciations; to develop whole-class, small-group, and individual activities designed to meet the desired outcomes; to utilize a wide variety of appropriate materials; and to employ both informal and formal evaluation techniques. As the class moves into neighboring junior high schools to make periodic observations of block-of-time classes, every student is asked to observe each lesson from a "what and why" viewpoint. He is directed to record the procedures employed by the teacher (the what) and the understandings, skills, or attitudes (the why) which, he believes, the teacher is attempting to develop through the procedures employed. As the students discuss, compare, and evaluate their findings, greater insight into the teaching–learning process becomes evident.

The Junior High School Practicum is typically scheduled full-time for the fourth quarter of the junior year. There is an intensive three-week preparation on-campus, building upon and adding to the Curriculum course, then students move into a neighboring junior high school where each is assigned to a core class for a period of four to five weeks. The college instructor or Practicum Coordinator "lives" with students in the school full-time so that each may receive individual guidance and supervision of his experiences in this public-school setting. Commonly, a student is assigned to a two-period block class each day where he begins by observing and participating, and gradually works into the responsibility for teaching this class, under the combined supervision of the teacher and the Practicum Coordinator. One period daily the student works on a school service project, such as adding data to guidance records, previewing audio-visual materials, classifying or cataloging instructional materials, working with small groups of pupils on special projects, and the like. At least one other period is spent each day in observing another class in action and one or two additional periods are provided for planning and conferring with the Practicum Coordinator. Approximately 120 hours are actually spent in the junior high school; some 45 hours are in observation, 50 hours in varied participation activities, and at least 25 hours in teaching. Thus each student is gradually introduced to the responsibilities which are to follow in student teaching.

In the senior year every junior high school major is assigned to a junior high school block-of-time program for Responsible Student Teaching. During this nine-week period he usually assumes responsibility for two block classes, and, in addition to the daily assistance of the cooperating teacher, he receives periodic visitations and suggestions from a college supervisor who is thoroughly acquainted with the functions and provisions of the junior high school program. In fact, the college supervisor is usually a member of the "faculty team" that has worked closely with the student in his previous professional courses and maintains a personal interest in his growth and potential for block-of-time teaching.[17]

During the early 1960's some colleges and universities designed their teacher education programs to include more special preparation of junior high school teachers. However, until distinct and separate programs for professional preparation of junior high school teachers are recognized as necessary and implemented by all training institutions, as illustrated by the Stewart Laboratory Junior High School, College of Education, University of Utah, and the New Jersey State College at Glassboro, a hiatus will continue to exist in teacher preparation.

The present deficiencies in most college and university programs offering training for junior high school teaching will not be overcome by universal teacher preparation programs which fail to recognize the distinctive nature of learning at the elementary school level, the junior high school level, and the senior high school level. This in no way negates the commonalities inherent in all learning; in analogy, we might think of a family consisting of three individuals residing in the same house but requiring unique resources to meet

[17] George A. Hays, "Preparing Teachers for Block-of-Time: The Glassboro Program," *The Core Teacher,* April, 1962, pp. 1-2.

their individual needs. When resources are non-existent or do not fill one member's needs, a state of disequilibrium is established within the family unit which reduces the strength and effectiveness of all members. This concept is strikingly applicable to the "family" of the three different and separately functioning school units.

Johnson's study at Cornell University of the problems experienced by six hundred junior high school teachers lends further support to the urgent need for special junior high school teacher education programs:

> . . . Nevertheless, a recent study at Cornell showed that among some 600 teachers who were surveyed, those teaching grades seven and eight were markedly less satisfied with their level of assignment than were teachers in grades below and above. When the reasons were analyzed, the nature of the curriculum (the ideas), rather than the nature of the pupils at this level, seemed to be predominant. . . .[18]

4. To what extent are principals and teachers specially certified by state departments of education?

The shortage of adequately prepared junior high school principals and teachers calls for an examination of the standards established by state departments of education for certification to teach in this middle school. The certificate standard maintained by every state school system plays a significant role in the development and design of programs which may effectively mediate this serious staffing problem.

In a study of patterns for teacher preparation and licensing for junior high school programs, the Indiana State Department of Education asked all chief state school officers to write a brief statement of their experiences or requirements for (1) teacher preparation for junior high school teachers, and (2) pattern for licensing junior high school teachers. The findings from this study are as follows:

> Forty-two of 47 chief state school officers replied, showing that they were interested in the study and willing to cooperate. While most of them reported that their position was similar to the one in Indiana, they recognized that the patterns for teacher preparation and the certificaion of Junior High School teachers warranted special consideration.
>
> The results of the tabulation showed that a majority of the states require for junior high school teachers a secondary license or an elementary license with some type of modification, endorsement, or requirement. A majority have no specific pattern for the certification of junior high school teachers, but 8 states said that they are studying the situation. Only one state, Georgia, reported a

18 Mauritz Johnson, Jr., "School in the Middle — Junior High: Education's Problem Child," *Saturday Review,* July 21, 1962, p. 42.

pattern for certification which might be construed as strictly a junior high school pattern. However, the standards for this certificate resembled the secondary ones to such an extent that this particular pattern could not effectively meet the needs of early adolescents.[19]

As this study illustrates, certification standards for teaching in the junior high school have not yet become generally accepted. The existing state certification requirements gravitate toward, or have been taken from, secondary and elementary standards. The aforementioned study additionally mentions the North Central Association of Colleges and Secondary Schools as entertaining the possibility of accrediting junior high schools. This accrediting agency currently requires the *same* kind of professional preparation for teachers of Grades 7, 8, and 9 in junior high school as for teachers in the four-year secondary schools.

Prominent educators in the secondary education field have responded to the current movement to provide special and separate preparation and certification standards by recommending that junior high schools be approved and accredited by representatives from one or more educational organizations visiting and assessing junior high school programs in addition to those of the senior high school. In discussing accreditation agencies Douglass states:

> Among the agencies which might be considered for carrying on accreditation are the following: (1) the regional accrediting association; (2) state departments of education; (3) state groups of secondary-school principals; (4) state groups of junior high-school principals; (5) a national board made up largely, if not entirely, of junior high-school principals.
>
> Although evaluation by the regional accrediting associations would no doubt be very helpful it seems rather clear to the author that a national board would most likely lead to the attainment of the values and objectives for evaluation of junior high schools. The membership of such a board should be made up largely of junior high-school educators, probably appointed by the president of the National Association of Secondary-School Principals, but it should also include at least one senior high-school principal, one superintendent of schools, one elementary-school principal, and one outstanding leader in junior high-school education among professors of education.[20]

The major problems of staffing junior high schools will be more amenable to constructive resolution when teacher training institutions, state departments of education, and regional associations for accrediting colleges and secondary schools perceive the junior high school as a distinct school unit. The creation of a national junior high school accrediting board, as recommended by Douglass, would, to the authors of this book, negate the value of regional and state

[19] Wilson, *op. cit.*, p. 100.

[20] Harl R. Douglass, "Junior High Schools Evaluated and Accredited." Reprinted by permission from *The Bulletin of the National Association of Secondary-School Principals,* February, 1963. Copyright: Washington, D.C. P. 126.

representation and lead to stratification of the curriculum and lockstep uniformity of school programs.

The development of knowledgeable criteria for professional standards is necessary before present and future junior high school principals and teachers can know and understand "whom they teach," "what they teach," "how they teach," and "where they teach."

SELECTED BIBLIOGRAPHY

Andrews, Joseph. "Resistance to Core: Real or Imaginary," *The Core Teacher* (published by the Curriculum Laboratory, Division of Secondary Education, College of Education, Temple University, Philadelphia), September, 1962.

Budde, Ray. "A Study of the Permanence of Seventh-, Eighth-, and Ninth-Grade Teachers in Michigan," *The Bulletin of the National Association of Secondary-School Principals,* 46:389-390, February, 1962.

Committee on Junior High School Education, National Association of Secondary-School Principals. "Annual Report of Summer Session Courses on Junior High-School Education in Colleges and Universities," *The Bulletin of the National Association of Secondary-School Principals,* 39:87-88, February, and 39:105-106, May, 1955; 40:151-160, March, 1956; 41:69-80, March, 1957; 42:395-414, April, 1958; 43:217-230, March, 1959; 44:140-157, March, 1960; 45:169-183, May, 1961; 46:232-251, April, 1962, and 47:165-189, March, 1963.

Conant, James B. *Education in the Junior High School Years: A Memorandum to School Boards.* Princeton, N.J.: Educational Testing Service, 1960. "System-Wide Recommendations, Recommendation 13: Size of System-Wide Professional Staff and Teacher Load, Grades 7-12."

Corbally, John E., Jr., T. J. Jensen, and Frederick Staub. *Educational Administration: The Secondary School.* Boston: Allyn and Bacon, Inc., 1961. Chap. 10, "Unique Tasks of the Junior High School."

Council for Administrative Leadership. *The Administrative Organization of the Modern Junior High School.* Albany, N.Y.: The Council, 1959. Pp. 1-48.

Dalton, Elizabeth L. *What Makes Effective Teachers for Young Adolescents?* Nashville, Tenn.: Department of Education, George Peabody College for Teachers, 1962.

DeVane, LeRoy Maxwell, Jr. "The Qualities and Qualifications of the Excellent Junior High School Teacher," *The Bulletin of the National Association of Secondary-School Principals,* 46:378-380, February, 1962.

Douglass, Harl R. "Junior High Schools Evaluated and Accredited," *The Bulletin of the National Association of Secondary-School Principals,* 47:125-128, February, 1963.

Faunce, Roland C., and Morrel J. Clute. *Teaching and Learning in the Junior High School.* San Francisco: Wadsworth Publishing Company, 1961. Chap. 14, "Preparing Teachers for Junior High Schools," and Chap. 15, "Administering the Junior High School."

Gruhn, William T., and Harl R. Douglass. *The Modern Junior High School.* New York: The Ronald Press Company, 2nd ed., 1956. Chap. 16, "Staff Problems."

Harrington, H. L. "Detroit Expands Its Junior High School Program," *The*

Bulletin of the National Association of Secondary-School Principals, 46:34-38, February, 1962.

Hays, George A. "Preparing Teachers for Block-of-Time: The Glassboro Program," *The Core Teacher,* April, 1962.

Jersild, Arthur T. *When Teachers Face Themselves.* New York: Bureau of Publications, Teachers College, Columbia University, 1955.

Johnson, Mauritz, Jr. "School in the Middle — Junior High: Education's Problem Child," *Saturday Review,* 45:40-42, July 21, 1962.

Junior High School Program, The. A Joint Study Conducted by the Commission on Secondary Schools and the Commission on Research and Service. Atlanta, Ga.: Southern Association of Colleges and Secondary Schools, 1958. Chap. 5, "Organization and Administration of the Junior High School Program," and Chap. 7, "Staffing the Junior High School."

Junior High School Program in Illinois, The. Springfield, Ill.: Office of the Superintendent of Public Instruction, 1961.

Lounsbury, John H. "What Keeps Junior from Growing Up?" *The Clearing House,* 34:301-303, January, 1960.

Lowe, Alton D. "Three Schools Within a School," *The Bulletin of the National Association of Secondary-School Principals,* 46:47-48, February, 1962.

McGlasson, Maurice A., Donald C. Manlove, and Gilbert R. Weldy. "Summary of Discussion Groups of the Junior High School Regional Conference — Indiana University," *The Bulletin of the National Association of Secondary-School Principals,* 47:37-43, February, 1963.

Noar, Gertrude. *The Junior High School, Today and Tomorrow."* Englewood Cliffs, N.J.: Prentice-Hall, Inc., 2nd ed., 1961. Chap. 7, "The Teacher's Role."

Nordberg, H. Orville, James M. Bradfield, and William C. Odell, *Secondary School Teaching.* New York: The Macmillan Company, 1962. Chap. 1, "The Role of the Secondary School Teacher."

Palmer, Roderick. "Student Teaching and Student Teacher," *The Clearing House,* 36:430-432, May, 1962.

Rollins, Sidney P. "A Survey of Problems of the Principal," *The Bulletin of the National Association of Secondary-School Principals,* 44:55-57, February, 1960.

Romine, Stephen A. "Opinions About North Central Association Accreditation of Junior High Schools," *The North Central Association Quarterly,* 36:193-200, Fall, 1961. (Junior high school principals approve accreditation to assist junior high school and its personnel in gaining greater status and security in the educational structure.)

Rose, Howard C. "A Study of the Competencies Needed for Junior High-School Principals," *The Bulletin of the National Association of Secondary-School Principals,* 46:404-406, February, 1962.

Scott, W. Joe. "Nine Schools Make One," *The Bulletin of the National Association of Secondary-School Principals,* 29:78-87, April, 1945.

Stone, William Jack. "Communities of Learning in a Large Junior High School," *The Bulletin of the National Association of Secondary-School Principals,* 46:53-54, February, 1962.

Wilson, William E. *The Junior High School.* Report Prepared by the Indiana Association of Junior and Senior High School Principals. Indianapolis: Indiana Department of Public Instruction, Bulletin No. 246, 1961.

14

Housing the Junior High School

The junior high school has remained the most neglected segment of the public school system not only in its program but even more in its physical plant. From the beginning it has been expected to assume the cast-off garments of the senior high school, and frequently of the elementary school. When new buildings were contemplated to care for overcrowded or expanding school communities, they were planned, almost by habit, for the elementary or senior high school years. An old building no longer thought adequate to meet the modern needs of the elementary or senior high school pupils, but considered too well built to be abandoned, was regarded as good enough, with occasional minor rehabilitation, for this newly created segment of the public schools. A corollary was the more serious tendency, until recently, to construct new junior high school buildings, if any, as slightly modified, smaller imitations of their senior prototypes.

Happily, this unfortunate attitude toward the junior high school is passing, and a new interest in the kind of physical plant and facilities most appropriate to its educational needs is emerging. Now, it is not uncommon for the junior high school and its unique requirements to receive first consideration when school buildings are planned.

1. What considerations are basic to junior high school plant planning?

It is a truism in modern education that the only justification for school buildings and facilities is their maximum usefulness in implementing well-defined educational purposes. Yet in all too many situations this principle has been honored more in the breach than in the observance. In the past conscientious architects frequently have complained that they were told to plan a building similar to one some school board had taken a fancy to in some other community but large enough to house a given number of pupils, or to produce a building of a given size to house a standard school program but not to exceed a certain cost. Little help was given them to plan a real educational plant. Implicit in this approach to school building was the assumption that a school program and its housing were not too closely related. Throughout the country, in the smaller communities particularly, this attitude is evidenced in many older, poorly conceived school buildings still in use. They reveal not only a minimum of educational planning, but the feeling of many former school boards that highly specialized school architects were not necessary; any architect or contractor capable of putting up a durable building was capable of building a school.

Today, building schools is regarded as a highly complicated and important business. It reflects the mounting general awareness that education is America's most important responsibility, and that the success of this enterprise depends not alone upon the adequacy of the school program and the competency of the school staff but also upon the kind and quality of the educational plant and facilities in which the program and staff operate. The importance of the educational plant to the success of education has been stated most succinctly thus:

> A suitable physical environment has a role so important that the degree of success of an effort toward program improvement is closely related to it. The best efforts of the most competent staff using the best curricular content, applying the best known methods of teaching, guidance, and evaluation, and working in a highly favorable climate of public opinion and acceptance cannot achieve success until an appropriate physical plant is provided.[1]

Strong words, these, but their basic correctness is more and more being realized. It is understandable that school buildings and facilities did not loom large on the horizon of communities, school boards, or even many educators of past generations. Until after the turn of the present century the educational program was simplicity itself, highly uniform in pattern, and the methodology of the classroom was characterized by a deadly, unimaginative sameness — the simple lecture or the recitation. Knowledge of the learning process was almost nil, and the educational competency of the school staff mirrored the general low status of the educational developments of the time.

Now a profound change has taken place. Much has been learned in the past few decades about the intricate nature of the learner and the learning process, and about the extreme importance of the environment in its effect

[1] Charles W. Bursch and John L. Reid, *High Schools Today and Tomorrow* (New York: Reinhold Publishing Corporation, 1957), p. 47.

upon the learning situation, the health of the learner, and the work of the teacher. As more attention is focused upon the complexity of individual differences, the traditional lockstep pattern of classroom work is giving way to procedures that emphasize attention to the individual and his needs, even where group processes are used. The old rigidity and uniformity of the curriculum has been superseded by flexibility of offerings to meet individual needs which must take into account the peculiar characteristics of each community. Thirty years ago, for example, one of the authors served on a state textbook commission, where by law a basic curriculum had been decreed for all the schools of the state. A single textbook for each approved course of study had to be adopted periodically for use in all schools. Consequently, the same textbook in agriculture was supplied to every school, whether it was in a rural or urban center, in a wheat-producing, horticultural, or cattle-ranch type of community.

This chapter will not dwell at length upon the educational guideposts that signal the kind of physical plant, facilities, and general environment needed for the junior high school period. These have been developed in the preceding chapters. Here they will be recalled only to point up their basic relationship. Two major aspects of this relationship need to be considered in this connection.

Nature of this period of development

Two major aspects of this period of development need to be noted briefly.

Transition from childhood to adolescence. From the time of Nicholas Murray Butler, John Dewey, and G. Stanley Hall, it has been recognized that the unique characteristics of this period in the life of the maturing child are the physical transition from childhood to adolescence, the maturation of the sex function, and the profound physiological and psychological effect this has upon the boy or girl. With the passing years educators have come to place greater emphasis upon the importance of this transition period.

Unevenness of adolescent development. Of equal if not greater significance to the educator is the early awareness of the irregularity of the approach of adolescence. It is now substantiated by a wealth of research evidence that approximately 70 per cent of girls have become pubescent when they enter the seventh grade, while almost the same percentage of boys who enter the seventh grade are still prepubescent in development. On a strict grade basis of division between the elementary and the junior high schools an appreciable number of children are more elementary than junior high school in outlook when they enter the junior high school.

Educational functions to be served during the early adolescent years

Functions of education in a democracy. It has been a widely accepted function of education to develop in each individual those ideals, understandings, and behavioral competencies that will enable him to become an intelligent, effective citizen of our democratic society. It is accepted as an equal corollary that this is best achieved as the child at every stage in his growth toward adulthood is enabled to meet new situations and changing patterns of living with continuously emerging power to cope with each one. Further, it is expected that ideally education will equip the learner with the intellectual and behavioral skills to meet new situations with progressively increased effectiveness until he has achieved the general competency to deal with problems of the adult world without the guidance of the school.

Functions of education in the junior high school. The junior high school, situated as it is at the close of the elementary school period and at the threshold of secondary education, has a unique function and a difficult task. On the one hand, it must fulfill its avowed purpose of taking the biologically maturing child out of an environment designed for childhood and inducting him into an environment designed for those who have begun pubertal development. On the other hand, as the elementary and junior high schools are now organized, it must accommodate itself to a large number who biologically belong still in the elementary school environment but socially and psychologically may be more at home with their age group in the early secondary school environment. This somewhat ambivalent situation puts a major strain on the junior high school. Its program as well as the physical plant and facilities must reflect this unique pattern of needs.

Thus the program outlined earlier for the junior high school years must be markedly different from that provided in the elementary school and quite unlike the program visualized for the senior high school. At the beginning of the junior high school there must be carry-over elements from the elementary school program to insure continuity of learning and to provide those transitional features so important to the smooth induction of the child into an appreciably changed environmental atmosphere of living and learning. At the other end of the junior high school period the program must anticipate the necessary transition to the senior high school with its more advanced learning demands and its more matured environment, which points definitely and ultimately to the adult status of the rapidly developing youth. This circumstance, too, makes more evident the need for a distinctly different type of school plant and facilities.

2. *What are the problems of the school plant environment?*

General considerations

Most school building specialists agree that the success of the school program is enhanced or hindered according to the wisdom exercised in selecting a building site. Here is one of the major sources of mistakes in the initial planning for a new school. In selecting a well located building site, these commonly recognized factors should be considered:

Accessibility. Consideration of a junior high school site should take into account at least three aspects of accessibility. First, and of primary importance, is its centrality to the pupils to be served — and in this connection future developments must be anticipated. It is assumed that junior high school pupils should not have to walk more than two miles from home to school. Second, since schools are being looked upon more and more as community centers, for adults as well as for youth, the school should be centrally located with this purpose in view. Third, important to both youth and adults, is the ready means of access and egress. There should be as few arterials as possible to cross in reaching the school, yet it must have most direct street connections from the homes it serves.

Relation to community development. Normally school sites are selected with the expectation that they will serve the community for many years. Therefore, the future expansion of the community should be kept in perspective. If it is clear that near-future development will appreciably shift the geographical center for school purposes, the school site should be chosen accordingly. Part of the community's youth of tomorrow should be safeguarded against having undue distances to travel, even though present youth may have to be denied the equalized advantages now enjoyed. Transportation facilities as they now exist, however, make distances less important than formerly.

Another factor of accessibility may outweigh those already mentioned. Too often it is not a simple question of locating the center of the educational needs of the community. When a new building is needed the community frequently is found to be pretty well built up. Sites moderately priced are often not available. It may be necessary to choose between a smaller, less desirable site central to the school population and a larger, much more ideal site somewhat off center. For the sake of the educational program it may be in the best interests of all to take the farther site.

Too often school boards have selected sites which meet the criteria thus far discussed but have not consulted the city zoning ordinances or planning commission, where such exist, to see how long the desirable features of an attractive site may be expected to remain permanent. In these days of rapidly changing conditions the character of parts or even of a whole community frequently is radically different within a few years. Unless sections of a community have been carefully zoned and changes in zoning ordinances are carefully watched, a flourishing residential district may in a decade or two become a factory district, a business district, or even a socially blighted area.

Aesthetic considerations. Educators increasingly recognize the value of beauty and an attractive environment in the learning process. Studies reveal clearly the tremendous potential of beautiful and pleasant surroundings in their effect upon student morale and the improved behavior that results.

Whenever possible, high ground should be chosen for a school site, particularly when other advantages are also present. The ability of the pupil to feel the inspiration of the surrounding landscape, even though it may not be so beautiful, is enhanced by such a site. At higher levels, too, the lighter, cleaner atmosphere brings more zest and vigor. Psychologists are agreed that a location on low ground where the view is limited and the atmosphere likely to be heavy is conducive to depressive moods, lethargy, irritability, and a tendency to unsocial behavior.

Wooded areas, parks, and lakes make an excellent environment for a junior high school. The majesty of nature appeals to youth at probably their most emotional and impressionable age. Moreover, such surroundings provide many opportunities to study nature as it is not experienced through books. When these desirable conditions are not available it is usually possible to locate a school in a quiet residential area, where the pupil is protected from the nervous strain, conscious and unconscious, of the noise of heavy traffic. A site away from airlanes with their disquieting overhead noise is definitely recommended. Many educators advise locating a school near a playground where that is feasible and in harmony with the criteria already mentioned.

Insuring maximum educational adaptation to environment

From the mute evidence of the mistakes of the past comes wisdom to give guidance for the future. Scattered over the country in small towns and large cities are school buildings on sites so circumscribed in relation to the educational program planned that it is practically impossible now to adjust their facilities to contemporary educational thinking. For example, the emergence of new ideas concerning outdoor education, dramatics, music, and nature study has rendered outmoded older sites purchased to provide for an indoor, rigidly conceived academic program. It is now advocated that sites be selected with possibilities for future expansion and radical modification of existing educational plans.

Size of site. There is general agreement that future sites for junior high schools, as well as for elementary and senior high schools, should be large enough to accommodate adequately modern educational programs and should anticipate expansion needs or possible changes in educational plans.

Frequently quoted in this connection is the recommendation of the National Council on Schoolhouse Construction which advocated a formula of a minimum base of ten acres plus one additional acre for each one hundred pupils in the junior high school. A school with an enrollment of seven hundred pupils, then, would need a minimum site of seventeen acres.[2] More recent authorities have recommended much larger sites. The Southern Association of Colleges and Secondary Schools has suggested that an ideal enrollment for a junior high school is 720 pupils and that a site of "up to 35 or 40 acres be purchased."[3] In their "Score Card for the Selection of School Building Sites" Engelhardt, Engelhardt, and Leggett recommend a minimum size of thirty acres for a junior high school site.[4] Herrick and others, in *From School Program to School Plant,* mention approvingly an eighty-acre site developed in Worthington, Ohio, for a School Community Center which houses separate junior and senior plants and provides extensive outdoor facilities.[5] It is important that the site be such that it can be of maximum use. A site oddly shaped even though of fair size may be extremely limited when it comes to future adaptation to educational needs. Engelhardt, Engelhardt, and Leggett suggest that the "golden" shape for greatest potential utilization should be of a three to five ratio. They also warn against swamp, poorly drained, or uneven and rocky terrain that may make large sections of a site uesless as an educational asset.[6]

Characteristics of a good site. There are many elaborate statements and checklists describing good secondary school sites. The following list of characteristics is largely an adaptation from the many groupings developed by students of this problem and is not presented as either original or complete. It includes those major characteristics upon which there appears to be general agreement and which the authors consider to be most pertinent to the junior high school, and gives the reader a quick perspective on the principal problems associated with providing a desirable environment for a modern junior high school.

1. Located near center of the community — present and anticipated.
2. Adequate size for present and possible future educational needs.
3. Aesthetically inspiring surroundings.
4. Safeguarded against undesirable zoning ordinances.
5. Where possible, adjacent to public park or playground.
6. Surrounded by social influences of high moral quality.
   a. Attractive, well-kept residential community.
   b. Absence of undesirable business activties, such as pool halls, dance halls, taverns.

[2] *Guide for Planning School Plants* (Nashville, Tenn.: National Council on Schoolhouse Construction, Peabody College, 1953), pp. 26-27.

[3] *The Junior High School Program* (Atlanta, Ga.: Southern Association of Colleges and Secondary Schools, 1958), p. 86.

[4] N. L. Engelhardt, N. L. Engelhardt, Jr., and Stanton Leggett, *School Planning and Building Handbook* (New York: F. W. Dodge Corporation, 1956), p. 187.

[5] John H. Herrick and others, *From School Program to School Plant* (New York: Henry Holt & Co., 1956), pp. 242-243. See also *The Junior High School Program in Illinois* (Springfield: Office of the Superintendent of Public Instruction, 1961), p. 101.

[6] Engelhardt, Engelhardt, and Leggett, *op. cit.,* p. 189.

7. Remote from industry, railroads, airfields, and airlanes.
8. Free from noise, dust, smoke, odors.
9. Free from transportation and traffic hazards.
10. Adequate fire protection.
11. Proximity of efficient utility services — water, communication, light, sewage disposal.
12. Accessibility of site, via sidewalks and transportation services.
13. Well located for community access and use.
14. Adequate areas for outdoor educational–recreational activities, nature study, gardening.[7]

3. *What does the school plant involve?*

Purposes served

The school plant has one purpose only: to facilitate and implement the educational program of the school. This fact cannot be too often or too emphatically reiterated. It should be obvious to all that buildings and facilities are important means by which the attainment of educational ends is made possible. Consequently, they should be looked upon as important adjuncts to a successful educational program. As indicated in the *Evaluative Criteria:*

> The school plant, consisting of the site, building, equipment, and services, is a major factor in the functioning of the educational program. The plant, as planned and equipped, is more than a place of instruction. It is, during school time, the physical environment which assists or limits student achievement of desirable learning outcomes.
>
> The school plant must provide the physical facilities to conduct a program designed to meet the educational needs of youth.[8]

Planning the school plant

In recent years there has been a definite tendency to move decision making from the local community to the state and national level. This has had its good and undesirable features. To the extent that state or national groups assume the responsibility for curriculum making, as is now being attempted by several national foundations, curriculum patterns will become stratified and

[7] For a more complete discussion of site selection for junior and senior high schools, see *Evaluative Criteria* (Washington: National Study of Secondary School Evaluation, 1960), pp. 303 ff.; Herrick and others, *op. cit.,* Chap. 12, "The School Site"; Englehardt, Englehardt, and Leggett, *op. cit.,* Chap. 9, "School Site Selection," and "Checklist of Items Affecting Size of Junior High Schools," p. 254. For a general discussion, see American Association of School Administrators, *Planning America's School Buildings,* Report of the AASA School-Building Commission (Washington: The Association, 1960), Chap. 10, "The Site."

[8] *Evaluative Criteria, op. cit.,* p. 301.

curriculum offerings made uniform in each school without much regard to local needs. This has been uniformly the result of such controls in highly centralized nations.

The movement toward state and national decision making in curriculum and school matters, as in other areas of human activity, has its desirable aspects where it is confined to the setting up of minimal standards to safeguard the quality of the services the citizen enjoys. Particularly at the state level it insures equality of educational opportunity for all irrespective of economic status or community residence. The present policy of state departments of education to set up minimum standards for school plants and facilities has protected the children and youth from health and safety hazards too often present in older school buildings. Too, most states now anticipate in their minimal plant standards a certain level of educational opportunity as provided in the general educational standards of the state.

The dangers that are inherent in state and national decision making in school matters flow from the evident inclination of the decisions to be arbitrary and dictatorial whereas what needs to be done is to set up broad minimal standards with built-in encouragement to communities to raise the quality of education offered *beyond* these minimal standards. For example, one state set up standards to govern certain school buildings which it would help local school districts finance. The standards omitted auditoriums and swimming pools. Thus only school districts financially able and willing to build their schools without state aid could offer these educational advantages to their communities, and they were criticized for exceeding the state minimal standards.[9]

Policies which tend to remove major decision making from the local school community definitely threaten to produce uniformity and stifle initiative. Even more serious is the danger that local citizens will lose interest in their schools. It has been awareness of the close relationship between contact of the public with its schools and interest in them that has led educational leaders to encourage local citizens to participate in school affairs. Where the members of the community participate in school activities, planning with the school administrator for new buildings and other educational advances, there is a loyal group of supporters. Where local school projects fail, it is largely because the school administration advances the plans but does not seek the cooperation of the public through consultation and the sharing of important responsibilities with them. The conspicuous examples of continued success in school financing and in the erection of notable school plants are accompanied by unusual interest and pride in the community schools by the citizens, who have shared responsibility with the school administration in the vital affairs of the school.

[9] American Association of School Administrators, *op. cit.*, p. 88.

Today educators agree that the members of the community must share responsibility with the administrator in major school plans,[10] and particularly in the planning and construction of school buildings. Not only is the school plant important to the administrator. It is even more so to the community; the education of the children takes place there, and it is becoming more and more the center of much of the community life.

There is scarcely an authority on school buildings who does not maintain that another group which should have an important part in school plant planning is the school staff. Some suggest that the pupils concerned should be consulted. All insist that the school plant must clearly mirror the educational program it is built to house. By the same token those who must carry out the educational program should share in the design of the building and facilities erected for it. The teachers, curriculum coordinators, supervisors, and guidance specialists, among others, who carry on the daily activities of the educational program, are the most competent to advise on the size, shape, and built-in features of the classrooms, and many auxiliary areas, such as the library. Referring to the necessity that all concerned with the school program participate in planning the school plant the following statement is most pertinent: "Group planning is time consuming. It is annoying, especially to school boards. . . . But it is also the only way a school can really be planned to serve the specific needs and purposes of the community in which it is located."[11]

The Office of Education is even more emphatic regarding community-wide participation in school plant planning: "In many communities the trend is toward cooperative functional planning, and an effort is made to include in their planning committees staff members, teachers, pupils, and lay citizens who will occupy and use the various facilities. . . . Teachers and lay leaders who will use the school's facilities should know better than anyone else what is needed."[12]

Trends in school building

As newer ideas about education, the curriculum, and teaching methods have come to the fore there has been a corresponding interest in the design of school plants to implement them. In fact, one of the most encouraging developments in school architecture is the apparent growing alertness and sensitivity of architects to the implications of these ideas for the design of

[10] See Lester W. Anderson and Lauren A. Van Dyke, *Secondary School Administration* (Boston: Houghton Mifflin Company, 1963), Chap. 17, "The Secondary School and Community Relations." Also, American Association of School Administrators, *op. cit.*, Chap. 5, "Public Relations."

[11] School Planning Laboratory, School of Education, Stanford University, *Planning Tomorrow's Secondary Schools* (Stanford, Cal.: Stanford University Press, 1954), p. 28.

[12] *The Secondary School Plant: An Approach for Planning Functional Facilities*, U.S. Office of Education, Special Publication No. 5 (Washington: Government Printing Office, 1956), pp. 45-46.

school buildings. They are also aware of the changing conditions that surround the future of our society and the changes that are taking place in educational thinking.

Flexible construction. Today a major concern is the construction of a school building with the utmost flexibility — the greatest capability of meeting unknown future changes in educational needs. One reason for their concern is uncertainty over population trends. We have been experiencing a postwar population expansion of unprecedented nature. Will it continue, or may we expect, as in Japan, an early leveling off? What effect will technological development have on shift of populations between and within communities? What direction will educational concepts — and consequently practices — take?

Whereas in the past schools were designed and built with the assumption that the community population and educational practices would remain relatively stable, now we know that both these elements will undergo radical changes, and better understanding of the nature of the learner and of the learning process is called for.

As far as is feasible, then, school sites are selected with maximum future change in view. School buildings are planned with maximum modification a possibility. Ideally now the interior of the building has no load-bearing walls, and the roof is supported entirely by the outer walls. The heating system may be embedded in the inner walls; ventilation and electrical systems may be carried in the ceilings; in any case walls are adjustable to provide for changing space needs of classrooms, offices, and services. Architects are now covering ceilings with removable sections to facilitate changes in heating, ventilation, lighting, and television connections as room interiors are adjusted. Even outer walls are planned as far as possible to allow for maximum change. As the president of the Educational Facilities Laboratories observed at a recent convention of the National Association of Secondary-School Principals, "It is not surprising, therefore, that the rearrangement of pupils and teachers is bringing about the rearrangement of school interiors. Literally the schools are bursting out of their boxes. Within a decade, it is quite possible that the capacity of a school will not be measured by units called classrooms but by zones of space."[13]

Single-story building. Within recent years there has been a movement away from multistoried school buildings except in metropolitan areas where land values make their elimination impractical or financially prohibitive. Single-story buildings can be readily added to, if the change is properly anticipated, and make interior room modification relatively simple. They are

[13] Harold B. Gores, "What Principals Should Know About New Developments in School Design," *The Bulletin of the National Association of Secondary-School Principals,* 47:190-200, April, 1963. See further discussion in American Association of School Administrators, *op. cit.,* pp. 38, 125-127.

much more susceptible to a wide range of educational design. They appear to be better adapted to the elementary and junior high school ages, although their advantages of management and availability of facilities apply as well to the senior high school.

Designs emphasizing smallness with largeness

The growing body of knowledge about differences between and within individuals has led to a more critical attitude toward large secondary schools, particularly at the junior high school level. However, efforts to get away from the impersonal, factory type of secondary school with its large enrollment has not been limited to the junior high school.

The emphasis of modern education has steadily moved in the direction of concern for the needs of the individual pupil. Grouping, team teaching, equal time for individual study, class and library study carrels, and other forms of individualization of instruction coming into vogue suggest not only a lively awareness of the individual within the group but also a determination to do something about his particular needs. Some have taken an extreme position and suggested a high school with its program largely centered around the individual. To provide an environment favorable to this educational plan a school plant design is proposed to give great flexibility to the program.[14]

There have been many efforts lately to give attention to individuals within the group and yet maintain the advantages that accrue from large numbers. At the secondary level a practical problem is that of keeping the student body small enough to make possible the identity of the individual in instruction and at the same time not make the costs of the auxiliary instructional units necessary to a well-balanced education prohibitive. Most junior high school groups feel that the lowest enrollment practicable for a three-year junior high school that maintains the auxiliary units or advanced courses essential to a sound educational program is between 600 and 900.[15] Judged by the many attempts to offer the enriched and varied curriculum financially feasible with a student body of 600-900 yet keep the advantages that inhere in a small student body of 300, educators consider a small student body preferable to a large one. The major attempts to figuratively "have your cake and eat it too" may be divided roughly into two over-all plans. The first

[14] For a discussion of the plan and the building design see Bursch and Reid, *op. cit.*

[15] The Southern Association of Colleges and Secondary Schools in its official publication *The Junior High School Program* suggests (p. 74) a junior high school minimum-maximum enrollment of 360-720, with 720 as the basis of the educational facilities recommended. The Indiana Public School Study Council, in *A Summarization of Trends in Junior High School Education* (Muncie, Ind.: Ball State Teachers College, May, 1961), p. 21, accepts 720 as the basis of its recommended plans, as does *The Junior High School Program in Illinois,* p. 101. James B. Conant, in *Education in the Junior High School Years* (Princeton, N.J.: Educational Testing Service, 1960), p. 40, recommends 750 as the desirable enrollment of a three-year junior high school.

would break up the larger group into small units of approximately 250-300 pupils under separate leadership, each unit meeting in separate parts of the same building but utilizing advanced courses and auxiliary educational services such as library, shops, auditorium, gymnasium and cafeteria in common. The second plan would be the same except that the small units would be housed in different buildings on a campus.[16]

Schools-within-a-school: single-building plan. Schools of this kind are usually organized in such a way that each unit of approximately 250-300 pupils occupies a wing of a building. Each unit is under an assistant principal and operates as a separate entity. It has its own student government organization and its own basic teaching staff, and regards itself as a distinct school. The pupils of all units use the library in common, although in some schools some assignment of library hours to each unit is made. The facilities of the gymnasium, shops, auditorium, cafeteria, and other auxiliary services are shared, but usually on a scheduled basis. Each unit is responsible for offering certain advanced courses for which it is assumed there is not sufficient demand for it to be repeated in each unit. The few students interested in an advanced course cross over to the unit where it is offered at the time the course is scheduled.

In most cases units of "schools-within-a-school" have a cross section of Grades 7, 8, and 9 to provide a balanced age group in each division — a normal junior high school group. A few schools are organized horizontally, with all the seventh grade in one unit and the eighth and ninth grades in their respective units. This has not been a popular plan for it introduces rigidity as well as an unnatural grouping of pupils for over-all school purposes. There is an over-all administrative and instructional organization between the units to provide integration and coordination of program and building use. In some schools the sections are known as houses and the one in charge is known as assistant principal house director.

The organization of "schools-within-a-school" is shown graphically in Figure 14.

A specific type of schools-within-a-school, sometimes called "cluster schools," has been developed at Flint, Michigan, in both its junior and senior high schools. Slight modification of the idea has taken place as it has been introduced progressively into new junior high schools within the school system. The Oliver Wendell Holmes Junior High School, built in 1962, includes three "academic houses" (schools) of approximately 300 pupils each. The

[16] For a general discussion of this idea see Stanton Leggett, "Trends in Educational Spaces in Junior High Schools," *American School and University, 1954-55* (New York: American School Publishing Corporation, 1955), pp. 219-228; Frank G. Lopez, "The New High School," *Architectural Record,* 10:205-206, October, 1955; "How to Make a Big School Little" (illustrated plans), *School Management,* 6:59-63, February, 1962. For a series of nine "plans" for such schools see "A Portfolio of 'Little School' Plans, A Better Way to House a High School," *School Management,* 4:65-75, February, 1960.

FIGURE 14

Schools-Within-a-School

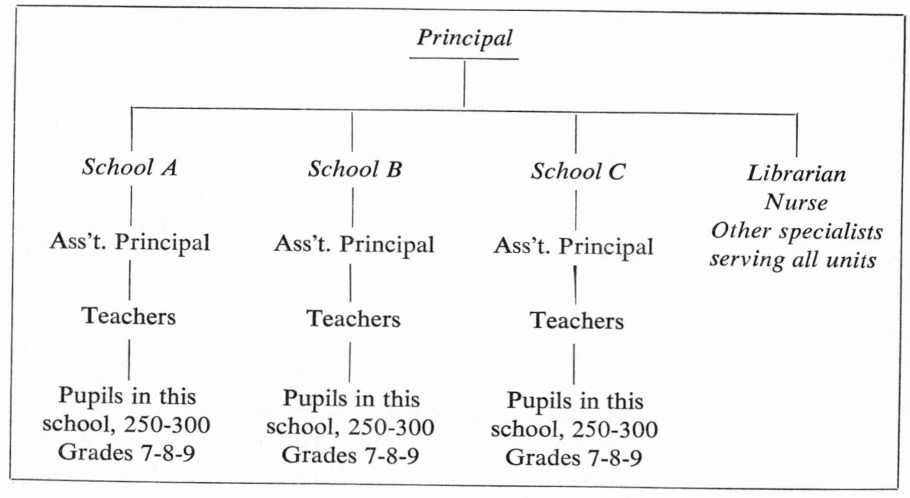

1. Total enrollment in the three schools-within-a-school approximates 750-900 pupils.
2. Some form of administrative and instructional committees with representatives from each school-within-a-school provide the over-all integration of the school.
3. In some schools one of the principals of a school-within-a-school functions as the principal of the whole school.
4. Each school-within-a-school usually has its own guidance counselor.

Adapted from Council for Administrative Leadership, *The Administrative Organization of the Modern Junior High School* (Albany, N.Y.: The Council, 1959), p. 42.

third house (school) is so designed that it can be expanded into a fourth, with anticipated increased enrollment, to duplicate the pattern of houses A and B (see insert, page 1). Ultimately this junior high school is expected to enroll approximately 1200 pupils. Each house is made up of Grades 7, 8, and 9 — a full complement of junior high school pupils. Each house has a house chairman, counselor, and teacher's aide. There is a principal, dean of boys, dean of girls, and general clinic to serve all houses.

The responsibilities of the house chairman are as follows:

A. Supervising the ordering of instructional materials of a general nature for members of the house.

B. Coordinating the use of clerical time assigned to members of the house.

C. Planning with the principal general house staff meetings called to gain faculty direction concerning problems relating to operational and procedural matters.

D. Assuming responsibility for seeing that new staff members assigned to the house are integrated into total operation.

E. Assisting subject matter coordinators with arrangements for special programs involving all pupils of the house.[17]

A unique aspect of the physical arrangement of this house plan is that the three (and ultimately four) houses surround the library, which is considered central to the work of the houses. The auxiliary services of general administration, cafeteria, shops, auditorium, gymnasium, music, and other special areas are separated from the academic houses by a patio, yet connected by corridors on each side of the patio.

The general curricular organization of each house is the same. Since the Flint junior high schools utilize the common-learnings idea, each house has a number of common-learnings double-period sections combining social studies, health, and science in the seventh grade and social studies and English in the eighth grade. These are supplemented by other courses in the academic areas and involve use of the special facilities — auditorium, shops, art, music, gymnasium, and homemaking — under special school scheduling.

To take care of a balanced program of special interest subjects that could not be supported with sufficient class enrollment in a given house, particular houses make available advanced courses which pupils from other houses may take, crossing over to the respective house for that class period. This procedure permits the offering of a range of advanced academic courses not feasible in a small school, but possible in a large school organized on the principle of schools-within-a-school.[18]

Schools-within-a-school: campus plan. This plan is basically like the one just described except in its plant arrangements. In the campus plan the "little schools" or "houses" are contained in separate buildings, usually clustered around a building housing the library. Other auxiliary services such as administration, auditorium, gymnasium, music, art, shops, home economics and cafeteria may be in separate or partially separated buildings.

The general plan of curriculum and administrative organization is essentially the same as that described for the junior high schools of Flint, Michigan. The differences are usually in some special features. Most of them in-

[17] This list of responsibilities of the house chairman was given to the authors in a personal letter from Dr. Jack A. Mobley, Principal of the Longfellow Junior High School, Flint, Michigan, July 9, 1963.

[18] There are many variations of this plan to be found throughout the United States both at the junior and senior high school levels. More innovations have taken place at the senior high school level than might be expected with the heavy emphasis upon the traditional curriculum and methods stressed in the senior high school. Study the plans in Hagerstown, Maryland, extensively described in "North Hagerstown High School," *Profiles of Significant Schools* (New York: Educational Facilities Laboratories, February, 1960). See brief descriptions of the Loy Norris High School, Kalamazoo, Michigan, and the school in Syosset, New York, in American Association of School Administrators, *op. cit.*, pp. 67-69. A quick check of the *Education Index* will reveal many other examples and suggest how popular this plan is becoming at both levels of the secondary school.

corporate some form of common learnings or core and class organization on a block-time basis as a part of the plan.[19]

The Topeka, Kansas, city school system has adopted the schools-within-a-school idea for its new junior and senior high schools. The Topeka West High School and the Jardine and Eisenhower junior high schools, opened during the school year 1961-1962, are of the campus type. The latter schools appear to have much the same approach to curriculum and administration as is found in the junior high schools of Flint, Michigan. A letter from Superintendent of Schools Dr. Merle R. Bolton, June 28, 1963, describes the organization of the campus schools:

> The administrative organization for our campus type schools includes the principal, who has the responsibility for the over-all supervision and coordination of the educational program conducted in the various buildings on this site. He is assisted by counselor-directors assigned to each building. The counselor-directors supervise the students and teachers in their respective little schools. In reality, the campus type school is administered by a "team" made up of the principal and the counselor-directors. This same basic idea is followed in both junior and senior high schools.

Jardine Junior High School is made up of a cluster of eight buildings (some connected) conveniently located with relation to each other. On page 2 of the insert is a picture of this school, which is typical of the modern campus school. It will be noted that space is provided for a possible fourth "little school," should it be needed.

Again, the format of the "little school" will vary with different communities, but a similarity is evident between the building plan of the "little school" of the Jardine Junior High School in Topeka and the "house" of the Oliver Wendell Holmes Junior High School in Flint. The building plan of the Jardine Junior High School as presented on page 2 of the insert can be readily compared to the Flint plan on page 1.[20]

Whether by accident or design a campus-type junior high school organized on the conventional total school unit plan, but with the buildings arranged so that it could easily be changed to a schools-within-a-school organization, has been built in Cincinnati.

The Heinold Junior High School, comprised of six separate buildings connected by breezeways, has been erected upon a commodious thirty-seven-acre

[19] The extreme variations in the campus plan have appeared most often at the regular or senior high school level. One variation which has become widely publicized because of the educational idea advanced as well as the novel plant design is known as "The Random Falls Idea," by school superintendent Archibald B. Shaw and architect John Lyon Reid. It was published in *The School Executive,* March, 1956, and then issued as a forty-two-page reprint.

[20] The attention of those interested in comparing building plans for campus schools is called to the eight site plans and building plans for high schools in "A Portfolio of 'Little School' Plans, A Better Way to House a High School," *School Management,* 4:65-75, February, 1960.

hilltop site. It is admirably arranged. Three academic buildings — two regular classroom buildings and a science building — are interconnected, at one end of the campus, with the arts and crafts building (containing the library, and arts and crafts and home economic rooms). The latter is centered between the three academic classroom buildings and the large building which houses the music department, gymnasium, and general service agencies such as administration, cafeteria, auditorium, etc. The shops building is on the opposite side of the campus site.

This design represents excellent educational planning. It clusters the academic program in close functional relation to the library. Placing the shops building at the other end of the campus brings it into close proximity to the special service functions of the school. A study of the aerial photograph shown on page 3 of the insert clearly indicates the careful placing of the six buildings with relation to their educational functions.[21]

A study of the arrangement of the buildings in the campus design suggests how easy it would be to change to a schools-within-a-school plan. Buildings 1 and 2 could, with minor change become "little schools," and building 3 could be converted into another one with not too much effort. The central position of the library makes an ideal schools-within-a-school setup possible.

Plant facilities

There are many ideas concerning the kinds of facilities the junior high school should have. Different patterns have been drawn up which reflect the educational thinking behind them: from ultraconservative to radical notions of what should constitute a junior high school education.

One carefully outlined statement of what plant facilities should be like that has found favor with many responsible groups is presented by the Southern Association of Colleges and Secondary Schools. It is the work of a joint study conducted by the Commission on Secondary Schools and the Commission on Research and Service.[22] This specification of facilities essential to a good junior high school program is based upon the assumption of a modified core curriculum. The facilities, however, would remain basically the same for any modern junior high school program. A junior high school enrollment of approximately 720 pupils is presupposed. In abbreviated form the plan is as follows:

1. General Purpose Classrooms. A sufficient number of general purpose classrooms to care for core classes, block-time classes, subject classes, ex-

[21] A model of this school was awarded a citation for excellence in planning and design by the American Association of School Administrators.

[22] *The Junior High School Program,* pp. 87-91. This plan was accepted in toto by the Indiana Public School Study Council (*A Summarization of Trends in Junior High School Education,* pp. 21-24), and with minor changes as a guide for the junior high schools of Illinois (*The Junior High School Program in Illinois, op. cit.,* pp. 101-108).

ploratory courses, and other activities not requiring special rooms. Such rooms should meet the following specifications:

(1) Rooms should be approximately square — containing at least 900 square feet or a 30 x 30 sized room. Sixteen rooms, it is estimated, will be needed.

(2) All fixed installations should be placed around the walls of the room and movable furniture installed to insure maximum flexibility.

(3) For the general purpose rooms — work benches, sinks, display cases, tackboard, blackboard, bookshelves, a variety of work surfaces, ceiling supports for hoists, electrical outlets, T.V. jack, and doors with access to corridors and patios. Some type of blackout provision should be made to make efficient use of television and other visual aids.

(4) The eight or ten core or block-time classrooms should have two small rooms between "every other room" of approximately 8 by 15 feet in size. This room can be used for student work groups, teacher-pupil conferences, and "for a teacher's office and materials room."

(5) Adjacent to core or block-time classrooms storage rooms should be provided for curriculum materials.

2. Special Rooms and Facilities. These should be planned carefully and contain at least 1200-1400 square feet. If, for example, exploratory courses in both art and crafts are to be offered and required of all students, then two laboratories will be required; otherwise only one will be needed. Special rooms are needed for "exploratory courses, physical education, student activities materials, health, administration and teachers' needs."
3. Arts and Crafts. Two laboratories will be needed for two exploratory courses and one elective of 1200-1400 square feet dimensions. Two sinks, plenty of counter and storage space for student art projects, a kiln, chalkboard, tackboard for display of art work and storage room for art supplies. The corridor wall outside the room should contain several display cases. Movable tables should be provided for individual and group work in the teaching area. Interest centers should be set up possibly for such activities as painting, clay modeling, pottery, jewelry, leathercraft, etc.
4. Manual or Industrial Arts. Two shops are suggested with areas of approximately 1800-2000 square feet. These should be general shops as vocational work is not contemplated at the junior high school level. The program, being exploratory, should be diversified for this age group.
5. Homemaking. Assuming both boys and girls are to have two exploratory experiences with an elective in the ninth grade, two laboratories will be needed of approximately 1300-1500 square feet each. It is suggested that each laboratory contain three or four unit kitchens, laundry appliances, clothing area, and a teaching or planning area, with a dining room between the two laboratories. These rooms should be planned as all-purpose homemaking laboratories.
6. Science, Photolab, and Solarium. Two general science rooms are needed of 100-1200 square feet each. Ten per cent space should be added for a solarium to serve both rooms. Adequate storage space for supplies and

Oliver Wendell Holmes Junior High School, Flint, Michigan

Courtesy of MacKenzie, Knuth & Klein, Architects, Flint, Michigan

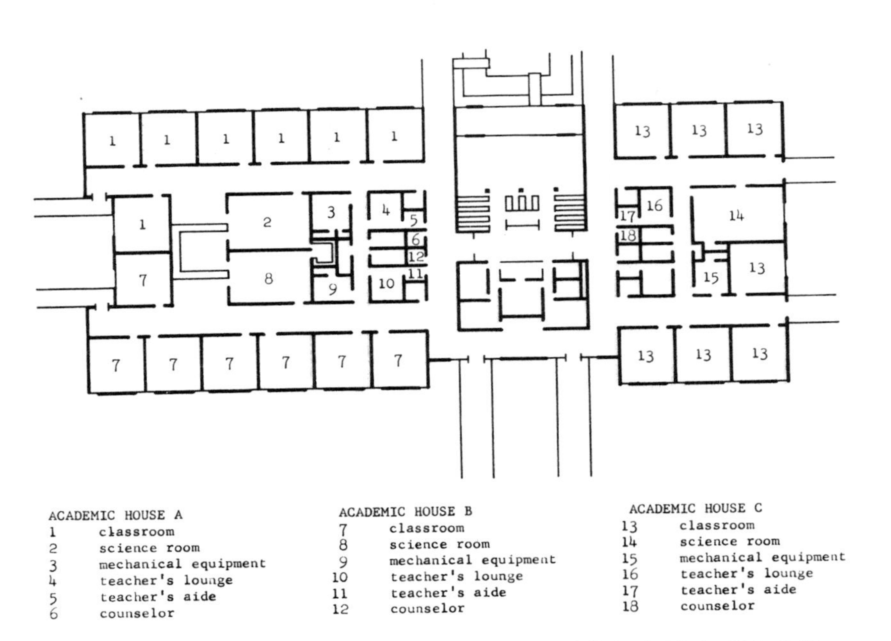

Courtesy of MacKenzie, Knuth & Klein, Architects, Flint, Michigan

Above: Architect's drawing of the new Oliver Wendell Holmes Junior High School at Flint, Michigan. "Academic Houses" A, B, and C are located in the large building in the foreground. *Below:* Floor plan of Academic Houses A, B, and C. Note that the plans have been drawn so that, should the enrollment reach 1200, Academic House C can be enlarged to create a fourth house. In this case, Houses C and D would exactly duplicate the plan of Houses A and B. The school opened with an enrollment of about 800.

Jardine Junior High School, Topeka, Kansas

Courtesy of the Office of the Superintendent of Schools, Topeka, Kansas

Courtesy of Williamson Corman & Associates, Topeka, Kansas

Above: Aerial view of Jardine Junior High School, Topeka, Kansas. Note the vacant space at the side of the three schools containing room for another "little school." *Below:* Floor plan of the three buildings shown at the right in the aerial view. The "little school" plan is the design used in each school-within-a-school of the campus-type Jardine Junior High School. The same general design is employed for all "little schools" in Topeka's campus schools.

Heinold Junior High School, Cincinnati, Ohio

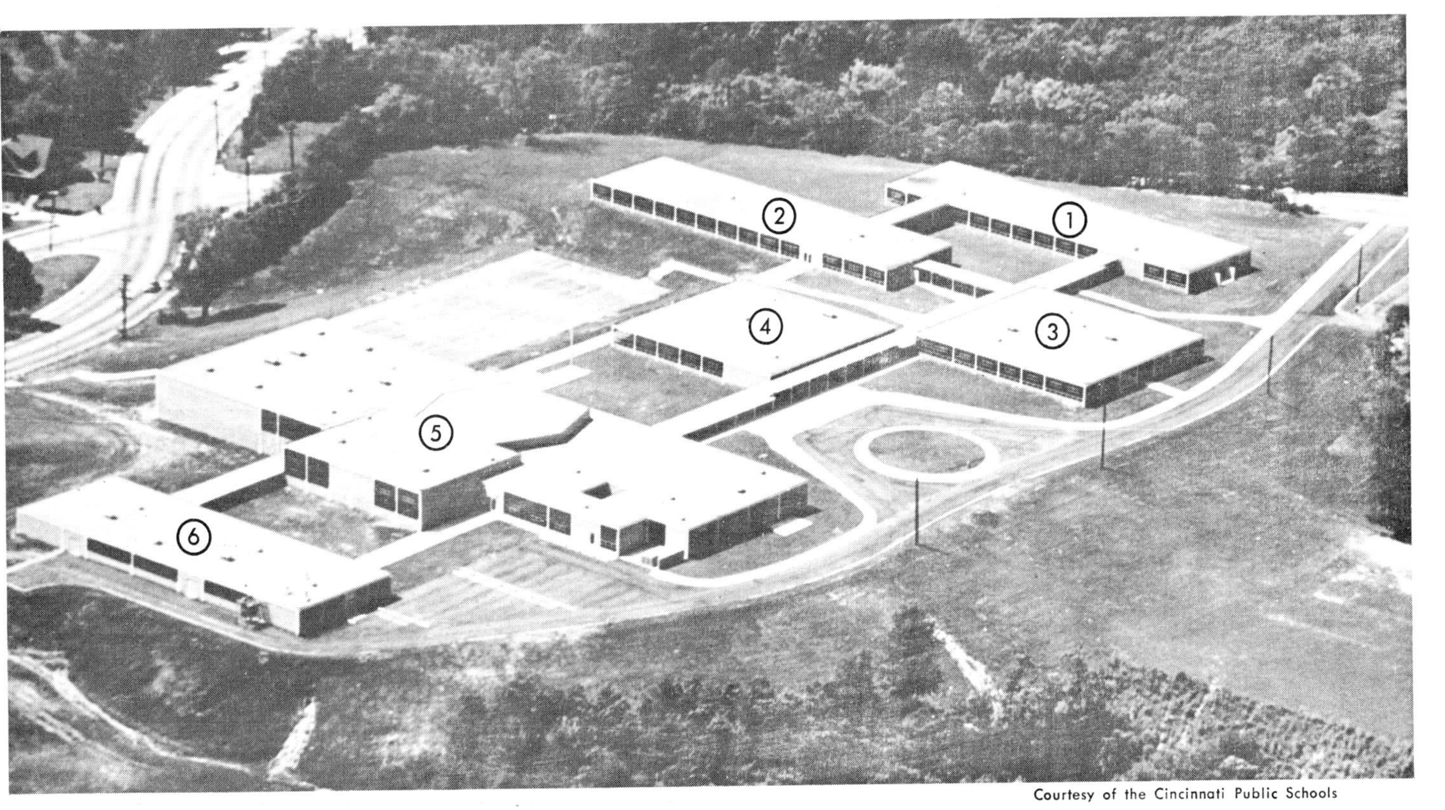

Courtesy of the Cincinnati Public Schools

Buildings numbered 1 and 2 contain twelve regular classrooms each. Building numbered 3, the science building, contains six classrooms for biology and general science. The building in the center, numbered 4, contains the library and arts-and-crafts and home-economics classrooms. The large building, numbered 5, contains administrative offices, lunchrooms, the auditorium, the gymnasium, instrumental and vocal music rooms, and auxiliary rooms. Building numbered 6 houses four industrial arts shops.

Junior High School Classroom Arrangements

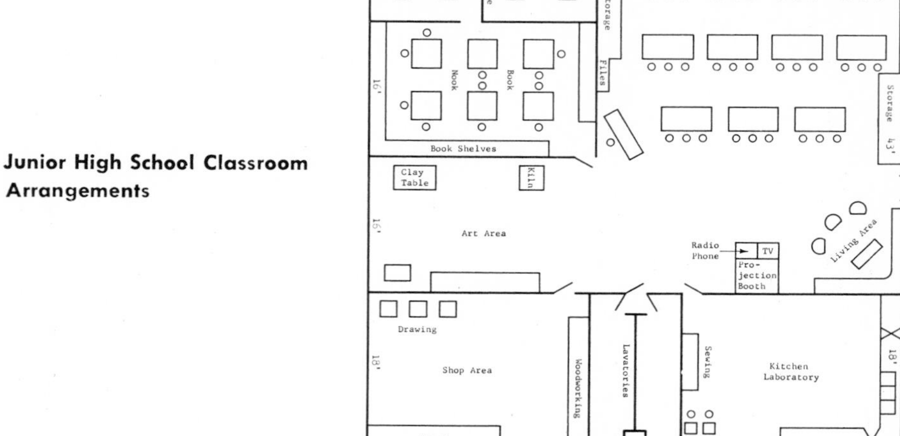

Above: A self-contained junior high school classroom, sixty feet square, designed to include in one room all the possible academic material needs of a group of pupils in a typical core program. *Below:* A core class arrangement devised by a teacher in a New York City junior high school.

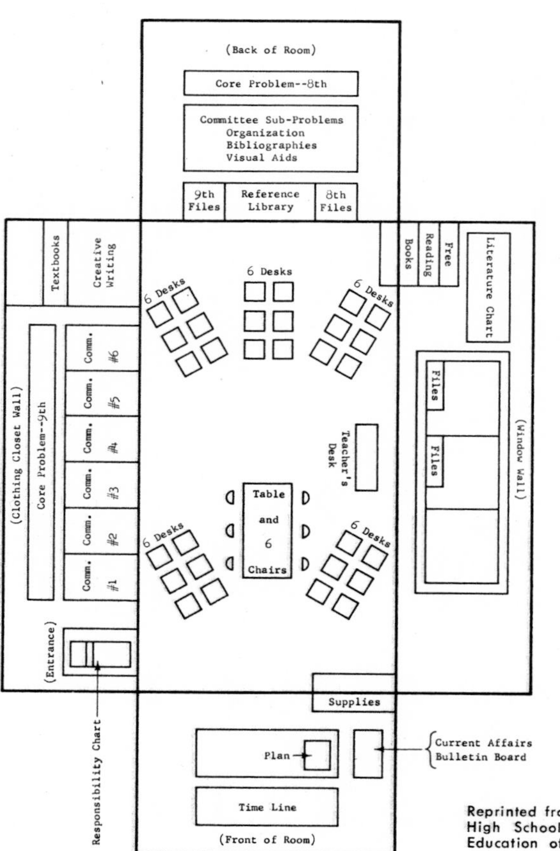

Reprinted from "Developing a Core Program in the Junior High School Grades," by permission of the Board of Education of the City of New York.

equipment, a photographic dark room, bookshelves and magazine racks. Laboratory work counters should be attached to the walls around the room. Eight to 15 sinks should be provided to accommodate 30 students at a time. Movable furniture and a demonstration table are needed in the teaching area.

7. Physical Education. This area should include space for a basketball court 76 x 96 feet and folding bleachers to seat ideally all the student body. It should be possible to divide the area by folding partitions to enable boys and girls to have some activities separately. Provision should be made for shower, locker rooms, toilets, offices, and storage, plus smaller rooms for group instruction and other purposes. It is emphasized that physical education is primarily planned for emphasis upon a general instructional program — not interscholastic sports.
8. Student Activity Room. A room at least 40 x 60 feet in size is needed. It should serve primarily as a student lounge, place of meetings of the student council and other student organiations. Movable furniture for flexibility is essential.
9. General Music. One room of 1000-1200 square feet should be adaptable to work in choral music and music appreciation and general music instruction. This room should be so located as not to disturb other classes. It should have special acoustical treatment.
10. Instrumental Music. This area should involve at least 1800-2000 square feet divided into a large practice room, storage provision for music and instruments, small practice rooms, and office. This area too should be insulated and isolated from the possibility of disturbing other groups.
11. Typing. A room of 900-100 square feet for exploratory experiences for each student and possibly for an elective in typing at the ninth grade [level]. This room should contain regular typing equipment.
12. Auditorium. It should be large enough to seat the entire student body. Including space for stage and storage it should have an area of 6500 square feet. It should be accessible to parking and the general public.
13. Lunchroom. The dining room and accessory areas will require 3800-4000 square feet. It should be readily accessible to pupils and have a service entrance.
14. Materials Center. This facility should be centrally located for easy access. All instructional materials and equipment should be kept here — audio-visual materials, curriculum materials, textbooks, etc. Provision should be made for a photographic laboratory, rooms for listening to records and previewing films, and workrooms for teachers and students. It should include a reading room of 1800-2000 square feet, and the materials center as a whole should have an area of 3000-3500 square feet.
15. Administrative Suite. This facility should be located where it is most accessible to the public and students. It should include as a minimum a reception room, offices for principal and vice-principal, conference room, two counseling rooms, vault, duplicating room, file room, toilets for men and women. About 1800 square feet is needed for this facility.
16. Health Suite. This area includes a reception room, nurse's office, cot room, storage, and toilets. Where medical or dental examinations are given an

examination room is needed. Approximately 600 square feet is needed for this facility.

17. Teachers' Lounge. "The teachers' lounge should be a pleasant, nicely furnished room where teachers may rest, take a coffee break and visit with each other. It should include an efficiency kitchen unit and toilets for men and women."
18. Recapitulation. Additional space is suggested as follows: 20 per cent of the total square footage for corridors, 5 per cent for toilets (1500), storage (720), janitorial (100), heating and maintenance shops (720).

The detailed enumeration of plant facilities for a good junior high school obviously applies to a typical total student body of approximately seven hundred. It does not anticipate the schools-within-a-school organization, although with some modification it could be fitted into the basic educational idea. It does represent a marked advance over the traditional educational program, still widespread, and the typical plant facilities at present in use. To appreciate the nature of the educational program for which these facilities were visualized the reader should review the chapters that precede this list.

It is of interest to note that proponents of the newer conception of the junior high school favor a shift from the older rectangular classroom to the square classroom. It is recognized that changing the concept of the nature of the educational process requires changing the concept of the function of the classroom. A classroom in which pupils sit and absorb what the teacher has to say is far different from a classroom — a *workroom,* really — where the pupil is busy working, discovering, and learning under the stimulus of a teacher who regards it as his function to assist the pupil to discover for himself. The learning situation in the latter instance requires space for freedom of movement and a variety of activities. The square rather than the rectangular classroom, it is now agreed, provides greater flexibility and efficiency as a learning environment.

A classroom thirty feet square is regarded as of minimum size. Many think a forty-foot-square classroom offers more flexibility for various approaches to learning; this is particularly the view of those who favor the self-contained classroom or some modification of it, where major emphasis is upon the classroom as a student workshop. An example of one of the most advanced types of self-contained classrooms at the junior high school level that has come to the attention of the authors is the sixty-foot-square classroom plan presented on page 4 of the insert. It was used in a school committed to the core curriculum idea.

An important omission in the building plan presented by the Southern Association of Colleges and Secondary Schools is the lack of provision for individual study so much emphasized in modern education, and in more recent school building plans. Most architectural authorities of the past few years have given a prominent place to this phase of library and classroom planning.

The introduction of study carrels (individual study stalls) is a unique feature of the newer plans.[23] They can be quite substantially built, as permanent features of a library or classroom, or can be made of light materials and folded into small space for storage when not in use.[24] Some schools use very inexpensive carrel devices made up of fiberboard or plywood; two sheets possibly 3′ x 4½′ hinged together form a V-shaped enclosure when opened, and a collapsible shelf, also V-shaped, can be quickly hooked up and braced with hinged supports to make a desk within the enclosure. The obvious advantages of this temporary carrel are its cheapness, ease of manipulation, flexibility of use, ease of storage, and economy of space. Imaginative teachers in other schools have used less satisfactory devices for individual study — tables and chairs or movable unit desks isolated from the main activity of the particular class period. No doubt the junior high schools of tomorrow will reflect the modern emphasis upon individual learning experiences by providing carrels or similar devices for individual study.[25]

Another feature of the junior high school plant that needs to be stressed is the general aesthetic effect of the interior of the building and the particular functional significance of the corridors in modern education. Many educators and school building specialists are advocating wider corridors and more commodious hall space with facilities inviting students to more informal socialization. This is made clear in the following statement: "The halls or passing corridors are not a mere avenue to expedite the flow of pupils between classrooms, but are vehicles of social training. The lighting, convenience, and atmosphere of auditorium, cafeteria, gymnasium, locker rooms, and even toilets determine to considerable extent the effective influences of the school in educating for desirable social behavior."[26]

Special facilities for core

It is of interest to note that most of the advanced features of the junior high school plant proposed recently by educators and building specialists have been in the direction of changes advocated generally by those who stress the core curriculum idea. The facilities discussed thus far in this chapter and outlined particularly in the plan offered in *The Junior High School Program* could be

[23] See the illustration in "Modern Education: Its Impact on School House Design," *The Nation's Schools,* 71:90, January, 1963. See also architectural journals for a wealth of suggestions in their building plans for the use of carrels.

[24] For illustrations of various types of what they call the "student work desk" with flexibility of design see Bursch and Reid, *op. cit.,* pp. 106-109.

[25] For further discussion see Charles W. Brubaker and Lawrence B. Perkins, "Space for Individual Learning," *The School Executive,* 78:43-58, February, 1959; J. Lloyd Trump, *Images of the Future* (Washington: National Association of Secondary-School Principals, National Education Association, 1959), p. 46; N. E. Hokanson, "School Library Plans for Individual Instruction," in American Association of School Administrators, *op. cit.,* pp. 64-65.

[26] *Planning Tomorrow's Secondary Schools, op. cit.,* p. 4.

accepted as basic to core. The provisions for special interest areas and auxiliary services would be ample, unless a degree of specialization questionable for the junior high school age were presumed.

Classroom. Two phases of the school plant important to the efficient operation of core need further consideration here. The minimum classroom size for core, which operates on the assumption that the classroom is essentially a workshop for pupil learning, should be 35 x 35 feet, and a room of 40 x 40 feet dimensions is regarded by many as more desirable for the multiphased activities of the core curriculum.

All furniture should be movable; the utmost flexibility in the use of the room should be the ideal. Blackboards, cork tackboards for display purposes, sinks, work benches, shelf space around the walls, bookcases and file cabinets and display cases, facilities for darkening the room for films and T.V. use are musts. Each room should be provided with small glassed-in rooms for the use of student committees or teacher conferences. Adequate storage space for large equipment and supplies should be adjuncts of each classroom. Some provision should be made for individual study in the classroom, library, or a part of the building set aside for the purpose.[27]

A classroom plan that offers many suggestions to the alert core teacher is one developed in New York City in connection with the core program. It represents an effort to adapt a regular classroom to meet the needs of a core teacher. It does not include all of the features enumerated in the above statement of what a core classroom should contain, but it does show what an imaginative teacher with a cooperative administrator was able to do to provide a highly desirable environment for her eighth- and ninth-grade core groups.

Attention again is called to the self-contained classroom extensively advocated for at least the seventh and eighth grades. Claims advanced for this form of curriculum and class organization were discussed in early chapters of this book. If such an educational idea is to be carried out in the junior high school, additional classroom features must be planned beyond those considered in the previous paragraphs. The floor plan of the sixty-foot-square classroom designed as a self-contained classroom was carefully prepared and used in a junior high school organized on the core plan. Almost every class need is provided for in this large classroom. (See page 4 of the insert.)[28]

[27] Note the discussion of the provision of carrels or student work desks in the preceding section of this chapter.

[28] At this point it may be of value to review the advantages claimed for the self-contained classroom in Chapters 5 and 7 or to read the summary reports of two pertinent research studies on the significance of the use of self-contained classrooms in the junior high school: Monroe L. Spivak, "The Junior High: Departmentalized or Self-contained?" *Phi Delta Kappan,* 38:134-135, January, 1957; Robert L. Shannon, "Student Self-Acceptance and Curriculum Organization in the Junior High School," *The Bulletin of the National Association of Secondary-School Principals,* 44:35-38, November, 1960. See also G. R. Koopman, "A New Theoretical Approach to Secondary School Planning," *The Nation's Schools,* 52:50-58, December, 1953.

Library. Next to the classroom the library is of most importance in core. Since problem solving and investigative skill development are basic in the philosophy of core, the library becomes the major service aid to the core teacher. Although the library, or materials center, is now strongly emphasized in the junior high school, it is given even greater emphasis where the core curriculum is used.

Cyphert, in his comparative study of library usage by core teachers and departmentalized class teachers in the junior high school, found the core teacher made much more use of the library and of the librarian. Since the library is a prime educational agency of core, the pupils in core classes were given much more rigorous training in the use of library resources. Consequently, the librarian was in greater demand in core classes for instruction in library usage. Inasmuch as it was a usual procedure for entire core classes and core class committees to use the library, the librarian was constantly called on to advise them in their search for source data. Cyphert found that library usage by the core classes was double that of the regular departmentalized classes. He recommended that any junior high school anticipating the use of the core curriculum should double the size of the library usually found in departmentalized schools.

It is clear that junior high schools where the philosophy of core prevails should give particular attention to the library needs of core. A greater emphasis upon the provision of current resource materials seems imperative. The concept of the library as a learning workshop adjunct to the classroom rather than just a storage place for books should prevail. This means much greater physical space, extensive provision for pupil use, more small glassed-in conference and committee rooms, more tables and chairs for use by pupils on library assignment from their classroom base. In such a library carrels or student work desks are most important. It is necessary to begin thinking of library usage in the junior high school, particularly where core predominates, the way one thinks of it in college, and this demands a revolutionary approach to the concept of the library and its physical facilities.[29]

SELECTED BIBLIOGRAPHY

American Association of School Administrators, National Education Association. *Planning America's School Buildings.* Report of AASA School-Building Commission. Washington: The Association, 1960.

Anderson, Lester W., and Lauren A. Van Dyke. *Secondary School Administration.* Boston: Houghton Mifflin Company, 1963. Chap. 20, "The Role of the Principal in School Plant Planning."

[29] For important implications for the junior high school library where the core philosophy is accepted, see Frederick R. Cyphert, "How Core Affects the Junior High School Library," *Library Journal,* 84:7-9 (615-617), February 15, 1959.

"Airborne Tour of the Best Ideas in New School Design," *School Management,* 6:69-83, September, 1962.

Blackwell, H. R. "Development and Use of Quantitative Methods for Specification of Interior Illumination Levels on the Bases of Performance Data," *Illuminating Engineering,* 54:317, June, 1959.

Brubaker, Charles W., and Lawrence B. Perkins. "Space for Individual Learning," *The School Executive,* 78:43-58, February, 1959.

Bursch, Charles W., and John L. Reid. *High Schools Today and Tomorrow.* New York: Reinhold Publishing Corporation, 1957.

Crouch, C. L. "New Methods of Determining Illumination Required for Tasks," *Illuminating Engineering,* 53:416, August, 1958.

Dalton, Elizabeth L., and Curtis P. Ramsey. *The Junior High School.* Cooperative Action Program for Curriculum Improvement, Capci Bibliography. Washington: Association for Supervision and Curriculum Development, National Education Association, in cooperation with NEA Research Division, December, 1960.

Engelhardt, N. L., Sr. "What Size School Sites?" *American School and University,* 1:65-70, 1956-57.

———, N. L. Engelhardt, Jr., and Stanton Leggett. *School Planning and Building Handbook.* New York: F. W. Dodge Corporation, 1956.

Engelhardt, N. L., Jr. "School Building Costs: Controls, Economy and Comparisons," *American School and University — 1958-59,* 1:284-296, 1958-59.

Evans, B. F. "Genealogy of the House Plan," *Educational Executive Overview,* 3:31-33, November, 1962.

Giaudrone, A., and H. R. Snodgrass. "School-Within-A-School Offers Pleasant Uncrowded Learning Atmosphere," *The Nation's Schools,* 69:58-62, June, 1962.

Gores, Harold B. "What Principals Should Know About New Developments in School Design," *The Bulletin of the National Association of Secondary-School Principals,* 47:190-200, April, 1963.

Guide for Planning School Plants. Nashville, Tenn.: National Council on Schoolhouse Construction, Peabody College, 1953.

Halfaker, Philip. *A Summarization of Trends in Junior High School Education.* For the Indiana Public School Study Council. Muncie, Ind.: Ball State Teachers College, May, 1961. Chap. 7, "The Junior High School Plant."

Herrick, John H., and others. *From School Program to School Plant.* New York: Henry Holt & Co., 1956.

"Junior High for the Complete Educational Program," *American School Board Journal,* 146:16-18, January, 1963.

Junior High School Program, The. Atlanta, Ga.: Southern Association of Colleges and Secondary Schools, 1958. Chap. 6, "Facilities for the Junior High School."

Junior High School Program in Illinois, The. Illinois Curriculum Program. Springfield: Office of the Superintendent of Public Instruction, Bulletin A-1, 1961. Chap. 10, "Facilities of the Junior High School."

Junior High Schools for Iowa Youth. Des Moines: Iowa State Department of Public Instruction, 1960. Chap. 6, "What Is a Good Junior High School Plant?"

Koopman, G. Robert. "A New Theoretical Approach to Secondary School Planning," *The Nation's Schools,* 52:50-58, December, 1953.

Koppes, Wayne F. *Potential Economics in School Building Construction.* Troy, N.Y.: Renssalaer Polytechnic Institute, 1958.

Lowe, Alton D. "Three Schools Within a School," *The Bulletin of the National Association of Secondary-School Principals,* 46:47-51, February, 1962.

MacConnell, James D. *Planning for School Buildings.* Englewood Cliffs, N.J.: Prentice-Hall, Inc., 1957.

Marsh, D. E. *Modern Junior High School Program and Its Implications for School Plant Planning.* Eugene, Ore.: University of Oregon, 1957. Bibliography.

"Modern Education: Its Impact on School House Design," *The Nation's Schools,* 71:49-100, January, 1963.

Moore, Hollis A., and William W. Caudill, "Designed for the Early Teenager," *The Nation's Schools,* 55:55-64, January, 1955.

Neutra, Richard. *Survival Through Design.* New York: Oxford University Press, 1954.

Nimnicht, Glendon P., and Arthur R. Partridge. *Design for Small Schools.* A Project of the Educational Planning Service. Greeley, Colo.: Colorado State College, 1962.

Planning Tomorrow's Secondary Schools. The School Planning Laboratory, School of Education, Stanford University. Stanford, Cal.: Stanford University Press, 1954.

Popper, Samuel H. *Educational Specifications — Architectural Program for Theoretical Junior High School.* St. Paul, Minn.: The Cerny Associates, 1962.

"Portfolio of 'Little School' Plans, A — A Better Way to House a High School," *School Management,* 4:65-75, February, 1960.

Proceedings of the Annual Meeting of the National Council on Schoolhouse Construction. Nashville, Tenn.: The Council, 1958. (See the annual reports of this organization. They contain valuable data on all aspects of school building construction.)

Ratliff, John A. "Junior High School Libraries Must Be Different," *The Bulletin of the National Association of Secondary-School Principals,* 43:61-65, November, 1959.

Reid, John Lyon, and Archibald B. Shaw. "The Random Falls Idea," *The School Executive,* 75:47-86, March, 1956.

"Schools Within a School May Be Answer," *Better Schools Spotlight Report* (National Citizens Council for Better Schools). November, 1957.

Smith, E. Berle, and others. "New Directions in School Design," *The School Executive,* 78:64-69, June, 1959.

Space Allocations and Facilities Needed for Physical Education Outdoor Teaching Stations for Elementary, Intermediate and Junior High Schools. Sacramento, Cal.: California State Department of Education, 1958.

Spivak, Monroe L. "Effectiveness of Departmental and Self-Contained Seventh- and Eighth-Grade Classrooms," *The School Review,* 64:391-396, December, 1956.

———. "The Junior High: Departmentalized or Self-Contained?" *Phi Delta Kappan,* 38:134-135, January, 1957.

Stone, William J. "Communities of Learning in a Large Junior High School," *The Bulletin of the National Association of Secondary-School Principals,* 46:52-58, 1962.

Sumption, Merle R., and Jack L. Landes. *Planning Functional School Buildings.* New York: Harper & Brothers, 1957.

Taylor, James L., and Ray L. Hamon. *The Secondary School Plant: An Approach for Planning Functional Facilities.* U.S. Office of Education, Special Publication No. 5. Washington: Government Printing Office, 1956.

"Two Versions of the 'House' Plan — Scarsdale and Niskayona, N.Y.," *The Nation's Schools,* 67:65-69, 94, June, 1961.

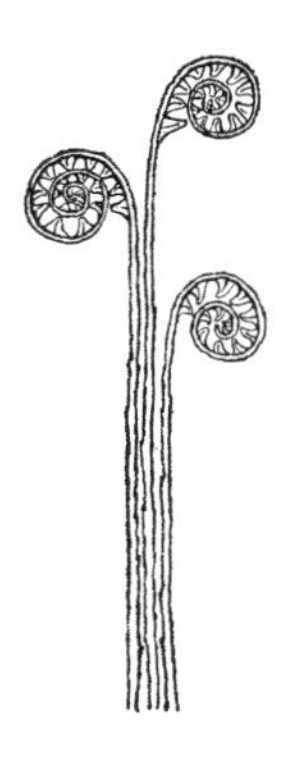

Part Five

SCHOOL RELATIONSHIPS AND EVALUATION

15

Problems of Articulation

Since the time of the Committee of Ten, wherever there have been two divisions of the secondary school the upper division has tended to dominate the lower. Gradual modifications of this situation have brought about a more nearly universal public education for all youth through Grades 1 to 12. Educators are increasingly aware that both school divisions have unique and separate educational requirements suited to their respective student groups.

1. What must be considered in the development of articulation aims?

The junior high school is now commonly designated as the connecting and articulating agent within the educational complex of the elementary school and the junior and senior high schools. In unified school districts the junior high school is expected to afford every student from sixth grade in the elementary school to tenth grade in senior high school continuous progression and to eliminate learning obstructions at the point of transfer from each school division to the one above.

Practices that guide students toward constructive management of anxieties and frustrations, so typically associated with changes in school settings, teachers, curriculum, activities, and peer group associations, facilitate continuous learning. *A Look at the Continuity in the School Program,* 1958 Yearbook of the Association for Supervision and Curriculum Development, National Education Association, supports this point of view:

"Continuity of learning experience" may indicate a clearer emphasis upon what is happening to the learner than does the term "articulation" as the latter has commonly been used. As already stated, discussions of articulation are too frequently, though not necessarily, devoted to the externals of school organization and curriculum planning. The fundamental test of efforts at improving articulation in schools is found in what happens to the learners in those schools. *Our aim is to further continuity of learning experience toward educational objectives.* We seek to give boys and girls in the schools those learning experiences which will help them achieve their own and the school's objectives in the most efficient manner possible. At times this involves prevention or removal of barriers to pupil progress in the course of being educated.

The term "continuity of learning experience" stresses the ongoing learning process rather than formal administrative structure or even sequences of curricular activities. The emphasis is placed less upon how the school is organized into grades and levels, less upon what learning activities are prescribed at various levels, and more upon what happens to the learner as he goes from level to level or as he reacts to the various learning activities. After all, what happens to school learners collectively represents the sum total of the school's accomplishments, good or bad.[1]

Student-focused articulation practices are basic to the effective management of the many changes in educational programs that insure learning progress. Educators from *all* units within a school system must anticipate imaginatively the varying degrees of regression and progression which their students may manifest in abilities, interests, and responses to various learning tasks as they approach the crucial problems of early adolescent growth and development.

When educators from the three major school units integrate these concepts, their perception of students as requiring continuous learning experiences is greatly increased. Recognition, too, of the individual differences in learning progress will eliminate the "peck system" in which one school unit staff holds another accountable for a student's regression in one or more learning areas, often concomitant with school level changes.

David H. Russell declares in his treatment of "Continuity in the Reading Program" that an all-school continuous instructional reading program for twelve or more years is essential to the attainment of adequate reading skill:

The comprehensive view of continuity, as expressed in terms of the learner's interests and abilities, must be translated into specific activities and materials. Teachers at all grade levels must understand how pupils grow in their reading abilities, and they must have acquired technical competence in methods and knowledge of materials which contribute to the growth of pupils. Some of the

[1] Association for Supervision and Curriculum Development, National Education Association, *A Look at Continuity in the School Program,* 1958 Yearbook (Washington: The Association, 1958), p. 6. By permission of the copyright © owner, The Association for Supervision and Curriculum Development.

characteristics of an all-school developmental program that may be of interest to both teachers and parents of school children are explained in the following descriptive statements.

In a number of schools and school systems, the developmental program provides for reading instruction for all pupils at all levels from the first grade through the high school or junior college, according to the existing organization. The program also provides for special help in reading on an individual or small-group basis for all children and especially for those significantly retarded or accelerated in reading ability. The administrative procedure is based upon the concept of the reading program as a selection of appropriate activities which involves not only the reading of textbooks and anthologies but also emphasizes experiences in reading and study in all subject-matter fields. Another feature of the developmental plan makes accessible abundant and varied reading materials which can be adapted to specific needs of individual learners at all classification levels. By the same token, the developmental program offers opportunities for free reading of an individualized nature and emphasizes opportunities for reading as an aid to social and personal development. The all-school developmental program also provides for continuous measurement of the effectiveness of the program at all levels by the use of standardized tests, informal teacher evaluation, and studies of pupils' use of reading in various school tasks. In addition to the foregoing statements regarding the plan and purposes of an all-school reading program, the arrangements are made for the evaluation of special phases of the program through pupils' reading habits and by means of action research on problems presented by teachers, parents, and children.[2]

The primary objectives of all distinctive processes in an educational complex must be consistent with contemporary junior high school philosophy. The unique features of a particular school and/or school system are to be considered in the formulation of articulation aims and procedures but must not obstruct the over-all purposes of junior high school education. It should be kept in mind that any number or variety of practices and curriculums may be established, but they are preordained for failure unless those who formulate and apply them fully accept the educational principle that continuous and connecting learning opportunities advance student progress whereas fragmented learning opportunities retard it.

Re-establishment of student equilibrium

Assisting students to re-establish a sense of equilibrium as they leave the past and encounter the new educational environs is a primary articulation aim. Its attainment requires attention from *all* educators, but particularly from those whose interest and activities place them in direct contact with preadolescent and early adolescent student groups.

[2] David H. Russell, "Continuity in the Reading Program," Chap. 13 in *Development in and Through Reading,* Sixtieth Yearbook of the National Society for the Study of Education, Part I (Chicago: The Society [distributed by the University of Chicago Press], 1961), p. 228.

Basic to the attainment of this aim is awareness and comprehension of the influences exerted on learning efforts by the complex emotional and physical growth struggles of early youth. Effective direction of learning progress through the stress accompanying changes in school levels is highly contingent upon the availability of external supports within school settings. These must be styled to the particular characteristics of each student group and sensitive to individual differences.

The routine use of identical articulation practices year after year is symptomatic of a school staff's failure to discharge its acknowledged responsibilities to formulate and implement *student-centered* procedures. It is necessary to recognize each student group as a potential transmitter of either constructive or destructive adaptations to changes in the educational situation. Understanding of the nature of these determinants within every student group will make it possible to augment constructive articulation.

The special purpose of articulation necessitates collaborative work between the elementary, junior high, and senior high school staffs. The unquestionable benefit of interstaff activities is clearly identified in uninterrupted student learning progress and the establishment of student equilibrium.

A brief search for the reasons for student disequilibrium during the change in grade and/or school levels reveals the student's concern, or fear of failure, associated with unknown learning demands. Students with specific learning deficiencies usually experience more acute and longer-lasting anxieties and may functionally withdraw from their learning situation. Junior high school staffs should consult with appropriate elementary school staff members in order to assess these deficiencies and institute remedial articulation measures.

Also important to this articulation aim is recognition of the additional problems of early adolescents confronted with simultaneous changes in school units, peer groups, and neighborhoods. The fact that they are quite vulnerable and defensive may appear in their behavior, which often provokes initial rejection from the new teachers and the new peer groups. The latter may be non-accepting because the "new ones" are frequently viewed as an intrusion or threat to the established peer group. When school staffs recognize the underlying fears of the "outsiders," they are better able to deal with their perhaps provocative attitudes and behavior in ways which lessen obstructions to continuous learning progress.

Continuity of learning progress

One of the prime considerations in articulation is the consistent and orderly instruction process which directs students from simple to complex learning and from the old to the new. Specific emphasis is placed on connecting the commonalities within learning demands by instructional material, extra-class assignments, and class activities. Feelings of bewilderment and trepidation which conflict with the student's desire to progress, or be "promoted," at the same rate as his contemporaries are modified by effective articulation practices. The professional responsibility of all educators to collaborate with their colleagues commits both teaching and administrative staffs to the single purpose of providing coordinated learning opportunities. This commitment must be system-wide if students are to fully realize continuity in learning.

Teacher proficiency in guiding students to integrate the various elements within curriculum content areas is augmented by formal and informal collaborative activities among school staff members: those from all school units within a school system, from single school units, and from the school units collectively serving the same area in the community. Such an educational approach encourages cross-fertilization of learning materials, methods, and goals represented within the participating staff groups. The organizational structure of these groups should foster functional activities which are directed toward improved perception of interrelated curricular content, which in turn reinforces sequential learning opportunities. The premise on which this activity is based is the well-established principle that the task of integrating knowledge confronting all students is a vital component of human learning and when recognized makes dysfunctional learning unlikely.

Effective student–teacher relationships

One of the most significant aims of articulation in junior high school is the establishment of productive student–teacher relationships. The teacher's approach to students should be based upon an empathetic perception of their individual learning assets and liabilities. A good student–teacher relationship is most influential in the student's development of positive learning attitudes, which are vital to effective learning progress at all school levels.

The formation of a creative student–teacher relationship demands awareness and acceptance of the student's earlier learning achievements, extra-school situation, attitude toward himself and his educational environs, and personal interests and ambitions. Thus, perceptive instructors are most strategically positioned to influence the healthy development of their students as they guide them toward successful integration of learning opportunities.

Positive and constructive learning attitudes are of such vital consequence that their development should bear the closest scrutiny by all concerned with this student group. Data available from the behavioral sciences increasingly attest to the importance of successful learning experiences upon the personality of early youth. (This point is discussed in detail in Chapter 3.) Rapport between teacher and pupil, so essential in learning–teaching situations, is often achieved by the teacher's sincere acknowledgment of whatever appropriate contributions a student may offer, as this confirms approval and acceptance. Being relieved of the necessity of coping with fears of failure and rejection by the teacher, the student may freely utilize his instructional help. The potential benefits to students from the attainment of this articulation aim are manifold.

2. *What articulation practices are required?*

Articulation practices involve numerous flexible and creative procedures. One is the effective orientation of students progressing from one school unit to the next. There should be opportunities for students and parents to actually preview the school building and its facilities, to meet the staff, and to be briefed on the most important initial activities they will encounter in the new setting. Perhaps most useful to the student to know are the *required practices.* These should be such as will contribute to his ability to cope with individuals and groups without impediment to his continuous progress from one grade and/or level to another.

Transition from elementary to junior high school

On a school system-wide basis it is necessary for the central and local school unit staffs to formulate a wide range of articulation practices which are adaptable to the unique needs of the elementary school groups. When these factors are overlooked, the practices invoked frequently aggravate the complexities they are supposed to alleviate. "Customized" articulation aids are of critical importance because late preadolescents and early adolescents usually evidence acute resistance to and concern with the new demands anticipated from their first school unit change.

Let us look at the articulation practices of the Jordon School District, Midvale, Utah. General management of student orientation activities is the responsibility of the pupil personnel department, with appropriate assistance from local principals, counselors, district consultants, students, and parents. The central school staff, who serve as consultants to the local staffs, allow the latter considerable autonomy. This organizational system makes possible the use of orientation programs that best meet the unique needs of each school group.

For a number of years all sixth-grade students in the Jordon School District have completed a questionnaire which is designed to clarify the nature of their attitudes and anxieties toward the impending move into junior high school. The following questions are asked:

> "Are you happy about going to junior high school? Why?
> "What fears do you have about going to junior high school?
> "What suggestions do you have for helping sixth-graders to become acquainted with the junior high school program?"
>
> The seventeen elementary schools in our system used these questions and in some cases added others. (Seventh- and eighth-graders attended three large junior high schools. While we recognized some of the problems this presented for the students, we also wanted to determine exactly what the sixth-graders were feeling and thinking.)

In answer to the questions many fears and concerns were expressed as well as many joys and anticipations. Some of the happy anticipations included such things as looking forward to meeting new friends, attending more parties and assemblies, enjoying different teachers and a greater variety of class activities.[3]

The major features of the "Orientation to Junior High School" are illustrated by describing the specific orientation activities provided by one elementary and one junior high school in the district. The elementary school program extends over the whole school year and affords the sixth-grade students anticipatory guidance in an effort to minimize their fears and tensions toward the forthcoming school change.

1. Early in the school year the students participate in class activities designed to prepare them to relate to more than one teacher for learning instruction. These opportunities are usually facilitated by having the teachers who demonstrate significant strengths in teaching physical education and/or music exchange class groups. If scheduling conflicts occur within these areas, arithmetic is substituted, with an exchange teacher. For six to seven months sixth-graders develop a limited awareness of the instructional system they will enter in junior high school.

2. During the year teachers assign a limited amount of regular homework similar in volume and complexity to what will be called for in junior high school. Care is taken to insure functional assignments which are varied in difficulty and in time required for completion. "Special emphasis was placed on functional work — not just *more*."

3. Five or six weeks prior to the close of the school year, the sixth-grade students, accompanied by their parents, have dinner in the elementary school cafeteria. After dinner the administrative staff and student leaders from the junior high school present a program in the school auditorium which includes brief introductory remarks by the junior high school staff and student leaders; color slides to illustrate some junior high school activities; information regarding school fees, regulations, and customs by former elementary school students; and preregistration materials, distributed to facilitate the forthcoming seventh-grade class schedules.

4. Either immediately preceding school dismissal in the spring or prior to initiation of the fall sessions the sixth grade students are escorted through the junior high school's physical facilities. They receive directions for locating their classrooms, the cafeteria, the library, and the gymnasium.

The staff of the Jordon School District prepared material on the "why" and

[3] Reprinted by permission of the Association for Childhood Education International, 3615 Wisconsin Avenue, N.W., Washington, D.C. 20016. From bulletin-D, "Orientation to Junior High School," 1962-63, p. 1. Prepared by members of the Jordon School District, Midvale, Utah; Julian Brown, Elementary Principal; Hulda Crossgrove, Guidance Department, Junior High School; P. M. Mickelsen, Director of Pupil Personnel; and Alta Miller, Consultant, Intermediate Grades.

"how" of their junior high school orientation program, and its unique features are discussed below:

> The seventh-grade student finds himself confronted with situations which call for reorganization of previous learning and for the learning of new concepts. Individuals in this kind of situation often use trial-and-error learning or conditioned response learning. Neither of these is high on the scale of maturity or efficient in terms of time and use of learning capacity. Without guidance the seventh-grade student may be expected to reorganize his experiences through imitation, suggestion, sympathy or a combination of these. Appropriate orientation seeks to utilize the present knowledge and skill of the student in a process of learning rather than to allow him to be a mere imitator, developing emotional frustrations and using up valuable learning time.
>
> All members of the school staff are involved in the orientation program; administrators, teaching personnel, custodians, cafeteria workers, bus drivers, clerks, and student council members. Just as the seventh-grade pupils will benefit from such a program, so will the school personnel with knowledge of the students they will receive. The program is directed by the Guidance Department with assistance from any or all groups, including members of the district office staff.
>
> How the members of the school staff respond to orientation depends on the philosophy that has been developed. Here the school counselors play an important role. The program must be explained to the entire staff and the role each will play indicated. How well it is planned and the enthusiasm with which it is presented are important. "What one is not up on, he is usually down on" is a good philosophy to follow.
>
> Parents and PTA groups are important members of this learning experience and are considered key people.[4]

They also formulated a "Seven-Point Program" as a guideline for the evolvement of orientation activities in their junior high schools. These seven points are summarized here:

1. Two or three times during the year the sixth-grade pupils and their teachers are invited to the junior high school auditorium to attend assembly programs which are of general interest.
2. At the conclusion of the first quarter the junior high school counselor visits the sixth-grade classes in the elementary school, becomes acquainted with the progress of the various groups and, in certain cases, confers with the teacher about individual student situations.
3. A few weeks before the close of the school year the counselor and student guidance committee members from the junior high school call upon the sixth-grade classes to offer information and answer questions regarding their forthcoming experiences in the junior high school.
4. During the final week of the school year the sixth-grade students from

[4] *Ibid.*, p. 3.

all elementary feeder schools convene in the junior high school auditorium to receive more preparation specific to their next year's school program. Student council members welcome the new students and indicate the expectations, traditions, and privileges attending their entrance into the junior high school. They are then directed to form small groups and, escorted by student hosts, tour and observe the junior high school in regular session. After completion of the tour, each student receives informational literature and registration forms to complete and return later to the sixth-grade teachers.

5. Ten days prior to the initiation of the fall school term, the junior high school counselors, student council, and guidance committee members meet to review their arrangements for assisting the incoming seventh-grade students to become acclimated to their new school environment.

6. The new seventh-grade student group and their parents receive written invitations to a special orientation program one week prior to the starting of regular school sessions. This program is conducted by members of the ninth-grade student council and student guidance committee under the direction of the school counselor. The activities which the new students will engage in during the first school day are reviewed in detail and questions are solicited.

7. When regular school sessions commence, each homeroom teacher, with supplementary aid from the counselor, introduces and discusses the role of student council, election to the council, the marking or grading system, attendance regulations, conduct standards, school activities, clubs, and the use of the student handbook.

The foregoing list is representative of all elementary and junior high school orientation programs within the Jordon School District. The school staffs evaluate the programs annually and complete whatever modifications are indicated to facilitate the students' transfer to junior high school.

Research and experimental findings. Research findings reported in the educational literature repeatedly attest to the necessity for "many and varied" articulation practices to effectively meet the student's requirements for stability and continuous progression preceding, during, and following his first move from one school level to another.

Denton's interesting study entitled "An Experiment with Selected Junior High School Orientation Techniques" describes an effort to identify orientation techniques, their effectiveness, frequency of application by junior high school counselors, and insight into the educational benefits as demonstrated in experimental teaching with seventh-grade junior high students. Denton reported these major findings:

> 1. The use of the guided tour and floor plan charts is effective as a means for orienting new students to the school plant.

2. The home-room program is effective as a device for orienting new seventh-grade students to the routine of the junior high school.

3. The upper class committee is not effective as a means for orienting the new seventh-grade student to the increased self-discipline and self-direction required by the junior high school.

4. The use of guidance class panel reports of teacher interviews is effective as a method for orienting the new student to the departmentalized instruction of the junior high school.

5. Group guidance using photographs is effective as a device for orienting new students to the larger faculty of the junior high school.

Further analysis of the statistics showed that orientation can have long-range implications since oriented pupils achieved significantly higher grade-point averages than non-oriented pupils, and significantly higher ratings were assigned to oriented pupils by the teachers indicating that orientation can have visible results. The analysis of the needs checklist showed no significant differences between groups.[5]

Denton's work provides further evidence that effective orientation techniques are essential to articulation. Encouraging students to manage the emotional stress occasioned by all that is *new,* they contribute significantly to student learning progression in all areas.

Another valuable study of effective articulation methods between the elementary and junior high school has been reported by Campanale. This study proposed to identify effective articulation practices within the seventh-grade classes of two junior high schools containing Grades 7, 8, and 9 and one junior-senior high school containing Grades 7 to 12 in Bloomington, Indiana.

Campanale compiled articulation practices from fifty educational literature sources pertaining to junior high school education. These were submitted to a jury of five junior high school principals with a request to identify "desirable" practices. The latter were then presented to a group of students and teachers of the Indiana University laboratory school, with instructions to appraise them in accordance with their perceptions of value.

A final inventory of twenty-six "desirable" articulation practices was obtained, classified, and submitted to 200 pupils (selected by a table of random numbers from 540 pupils in the seventh grade), their parents (74 responding), and 42 seventh-grade junior high school teachers. The respective respondent groups were requested to indicate, first, whether or not they believed

[5] William D. Denton, "An Experiment with Selected Junior High School Orientation Techniques." Reprinted by permission from *The Bulletin of the National Association of Secondary-School Principals,* February, 1962. Copyright: Washington, D.C. P. 325. See also these research studies: Richard S. Byers, "Articulation in the Junior High School" (1955), *The Bulletin of the National Association of Secondary-School Principals,* 46:416-418, February, 1962, and James W. Brinkopf, "Transition from Sixth to Seventh Grade Made Easy at Cherry Creek" (1960), *The Bulletin of the National Association of Secondary-School Principals,* 46:70-73, February, 1962.

the twenty-six practices were utilized, and if so, whether they were considered helpful.

From the schedule of twenty-six articulation practices, three-fourths of each respondent group (students, parents, teachers) indicated that these thirteen articulation practices were applied and considered helpful:

Club membership.
Student council representatives.
Information disseminated to incoming seventh-grade pupils.
Visits by sixth-grade pupils to the junior high school.
Relationship in subject-matter content.
Pupil-organized activities.
Aid to seventh-grade pupils early in their careers.
A continuous orientation program.
Parents' visit to the junior high school.
Opportunities for leadership.
Teachers for more than one period (block-time classes).
Social activities.
Parent-teacher conferences.

The respondents from the three groups indicated that these two practices were *not* used:

Visits of the junior high school principals to the elementary schools to explain the junior high school to the sixth-grade pupils.
Visits of seventh-grade pupils to the elementary school for the same purpose.

A quarter or more of the respondents from the three groups indicated that these eleven practices were not used and/or were of no value:

Similar grading system.
Faculty attitude toward conduct.
Distribution of handbooks to sixth-grade students before they enter the seventh grade.
Orientation discussions in the classroom.
Special assemblies.
Administration and teachers' explanation of school program to parents.
Printed or mimeographed materials for parents.
School news in the local newspaper.
Guidance program in pupil-teacher acquaintanceship.
Teacher-pupil conferences.
Increase in elective courses from Grade 7 to Grade 9.[6]

[6] Eugene H. Campanale, "An Appraisal of Elementary and Junior High School Articulation in the Bloomington, Indiana, Schools," Ed.D. dissertation, School of Education, Indiana University, 1961, pp. 113-114 (adaptations of Tables 8 through 33, pp. 59-90).

The assessment of the practices which were identified by the study respondents as "not used" and/or of "no value" must not be perceived as valid for these particular practices since they were not operatively observed; assignments of "no value," then, are incongruous with basic reliability. The study findings are indicative of the Bloomington school staff's possible need to evolve a clearer perception of articulation aims.

The articulation practices between Grades 6 and 7 in the Bloomington junior high schools suggest both strengths and weaknesses. There are definite indications that more collaboration between the elementary and junior high school staffs would help them advance the students' attainment of a unified view of the conditions attending the various learning areas, thus affording them increased *unity* in their outlook and attitudes.

Transition from junior to senior high school

Research findings point up the urgency of having *all* youth from all intellectual and social levels of society provided the opportunities and motivations which will sustain them in the successful completion of secondary educational programs. This has become a prime requisite for productivity in the contemporary socioeconomic system.

These societal conditions place a heavy responsibility upon educators to supply youth with the incentives to continue in school, through realistic and radical changes in the curriculum and instructional procedures to make education functional for all and through the development and competent application of effective articulation devices. The importance of the availability of these devices, which are related to multiple and diverse learning requirements evidenced by youth during the ninth and tenth grades, cannot be questioned. Society can no longer afford a membership burdened with educational impairments which obstruct functional productivity.

O'Brien investigated twenty-seven New Jersey junior and senior high schools in an effort to determine the extent to which theoretical articulation practices represented in the literature were actualized and to suggest possible procedures specific to articulation needs for ninth- and tenth-grade students in the Linden, New Jersey, Public Schools.

Staff members from the twenty-seven schools (located in Camden, Elizabeth, Newark, and Trenton, New Jersey) were asked to rate, in terms of their current articulation practices, the practices O'Brien had derived from the literature. These schools were selected because of their outstanding articulation practices between the ninth and tenth grades. Another twenty schools were selected out of 120 suggested by forty-seven state departments of education and other authorities on articulation in secondary schools. An analysis of the rating assigned to these articulation practices by all respondents is given below:

1. Most of the articulation practices enumerated in the educational literature were in use in the twenty-seven New Jersey schools.

2. The counselor, or a combination of principal, vice-principal, and counselor, was responsible for administering the articulation program.

3. Over-all responsibility for promotional policies was assigned to the vice-principal, counselor, teacher, and, infrequently, the principal. The teachers determined specific promotion practices based on establishing standards within their local senior high school.

4. The New Jersey respondents considered these articulation practices effective between ninth and tenth grades:

Student records.
Course selection.
Junior high school (pupil) visitation to senior high school.
Joint meetings of junior and senior high school staffs.
Senior high school counselor and pupil participation in ninth-grade orientation program.
Orientation programs at the opening of school.
Parent participation.

5. The New Jersey respondents designated these articulation areas as inadequate and in need of improvement:

Professional meetings.
Cooperation of professional staffs.
Course information.
Parent participation.
Visitation to senior high school.
More involvement of the school psychologist and social worker in problem cases.[7]

Another important study of articulation between junior and senior high school has been reported by Frey.[8] It included 206 junior and senior high school principals in 6-3-3 schools and 108 principals in 6-6 systems from nine states and inquired into the articulation problems involved in the areas of "administrative organization, curriculum, guidance programs, teaching staffs, and extra-class programs." Five tables are presented showing the degree of articulation difficulties found in these areas. They are combined and summarized here in Table 29.

[7] John L. O'Brien, "Articulation in Selected New Jersey Junior and Senior High Schools," Ed.D. dissertation, Rutgers University, *Dissertation Abstracts* (University Microfilms, Inc., Ann Arbor, Michigan), 20:3633, March, 1960.

[8] Sherman H. Frey, "A Descriptive Study of the Problems and Procedures of Articulation Between the Junior and Senior High Schools Accredited by the North Central Association in Public School Systems Organized on a 6-6 or 6-3-3 Basis," Ph.D. thesis, State University of Iowa, 1962, and reported by the author in "Articulation Between the Junior and Senior High School," *The Bulletin of the National Association of Secondary-School Principals,* 47:35-43, October, 1963.

TABLE 29

Principals' Evaluations of the Degree of Trouble Presented in the Administrative Organization, Curriculums, Guidance Programs, Teacher Assignments and Loads, and Extra-Class Programs of the Junior and Senior High Schools

Articulation Problems in Different Areas	Junior and Senior High School Principals in 6-3-3 Schools (N = 206)*		High School Principals in 6-6 Schools (N = 108)	
	Per Cent Reporting No Trouble	*Per Cent Reporting Minor, Moderate, or Major Trouble*	*Per Cent Reporting No Trouble*	*Per Cent Reporting Minor, Moderate, or Major Trouble*
Administrative Organization				
Physical facilities	57.8	42.2	22.2	77.8
Student records	51.9	48.1	66.7	33.3
Class recitation schedules	76.7	23.3	52.7	47.3
Pupil promotion policies and plans	54.9	45.1	58.3	41.7
Granting course credit	80.6	19.4	76.9	23.1
Pupil grading policies and plans	65.5	34.5	54.5	45.5
Curriculums				
Grade placement and sequence of courses	50.0	50.0	64.3	35.7
Course content	36.4	63.6	33.3	66.7
Provisions for individual differences	26.2	73.8	13.9	86.1
Guidance Programs				
Orientation services	15.1	84.9	22.2	77.8
Counseling services	22.8	77.2	32.4	67.6
Student appraisal services	24.3	75.7	17.6	82.4
Information services	29.1	70.9	23.2	76.8
Teacher Assignments and Loads	50.0	50.0	34.3	65.7
Extra-Class Programs				
Scheduling of extra-class programs	34.9	65.1	21.3	78.7
Types of extra-class programs	38.8	61.2	22.2	77.8
Use of facilities for extra-class programs	44.2	55.8	19.4	80.6

* The "N" includes both junior and senior high school administrators.

A combination and summarization of the findings of Tables 1-5 as they appear in *The Bulletin of the National Association of Secondary-School Principals,* 47:37-41, October, 1963.

While over half of the principals appear to find articulation problems in administrative organization virtually nonexistent, a large number find them in the areas of physical facilities, student records, pupil promotion policies, and pupil grading policies and plans; a majority find the curriculum a source of greater difficulty, particularly problems associated with adequate provision for individual differences and continuity in course content; and approximately half are concerned with problems of sequence of courses and proper grade placement. Guidance and adequate facilities for extra-class activities appear to pose major problems of articulation for a heavy majority of the principals.

The most successful articulation practices in these situations were found to be: in respect to articulating the use of physical facilities, for one principal to assume coordinating responsibility in the 6-6 type of organization and for joint planning by the principals in the 6-3-3 schools; to care for individual differences, "counseling, ability grouping, and the enriching courses at both the junior and senior high school levels" appeared most effective; the use of a continuous text series and the use of joint faculty committees proved most satisfactory for articulating course content; the use of joint faculty committees and the adoption of continuous textbook series also proved the most effective way to care for grade placement and sequence of courses; the most successful articulation devices in guidance involved "forwarding guidance records from the junior to the senior high school, having similar guidance objectives and procedures in both schools, having certified counselors in both schools, having conferences attended by the counselors of both schools, and using all the records of both schools in counseling"; in articulating extra-class activities joint scheduling of programs and the employment of a single athletic director for both schools or levels seemed most feasible.

Articulation practices found most helpful in this study are summarized by Frey:

> Communication by means of conferences and meetings was widely employed as an articulation practice. Another widely used practice was having one person responsible for the program or activity from grades seven through twelve. . . . Theory in articulation rests essentially on the idea of good communication between the units concerned. This communication takes place in various forms, either through direct verbal contact or through the use of sequential curricular materials of different kinds. The practices in articulation which were most frequently used and effective were those that kept the lines of communication open.[9]

When students reach senior high school they are entering the young adult phase of development with its attendant distinctive social, intellectual, physical, and emotional modifications and requirements — far different from those associated with their entrance into junior high school. Articulation practices

[9] *Ibid.*, pp. 42-43.

must be tailored to their diverse learning interests, attitudes, aptitudes, abilities, and liabilities, and directed to supporting their inner motivations toward continuing the new, larger, and more advanced program of the senior high school.

3. *How are practices represented in instruction and administration?*

Articulation practices are often implemented within the regular junior high school instructional program. The 1958 Yearbook of the Association for Supervision and Curriculum Development has an excellent description of the way a class in social studies is used to introduce the student to the mysteries of the senior high school:

> Orientation to high school is a part of the planned curriculum. The 9A social studies course includes a unit on the senior high school — training possibilities, requirements for 10B's, and organization of the school. The dean teaches this unit, counsels with the group and with each individual, and registers them for senior high school. Parents are contacted concerning this program through letters and bulletins and are encouraged to become acquainted with the dean.
>
> One night meeting is held when the principal, dean of boys, and dean of girls from the high school come to the junior high school to meet the pupils and their parents. They participate in a roundtable discussion giving parents and pupils an opportunity to ask questions about the senior high school.
>
> The 9A's have always been invited to the senior high school for a part of the day, usually in the afternoon when many of the upper-classmen will be gone. They meet with the student council for a discussion of the school activities and are given an opportunity to ask questions. Later they are taken on a tour of the building.[10]

The foregoing is an example of the integrative aspects of articulation practices. This instructional approach fosters student interest and motivation in learning as immediate and purposive, and pleasurable implementational opportunities are readily available. Further, these learning experiences involve broad problem-solving methods with a variety of interchangeable features which advance creative and imaginative learning.

Block-time and core classes

Block-time or core classes afford numerous opportunities for integration of articulation principles in junior high school instructional programs. The following is illustrative, rather than exhaustive:

[10] Association for Supervision and Curriculum Development, National Education Association, *A Look at Continuity in the School Program,* 1958 Yearbook (Washington: The Association, 1958), pp. 193-194. By permission of the copyright © owner, The Association for Supervision and Curriculum Development.

1. The instructional organization is in harmony with the late preadolescent and early adolescent student's demand for consistent and sustained situations with sequential continuity which extends learning progression.

2. The block-time system provides adequate time for teacher-student relationships which realistically accommodate the student's struggle to adjust to the stresses inherent in the transitional situation.

3. Counseling is an important aspect of block-time instruction, offering educators opportunities to exercise constructive influences upon their students during the critical growth and development period of early adolescence.

Administrative practices and the realization of articulation aims

Administrative guidelines relative to promotional policies and practices should be provided for all school staffs.

The aims of a universal and continuous educational development imply an orientation to promotion from one grade and/or school to another as a prime responsibility to the learner and his growth needs.

Many school systems indicate their awareness of problems attending student graduation programs upon completion of elementary or junior high school and are rapidly converting to a single graduation, or commencement, program. This acknowledges and symbolizes the student's completion of the highest level in senior or vocational high school. Too often the graduation program at the end of elementary or junior high school gives youth the false idea that they have completed school, when they are actually in the middle of their common school program. With only one graduation from school, a smaller number of children yield to the temptation to drop out before experiencing their first graduation.

Value of the cumulative school record

Staff members in all school units should enter all pertinent information regarding students and their progress in the cumulative record. When this ideal is approached, effective student guidance and counseling is possible, an essential factor of good articulation at every grade and school level. The primary purpose of the cumulative record is to provide a comprehensive, informative, organized school record or profile of every student, which contributes to articulation and continuity in learning progress. The cumulative record should be begun prior to actual student entrance; additional entries are made throughout the school experience; and the record is closed only upon completion of high school.

Cumulative records that are orderly and up to date offer teachers and other appropriate staff members more assistance in their guidance of students than any other record in the history of child accounting. They are basic to the guidance process and contribute to the maintenance of continuity in learning from one grade level to the next, and from one school unit to the next, until senior high school is completed. It is believed that programs incorporating this articulation principle afford non-fragmented, student-centered learning experiences, as well as minimizing the frequency and degree of regression in the learning process.

The student's repeated surmounting of obstacles is a significant factor in reducing the level of anxiety always experienced in some degree in educational progression. Student learning ability is frequently obstructed by apprehension and fear of failure; it is best nurtured by bringing into view past achievements in learning, which minimizes regression. The usefulness of this articulation principle is of extreme value in junior high school, the link between elementary and senior high school. Consequently, educators should use articulation practices that will afford students successful experiences within new learning situations in order that learning may become progressively more comfortable and satisfying.

SELECTED BIBLIOGRAPHY

Association for Supervision and Curriculum Development, National Education Association, *A Look at Continuity in the School Program.* 1958 Yearbook. Washington: The Association, 1958.

Austin, David B., Will French, and J. Dan Hull. *American High School Administration: Policy and Practice.* New York: Holt, Rinehart & Winston, Inc., 1962. Chap. 21, "Communities — Local and Beyond — and the High School."

Ball, Arthur L. "Factors Affecting Articulation in the Transition of Pupils from Eight-Grade Elementary Schools to Secondary Schools," *The Bulletin of the National Association of Secondary-School Principals,* 46:418-419, February, 1962.

Brinkopf, James W. "Transition from Sixth to Seventh Grade Made Easy at Cherry Creek," *The Bulletin of the National Association of Secondary-School Principals,* 46:70-73, February, 1962.

Byers, Richard S. "Articulation in the Junior High School," *The Bulletin of the National Association of Secondary-School Principals,* 46:416-418, February, 1962.

Campanale, Eugene A. "An Appraisal of Elementary–Junior High School Articulation in the Bloomington, Indiana, Schools," Ed.D. dissertation, School of Education, Indiana University, 1961.

Conant, James B. *Education in the Junior High School Years: A Memorandum to School Boards.* Princeton, N.J.: Educational Testing Service, 1960. "System-Wide Recommendations, Recommendation 12: Coordination of Subject-Matter Instruction," pp. 33-34.

Cramer, Roscoe V., and Otto E. Domian. *Administration and Supervision in the Elementary School.* New York: Harper & Brothers, 1960.

Denton, William D. "An Experiment with Selected Junior High School Orientation Techniques," *The Bulletin of the National Association of Secondary-School Principals,* 46:324-325, February, 1962.

Faunce, Roland C., and Morrel J. Clute. *Teaching and Learning in the Junior High School.* San Francisco: Wadsworth Publishing Company, 1961. Chap. 6, "The Program of Student Activities." (This chapter contains a discussion of articulation with the curriculum.)

Franzén, Carl G. F. *Foundations of Secondary Education.* New York: Harper & Brothers, 1955. Chap. 7, "The Educational Ladder: Presecondary Education."

Frey, Sherman H. "Articulation Between the Junior and Senior High School," *The Bulletin of the National Association of Secondary-School Principals,* 47:35-43, October, 1963.

Gruhn, William T., and Harl Douglass. *The Modern Junior High School.* New York: The Ronald Press Company, 1956. Chap. 15, "Problems of Organization and Articulation."

Harris, Samuel D., Jr. "A Study of the Relationship Between the Sixth-Grade Student's Beliefs About Junior High School, His Concept of Self and Others, and His Socio-Economic Status," *The Bulletin of the National Association of Secondary-School Principals,* 46:275-276, February, 1962.

Job, Kenneth A. "A Social Studies Resource Unit Based on Adjustment Problems of Entering Junior High School Students," *The Bulletin of the National Association of Secondary-School Principals,* 46:200-201, February, 1962.

Juckett, E. A. "A Pleasant Bridge in the Hyde Park Schools," *The Clearing House,* 29:81-83, October, 1954.

Koenig, Isidore M. "A Comparison of the Forethoughts of Sixth-Grade Students Concerning the First Year of Junior High School with Reality as Seen Through Their Afterthoughts at the End of the First Year of Junior High School," *The Bulletin of the National Association of Secondary-School Principals,* 46:312-314, February, 1962.

Kroth, Roger L. "Orientation in Action," *The Clearing House,* 36:91-92, October, 1961.

O'Brien, John L. "Articulation in Selected Junior and Senior High Schools," Ed.D. dissertation, Rutgers University, *Dissertation Abstracts* (University Microfilms, Inc., Ann Arbor, Michigan), 20:3633, March, 1960.

"Orientation to Junior High School," Membership Service Bulletin-D, 1962-63, prepared by members of the Jordon School District, Midvale, Utah: Julian Brown, Elementary School Principal; Hulda Crossgrove, Guidance Department, Junior High School; P. M. Miceklsen, Director of Pupil Personnel; and Alta Miller, Consultant, Intermediate Grades. Washington: Association for Childhood Education International, 1963.

Otto, Henry J. *Elementary School Organization and Administration.* New York: Appleton-Century-Crofts, Inc., 1954.

Romine, Stephen A. "Articulation: A Look at the Twelve Year Program," *The North Central Association Quarterly,* 34:274-277, April, 1962.

Rush, Joseph. "For Junior High Adjustment," *The Instructor,* 72:97, 99, 134, August 28, 1962.

Russell, David H. "Continuity in the Reading Program," Chap. 13 in *Development in and Through Reading.* Sixtieth Yearbook of the National Society for the Study of Education, Part I. Chicago: The Society (distributed by the University of Chicago Press), 1961.

16

School–Community Relations

Since the turn of this century there has been a steadily growing emphasis upon the importance of education's breaking out of the narrow confines of the classroom and becoming involved in the total life of the community. It is nearly impossible to pick up an educational book which focuses upon the function or program of the school that does not have a chapter on the relation of the school to its community and vice versa. Moreover, sociological books consider the school as an important social institution enmeshed in the life of the community it serves.

1. Why school–community relations?

Importance

As far back as the beginning of the century the farsighted John Dewey noted the necessary relationship between school and community: "From the standpoint of the child, the great waste in the school comes from his inability to utilize the experiences he gets outside the school within the school itself; he is unable to apply in daily life what he is learning at school."[1]

Even more emphatic is a contemporary spokesman for education, James B. Conant: ". . . the nature of the community largely determines what goes on in the school. Therefore, to attempt to divorce the school from the community is to engage in unrealistic thinking, which might lead to policies that could wreak havoc with the school and the lives of children. The community and

[1] John Dewey, *School and Society* (Chicago: University of Chicago Press, rev. ed., 1915), p. 3.

the schools are inseparable."[2] Conant presses on from this general statement to give examples of the effect of homes upon the life and needs of youth at school. Although strongly recommending "homework" for students in his previous book *The American High School Today,* after a description of a home visited in a city slum area he comments pointedly, "Homework has little relevance in a situation where home is a filthy, noisy tenement."[3]

An educator who has given much of his life to the problems of the school in its community setting asserts:

> The school and community movement is coming of age. Even its critics no longer dismiss this major trend in American education as merely another in a series of professional fads, popular today, ignored tomorrow. On the contrary, this general determination to make school instruction really effective by relating it closely with essential community and human needs is the most significant, far-reaching educational emphasis and advance of this century.[4]

At the risk of seeming to press a point we present the reasoned thinking of another well-known educator who stresses the importance of the school-community relationship and at the same time gives some indication of a reason for this emphasis, which he finds in the nature of the educative process itself:

> People who think about education in broad terms, as a process of teaching children the concepts and attitudes of their society, and of teaching them how to behave in their social, civic, and economic relations, tend to think of the whole community as an educative agent. From this point of view, the school alone cannot do the job of education, nor can the school and family together. Education is the result of living and growing up in a community.
>
> . . . .
>
> Because the community is important in the education of children, educators are interested in finding the best combination of school and community experience for educational purposes.[5]

Historical evolution

The history of school and community relations in America has been a checkered one. As early as 1642 and 1647 the people of Massachusetts established what might roughly be considered schools for children and young adolescents. The grammar schools became not only the center of education for early adolescents but the center of community social and cultural life.

[2] James B. Conant, *Slums and Suburbs: A Commentary on Schools in Metropolitan Areas* (New York: McGraw-Hill Book Co., Inc., 1961), p. 20.

[3] *Ibid.,* p. 22.

[4] Edward G. Olsen, ed., *The School and Community Reader: Education in Perspective* (New York: The Macmillan Company, 1963), p. vii.

[5] Robert J. Havighurst and Bernice L. Neugarten, *Society and Education* (Boston: Allyn and Bacon, Inc., 2nd ed., 1962), p. 310.

In these days there was a close relationship between the parent, the community leaders, and the school. Many schoolmasters "boarded round" in the homes of the children and youth who attended the school. Thus parents became closely identified with what went on in the school, and the teacher became intimately acquainted with the background of each pupil. The local community accepted somewhat direct responsibility for the curriculum and quality of the instruction through its "committee of examiners," which visited the schools and examined each pupil carefully as to his school progress. "In New England during the colonial period the idea of having a committee of the town selectmen to run each local school was established. This arose partly because of the difficulty of communication from one school to another and partly because of the desire of the parents of each school to have control. Local school committees eventually became boards of education."[6]

As the communities and schools grew, the secondary school, particularly, began to offer a more complex curriculum, and control of the school in many details shifted to the state legislature. In consequence parents lost touch with the school. The curriculum increasingly felt the pressures of the Boston Latin Grammar School and the general idea of the times that the primary responsibility of the secondary school was to prepare its students for college. The close relationship that had originally existed between the school and the community gradually faded away.

With Franklin's unique academy, although it had lost many aspects of community relationships envisioned by Franklin by the time it was finally established in 1751, there was still some return to the earlier identification of the institution with the community. In particular, the curriculum of part of that early academy was tied into the practical life of the community, though not to the extent outlined in the "proposals" for it. But the more rural the academy setting, the more it became identified with the life and needs of the community, and the center of many community activities.

Except for the smaller places where the schools remained close to the people as a community center, the secondary school, through its greater academic emphasis upon classical subject matter, became less and less concerned with any practical relationship to community needs. The educational program, it was believed, could be fully met within the confines of the classroom. This remained largely the situation before the turn of this century, and in many schools today an attitude of cloistered academic sufficiency either still exists or is giving way most slowly and reluctantly before the pressures of newer educational concepts.[7]

[6] Ralph L. Pounds and James R. Bryner, *The School in American Society* (New York: The Macmillan Company, 1959), p. 69.

[7] For a brief discussion of the early development of school–community relations see M. W. Rodenhaver, W. B. Axtell, and R. E. Gross, *The Sociology of the School* (New York: Thomas Y. Crowell Company, 1957), Chap. 12, "The Community and the School."

2. *Why is education a school–community task?*

Relation of school and community

Sometimes it is necessary to repeat what all informed readers of this book know full well: the schools belong to the public. This is so fundamental and universally accepted a principle of school–community relationship that it would seem to need no discussion. However, the connection is not always made.

From the earliest days of primitive society the institutional agency employed for the educational induction of the adolescent youth into the adult life of the tribe was the time-honored "initiation rites" carried on by the tribesmen, or a group selected from their number for the purpose. This is the forerunner of the complex and often physically massive institution we call the school. It is just as surely the instrument of the people for the education of today's child. At times the modern school seems to have devious lines of control which extend beyond the local community, but these represent only strands of the larger community that makes up society.

It is an axiom that the school exists to perpetuate the ideals and way of life of the society that supports it. In our democratic society the school has the important additional function of so educating its youth that they will be alert to changing conditions and possess the imagination and genius to improve the functioning of this democracy to progressively enrich the way of life of all citizens. As Pounds and Bryner have pointed out, "The school as an institution in most cases has been developed consciously by a people in order to carry out certain ideas deemed appropriate to them. Although the school as an institution sometimes has lost touch with its society and has tended to become a conservative force, it has always been established as an agency of society to carry out its purposes."[8]

The founding fathers recognized the importance of education as an instrument of national well-being. The national government declared, through the Ordinance of 1787, "Religion, morality and knowledge being necessary for good government and the happiness of mankind, schools and the means of education shall be forever encouraged." However, responsibility for the maintenance of schools was left to the states. They in turn delegated major responsibility for the conduct and support of schools to the local communities; hence the healthy interest in the schools by early American pioneers.

In time both the state and the federal government stepped up their support of the schools. The state now approaches 50 per cent of the underwriting of local school financial support, while the federal government has increased its special grants to education in amount and in a variety of forms. The state has

[8] Pounds and Bryner, *op. cit.*, p. 55.

gradually taken over more of the larger phases of school regulation to insure a uniformly higher minimum level of educational standards for children and youth of all communities. These prescriptions have been directed particularly to minimum standards for teacher certification, length of school day and year, curriculum, school facilities, and the amount of money spent for each pupil. Beyond the minimum standards, the local school community is free to advance its educational program as far as it desires. In fact most communities have regarded it as something of an obligation to move beyond the minimum standards set up by more remote governmental agencies. These efforts to safeguard the privilege of all children to a general level of educational opportunity consonant with their rights as American citizens in no way limits the freedom of the community to improve the quality of the education of its youth as it may choose.

Should education be a cooperative task?

To most educators this question will appear to be superfluous. Some would quickly reverse the question to read, "Can education be other than a cooperative task?" so completely has contemporary knowledge of the learning process permeated the teaching profession.

It must be acknowledged that the concepts of learning held during past centuries have encouraged the belief that the educational process could be carried on best in isolated schools and insulated classrooms, where window-sills were so high no outside distraction would be visible to the class. That notion of education, fortunately, has given way to the recognition that education includes the total environment of the child. The title of a book, *They Learn What They Live,* dramatizes succinctly the present-day learning theory that the child learns from all that impinges upon him and that in a real sense the learner is the product of his whole community environment. This fact is most pointedly stated thus: "Modern programs of education are built around the central idea that the child is a whole being who is educated by his total life experience — out of school as well as in it. Schooling and education are never synonymous. Every experience of his life educates the individual in some way, some degree, some respect."[9]

The implications for the community are tremendous. This concept of learning means that, for good or ill, the pupil learns what his environment exposes him to. His learning may be wholesome and constructive, representing the best the community can offer, or undesirable, the result of his contact with the seamy side of life. It is of the utmost importance, therefore, that school and community work together to see that the learning experiences at all points, both in and out of school, reflect the same wholesome ideals.

It should be constantly kept in mind that the six or seven hours the child or youth spends in school are a very unequal match to the seventeen or

[9] Olsen, *op. cit.*, p. 240.

eighteen hours he spends at home and in the community. What is learned outside of school may nullify the ideals and behavioral patterns the school tries to inculcate within its own environmental milieu. It must never be forgotten for a moment that the *child learns what he lives.* This is true to a much greater extent of the early adolescent who, as he grows older, begins to explore the farther reaches of his local community and even beyond. As he becomes less and less limited to his school and home, his experiences arise from a more extended and complex environment. The tremendous power of the community as educator is emphasized by Thelen: "The learning of the child is actually influenced will-nilly by all his experiences in the community. . . . We need a complete reinterpretation of the place of the community and the school in the enterprise of education."[10]

3. What important personnel relationships exist?

Teacher–pupil relationship

One of America's most important educational organizations makes this sweeping statement: "The most important single factor in school–community relations is the teacher–pupil relationship."[11] This relationship is of equal importance from the educational point of view, and never is it more important than during the junior high school years. At this critical period the youth is emerging from childhood into adolescence. Up to this time, by and large, the child from the typical home has had a somewhat sheltered life within the limits of his home and school. Except for the more precocious and adventurous, radio and television have been the most frequent sources of his experiences beyond the home and school, church possibly excepted.

The emerging adolescent is more aware of selfhood. He begins to see himself as an individual — a personality — though somewhat confusedly. He becomes acutely sensitive to his peers, and to social situations that little concerned him before. Too, in this situation he is somewhat blindly though nonetheless surely striking out against the restraints of the home, which he regards as unnecessarily restrictive to his freedom of expression, freedom to learn, to know, to become. In modern youthful parlance he is likely to look upon his parents as "squares." They have lost touch with the real world and do not understand him. He shares the thinking made famous by Mark Twain's characterization of the boy who at age twelve could not understand how his father could be so impossibly ignorant but at eighteen marveled at how much

[10] Herbert A. Thelen, *Education and the Human Quest* (New York: Harper & Brothers, 1960), p. 55.

[11] American Association of School Administrators, National Education Association, *The Superintendent as Instructional Leader,* Thirty-Fifth Yearbook (Washington: The Association, 1957), p. 101.

his father had learned in a few short years. As one student of young adolescents observes, "Whether they show it or not, most adolescents are quite insecure and frightened; everything is so new."

An extended study was made of teen-agers in Grades 7-11 to discover the range and nature of their problems as these early adolescents saw them. They are presented below in slightly adapted form, listed in general order of frequency of mention:

Worries

Marks (mentioned twice as often as any other worry).
School (includes worries other than those associated with marks).
Opposite sex (never mentioned by seventh-graders, only eighth- and ninth-graders; girls and boys in about equal numbers).
Being popular.
Family relations.
My future.
Myself.
Being accepted.
Money.
My appearance.
Failure.
Health.
Lack of time.
Nothing (a good many left the questionnaire blank, stating they had no worries).
Temper.
The world situation.

When an attempt was made to assemble the list of worries presented into large categories they appeared to fall into three major divisions:

School, 41% (failure, marks, homework, etc.).
Myself, 40% (appearance, being accepted, popularity, future, relation to opposite sex, etc.).
Others, 19% (family, friends, money).

What They'd Like to Change

Family.
Myself.
Nothing (some would make no changes in their lives).
School.
Get good grades.
My age (boys only mentioned this; possibly an interesting commentary on differences in maturation levels of boys and girls).
Place of residence.
Be more popular.

Have more money.
Be more intelligent.
Stop worrying.
World situation.
The future.[12]

It is clear from this study that early adolescence is a time of real problems. The youngster needs help. He wants answers to many questions, but at this age he shies away, for the most part, from asking many of these questions of his parents. The teacher who looks upon his function as fundamentally that of helping youth to come to an intelligent understanding of themselves, their immediate environment, and their world may be the key person in the community to whom junior high students flock for counsel. Or, in the Rogerian sense, he may be just someone with whom they feel they can talk over the problems they find themselves unable to handle. It has been the contention of the authors throughout this book that this *is* the primary function of the junior high school teacher, and that the teacher who thinks his supreme task is to supervise the mastery of large segments of subject matter is missing the real challenge and opportunity of teaching and in reality is "selling his birthright for a mess of pottage."

Teacher–parent relationship

From the standpoint of the immediate education of the pupil the teacher–parent relationship doubtless stands next to that between teacher and pupil. In many respects teacher, students, and parent are closely intertwined in the educative process.

In the first part of this chapter and elsewhere in the book stress has been placed upon the unique concept of modern education and learning as it relates to the total environment which the community provides as a learning situation for the pupil. The most important single factor during the early adolescent period is the home. A proper home environment can do much to offset the educational influences of undesirable community situations. If the school and home maintain a united educational front, a poor community environment can to a large extent be nullified or overcome. There is no possibility that pupils can completely bypass pervasive deleterious community influences when they are exposed to them. The more serious these environmental influences are, the more harmful their effects on pupils in the community. Obviously, then, the most effective cooperation should exist between teachers and parents. As Max Lerner, in an address before the National Education Association, observed somewhat pessimistically, "Speaking as a teacher, I would like to say that it is very hard to get the life of the mind across to a child in school if the child comes from a home in which there are

[12] Adapted from Eric W. Johnson, *How to Live Through Junior High School* (Philadelphia: J. B. Lippincott Company, 1959), pp. 34-38.

no books and in which there is no reading. If the home does not furnish a context and background of devotion to ideas, then the school can do very little."[13]

It is clear that meaningful and dynamic relationships between the junior high school and the home, the teacher and the parent, are essential to all attempts to guide the early adolescent in the development of human dignity and the knowledge of the worth of the individual. If these concepts are not evidenced in the home it is hard to develop them adequately in the school.

There is a relation between juvenile delinquency and home environment, although the home cannot be charged with full responsibility for our delinquency problems, as will be pointed out later. Juvenile delinquency has increased nearly 100 per cent in the United States since World War II, and its highest incidence is generally reported in depressed rural areas and the slums of our cities, where there is a large proportion of deprived families, with many children, often broken homes, bad parental relations, and neglected children.[14]

When parents become delinquent in assuming the caretaking responsibilities of their children, whether through neglect, ignorance, or because of substandard homes in lower socioeconomic families, it is important that the school — through its teachers, particularly, and other staff, such as counselors and social workers — contact and work with parents. This obligation is becoming increasingly important in homes where the physical conditions of living are normal or above, but distance from work and the demands of office and professional life require the father to be away from home much of the day, sometimes for extended periods. The seriousness of this situation is being intensified further by the fact that more and more married women are being employed in the market place. Often they leave home for work before the children are off to school and return home long after the children assumedly have gotten back from school. These problems may rapidly be passing beyond the reach of solution on a limited teacher–parent basis. The crisis of the disintegrating home, whatever the cause, particularly at the formative elementary and junior high school periods, is extremely grave, as is pointed out by Remmers and Radler:

> It seems clear that the attitudes of the American teenager, to a very great extent, are the attitudes of the American adult. Apparently the real foundation for citizenship must be laid at an early age in the home. Formal education does contribute substantially, of course, and, as we have seen, students reflect both their education and the attitudes of their teachers. But the true wellspring of an integrated, healthy and happy personality lies within the walls — large or small,

[13] Max Lerner, "One of the Sacred Cows," *Addresses and Proceedings,* National Education Association, 1958, p. 52-62.

[14] For vivid details of this problem as it relates to the school and home see Conant, *op. cit.,* pp. 23-27.

many or few, bare, painted or tapestried — of the teenager's home. "Home is where the heart is" — and the heart, of course, is the figurative seat of the feelings and attitudes which determine so largely the kind of man or woman the teenager will become.[15]

Much of the difficulty experienced with youth in school can be ameliorated through intelligent cooperation between teacher and parent. While many troubles seem to develop in school, often they can be greatly decreased or overcome with the help of sympathetic parents who back up the work of the school and classroom. Sometimes parents are unaware of the nature of these problems or even of the existence of problems their children may be having in school. Most parents are eager to see their children make a success of their school experiences and are ready to provide substantial encouragement when they understand what the problems are and what specifically might be done to improve the situation. Frequently the student needs only to sense the parental support of the school and teacher to adopt a more responsive, cooperative attitude toward the teacher.

Even more often the teacher needs to understand the attitudes of the parent or the conditions in the home to appreciate the difficulties of the pupil and how best to help him. As class schedules now operate, the teacher in the junior high school usually conducts five to six classes a day, each attended by 25 to 35 pupils and sometimes more — a total of 125 to 200 or more pupils daily. It is futile to think that under these circumstances each student will receive the personal attention he deserves, or to expect the teacher to make frequent visits to the home to find out what makes George tick as he does in school, or to seek the parents' cooperation in the solution of their son's problems. Yet the enterprising, conscientious teacher can do much to elicit parental cooperation.

Three major changes are taking place in the junior high school today that encourage and facilitate possible teacher–parent understanding and cooperation. The first is the rapid shifting to block-time organization of the class schedule. This makes possible a reduction in the number of youth for whom each teacher is daily responsible to a normal sixty to seventy. Thus each teacher can have sufficient daily association with his pupils to become reasonably well acquainted with them and their problems, and there will be greater opportunity to establish that rapport so essential to teacher–pupil mutual confidence and understanding. It is much more reasonable to expect the teacher to become better acquainted with the parents and the home conditions that may be at the source of many of the learning and personality problems of the pupil. The teacher has more time and incentive to seek parental cooperation and counsel, as well as the time and inclination to respond to the approach of

[15] From *The American Teenager* by H. H. Remmers and D. H. Radler, copyright © 1957 by H. H. Remmers, reprinted by permission of the publishers, The Bobbs-Merrill Company, Inc. P. 250.

troubled parents. In the block-time and core curriculum organization another valuable asset is the growing practice of keeping teacher and pupil together in classes for a year or more.

The second change that is rapidly being accepted is the introduction of school reports to parents which evaluate personal-social behavioral growth as well as academic achievement, and all in relation to what the teacher considers the potentials of each student. This makes possible a better comprehension on the part of the parents of the total educational progress of their child. Such an evaluative report to parents, supplemented as it is increasingly with a teacher–parent conference to discuss its implications, provides an invaluable basis for teacher–parent understanding, and, where remedial work is suggested, an excellent opportunity for planning whatever cooperative action the situation warrants.

The third change may at first appear not to be a particular innovation of the junior high school, for the National Congress of Parents and Teachers has been in existence since before the turn of the century. However, it has been hitting its stride as an important medium of teacher–parent cooperation at the same time the junior high school has been emerging as an important educational organization. The National Congress of Parents and Teachers is increasingly being recognized as an organization of tremendous potential in a period of the school life of the early adolescent where cooperative effort by parent and school, represented predominantly by the teacher, is of strategic importance. It is at this point that the developing adolescent becomes such a source of bewilderment and worry to his parents and a problem to the school. An organization designed to bring parents and teachers together can make a big contribution to both home and school as its members explore and consider together common problems. This organization has been accepted increasingly in recent years as an invaluable adjunct to the junior high school.[16]

Administrator–community relationship

It is clear that many problems of the school and home are beyond the province of the teacher and pupil or teacher and parents, as isolated units, to settle. These problems become the concern of the total school and community together. In the smaller school district the superintendent normally accepts this educational leadership.

As school districts become larger it is necessary for the principal to assume more leadership responsibility for his local school community. There are many conspicuous examples of dynamic, educationally alert principals who have accepted the challenge for educational leadership within their communities. They have been particularly noticeable in the rapidly developing

[16] For an extended discussion of the ways in which parents and teachers may work together see Ernest Osborne, *The Parent–Teacher Partnership* (New York: Bureau of Publications, Teachers College, Columbia University, 1959).

junior high school movement where efforts have been made with some sense of realism to fit the general school program to the needs of early adolescents and to the needs of the adults of the community, and through the cooperative efforts of school and community to raise the level of home and community living.

One such junior high school principal reported that in the early fall meeting of the principals of nearly a dozen junior high schools of the city, in which his was second largest in enrollment, several schools reported over forty juvenile court cases from each of their student bodies and one school reported eighty-one, while his own school had but one. This in spite of the fact that his school was in a middle- to lower-class community, economically and socially speaking, and further, that this principal had made it a practice to take into his school disciplinary cases from other parts of the city. His school, however, was noted for its effort to provide a curriculum and atmosphere challenging to the students and appropriate to the needs of the community. His rapport with his community was such that later, when the city district adopted a policy of discouraging individual schools from making innovations in their school programs, his community overwhelmingly supported him.

One of the authors was visiting in a junior high school of a metropolitan center which had received national attention for its unique school program in a community of low economic level. While visiting classes and special projects with the principal, who escorted him around the building, the visitor chanced to remark as they moved from floor to floor and corridor to corridor that he was intrigued by the absence of any evidence of policing, referring to the customary school practice of corridor monitors. The principal misunderstood the reference to policing to mean police, and quickly replied: "No, we do not use police here. We depend upon a challenging educational program to engage the serious interest of our students, but I can take you to junior high schools in this city where police are used to keep order."

It is the responsibility of the administrative leaders to see that equality of educational opportunity and adequate modern school facilities and staff are available to the community. It is he who represents the community with the larger school district offices in behalf of such equality of facilities and staff. For it is in part the negative influence of inadequate and unattractive school facilities that militates against even the best of programs, although poor programs are likely to accompany poor physical conditions. The Educational Policies Commission has pointed up this problem quite clearly:

> Thus, in working with disadvantaged children, the school is itself handicapped by home and community conditions and often by its very inheritance of a traditional concept of schooling. There are notable exceptions, but in many communities the problems are grave. Rates of absenteeism, failure, and dropouts are frequently high, achievement low, and classroom response is inadequate. Classes tend to be large, and half-day sessions are common. Staff and

student turnover is often high and morale low. The often-obsolete school buildings are costly to maintain; yet they tend to be unattractive and to lack necessary teaching facilities.[17]

It is the principal who must see the schools as the major asset of the community and the community as the tangible living curriculum resource of the instructional program of the school. It is his responsibility to help his community see the school as its personal and community asset, and to encourage his staff to utilize the rich resources of the community as a means of giving the curriculum meaning and vitality. As he becomes involved in the life of the community he wisely encourages the school staff to become involved also as a means of better understanding the community and the children whom they teach. As the leader of a small community school was discussing with his staff a young adolescent boy who had become a school problem, he remarked, "Have any of you teachers ever been in this boy's home?" He then went on to describe vividly but sympathetically the conditions he had found on several visits. "If you would visit his home and his parents I think you would appreciate more fully the boy's background, his personal problems, and what our educational problem with him is," he said. It was at this meeting that the teachers volunteered as a staff to set a minimum goal of a visitation to each student's home each semester.

The principal has the responsibility of gaining the confidence of the community and, with the cooperation of his staff, leading the community to a higher quality of living and an understanding, loyal support of the educational forces of the community. The possibilities for far-reaching educational leadership are almost limitless to the intelligent, educationally alert, community-minded school administrator. And unless he provides such leadership there is strong likelihood the community will have little or none.

4. *What is the school–community educational task?*

Community resources for student use

There are two major approaches to the use of community resources. The first represents the myriad ways in which the community serves as a medium or environment for the learning experiences of its students. The second involves the cooperation of the citizenry in the determination and furtherance of policies and plans for the educational life of the community.

The wealth of opportunity offered in the assets of the community for practical or vivid learning experiences will vary, of course, in terms of the richness

[17] Educational Policies Commission, National Education Association, *Education and the Disadvantaged American* (Washington: The Association, 1962), p. 13.

and complexity of the community itself. Some of the most common community resources schools have found helpful are suggested here briefly.

Utilizing people in the community. Possibly one of the richest sources the school has available is the large pool of people of varied backgrounds of experience and education within the average community. They can vivify the cold facts of much of the recent history narrated in textbooks. In a world that is changing rapidly history is made quickly, and many in the community normally have lived through periods of important events such as our two world wars, the first use of the atomic bomb, the emergence of Russia and China as communist nations. People who have visited other countries of the world can make them and their peoples live. Often they have valuable collections of film or colored slides portraying various facets of their life and customs. Many immigrants possess heirlooms and bric-a-brac from their native countries which they are proud to show.

In a class the question of who were Americans and what constituted an American arose. Instead of settling the question in typical academic fashion, a show of hands revealed that most of the class were only a generation or two removed from some other land. The teacher suggested that each one bring to class a graph of his ancestry for at least three generations if possible and in the meanwhile try to figure out what varied national strains flowed in his veins and in what ratio. This led to a charting on the board of the nationalities from which each was a descendant, and to what degree. Ultimately the contribution of each country to the culture of America was considered; prized heirlooms from other countries were displayed; stories of life in the "old country" were elicited from parents and grandparents; and friends from other countries visited the class to describe life in their homeland as only those so experienced could.

Does the class want to know more about a profession or a vocation — have intimate sidelights on the personal experiences, life, and activities associated with being a doctor, a lawyer, an engineer, a plane pilot, or a politician? The study of these occupations is made real and meaningful when persons engaged in them speak to the class and answer the eager questions of boys and girls exploring vocational possibilities.

Field trips. What has been said above can be carried out in reverse. All the personalities suggested as possible speakers or visitors to the class can be seen in their homes or places of business, sometimes to advantage. Things not conveniently moved, or not possible to bring to class, can be seen where they are. And sometimes the situation appears much different when seen in the working environment, let us say, of a vocation or business. While persons can frequently find it possible and pleasurable to meet with an eager class, there are factories, and governmental, social, civic, and historical places that require the class to come to them. Wide-awake schools have ready inventories of things in the community that it may be desirable for classes, groups, or individual students to visit. A typical listing of the resources available in the immediate community of the school and in the larger city environs is one prepared for the common-learnings classes in a junior high school in Kansas City, Missouri, of which one of the authors was principal. These sources were suggested as usually most appropriate for the grade noted:

Grade Seven

City market in a study of fresh vegetables and foods, and where they were grown.
Nelson-Atkins Art Gallery for "Early American Tour."
Kansas City Museum planetarium and exhibits of Indian and pioneer ways of living in America.
General Post Office during the historical study of American postal system.
A tour of thirteen significant places in the Battle of Westport, one of the decisive battles of the Civil War, where Kansas City, Missouri, is now located.
The Science Fair of Greater Kansas City, Missouri.
Public Housing project in the neighborhood of the school.
Kansas City Star in a study of the growth and development of newspapers in America.

Grade Eight

Kansas City Power and Light Company, Light Institute.
Southwest Bell Telephone Company, a study of communication.
Ford or Buick, Oldsmobile, and Pontiac assembly plants as an example of American industry.
Municipal Airport, a unit of transportation.
Weather Bureau, a governmental unit of service.
Liberty Memorial Building of World War II, a social studies-English unit.
Science Fair of Greater Kansas City, Missouri, exhibits of projects in mathematics and science.
Nelson-Atkins Art Gallery, modern American art.
The Office of Election Commission, to learn how to register and vote by use of voting machines.

Grade Nine

Truman Library, a study of the executive department of the federal government.
Police Department, a unit in the prevention of crime.
Circuit Court in session, including a case of trial by jury.
County Court and City Council meetings.
Power and Light Plant, a study of public utility.
Flood control by the federal and state governments.
Water Plant of Kansas City, Missouri.[18]

[18] Roscoe V. Cramer, principal, West Junior High School, Kansas City, Mo.

Community studies — improvement projects. A unique community study made by students of West Junior High School, Kansas City, Missouri, arose as a result of the city's publication of a monthly bulletin, *The City Pulse.* Each month throughout the year it gave the number of youths under age sixteen who were arrested in all the junior and senior high schools of the city and the causes of the arrest. In each grade of the West Junior High School the students accepted the proposition to try and reduce sharply the number of arrests of youths in their school district. This project was carried on from 1950 to 1958 while the monthly bulletin was published. The annual report for 1958 of *The City Pulse* revealed that there had been a 60 per cent reduction in the number of arrests of early youth in this junior high school district — an interesting commentary on what a school group can do when committed to a specific project of their own for community betterment.

In a small community with a junior-senior high school staff alert to community problems, the class in science was studying the topic of communicable diseases. It became aroused over the fact that there was a constant recurrence of typhoid fever in the community. The class decided to try to discover the cause. Studying what the nature of the disease was and how it was spread, they were led to suspect that it might be spread through the water supply of the community homes which were supplied from open wells. The students learned how to take samples of water in germ-free containers. Two samples were taken and labeled for each well in the community, one for their own laboratory analysis and the other to be sent to the state board of health for confirmation analysis. Their analysis, confirmed by the state board of health, revealed that 60 per cent of the wells were contaminated with typhoid bacteria.

The class then sought the likely sources of contamination. They found that in communities with open wells it most often was caused by the proximity of barns, cesspools, or outhouses to the wells and their draining into them. Investigation showed that this was the most probable cause of well water contamination.

The class next asked, "What have communities with such a situation done about it?" The most successful means of correcting the difficulty, it turned out, was to establish either a community water system or a sewer system, and to have both was the surest way to safeguard the public health.

At this point the class was not ready to stop. They investigated the relative merits and costs of the alternative solutions, for it became clear that the economically underprivileged community could not construct both a water and a sewer system. A water system was the better of the two solutions to their problem, so the class undertook to establish the approximate cost of a water system. By this time others could be enlisted in the study where technical aid was necessary. The class surveyed, estimated the cost of laying water mains, pipes, a well, etc. Armed with the facts of their study they met with the village council and sold them on the project. Now that village has a water system, and typhoid fever has become a dimming memory.

A much different type of a project utilizing the facilities of the community to make an exploration guidance course more meaningful and functional was conducted in the Washington Irving Junior High School in Tarrytown, New York. In order to assist what the school recognized as the disadvantaged student, the guidance and shop classes were incorporated into one specially designed course, the "Discovery Course," composed of boys and girls under the direction of a teacher with training in both guidance and industrial arts. Block-of-time or double-class periods were scheduled in the afternoon for these disadvantaged students. Such scheduling permitted the completion of projects or field trips without conflicting with other school activities. The "Discovery Course," utilizing real life situations in the community, is described briefly by Louis Bender, the principal, and William Sharpe, the guidance director:

> All of the teachers working with this group, whether teachers of academic subjects or of the special subjects, work as a cooperating group assisting the Discovery Course teacher. Time is provided for them to plan and coordinate units of study. Thus an integrated approach toward concrete experiences is achieved when the Discovery teacher, assured the students are being introduced to concepts by cooperating teachers, exposes the group to practical problems of measurement, communication, etc., as faced in the world of work.
>
> The course has been designed around units of study especially selected to include job opportunities of the Tarrytowns' area. The present plan includes visits or field trips to make concrete in the minds of the students the types of employment which are being studied. After such a visit, the students return to the shop and then seek to perform some of the job functions which were observed.
>
> An illustration of such a unit might be the decision of the teacher to study assembly line technique. An assembly line was visited and analysis of the different kinds of operations was studied and observed by the students so that, upon their return, they could establish an assembly line of their own for the actual construction of some project. In this case, it was metal ash trays and serving trays. Each operation of the assembly technique was directly experienced by each of the students in the class and a practical, concrete, rather than abstract concept was thereby gained.
>
> The group is a co-ed group, small in size, and operates within a framework sufficiently flexible to permit both male and female job characteristics to be taken advantage of by a single teacher. One of the major requirements for such a course, in addition to constant coordination, is the opportunity for the teacher to adjust or modify his program as he sees fit.[19]

[19] Louis W. Bender and William C. Sharpe, "A Junior High School Course for Disadvantaged Students." Reprinted by permission from *The Bulletin of the National Association of Secondary-School Principals,* March, 1963. Copyright: Washington, D.C. Pp. 129-130.

Another reason for scheduling the course for an afternoon double class period is that it is most impractical to expect to maintain the traditional fifty-minute class schedule and use extensively the community resources that cannot be brought to the classroom. And although important fixed resources cannot be visited in a fifty-minute period, to use more than the regular class period can lead only to confusion for students in their class schedules and to ill will among teachers. This is one of the reasons why so many junior high schools have moved to the long block-time period, now averaging two and a half hours, and some are shifting to a half-day period.

The educationally alert principal and staff of a large city junior high school with a core curriculum naturally considered the use of community resources an educational *must*. This staff was so concerned to equalize the use of all forms of away-from-school community resources that core teachers, on extended block-of-time schedules, alternated every other day from morning to afternoon and vice versa. The assumption was that some community resources could be used to advantage in the morning and some were better used in the afternoon. The extensive use of fixed community resources will necessitate a radical change in the schedule organization of many junior high schools.

Community resources for the school

An important area of profitable community–school interaction involves an identification of the adults who can help the school serve the community in more effective ways.

In many places the principal of the school, or in a small system the superintendent, has been able to secure a cross section of the leadership of the community to work on an educational advisory committee with representatives of the teaching staff. Some of these committees have given yeoman service in painstakingly analyzing the needs of the community youth and adults and making sound recommendations for curriculum improvement or school services.

In one community such a committee became concerned with the out-of-school recreational and entertainment facilities. The American Association of University Women volunteered to be responsible for much of the detail of a study the committee felt necessary of what actually was available for youth when out of school besides the movies, which in general were not of a high cultural quality. Careful study of community resources revealed that not a single public tennis court existed in the town. Committee discussion led to the project of developing a teen-age canteen. Again the AAUW offered to investigate possible facilities which in the beginning might be rented and furnished. No desirable place seemed available, when someone on the staff mentioned the fact that much of the basement and the whole area under the auditorium of the junior-senior high school was excavated but not completely finished. The school board found some money it could use and the American

Legion post offered a gift of nearly two thousand dollars toward the project. With the assistance of other public-spirited groups rooms were finished off for various types of activities; a snack bar, juke box, recreational games and reading material were added; and with the cooperation of community and teacher volunteers for supervision services, the teen-age canteen was opened six nights a week.

In still another town a citizens committee of twenty-five members representing six geographical divisions of the community was secured. It met at the beginning of the school year to consider what might be done. In cooperation with representatives of the school the committee members made careful studies of the curriculum and finally concluded that the school was neglecting the important matter of family living. They recommended that adolescents should receive thorough instruction in matters of sex and the larger problems of family and home, and went so far as to outline certain broad areas of the subject they felt should receive attention in the school.

In many respects this is one of the most useful types of committees the administrator can have assisting him. It is flexible and adaptable to his needs. The curriculum is always in need of adjustment to keep abreast of changing conditions. Particularly to be of utmost service to the community, the educational program should be constantly studied by members of the community and the staff. As has been well said, "Any school system, especially any program of instruction, that gets too far ahead of its community is due for violent reaction. Any school that gets too far behind its community is due for revolt."[20]

In another community the junior high school principal was instrumental in getting a Community Council organized composed of some forty of the influential town leaders. This group, sparked by the dynamic personality of the principal, in numerous ways contributed to the needs of the school, provided library and recreational facilities, and made possible medical clinic services to the children and youth of this underprivileged community.

A problem that is receiving increased public attention and promises to reach major proportions in the future concerns the formulation of a master plan whereby youth can be identified in some vital way with the life of the community. To involve youth of both the junior and senior high school years will require the utmost cooperation and planning by the leadership of the community and of the school. It must be essentially a community-wide responsibility. There has been an awareness for several years that those of adolescent years were in a real sense disfranchised, with no vital place in the life scheme of the community. The situation has been rather startlingly described by Patterson:

[20] American Association of School Administrators, *op. cit.*, p. 99.

> In a certain sense, American youth today are exiles, and they know it. We adults have been remarkably successful in excluding youth from roles that are significant and necessary in their immediate context. Increasingly, we have placed youth in a social vacuum with nothing to measure themselves against except standardized academic achievement scores and peer standards that are evoked by advertising, consumer persuasion, and the disc jockey. The chief remaining roles for youth are those of passive students, consumers, dependents, and bored observers of the adult rat race.
>
> Identity is familiar to us as an essential quest of adolescence. But the quest for identity now is increasingly stalled for many adolescents and carried over unfulfilled into adulthood. . . . The questions of adolescence, the really crucial ones that begin to be asked in the junior high school years — "Who am I?" "Where am I going?" "What is the meaning of life?" — become harder and harder to answer in ways that are stable, satisfying, and socially constructive.[21]

This same problem is receiving serious attention at the national level. The *NASSP Spotlight* for November-December, 1963, comes to my desk as this is written. It is burdened by the same problem of a disfranchised youth. The issue opens with the statement "A million youngsters have no useful place in our country. They have nothing to do; they are going nowhere."[22] And it is pointed out that by 1970 there will be approximately two million in this category. And this is not the complete picture, for it is estimated that by 1970 there will be possibly 7.5 million dropouts added. These represent the exiles Patterson refers to who have been unable to adjust to the school situations and have quit school. In a later paragraph the finger is placed on the issue of disfranchisement as a major problem faced by our society and the schools:

> But jobs are only one element. There is the deadly disease called alienation, which Havinghurst and others estimate to be gnawing at the heart of 15 percent — even 40-50 percent in some schools. It is a dreadful thing to be walled off from the grown-up world just when one should be busily growing into it. Our society is a hard one to grow into — maybe the hardest in all history. It lacks easy gradients into the world of work and the whole of adult life. Adolescence craves significance and responsibility, and we offer only childhood. So delinquency and crime keep rising year by year — even in "good" neighborhoods and rural areas; so adolescents "clam up," form their private subculture, model on one another instead of real adults, and join a formless rebellion against the world they yearn to join.[23]

[21] Franklin Patterson, "The Adolescent Citizen and the Junior High School." Reprinted by permission from *The Bulletin of the National Association of Secondary-School Principals,* May, 1962. Copyright: Washington, D.C. Pp. 69-79.

[22] *NASSP Spotlight on Junior and Senior High Schools,* published by the National Association of Secondary-School Principals, Washington, No. 60, November-December, 1963, p. 1.

[23] *Ibid.*

Not a pleasant picture, but one that must be accepted. Steps should be taken immediately to correct it. The start must be made at the point where adolescence begins — the junior high school. It involves some realistic, cooperative planning on the part of the school and the community to bring the adolescent into a place where he is identified as an integral part of the community with responsibilities and recognition commensurate with his maturity and talents.

There are many community services of real value which adolescents can render, and which can give them a sense of belonging and worth-while achievement. For example, it has been pointed out that in Boston 194 high schools provided 3600 student volunteers who gave a total of 386,000 hours of service to 84 Red Feather welfare agencies in one season.[24] Projects of civic improvement and responsibilities of a continuous nature can be given over to adolescents to perform, and others should be developed that will contribute to a better standard of community living at relatively little extra cost and provide a valuable contribution to citizenship responsibility.

School service to adults

Thus far concern has been expressed for the education of the early adolescent as a school–community obligation. In addition, the school carries a major area of responsibility for the adults of the community. In recent years this has become an important part of the school's service to its public.

With the rapidly changing nature of society and the accelerated growth in knowledge and skills as well as their rapid obsolescence, people have become concerned with ways and means of keeping up to date. Then there are those, now millions of them, who are eager to make up as far as possible for deficiencies in their education. The junior high school becomes a natural center for classes for these community residents with their varied needs.

At first the schools offered lectures and study group facilities to select adult groups, who frequently provided their own leaders from among the competent people in the community, even paying for light, heat, and supplies. Gradually, however, the school became cognizant of what it is — a community institution definitely answerable to its adults as well as its children. Tax money has been provided for the support of the program, and responsibility assumed for teachers or specialists where needed. Schools are open evenings as the demand warrants. Increasingly community schools stay open from possibly 8:30 A.M. to 10:00 P.M. The day session is for the youth, and at four o'clock or later the school shifts to its evening staff.

The second session usually centers around the particular interests of those who attend and is quite flexible. Many desire to make up regular school de-

[24] Franklin Patterson, "High Schools for a Free Society," a mimeographed report of proceedings, Twentieth Annual Convention, National School Boards Association, Chicago, 1960.

ficiencies, others to perfect skills or replace those now obsolete; some wish to acquire hobbies or avocational skills while still others are concerned with cultural lectures, formal courses, or individual or small-group projects. Often arrangements are made for the offering of extension courses in connection with the evening classes. A single evening at a junior high community center might involve the following offerings:

Arts and crafts
Furniture refinishing
Home interior decorating
Typing for personal use
Woodworking
Ceramics
Knitting and needlecraft
Photography
Shorthand
Study of contemporary Russia,
China, or some other part of the world
Spanish conversation
Newer developments in science
Regular academic courses as desired

A tremendous development in adult education lies in the future. What has been described represents the pioneering efforts in this direction. Future adults will continue to utilize in varying degrees the adult education program provided for the community through the school.

5. *What is a community school?*

Thus far the terms "community," "school and community," even "community school" have been used interchangeably to refer to the relation of the school to the functional group it serves. In this chapter reference has mostly been to the junior high school and the homes and persons most influenced by it. Throughout this book our concern has been basically with the junior high school as an institution, and as a center for community life the junior high school is superior to either the elementary or the senior high school. One is too small and the other normally covers too wide a physical area for people to feel any cohesion of interest — or it involves too many diverse group (community) interests which further dissipates what common feeling might otherwise be present. Books have been written in an attempt to define the community, and sociologists have gradations of communities that often pass beyond a political unit to involve state or larger area limits. Possibly a sufficient concept of the community for our purposes is set forth in the following seven characteristics:

1. A population aggregate.
2. Inhabiting a delimitable contiguous area.
3. Sharing a historic heritage.
4. Possessing a set of basic service institutions.
5. Participating in a common mode of life.
6. Conscious of its unity.
7. Able to act in a corporate way.[25]

If this somewhat general concept of the community is accepted, then the community school might be characterized as one enmeshed in the life of the community it serves, utilizing resources of the community for the enrichment of the community's youth and also to serve the adult members of the community.

Many definitions and lists of characteristics of the community school have been developed over the past three decades. A list given by one who has been a recognized leader in the community school movement may provide the perspective needed:

1. The Community School Improves the Quality of Living Here and Now.
2. The Community School Uses the Community as a Laboratory for Learning.
3. The Community School Makes the School Plant a Community Center.
4. The Community School Organizes the Curriculum Around the Fundamental Processes and Problems of Living.
5. The Community School Includes Lay People in School Policy and Program Planning.
6. The Community School Leads in Community Coordination.
7. The Community School Practices and Promotes Democracy in All Human Relationships.[26]

It should be clear that all that has been discussed in this chapter has pointed to the community school. When the community is used by the school and the school by the community in a cooperative effort to make the school serve the community in the most effective way possible, it will represent the community at its best and will fulfill its highest obligation to it and to society at large. Possibly the values of the community school have been spelled out most clearly by McCluskey in these eight propositions:

Proposition One: The community school is a demonstration of the law of increasing returns.

Proposition Two: Increased use of facilities by the community school leads to better support of the school by the community.

[25] Lloyd A. Cook and Elaine F. Cook, *A Sociological Approach to Education* (New York: McGraw-Hill Book Co., Inc., 1950), pp. 48-49.

[26] Edward G. Olsen *et al., School and Community,* Second Edition. © 1954, by permission of Prentice-Hall, Inc., Englewood Cliffs, N.J. Pp. 14-18.

Proposition Three: The community school is an agent of cohesiveness in both the neighborhood and the larger community.

Proposition Four: The community school may be a center for the assessment and management, if not solution, of problems unique to the neighborhood in which the school is located.

Proposition Five: The community school is a major and indispensable characteristic of the educative community.

Proposition Six: The community school helps create a set of common values which contribute to the intellectual and spiritual health of the community.

Proposition Seven: The community school is an educational ideal greatly respected by many other nations and, because of this fact, gives the U.S.A. a basis of meaningful communication with people and their leaders in different sections of the world.

Proposition Eight: The educative community is the ultimate test of the validity of American ideals. Democracy must be a living reality in the home community where people have most of their primary experience.[27]

SELECTED BIBLIOGRAPHY

American Association of School Administrators, National Education Association. *The Superintendent as Instructional Leader.* Thirty-Fifth Yearbook. Washington: The Association, 1957.

Bell, Robert R., ed. *The Sociology of Education: A Sourcebook.* Homewood, Ill.: The Dorsey Press, 1962.

Bossing, Nelson L. *Principles of Secondary Education.* Englewood Cliffs, N.J.: Prentice-Hall, Inc., 2nd ed., 1955. Chap. 16, "How to Develop the Community School?"

Campbell, Roald F., and John A. Ramseyer. *The Dynamics of School–Community Relationships.* Boston: Allyn and Bacon, Inc., 1955.

Conant, James B. *Slums and Suburbs: A Commentary on Schools in Metropolitan Areas.* New York: McGraw-Hill Book Co., Inc., 1961.

Counts, George. "Social Understanding for Survival," *Educational Leadership,* 18:485-488, May, 1961.

Cramer, Roscoe V. "What Educational Program Is Needed in the Junior High School?" *The Bulletin of the National Association of Secondary-School Principals,* 39:324-330, April, 1955.

——— and Otto E. Domian. *Administration and Supervision in the Elementary School.* New York: Harper & Brothers, 1960.

Douglass, Harl R. *Modern Administration of Secondary Schools: Organization and Administration of Junior and Senior High Schools.* Boston: Ginn & Company, 2nd ed., 1963. Chap. 23, "Community and Public Relations."

[27] Howard Y. McCluskey, "Some Propositions in Support of the Community School — A Summary," *Journal of Educational Sociology,* 23:179-83, December, 1959.

Educational Policies Commission, National Education Association. *Strengthening Community Life: Schools Can Help.* Washington: The Association, 1954.

———. *Education and the Disadvantaged American.* Washington: The Association, 1962.

Gross, C. H., S. P. Wronski, and J. W. Hanson. *School and Society: Readings in the Social and Philosophical Foundations of Education.* Boston: D. C. Heath & Company, 1962.

Havighurst, Robert J. "Do Junior High School Youth Grow Too Fast?" *The Bulletin of the National Association of Secondary-School Principals,* 47:161, April, 1963.

———, and Bernice L. Neugarten. *Society and Education.* Boston: Allyn and Bacon, Inc., 2nd ed., 1962.

Johnson, Eric W. *How to Live Through Junior High School.* Philadelphia: J. B. Lippincott Company, 1959. (This book is written for parents.)

Lonsdale, Richard C. *The School's Role in Metropolitan Area Development.* Syracuse, N.Y.: Syracuse University Press, 1960.

McCluskey, Howard Y. "Some Propositions in Support of the Community School — A Summary," *Journal of Educational Sociology,* 23:179-183, December, 1959.

Norberg, H. O., J. M. Bradfield, and W. C. Odell. *Secondary School Teaching.* New York: The Macmillan Company, 1962. Chap. 17, "Working with Parents and the Community."

Nutting, Willis D. *Schools and the Means of Education.* Notre Dame, Ind.: Fides Publishers Association, 1959.

Olsen, Edward G. "Is the Community School Anti-Intellectual?" *The School Executive,* 78:23-25, October, 1958.

———, ed. *The School and Community Reader: Education in Perspective.* New York: The Macmillan Company, 1963.

Osborne, Ernest. *The Parent-Teacher Partnership.* New York: Bureau of Publications, Teachers College, Columbia University, 1959.

Patterson, Franklin. "The Adolescent Citizen and the Junior High School," *The Bulletin of the National Association of Secondary-School Principals,* 46:68-79, May, 1962.

Pounds, Ralph L., and James R. Bryner. *The School in American Society.* New York: The Macmillan Company, 1959.

Remmers, H. H., and D. H. Radler. *The American Teenager.* Indianapolis: The Bobbs-Merrill Company, Inc., 1962. Chaps. 1-2.

Rodehaver, M. W., W. B. Axtell, and R. E. Gross. *The Sociology of the School.* New York: Thomas Y. Crowell Company, 1957.

"Settle Problems Together," *Parent-Teacher Manual.* Washington: National Congress of Parents and Teachers, 1960.

Thelen, Herbert A. *Education and the Human Quest.* New York: Harper & Brothers, 1960.

17

Evaluation of the Program

1. What is evaluation?

For many years books that were devoted to ways and means of determining the extent to which anything existed carried the word "measurement" in their title in some form — *Measurement of Achievement, Measurement of Intelligence* — depending upon what was being measured. A popular quotation from a pioneer measurement specialist reads, "Whatever exists exists in some degree, and whatever exists in some degree can be measured."

In the past educational measurement usually centered in efforts to discover the degree of intelligence possessed or to create tests that would give some idea of the schoolroom achievement of pupils. Since in the early decades of this century relatively little was known about the complex nature of the learning process, most tests were devised to measure the most obvious things. Achievement of classroom-taught knowledge and skills was most in evidence and most easily determined. Even this could be measured only in its simpler forms. Measurement consequently became concerned primarily with the extent of the memorization of quantities of factual information.

This procedure harmonized well with the dominant psychological concept that mental activity consisted of storing in the brain, thought to be a non-leakable container, encyclopedic quantities of factual material. It led most naturally to the concept of the curriculum as a compendium of facts classified by subject, and to a limiting stratification of curricular content. It led naturally, too, to the nation-wide practice during the forepart of this century of using state-devised examinations for all public schools, the examinations being almost exclusively factual in nature and based upon state-adopted textbooks.

Thus interpretation of the results of measurement was simple and relatively superficial. As our knowledge of the learner and the learning process has changed and has become more complex, both measurement and the interpretation of its results have become more difficult. Too, the growing variety and complexity of the problems of education have made vastly complicated the nature of measurement and emphasized the need for techniques that help us understand the less tangible and objective facets of education.

Concept of evaluation

There has been a definite movement toward the use of a term that combines all the subtle nuances that now surround the concepts of measurement and interpretation, possibly with greater focus upon the significance of interpretation as its implications have broadened. As one glances at the titles of articles classified in *The Education Index* it is commonplace to read titles such as "Evaluating Pupil Progress," "Evaluation of the Schools' Facilities," "Conference Objectives: Prelude to Evaluation," "How to Analyze and Evaluate Educational Objectives'; titles of publications on the author's desk as he writes are *Evaluation Criteria, Criteria for Evaluating Junior High Schools, Measurement and Evaluation for the Secondary School Teacher*.

It is clear from these widely varying titles that the term "evaluation" is comprehensive in meaning and usually implies the inclusion of measurement techniques. *Evaluation is the process of determining the extent to which given purposes, goals, or standards have been or are being attained.* This definition shows that the term "evaluation" has many facets, but they all focus upon a common denominator. One facet may be concerned with the degree in which school sites, buildings and facilities, curriculum, and staff meet the standards set up for them; e.g., "The school site is large enough to provide for all possible future needs." A second facet may relate itself to how closely classroom procedures approach this criterion: "Pupils and teachers together set up the goals and standards that govern their classroom activities." A third facet may focus attention upon the product of learning as involved in these criteria: "The pupils showed marked improvement in the development of problem-solving and investigative skills" or "The minimum standard for passing this course in typewriting is the ability to type at the rate of sixty words a minute with not more than two errors during a five-minute dictation period."

Purposes of evaluation

It has been well said that "The goal of universal and free education in the United States has been achieved, in a large measure, during the last fifty years. This quantity aspect of public education is not likely to be lost. The greatest need in the second half of the twentieth century is for the members of the profession to develop the quality aspect of the educational product."[1] By "quality" is meant the extent to which our education is effective in the realization of its major purposes, the extent to which the junior high school in particular is helping the early adolescent to understand himself and his relationships in, for him, an emerging heterosexually complex world, and to develop those behavior skills essential to a democratic society.

To achieve "quality" education it is necessary not only to evaluate what we are doing in education but to set up clearly the purpose of that evaluation. Many statements of purpose are to be found in the literature of education. We mention some of the more important ones as they apply to the junior high school.

To determine the acceptability of the junior high school program. This involves a careful study of the philosophical and psychological basis of the junior high school program in relation to the total twelve- or fourteen-year public school program. It requires an appraisal of the program in terms of the generally accepted purposes of a modern junior high school. There is always the presumption that if the school program meets desired goals and standards the results will be good, but unless the program is sound in purpose and structure the results are likely to be unsatisfactory. This has been the justification for state departments of education and other educational groups setting up standards.

To determine the effectiveness of the program. It is important to see that the expressed purposes of the junior high school are in harmony with the best educational thinking for this period of early adolescence. But more important, is the program realizing in the school product the goals it professes? It is well known that often there is a wide disparity between professed goals and achievement. The acid test of a program is its product. The degree of success of the program will often not only point up its strengths and weaknesses but suggest the reasons therefor. Where these are not clear it is the function of evaluation to seek the causes for success and failure. It may not be amiss to point out that it is as important to assess the reasons for success as to know why the program has failed.

To determine individual pupil progress. A school program may be rated generally good as judged by its over-all product yet be seriously weak in meeting the individual needs of boys and girls. A school in a community of predominantly superior pupils may show a high average attainment for the school on a set of standardized tests but be very inferior in its diagnosis of and assistance to its weaker pupils. For example, a school with a high average

[1] *The Junior High School Program in Illinois,* Illinois Curriculum Program, Bulletin No. A-1 (Springfield: Office of the Superintendent of Public Instruction, 1961), p. 111.

achievement score for its pupils may have an inadequate remedial reading program or none. Failure to assure adequate pupil growth and progress may be covered up by an abnormally heavy dropout rate.

Each year the evidence of research increases the awareness of the complex nature of individual differences and directs more and more attention to the individual pupil and his rate of educational growth. This book indicates abundantly and clearly the growing emphasis upon the learning problems of each pupil. In recent years there has been a sharp rise in the insistence upon streamlining the curriculum to fit individual needs and upon individualization of classroom methods.

Part of this reaction flows from the lockstep teaching that persists in the schools, with its tendency to produce uniformity rather than diversity in pupils. Probably no one has made this point more clearly and forcibly than Charles W. Eliot did nearly three-quarters of a century ago:

> It has always seemed to me that a teacher who did not discharge his pupils at the end of the year much more unlike in powers and acquisitions than they were at the beginning was a proved failure. We all know that children . . . are not alike, but infinitely different; that the object of education . . . is to develop to the highest possible degree the natural and acquired capacities of each individual.[2]

Any approach to evaluation today must have the determination of the nature and rate of progress of each pupil as a major purpose.

To help the school improve its educational procedure. It is not enough to think of evaluation as a way of determining the success of the school in the attainment of its goals. Evaluation must also reveal to the school ways and means of overcoming its weaknesses and conserving its strengths. As envisioned in the three purposes thus far discussed, evaluation could scarcely take place on a high level of efficiency without at least incidentally providing some implications for procedural improvement in administration as well as in classroom methods. However, evaluation now carries implicitly at least the responsibility of providing leads to the improvement of school procedures where these are obviously at fault.

To provide the basis for reporting pupil progress. Any comprehensive evaluation of the school program should provide much necessary information for such reporting. At the junior high school level these data should be useful (1) for the administrative personnel of the school as it reports to the senior high school what it will need at this stage in the educational guidance of the pupil, and (2) in the needed immediate relationship between school counselor,

[2] Charles W. Eliot, "Undesirable and Desirable Uniformity in Schools," *Proceedings of the National Education Association,* 1892, p. 83.

teacher, and parents. Most parents are no longer satisfied to have a simple letter grade report on the child's school progress. They insist upon a more detailed report on scholastic and social development; they want specific information concerning the reasons for the strengths and weaknesses reported, particularly with reference to the pupil's shortcomings, plus some indication of what the home may do to assist the school at these points.

2. *What are the approaches to evaluation?*

The evaluation of the educational purposes of the school discussed above must encompass the total school impact upon the pupil. This will involve the more tangible aspects of the school situation and the learning product that results from the total influence of this environment upon the learner.

The over-all school approach

Every feature of the school environment that affects the learning situation is to be appraised, from the statement of philosophy and purposes that gives direction to the educational program to the physical environment which implements it. Attention is here directed to the principal features that have been considered in detail in previous chapters.

Statement of philosophy and purposes. In any basic approach to an evaluation of the school itself the point of beginning focuses upon what the school personnel believe about the functions of education in our form of democratic society, and particularly upon the expression of that socio-educational philosophy in a statement of purposes which they believe should characterize the educational goals for this school. The statement of philosophy and purposes should be evidenced in the thinking of all concerned with the school. It should be clear that it has been thought through and cooperatively developed by the administration, the teachers, and the community.

Curriculum. The heart of the school program is the curriculum. It is expected to spell out in practical detail the statement of philosophy and purposes in the content of the educational program. Evaluation will be concerned with the degree to which the curriculum mirrors the school's statement of its philosophy. A critical study of the curriculum will reveal, too, the extent to which the local school understands its own statement of philosophy and purposes. It may indicate quite clearly the situation that exists in many schools where the statement of philosophy has been prepared by the administration or a staff committee and perfunctorily accepted by a faculty, the majority of whom do not understand its implications for the curriculum.

Instructional process. In modern educational thinking curriculum and methods are closely intertwined. A generation ago general textbooks on curriculum seldom if ever discussed methods of instruction. Today it is impossible to find a general curriculum book which does not interrelate content and method. The same is true with books on instructional methods.

Evaluation will of necessity be concerned with the extent to which modern instructional procedures are utilized in the school's classrooms. If the investigation reveals the total or predominant use of the formal lecture or recitation method by the teachers it will matter little how much the avowed educational philosophy reflects advanced educational thinking or how relevant the stated curriculum pattern is to this modern declaration of philosophy. The teaching in that school will be traditional and out of harmony with the stated educational purposes and curriculum professed by the school.

Staff. It has been well said that the effectiveness of the school program depends upon the competency of its staff — not only on the general level of education and professional preparation of each member of the staff but on his particular qualifications for a special type of educational program. It would seriously jeopardize a planned general education type of curriculum or a core curriculum, for instance, where a teacher of extremely broad background or wide range of subject-matter preparation was required, to attempt to staff such a curriculum project with teachers who were traditional, highly specialized subject majors. Through no fault of their own they would be inadequately prepared for the task assigned, and failure would probably be the lot of both teachers and program.

Even more important to a school program is individual or group morale. This can be affected by the assignment of staff members to tasks for which they feel unqualified, as in the theoretical case mentioned in the previous paragraph, or for which they have no sympathy, as where teachers are arbitrarily assigned to teach core even though they disagree with its basic concepts. Usually people are not happy to take on tasks they are not trained for or in which they do not believe. This is particularly the case with teachers. Evaluation must distinguish between success and failure due to staff education or morale or both.

School plant facilities. Too often evaluation has stopped here. Only within relatively recent years has the school plant come to have an important place in the planned success of the educational program.

As the concepts of education have become more complex and the curriculum has been diversified, modifications have been necessary in school building design to care for such major additions as home economics, industrial arts, and physical education. Classrooms designed to accommodate newer ideas of curriculum and method are still slow to catch the public imagination or even that of traditionally educated teachers. The need for a radical change in the size and design of the school library, for instance, which no longer serves basically as the repository of books but is a workshop for the extended and intimate use of students who require a wide range of different types of source materials is slow to be recognized by the public and many teachers.

It was a pioneer book in supervision that seriously advanced the idea that the aesthetic qualities of a classroom had a vital relationship to class morale, class achievement, and class social behavior. A situation was described in which the classrooms of the school were dark, dingy, poorly lighted, and drab. The desks were shabby. There had been a succession of teacher failures largely due to disciplinary problems and unsatisfactory work. Then came a decision to repaint and to some extent refurbish the classrooms. To the surprise of the supervisory staff the atmosphere and morale changed. A bright interior, some flowers, and attractive window curtains seemed to raise the morale of the children and markedly improve their behavior. Teachers now remained. All this was attributed primarily to change in the asethetic environment of the learners.[3]

Evaluation would be wide of the mark and unreliable if the school plant were not considered an important factor in the educational product. We are just beginning to sense the significance of the less obvious aspects of the school plant environment in relation to its pervasive influence upon the educational process.

Community-school relations. Any attempt at a school evaluation that did not take into consideration the important part the community plays in the local school program would be incomplete and inaccurate. Experienced educators know that some schools would not deserve the evaluation they would probably receive on the basis solely of school plant and the other facets of the educational program thus far considered. One community prior to mid-century was known widely and envied for its palatial school plant and elaborate facilities, the superior academic training of its staff, and the quality of its academic curriculum. Those who knew it best, however, were deeply conscious of the gap that existed between the high standard of excellence maintained within the framework of a conventional, unimaginative curriculum and the kind of highly functional curriculum that could have been of immeasurable service to the peculiar needs of the community and its children under dynamic and highly imaginative leadership.

The nature of the community — its racial stocks, its wealth, its cultural level, the concern of its people for education — will have tremendous bearing upon what leadership is provided the school, and what the educational leadership is able to develop in an all-over educational program. No evaluation can be complete that does not take into account the cooperation or lack of it that exists between the community and the school.

[3] See Chapter 14 for further discussion of the effects of aesthetic environment upon the morale and learning experiences of junior high school youth.

The pupil-product approach

While the evaluation of the school environment is essential in appraising educational opportunity, it is necessary constantly to keep in mind that this is but a means to an end. The most important part of any appraisal program concerns what has happened to the learner — what changes have been produced in him.

Academic achievement. Though traditionally considered the key to the success of the educational program, the acquisition of knowledge is still regarded as an important phase of learning. It is recognized by all that one does not think in a vacuum, that facts are essential as the basis of thinking. Other products of learning are now given more emphasis, for which, again, knowledge is accepted as a means to an end and less, as in the past, for its own sake. As progressing in subjects is systematized in most of our schools, evaluation of a pupil's knowledge essential to more advanced study is important for many pupils.

Pupil attitudes and morale. Problems of discipline and *esprit de corps* in the school often arise from the attitudes prevalent in the student body or dominant among key pupil leaders. Low pupil morale can noticeably affect the quality of school relationships in all phases of school life. Some causes of this situation were discussed early in this chapter. Evaluation should consider the effectiveness of the school in creating wholesome pupil personality.

Citizenship-leadership competency. Earlier in this book it was pointed out that education has changed its focus from what one knows to how one acts. Educational objectives are now expressed in terms of behavioral goals. Psychologically it is assumed that one has not truly learned unless knowledge is translated into appropriate behavioral skills. The schools have been shifting their educational emphasis to the development of those behavioral skills essential to effective participation in our democratic society. Evaluation of the school product now scrutinizes the evidence of pupil citizenship as expressed in the normal give-and-take of living within and without the immediate school community. Attention is also given to the extent to which leadership is being developed in the school.

Success of graduates. For practical purposes the evaluation of the success of the school in developing behavioral skills has been confined to the school life of the learner. Many schools now carry on comprehensive follow-up studies of their graduates to evaluate the degree of success they have had in problems of personal adjustment, leadership within and beyond the local community, vocational success, etc. At the junior high school level follow-up will be limited largely to the evidence of citizenship and leadership skills exhibited in the early years of the senior high school.

School retardation and dropouts. A study of the success of a school through its product cannot be complete without an appraisal of its retardation and dropout problem. The problem of dropouts as part of an evaluation of the junior high school is complicated by the fact that compulsory attendance laws in most states compel the attendance of pupils through the junior high school years. Evaluation is further rendered questionable if the effectiveness of education in the junior high school is to be judged mainly by the dropout problem in the senior high school. The serious cleavage in the educational purposes of the two school systems would seem to enhance the dropout rate in the senior high school. Pupils who have been concerned primarily with the business of growing up, reorienting themselves from an elementary school environment with its emphasis upon the needs of childhood to one that stresses the needs of early adolescence, will find it difficult to make the transition to a school markedly different in emphasis and organization. The disparity that generally exists between the two secondary schools is quite likely to create confusion and discouragement and lead to a heavy dropout rate in the senior high school.

It would be difficult to assess the degree of responsibility that belongs to each school. A recent study of the future school intentions of seventh-grade pupils in Oklahoma schools revealed that, of a 66 per cent participation of all seventh-graders, 90 per cent of the boys and 95.3 per cent of the girls expected to complete high school. This would indicate at least a favorable attitude toward school at the beginning of the junior high school.[4] Another report enumerates the personal characteristics most commonly associated with dropouts. While some of these are more likely to manifest themselves at a later time, most of the symptoms are evident in the junior high school period, and some even before. The alert school properly organized and staffed could do something to alleviate a number of the conditions that lead to school withdrawal.[5]

Much of the evidence on retardation and dropouts indicates the slow build-up of retardation; it often begins in the elementary school, gains momentum in the junior high school, and culminates as a dropout in the senior high school. Sometimes the milder types of retardation hold on until the students reach college, where they eventually fall by the wayside. Evaluation has a responsibility to help the junior high school become aware of its potential failures and suggest possible ways of correcting some of the major weaknesses.

[4] Harry J. Parker, "High School Dropout Intentions of Seventh Grade Pupils," *The Bulletin of the National Association of Secondary-School Principals,* 46:119-121, October, 1962.

[5] Among other sources see Russell N. Cassel and Jack C. Coleman, "A Critical Examination of the School Dropout, Reluctant Learner, and Abler Non-College Student Problem," *The Bulletin of the National Association of Secondary-School Principals,* 46:60-65, November, 1962.

3. *Who evaluates?*

In most school evaluations in the past, an outside group has been interested in looking at many aspects of the school program and the instrumentalities involved in the school's functioning: philosophy and objectives, curriculum, staff, physical plant, and community. Usually the direct evaluation of the product is a matter of local responsibility.

Evaluation of the school as a whole

Some of the more important agencies and groups that have evaluated schools need to be considered.

The local school community. There has been a noticeable trend toward encouraging the local school staff, with the cooperation of important elements in the community and the students, to make its own evaluation, using criteria that have been prepared by responsible educational groups. It has been accepted as a principle of evaluation that the appraisal carried on in the school will be effective in school reform to the extent that the local school staff and community elements participate. A number of instruments for self-evaluation have been developed, as well as instruments designed for cooperative use which could be adapted for use exclusively by local school communities.[6]

State departments of education. Most states have state departments of education which serve as the official accrediting agencies of the schools of the state. Standards are set up which become minimal for any school to be placed upon the state approved or accredited list. Certain financial or other advantages may accrue to schools which fully meet the prescribed standards. Generally state departments of education maintain staff members whose responsibility is the accreditation of schools, which is accomplished in two ways: first, the school submits data showing how it has tried to comply with the state's standards; second, the accreditation officials visit the school to inspect its program and to determine whether its efforts to meet the standards are acceptable. The educationally alert states assume that their standards are minimal and will be exceeded by the more progressive schools.

In recent years there has been a trend toward setting up evaluative criteria to be used cooperatively by the local school staff and state department of education officials in evaluating the school. An important purpose of the co-

[6] Typical of this kind of evaluative instruments are the following: Wendell G. Anderson, *An Instrument for the Self-Evaluation of Junior High Schools* (Urbana, Ill.: The author, 1959); *An Assessment Guide for Use in Junior High Schools* (Hartford: Connecticut State Department of Education, June, 1960); Texas Study of Secondary Education, *Criteria for Evaluating Junior High Schools*, Research Study No. 37 (Austin: The University of Texas, 1963). Many of the cooperative evaluation instruments could be adapted for self-evaluation purposes, such as those developed in Oklahoma and Utah, to be mentioned later.

operative evaluation approach is to stimulate the local school staff and its community to study their own community and its educational needs and achievements in the light of modern principles of education as cast in the framework of the evaluative criteria used. After the local school community has given considerable time to self-evaluation and formulated its conclusions, a visiting committee of educators and state department representatives studies the school for several days, reviews the local group's conclusions, and arrives at its own evaluation. The evaluations may or may not be used officially by the state department for accrediting purposes.[7]

State educational associations. The California Association of Secondary School Administrators probably can lay claim to being the first state secondary school organization to develop an evaluative device for the junior high school. Others have worked cooperatively on such instruments. Originally this association developed what was called the *CASSA Appraisal-Accreditation Program* for senior and four-year high schools. Experimenting with these appraisal forms in the junior high school proved unsatisfactory. A committee of junior high school administrators in collaboration with the CASSA Evaluation Committee has now designed an instrument called *Procedures for Appraising the Modern Junior High School.*

The same general plan of evaluation used in the *CASSA Appraisal-Accreditation Program* is employed with the junior high school instrument. Stress is placed upon the involvement of the total school staff and community representatives in self-evaluation studies. The study committees consist of (1) administration, (2) instructional staff, (3) classified staff, and (4) students. These committees work independently of one another, but their work is coordinated by a central committee consisting of the group chairmen. After the groups have completed their work a visiting committee of five persons representing a college or university, a county school office, the California State Department of Education, a secondary school administrator, and a curriculum specialist spends not less than two days studying the school. Having studied the reports of the local committees the visiting group meets with them to discuss the evaluation.

The visiting committee, after its report to the school committees, prepares a written report of "the total appraisal experience." It then recommends to the CASSA Accreditation Commission the extent of the accreditation the school should receive. In turn the CASSA Accreditation Commission reports back to the local school the results of the appraisal and its recommendations.

[7] Typical of the evaluative instruments that may be used in such cooperative studies are Oklahoma Curriculum Improvement Commission, *A Manual of Evaluation for a Junior High School* (Oklahoma City: State Department of Public Instruction, 1959); *Junior High School Evaluative Criteria* (Salt Lake City: Utah State Department of Public Instruction, 1960); *Descriptive Analysis for New Jersey Junior High Schools: A Device for Assisting in Evaluation Procedures* (Trenton: New Jersey Department of Education, 1958).

The advantages claimed for this approach are that it is a total evaluation of the school and the accreditation report is certified to the community concerned. It carries with it no penalties such as result from an adverse evaluation by a university, state department, or regional organization. It is conceived entirely as an educational project in which the community benefits from its own careful appraisal of its schools supplemented by the judgments of representatives of influential educational groups. The prestige of the outside evaluators is assumed to have great influence in the community in support of needed school improvements.[8]

Regional accrediting associations. Such organizations as the North Central Association of Colleges and Secondary Schools and the Southern Association of Colleges and Secondary Schools are part of a system of regional associations covering the United States and affiliated schools in other countries. Although these associations are concerned with all secondary education, primary attention in the past has been on the relation of the high school, principally Grades 9-12, to the higher institutions of learning. Their major concern has been with evaluation and accreditation problems of high schools and of colleges and universities, and with the quality of colleges and universities.

The school communities that wish their schools to be fully accredited, that is, accepted by other secondary schools on an equal basis or having their graduates favorably looked upon by colleges and universities for admission purposes, seek an evaluation by the association for the schools in that region.[9] The association then sets up an evaluation procedure quite uniform for all schools. The first part consists of a preliminary appraisal of the school by the local school staff on evaluation forms provided by the association. This self-evaluation phase usually involves several months to a year. Then the association representatives of colleges, state departments of education, and secondary administrators conduct a visitation appraisal and report to the association leadership their evaluation and recommendations.

Although the regional associations have heretofore focused chiefly upon

[8] *Procedures for Appraising the Modern Junior High School* (Burlingame, Cal.: California Association of Secondary-School Principals, 1960). For description of this new evaluation instrument see A. Winston Richards, "What Are the Best Ways to Improve Junior High School Programs Through Appraisal?" *The Bulletin of the National Association of Secondary-School Principals,* 44:244-245, April, 1960.

[9] Those fully aware of the significance of a school's being accredited by one of these regional associations will understand that accreditation does not automatically admit a student to any college or university. Most of the large universities maintain accrediting officials of their own, and many admit only by examinations they give all applicants for admission, or on the basis of results accepted through such instrumentalities as the National College Board Examinations. Smaller colleges and universities generally accept the accreditation of high schools by these associations as at least a part of the admission requirements for students. A discussion of the evaluation of colleges and universities in these associations has not been considered relevant here.

the upper years of the secondary school, traditionally the four-year high school, there is some indication that the early years of the secondary school will receive more attention in the future. Within recent years the educational importance of this period of emerging adolescence has caught the imagination of educators. Most of the evaluative criteria for the junior high school have been developed since 1955. One of the important recent documents of the Southern Association of Colleges and Secondary Schools is *The Junior High School Program* (1958). It might well be accepted as a set of standards for the junior high school. Now that the National Study of Secondary School Evaluation has developed *Evaluative Criteria for Junior High Schools,* the North Central Association and its affiliate regional accrediting associations may be expected to use it in evaluating junior high schools. The *Evaluative Criteria,* produced by the same organization that created the evaluative instrument for the junior high school, have been used almost exclusively by the North Central Association and its affiliates as an evaluation instrument.

National evaluation organizations. The direct organizational approach to evaluation which has been discussed thus far, at the state, association, and regional level, at present does not exist on a national basis. There are, however, some important national agencies which indirectly vitally influence evaluation in the upper years of the secondary schools and to a lesser degree the junior high school.

The National Study of Secondary School Evaluation, which produced the well-known *Evaluative Criteria,* an instrument used throughout the United States since 1940, has been closely associated with the six regional associations that have dominated the accreditation of secondary schools throughout the United States. Indirectly, since the use of the *Evaluative Criteria* has become standard in appraising secondary schools, this organization may be considered a national evaluative agency. The recent *Evaluative Criteria for Junior High Schools,* modeled after the *Evaluative Criteria,* will now tend to become the standard evaluative instrument of the regional groups. Since these publications no doubt will overshadow all others as the applied instruments for the accreditation of secondary schools in the future, the NSSSE may be looked upon as a powerful, if indirect, agency for junior high school evaluation.

Two other types of organizations will be mentioned as examples of the subtle, and not so subtle, agencies that indirectly evaluate and influence the junior high school in its goals and program. The first type represents the national foundations that since the Sputniks have essayed to set up a national curriculum in their subject areas, some proposing inclusive curriculums for Grades 1-12. Junior high schools that are found not to be using these curriculums are regarded as inferior and are under pressure from these foundations, the national subject organizations, and higher institutions of learning to meet their standards. Many educationally alert principals complain that the pressure of these agencies in their extreme emphasis upon certain academic subjects throughout each of the junior high school years makes adjustment of the curriculum to meet the functional needs of early adolescence virtually impossible.

Another group of national agencies reaching down into the junior high school, albeit indirectly, is made up of those trying to popularize college entrance examinations on a nation-wide basis; an example of this type is the well-known College Entrance Examination Board. This group has its counterpart in the national testing agencies which seek to set a standardized testing program for all secondary schools, thus directly and indirectly evaluating and controlling the educational program of the junior high school. The emphasis which these examinations give to subject-matter areas, and aspects of these areas, inevitably circumscribes the curriculum and gives specificity to its content. A specific curriculum can be developed for any test that can be constructed.[10]

Evaluation of the school product

The evaluation of the product, the extent of the education achieved by boys and girls, can be approached in maximal degree only by the school community. Modern educators recognize that there are limitations which even the school community confronts as it attempts to evaluate the behavioral changes wrought in each learner during his school career, or any phase of it.

Fifty years ago it was believed possible even for an outside agency to evaluate what the pupil had learned. This was the justification given for the widespread use of state-created examinations for schools. Some of that early naïvete appears still to persist. As the range of individual differences and the complexity of the learning process are better understood, evaluation will be accepted as the responsibility of the entire school community.

The teacher. Central in the educational scheme stands the teacher. It is generally agreed today that no one, not even the parent, normally knows as much about the pupil as the teacher. With acceptance of the counseling function as a teacher responsibility, evaluation in its multiple aspects rests more and more with the teacher. It is the recognition of the key place of the teacher in the total educational process that has led schools to provide for greater continuity of teacher association with the pupil and larger blocks of time daily for teacher guidance of and acquaintance with the pupil.

The staff personnel. Now that learning is defined as the change in be-

[10] The influence of these groups upon the thinking of some educational leaders and the import of their recommendations are clearly reflected in two documents that have had a far-reaching influence upon the junior high school: James B. Conant, *The American High School Today* (New York: McGraw-Hill Book Co., Inc., 1959), and, by the same author, *Education in the Junior High School Years* (Princeton, N.J.: Educational Testing Service, 1960).

havior that results from the myriad experiences the pupil has in all his environmental contacts, the education of youth is no longer considered the sole responsibility of the teacher. Everyone connected with the school, in greater or lesser degree, from principal to custodian, shares in the quality of the environmental contacts provided for the pupil and is in a position to observe his behavior in and around the school. Some persons have more contacts than others with pupils, as in the case of the guidance personnel or those responsible for special phases of student activities. All must accept their share of responsibility for evaluating the learning of pupils who have come under their observation. Schools alive to this concept of learning are developing techniques by which the evaluation of pupil learning becomes a group activity.

The community. The concept of learning presented in this book, and reiterated in the previous section, obviously projects learning beyond the school into the total community. Since learning experiences can no longer be thought of as reserved to the school and classroom, but pervade the waking hours of the pupil, the community too becomes an important part of his learning environment.

By the same token evaluation of the learning of the pupil must be a responsibility the community shares with the school. Probably the school is better equipped to evaluate the pupil's acquisition of factual materials, but it alone cannot evaluate patterns of social behavior and its concomitant attributes of attitudes. Parents should prove to be most effective in the cooperative evaluation of the change in behavior of the pupil as expressed in the environment of the home and school. The acid test of whether patterns of behavioral change have taken place is the extent to which these are in evidence in the school, the home, and the wider reaches of the community.

Evaluative instruments for the institutional aspects of the junior high school are of recent origin and thus are limited in number and still experimental in nature. Information about them is scarce. Only since 1950 have evaluative criteria been specifically created for the junior high school. Much of this development has come near the beginning of this decade and since. A book on the junior high school at this time would surely be incomplete if it did not at least consider these important instruments.

Self-evaluation instruments. One of the first major instruments devised for the evaluation of junior high schools was prepared by the Texas Study of Secondary Education in 1954 and revised in 1956 and 1963. Use of this instrument for "self-appraisal and improvement" is stressed in the introduction. Following a brief statement on the use of the instrument there are eleven sections devoted to evaluation. The final or twelfth section provides a selected bibliography. All sections but the last one are divided into two major divisions: (1) the "Overview," which includes pertinent data that became a basis for intelligent understanding of the section for evaluation, and (2) the "Criteria," a list of items used as standards for evaluation. The twelve sections are listed here with some amplification of some sections to indicate clearly the nature of their instrument.[11]

Criteria for Evaluating Junior High Schools

Section I. School Community and Pupil Population.

Section II. Junior High School Administration.

Section III. School Plant, Facilities and Equipment.

Overview — A half-page discussion of the importance and use of the school plant and its facilities.

Criteria — Thirty-four items characteristic of a good plant and facilities are listed. At the right-hand side are three columns to check: *none, some, much.*

Sample criteria

1. The school plant is built for a comprehensive program and not simply to provide classrooms.
2. The school plant is built to provide for the future growth of the community.
3. The classrooms have facilities for carrying on a forward-looking program of education.

This list of criteria is followed by two sections to be filled in entitled: "Features of the Program That are Commended," "Features of the Program That Need Improvement."

Section IV. The Staff.

Section V. The Junior High School Pupil.

This division is constructed differently from the preceding criteria. There are eight major categories of "Characteristics of Junior High School Pupils." Each of these characteristics appears at the top of a page. Below it the page is divided into two columns.

Column A	*Column B*
Ways in which this characteristic is revealed (Ten or more items listed)	Some ways in which schools meet these situations (Ten or more items listed)

The opposite page is divided into two columns in which the evaluator writes —

Specific practices in this school that are used for this area.	Other practices that might help.

[11] Adapted from the Texas Study of Secondary Education, *op. cit.*

Section VI. The Educational Program of the Junior High School.
Overview.
Criteria.
In the first part of this section, pages 45-50, an over-all evaluation of the total educational program of the junior high school is undertaken with a single-page "overview" statement, followed by a division on "criteria" with twenty-eight items which are to be rated on a three-point scale of the degree of presence of the item — *none, some, much.* The last page has two divisions: Features of the Program That Are Commendable," "Features of the Program That Need Improvement."

Section VI, a-m Follows the same form as above beginning with evaluation a: "The Core Program in the Junior High School." This in turn is followed by an evaluation of every subject thought likely to be offered in a junior high school.

Section VII. Library Service.

Section VIII. Pupil Activities.

Section IX. Guidance Services.

Section X. Special Provision for Potential Drop-Outs.

Section XI. Staff Utilization Practices.

Section XII. General Bibliography.

The second self-evaluation instrument considered here is one prepared under the auspices of the Connecticut State Department of Education. The purpose of this evaluation is as follows:

> This *Assessment Guide* has been prepared to aid junior high school professional staff members in appraising their schools. . . . This *Guide* is not designed to evaluate or rate any junior high school against any other high school. . . . Rather, through its use, it is hoped that each school staff may gain insight and develop understanding of its own students and will then proceed to improve in its unique task of educating them as individuals.[12]

The guide is composed of five major sections which are broken down by subheadings. At the right of the page opposite the criterion items is a five-fold scale for evaluating each item by its presence and effectiveness in the school situation. The items are to be evaluated (5) Superior, (4) Excellent, (3) Adequate, (2) Inadequate, (1) Not provided at all. A special feature of this evaluation form is that it does not attempt to appraise subjects as do most

12 *An Assessment Guide For Use in Junior High Schools, op. cit.,* p. 1.

evaluative instruments at present available. Instead it tries to focus attention upon the functions of the junior high school and then evaluate each phase of the curriculum in terms of its relevance to these functions. It uses the Douglass-Gruhn well-known six functions. They are listed under Part III of the outline. Two advantages appear obvious for this approach. First, the evaluator's attention is kept focused upon the basic purposes of the program, not the realia; second, the evaluation is not committed in advance to any particular theory of curriculum organization. This is fundamental if progress in curriculum thinking is to be encouraged rather than stymied, as happens with the structured forms of most current instruments of evaluation even at the junior high school level.

The general divisions of this guide appear as follows, with Part III expanded to clarify the comments offered at the close of the last paragraph.[13]

Part I. Who Are Our Pupils?

Part II. What Is Our Philosophy?

Part III. What Program Does This Philosophy Require?

- A. Articulation (twenty-four items to be appraised).
- B. Guidance (fourteen items).
- C. Exploration (three items).
- D. Integration (six items).
- E. Differentiation (seven items).
- F. Socialization (twelve items).

Additional Pertinent Comment.

Part IV. What Staff Does Our Program Require?

Part V. What Physical Plant Does This Program Require?

Instruments for cooperative use. The *Evaluative Criteria,* well-known to all secondary school educators, has been used in its present form, or with modifications, as an instrument of evaluation and accreditation in many sections of the country. Although much better adapted to the upper years of the secondary school, until evaluative instruments better suited to the junior high school were developed, it was used with reservations. This evaluative instrument first appeared in 1940, and since that time has followed a plan of revision and republication at ten-year intervals.

The same organization that produced the *Evaluative Criteria* developed the *Evaluative Criteria for Junior High Schools* in 1963. This instrument has followed almost slavishly the format and schemata of the *Evaluative Criteria.* The Table of Contents is almost identical except for the omission of four

[13] In addition to *An Instrument for the Self-Evaluation of Junior High Schools* developed by Wendell G. Anderson, a number of evaluation instruments designed for staff and official visitor groups might be used. A number of these were mentioned earlier. The two considered here were prepared for self-evaluation purposes and at significant points are different in design.

subject areas clearly more appropriate to the upper secondary school grades. Except for the section on "Philosophy, Objectives, and Functions," there is little to differentiate the content of this instrument from the one it so painstakingly imitates. Consequently, no effort will be made to describe its contents and organization since most, if not all, of those concerned with junior high school evaluation are well acquainted with the *Evaluative Criteria.*

Among the many cooperative evaluation instruments for junior high schools now available, the one developed through the combined efforts of the Utah Department of Education and the Utah Secondary School Principals' Association entitled *Junior High School Evaluative Criteria* is described briefly because it is in many ways unique, is adaptable to self-evaluation, and has become well known.

It has been set up as a cooperative evaluation project between the school community and a visiting committee. Preceding the appearance of the outside visiting committee of selected educators the local school will have made an extensive self-evaluation. Its rigor is indicated by the "Organizational Procedures" recommended in the manual, and by the fact that the self-survey is expected to require a year to complete. The committees recommended are (1) steering committee, (2) subject area committees, (3) service area committees, (4) student committee, (5) parent visiting committee, and (6) visiting committee.

Certain of the self-evaluation reports are to be made available to the visiting committee, which is expected to spend "approximately three days" in the local school. It is important to note in this plan that parents and students have a definite part in the evaluation scheme.

There is a broad similarity between the marking devices in most evaluation instruments and the system used here. This is more involved than most in its mechanical features. For the purposes of our brief summary it is essential to point out that to the left or right of each item for appraisal there is a blank to be checked on a five-fold scale.

In the organizational scheme the plan of three divisions for each area is generally followed — Contents, Overview, Evaluation. This represents a modification of the Texas plan, where "Overview" was followed by "Criteria."[14]

The evaluation document is organized to cover the following topics:

I. Basic Information.
   - Instructions.
   - Characteristics of Junior High School Youth.
   - Needs of Junior High School Youth.
   - Functions of the Junior High.
   - Pupil Population and School-Community Data.

[14] See Texas Study of Secondary Education, *op. cit.,* p. 1.

II. School Evaluation.
  Subject Areas.
    Individual subjects found in the school program are listed for evaluation.
  Service Areas.
    Administration.
    Library.
    Guidance.
    Special Education.
    Student Activities.
    School Plant.
  General Appraisals.
    Student Appraisal.
    Parent Appraisal.

The section on "Characteristics of Junior High School Youth" follows the plan of the Texas "Criteria" in its extensive list of characteristics with the broad divisions followed by a divided page of two columns respectively entitled "Characteristics of Students" and "Implications for the Curriculum."

The organization of this evaluative instrument departs markedly from that of the Connecticut evaluation form described earlier, on the divisions related to "program of studies." Where the Connecticut instrument lists six functions of the junior high school under the division of "program of studies" but omits a list of subject areas, the Utah instrument includes these functions, with an additional one, under the general division "Functions of the Junior High School." The division "Program of Studies" in the Utah plan has two sections: the first involves an evaluation of the total subject program in five particulars: (1) Content and Organization, (2) Evaluation, (3) Behavioral Outcomes, (4) Extent of Offerings, and (5) Specific Characteristics; the second is given over to the conventional list of subjects found in the usual school.

The aspects of each subject to be evaluated, ten in number, indicate that a minute appraisal is contemplated:

I. Procedures for Creating the Learning Environment.
II. Teaching Format.
III. Outcomes and Evaluations.
IV. Physical Provisions.
V. Material Facilities.
VI. Sectional Profile.
VII. Plans for Action.
VIII. Visiting Committee Summary.
  A. Commendations.
  B. Recommended Improvements.
IX. Teacher Preparation and Assignment.
X. Influencing Factors.[15]

[15] Adapted from *Junior High School Evaluative Criteria, op. cit.*

It is important for the junior high school that attention finally is being focused upon a critical appraisal of its functions and achievements in relation to the needs of the early adolescent years it is supposed to serve. These instruments represent pioneer efforts to set up competent devices by which to appraise the adequacy of the institution of the junior high school. Some show imagination and a courageous attempt to recognize the unique educational responsibility of the junior high school, and as is to be expected in any such effort, some leave much to be desired. The next few years should see a definite advance in the clarity with which the particular functions and program of the junior high school are understood, and a corresponding improvement in the evaluation instruments made available with which to determine their effectiveness.

SELECTED BIBLIOGRAPHY

Anderson, Wendell G. *An Instrument for the Self-Evaluation of Junior High Schools.* Urbana, Ill.: The author (2507 East Main Street), 1959.

Assessment Guide for Use in Junior High Schools. Hartford: Connecticut State Department of Education, June, 1960.

Brickell, Henry M. *Organizing New York State for Educational Change.* Albany, N.Y.: State Education Department, December, 1961. Pp. 78-84.

Criteria for the Evaluation of Six-Year High Schools in Minnesota. St. Paul: The Minnesota State Department of Education, 1958.

Descriptive Analysis for New Jersey Junior High Schools. A Device for Assisting in Evaluation Procedures. Trenton: New Jersey Department of Education (Office of Secondary Education), 1958.

Doolin, Ruie B., and others. *The Report of the Evaluation Committee of the Cedar Rapids Junior High School Curriculum Study.* Cedar Rapids, Iowa: The Cedar Rapids Public Schools, 1956.

Douglass, Harl R. "Evaluating and Accrediting Junior High Schools," *The Bulletin of the National Association of Secondary-School Principals,* 47:125-128, February, 1963.

"Evaluating and Reporting Pupil Progress," *Junior High School Manual,* Publication 104. Akron, Ohio: Akron Public Schools, 1954, pp. 27-33.

Evaluative Criteria. Washington: National Study of Secondary School Evaluation, 1960 edition.

Evaluative Criteria for Junior High Schools. Washington: National Study of Secondary School Evaluation, 1963.

Faunce, Roland C., and Morrel J. Clute. *Teaching and Learning in the Junior High School.* San Francisco: Wadsworth Publishing Company, 1961. Chap. 13, "Evaluating the Junior High School."

Frasier, James E., Winston Richards, and others. "What Are the Best Ways to Improve Junior High School Programs Through Appraisal?" *The Bulletin of the National Association of Secondary-School Principals,* 44:243-247, April, 1960.

Gruhn, William T., and Harl R. Douglass. *The Modern Junior High School.* New York: The Ronald Press Company, 2nd ed., 1956. Chap. 14, "Evaluating, Reporting and Recording Pupil Progress."

Guide to the Evaluation and Accreditation of Secondary Schools. Atlanta, Ga.: Southern Association of Colleges and Secondary Schools, 1958.

Holloway, R. L. "Characteristics of a Good Junior High School," *The Bulletin of the National Association of Secondary-School Principals,* 40:436-440, April, 1956.

Junior High School Evaluative Criteria. Salt Lake City: Utah State Department of Public Instruction, 1960.

Junior High School Program in Illinois, The. Illinois Curriculum Program. Springfield: Office of the Superintendent of Public Instruction, Bulletin No. A-1, 1961. Chap. 11, "Evaluating the Total Program of a Junior High School."

Junior High School Program, The. Atlanta, Ga.: Southern Association of Colleges and Secondary Schools, 1958. Chap. 8, "Evaluation in the Junior High School."

Junior High Schools for Iowa Youth. Des Moines, Iowa: The Iowa State Department of Public Instruction, 1960.

Manlove, Donald C., Otto Hughes, and Carl G. F. Franzén. "The 1960 Evaluative Criteria and Indiana Secondary Schools," *Bulletin of the School of Education,* Indiana University, March, 1962.

Matthews, Roderic D. "Evaluative Criteria for Junior High Schools," *The Bulletin of the National Association of Secondary-School Principals,* 44:111-113, October, 1962.

Morris, C. S., Jr. "What are the Most Crucial Elements in Evaluating a Junior High School and How Can It Be Done?" *The Bulletin of the National Association of Secondary-School Principals,* 46:25-26, October, 1962.

Nelson, I. I. "Criteria for Evaluating Junior High Schools," *The Bulletin of the National Association of Secondary-School Principals,* 39:346-351, April, 1955.

Nickerson, N. C., and A. Gruber, "Evaluating the Junior High School," *The Bulletin of the National Association of Secondary-School Principals,* 45:38-41, September, 1961.

Oklahoma Curriculum Improvement Commission. *A Manual of Evaluation for a Junior High School.* Oklahoma City: State Department of Public Instruction, 1959.

Organization and Functions of Oregon Junior High Schools, The. Salem: State Department of Education, 1959.

Romine, S. A. "Opinions about North Central Association Accreditation of Junior High Schools," *North Central Association Quarterly,* 36:193-200, Fall, 1962.

Samuelson, E. V. "Accreditation of Junior High Schools by the North Central Association of Colleges and Secondary Schools," *North Central Association Quarterly,* 37:233-236, Winter, 1963.

Schindler, W. A., and others. "We Review the Qualities of a Good Junior High School," *The Junior High School in Nebraska.* Lincoln: Division of Supervision, Nebraska Department of Education, 1960.

Secondary Schools: Standards for Classification. Part II, Standards for the Approval of Junior High Schools. Charleston: West Virginia State Department of Education, 1957.

Shannon, G. "Planning for Evaluation in the Junior High School," *The Bulletin of the National Association of Secondary-School Principals,* 44:12-15, February, 1960.

Texas Study of Secondary Education. *Criteria for Evaluating Junior High Schools.* Research Study No. 37. Austin: The University of Texas, 1963.

Trump, J. L. "Two Instruments for Evaluating Junior High Schools," *The Bulletin of the National Association of Secondary-School Principals,* 44:130-132, November, 1960.

Van Til, William, Gordon F. Vars, and John H. Lounsbury. *Modern Education for the Junior High School Years.* Indianapolis: The Bobbs-Merrill Company, 1961. Chap. 19, "Obtaining and Evaluating Instructional Materials," and Chap. 21, "Evaluation and Reporting."

Wrightstone, J. Wayne, Joseph Justman, and Irving Robbins. *Evaluation in Modern Education.* New York: American Book Company, 1956.

Wyatt, S. L., and others. "Utah Uses State-wide Approach in Studying Utilization Effect of Junior High School Evaluative Criteria, Physics Films, and Core Programs," *The Bulletin of the National Association of Secondary-School Principals,* 42:168-173, January, 1958.

Index